THE AUTISM MATRIX
The Social Origins of the Autism Epidemic

GIL EYAL, BRENDAN HART, EMINE ONCULER, NETA OREN, AND NATASHA ROSSI

polity

First published in 2010 by Polity Press

Polity Press
65 Bridge Street
Cambridge CB2 1UR, UK

Polity Press
350 Main Street
Malden, MA 02148, USA

ISBN-13: 978-0-7456-4399-1
ISBN-13: 978-0-7456-4400-4(pb)

A catalogue record for this book is available from the British Library.

Typeset in 10.5 on 12 pt Sabon
by Servis Filmsetting Ltd, Stockport, Cheshire
Printed and bound at MPG Books Group, UK

The publisher has used its best endeavours to ensure that the URLs for external websites referred to in this book are correct and active at the time of going to press. However, the publisher has no responsibility for the websites and can make no guarantee that a site will remain live or that the content is or will remain appropriate.

Every effort has been made to trace all copyright holders, but if any have been inadvertently overlooked the publisher will be pleased to include any necessary credits in any subsequent reprint or edition.

For further information on Polity, visit our website: www.politybooks.com

CONTENTS

CONTENTS

ACKNOWLEDGEMENTS

Many individuals provided us with useful comments after reading drafts of the manuscript or attending presentations of its main argument and findings, others have helped us through various stages of the research that led to this book. Thanks are due to: Peter Bearman, Dalia Ben-Rabi from JDC-Brookdale Institute (Israel), Douwe Draaisma, Vivian Ducat, Dani Eshet, Dahava Eyal, Ayelet Fischer, Marion Fourcade, Gyorgy Gergely, Kim Gilbert, Robin Gurley and Marguerite Kirst Colston at The Autism Society of America, Ian Hacking, Barbara Harmon, Haim Hazan, Noa Herling and Dafna Erlich from ALUT (Israel), Dagmar Herzog, Marissa King, Eric Klinenberg, Andrew Lakoff, Tanya Luhrmann, Carol Markowitz, Xue Ming, Anne Montgomery, Dan Navon, Ari Ne'eman, Molly Ola Pinney, Beatrice Renault, David Schelly, Chloe Silverman, Regina Skyer, Kathy Small, Michael Staub, Rachel Tait, Zsuzsanna Vargha, Lynn Waterhouse, Juliette de Wolfe, participants in Gil Eyal's Sociology of Expertise seminar at Columbia University, and the many parents who graciously took the time to share their stories and opinions with us. Thanks are also due to the editorial team at Polity Press. John Thompson shepherded the whole process with a sure hand and sage advice, and Ann Klefstad read the whole text and made useful corrections designed to make the book more communicative. Part of the research for this book was conducted with the generous support of the National Science Foundation under Grant No. 0719823. Any opinions, findings, and conclusions or recommendations expressed in this book are those of the authors and do not necessarily reflect the views of the National Science Foundation. Some of the manuscript was written while Gil Eyal was resident fellow at the Center for Advanced Studies in Stanford, California. Our thanks to the Center's director Claude Steele and deputy director Anne Petersen for their generous support.

INTRODUCTION: THE AUTISM MATRIX

Autism has become highly visible. Once you begin to look for it, you see it everywhere. Search the archived pages of major newspapers, and you will find countless reports on scientific advances in the detection, understanding, and treatment of autism; letters to the editors protesting insurers' miserly reimbursement for treatment options; dispatches from the battlefronts of special education; stories of parents' love and determination in the face of tragedy, of their dogged advocacy for their children. Type the keyword "autism" into Yahoo! Groups and you will get 3,072 entries, from "Texas-Autism-Advocacy" to HBO (hyperbaric oxygen) therapy for autism. Many of these sites contain lively discussions among parents, professionals, and other interested parties who have banded together virtually for this purpose and are communicating across county and state lines, across national borders. Sort through your mail or take a walk in your neighborhood reading car stickers, and you will surely discover that April is International Autism Awareness Month, that not far from you there is a special preschool or after-hours program dedicated to autism. Stroll into your local library or bookstore and you will discover whole shelves dedicated to autism sourcebooks, advice to the parents of autistic children, memoirs of individuals with autism or of their parents. Then start talking to somebody who is also browsing through these titles.

A few clicks away, a simple question addressed to a stranger, and you will be introduced to a host of strange terms that, you recognize, you had heard mentioned before but preferred to ignore: most important, you will learn about "the spectrum," about "high functioning" and "low functioning," about "Asperger's syndrome." You will hear talk about GFCF diets, chelation and mercury in vaccines. You will encounter numerous references to therapies going by various

1

acronyms such as ABA, DIR, RDI, RPM, PRT. You will learn to refer to children as being "very sensory," having "OT (occupational therapy) issues," and, most alarming of all, you will begin to look at your own children, or any other children around you, differently: Do they make eye contact? How long and how well? Do they walk around on their tiptoes and like to flap their hands? Do they know how to make friends? Do they like to run their hands over the soft fabric of toys rather than play with them? Autism has not only become highly visible, it's become the center of a social world, a universe of discourse complete with its own idioms, modes of seeing and judging, its own objects and devices. Wait but a little time, and you will begin to scrutinize not only children's behavior, but your own, your parents and siblings, your childhood memories, for the telltale signs.

Why is autism so visible now? We all know the answer. There is an epidemic. In the U.S., the Center for Disease Control estimates that the prevalence of autism has increased from 4 per 10,000 in 1989 to 66 per 10,000 in 2002; that is, from 1 in 2,500 to about 1 in 150 children.[1] A recent article in *Pediatrics* provided an estimate of 110 in 10,000 (1 in 91) based on parental reports (Kogan et al. 2009). Likewise, data from California show that between 1987 and 2003 the number of autism cases handled by the California Department of Developmental Services increased 634 percent. Around the globe, the incidence of autism is estimated to be rising – to 1 in 100 in the U.K., 1 in 250 in India, 1 in 1,000 in China – though the reliability of these estimates is very uneven.[2] We all know what an epidemic is – a public health emergency. A serious and devastating illness is spreading rapidly in the population. We all know what needs to be done about epidemics. It's a call for action. Detection centers must be established so new cases are rapidly identified, isolated, and treated. Money, lots of money, must be "thrown" at the scientists so they will come up with an explanation and a solution. The number of new cases must be brought down, the trend reversed.

But can this really be the answer? There are many who think it was exactly the other way around: it was not the epidemic that made autism visible, but the visibility of autism that made the epidemic. They say that changed diagnostic criteria, greater awareness, and better detection services have increased the frequency with which autism is diagnosed. We will address this argument in more detail in a few pages, but for the moment we note that from this point of view, we can think about claims of an epidemic as attempts to establish a discursive link, to throw an improvised rope bridge across from the autism social world to the worlds where decisions are made, resources allocated, and actions taken – the worlds of politics, economics, medicine and science. In these worlds, what do they care if children make eye contact? But they do care about epidemics; that is their business. The claim of an epidemic is salutary if it makes visible the plight of suffering children and their parents, but we think that on balance, it does more harm than good. It raises the alarm, and we must admit that we ourselves initially became interested in autism because we heard talk about an "epidemic." We asked: why are the numbers of diagnoses rising? What are the processes and causes leading to the current autism epidemic? Only slowly and painfully did we come to realize that this was a simplistic question. The search for the epidemic's cause was as good a place as any to start, but ultimately blinkered our vision. The claim that there is an epidemic constrains the communication between the autism world and these other worlds where decisions are made. As a discursive link it is self-defeating. It provokes a futile and barren debate about whether there is an epidemic or not (Shattuck and Durkin 2007), whether it is "socially constructed" or real. Are new cases evidence of children poisoned by vaccines or of an overzealous psychiatric profession?

In this book, we would like to change the terms of the debate. We would like to provide a different interpretation for the rise in the number of autism diagnoses and a different way of establishing a discursive link between the autism world and its interlocutors. The current rise in autism diagnoses, we argue, should be understood as an aftershock of the real earthquake, which was the deinstitutionalization of mental retardation that began in the late 1960s. The deinstitutionalization of mental retardation was a massive change, not only materially – large institutions emptied, some razed to the ground, some converted into more humane service centers – but also symbolically. Deinstitutionalization acted as a sort of "moral blender" into which disappeared the old categories that reflected the needs of custodial institutions (moron, imbecile, idiot, feebleminded, mentally deficient, mentally retarded – whether deemed educable or trainable, or neither – emotionally disturbed, psychotic, schizophrenic child, and so on). The moral blender of deinstitutionalization scrambled these categories, giving rise to a great undifferentiated mass of "atypical children" (we will explain later why we are using this term). Then, gradually, new categories began to be differentiated within a new institutional matrix that replaced custodial institutions – community treatment, special education, and early intervention programs. It is this institutional matrix and the therapies that populate it which gave rise to our current notion of a spectrum of autistic disorders running

3

the whole gamut from children with severe disabilities who speak little and require round-the-clock care to semi-genius teenagers with Asperger's disorder. Beginning in Chapter 2, after we have laid the necessary groundwork of the book's argument, we will give a historical account of this matrix and how it was assembled.

As well as giving rise to the new institutional matrix, and intimately connected to it, the deinstitutionalization of mental retardation signaled a massive change in the social organization of expertise. It was pushed forward by challenges to psychiatry from relatively marginal groups – special educators, occupational therapists, behavioral psychologists, activist social scientists identified with the anti-psychiatry movement – and parents. In the U.S., the National Association for Retarded Children (NARC) played a crucial role, and as we shall see in later chapters, so did the National Society for Autistic Children (NSAC) – both parents' groups. They all sought to undermine the dominance of the psychiatric profession, which had in the past ignored or belittled their expertise. Rather than unseating or replacing psychiatry, the challengers maneuvered around and beneath it, so to speak. In doing so, they opened up a vast contested space between professional jurisdictions into which entered all sorts of entrepreneurs from adjacent fields – psychiatrists, no doubt, but also academic psychologists, occupational therapists, speech therapists, special educators, activists, and parents – each peddling a different typically low-tech therapy tailored to suit the needs of the new institutional matrix. In the past, psychiatrists used to rule the roost by virtue of their monopoly over the directorship of large state institutions for the mentally retarded. The new institutional matrix of community treatment, special education, and early intervention, however, acts as a great leveler, putting the psychiatrist on equal footing with occupational therapists and special educators, since all must appeal to and strike an alliance with parents. In the custodial matrix, the psychiatrist acted *in loco parentis*, absolved the parents of their responsibility and expropriated their knowledge.[3] To succeed in the new institutional matrix, on the other hand, one must pay homage to its oft-repeated mantra that "parents are experts on their own children" and make room for meaningful interchanges between their expertise and one's own. Psychiatrists were the least prepared to adapt to such changes. No surprise, then, that they were outmaneuvered by swifter opponents.

To substantiate these arguments, we will first analyze, in Chapter 1, the international variation in autism prevalence rates, as well as between U.S. states, and show that it systematically correlates with indices of deinstitutionalization and parent activism. The bulk of

4

what follows through Chapter 11 is historical analysis of how the autism spectrum became the preferred way to represent and intervene in childhood disorders, showing the contribution to this process of deinstitutionalization, parental activism, and the reorganization of expertise. The analysis in this book is based mostly on texts: articles, published interviews, reports, and manuals. We also conducted interviews with parents, therapists, and advocates, and participant observations at therapy and diagnostic centers. We will analyze this data in depth in our second book, which will focus on the moral career of the autistic child. Occasionally, however, we will use data from interviews and observations to illustrate some of the arguments in this book.

So what does the deinstitutionalization of mental retardation have to do with autism after all? One can imagine the psychiatrists being relieved by no longer having custody over mental retardation. There was never much profit or prestige in it anyway, only trouble. The mentally retarded were severely underfunded and highly stigmatized, and the stigma infected whoever was in charge of them. Mental retardation was uninteresting for psychiatrists since there was very little to do about it. It should not have been the charge of psychiatry – whose role is to treat mental illness – to begin with. Isn't autism mental illness? Doesn't its story begin in 1943, before the deinstitutionalization of mental retardation, when the leading child psychiatrist Leo Kanner discovered it? Shouldn't we trace autism's origin back to the moment Kanner wrote his landmark article "Autistic Disturbances of Affective Contact" and introduced the world to a curious group of eleven children he had seen in his Baltimore practice, the first eleven people diagnosed as autistic in history? Unlike mental retardation, autism was always exciting for the psychiatrists, a mysterious disorder through which they hoped to catch a glimpse of how the normal mind/brain works (Rimland 1964, 3). They fumbled around for a while, no doubt, misled by psychoanalytic dogmatism and charlatanism. But as psychiatry became more scientific, more securely founded in neurochemistry, genetics, and brain imaging, it took up again Kanner's sound empirical observations, followed the thread untangled by his clinical wisdom, and is now hard on the heels of an explanation. Soon it will identify the genes and brain mechanisms involved and will devise a treatment. In the meantime, it has reiteratively modified diagnostic criteria to reflect its better understanding of the disorder, thereby producing the rise in the number of diagnoses.

One notes, of course, that it is not at all clear or self-evident why a better scientific understanding of autism should produce a dramatic rise

Digression: On terminology

Why are we using this offensive term "mental retardation"? Hasn't it been replaced by a more sensitive vocabulary?[4] Throughout this book we refer to "mental retardation," "mentally retarded" children, "the mentally retarded" and, worse still, to "retardates," "morons," "imbeciles," and "idiots" (we further explain the latter three terms in Chapter 9). Where it is historically accurate, we also employ the term "intellectual disability," as well as other terminology now in fashion. Words like "mentally retarded" may be unpalatable to many readers. These labels might have been used to deprive a loved one of services, or to devalue the richness of his or her experience. Our use of them is purely *historical*. In other words, we use the terms as they were used by researchers and physicians at particular historical moments. There are sharp differences in the moral images and ethical responses associated with these different terms and the sense conveyed by each has shifted dramatically over time. This book considers how these categories – autism and mental retardation in particular – have rearranged in relation to one another over the span of little more than half a century.

Let us be clear here. We are not claiming that people who are *really* mentally retarded have secretly infiltrated the autism spectrum. Nor are we suggesting that people who were *truly* autistic were mislabeled as mentally retarded in the past. We are arguing, rather, that the ways in which we think about and deal with childhood and developmental disorders, the very distinctions that we make, are what have changed. In the wake of deinstitutionalization, mental retardation sat at the center of the emergent domain of "developmental disabilities" (see Chapter 9) as the prototypical form of developmental disability. We argue, however, that it has lost this centrality in favor of autism, which is gradually coming to occupy the bulk of this domain as a multidimensional spectrum of pervasive developmental disorders. Mental retardation qua intellectual disability is now on the margins of this domain.

Today we grimace at the term "mental retardation," and prefer euphemisms such as "intellectual disability" or "developmental disability." Yet, when the term "mental retardation" was first used it was itself introduced as a *euphemism*. It was originally invented to denote those with only a mild deficit, those who were *merely* retarded rather than "idiots" or "imbeciles." In fact, it took over from terms such as "mental deficiency" or "feeblemindedness," each of which in their turn went through the same cycle. Each began as a euphemistic term for those slightly below "normal," then extended in a benevolent gesture to cover the whole realm of "mental defect," by virtue of which each gradually acquired a pejorative and ugly connotation which made it less and less useful. Then a new euphemism would be invented and the whole cycle would begin again (Wallin 1949, 5–6).

Before ending this digression, we must mention one other point of contention. Some readers may feel we should use "person-first" language. We refer at times to "autistic children" and even "autistics." Some disability studies scholars and advocates have argued that we ought to put the person first, before the label. We should refer to "people with disabilities" or more specifically in our case "a child (or adult) with autism." However, in deviating from person-first language at certain points, we are following autism advocates and accentuating a point about the novelty of autism.[5] Parent-activist-researchers, like Bernard Rimland (1993), have argued against person-first language because they think "autistic child" conveys how much autism pervades every aspect of their child's experience better than "child with autism." Jim Sinclair, a leading self-advocate, has also eloquently described why he himself does not use person-first language. "Saying 'person with autism,'" he writes, "suggests that the autism can be separated from the person. But this is not the case . . . If I did not have an autistic brain, the person that I am would not exist. I am autistic because autism is an essential feature of me as a person" (1999). Finally, we follow this use of terminology because it expresses a key aspect of the autism discourse we are describing: autism, on this view, is not something added to a person, like a disease that you can catch and later cure; it is a way of being that pervades every aspect of one's experience in the world.

in the number of diagnoses unless one assumes that the condition has been misdiagnosed in the past and was hiding under some other designation. This leads one back to mental retardation and to the mounting evidence – discussed in Chapter 1 – that a great deal of the rise in the number of autism diagnoses was caused by diagnostic substitution from mental retardation. So we are back to square one, to the deinstitutionalization of mental retardation. It created the institutional conditions of possibility for this diagnostic substitution, the ground upon which our current mode of representing and intervening in autism took shape. We have grave doubts whether psychiatry or a better scientific understanding had very much to do with this transformation.

We became interested in the deinstitutionalization of mental retardation because we noted two simple facts about autism. First, since there is still no medical treatment for autism, the bulk of the work in this field is done by paraprofessionals deploying behavioral, speech, occupational, or other therapies. Psychiatrists diagnose autism and (increasingly) prescribe medications, but these are merely meant to control mood or undesired behaviors, not to treat the core of the disorder. The bulk of therapeutic work – even though some of it is characterized as "biomedical" – escapes the jurisdiction of psychiatrists, though they may endorse it or even undertake to provide it themselves.

Second, as we shall show in Chapter 7, many of these therapies were not originally developed for treating autism but for mental retardation. More precisely, as we came to recognize once we delved into the history of these therapies, what they have in common is that they blur or hybridize the boundary between mental retardation and mental illness. Some, like Sensory Integration Therapy (SIT), originated in the field of mental retardation yet projected themselves outside it because they treated retardation as "brain injury," a semi-illness that could be cured. Others, like Applied Behavior Analysis (ABA), worked in the opposite direction: originating in the field of mental illness, they projected themselves outward because they treated illness as a bad habit or a lack of skills that could be corrected by means of behavior modification. These therapies date from the mid-1960s when they were fairly marginal. Certainly psychiatrists had very little to do with their invention or diffusion. Their moment came with deinstitutionalization. Their blurring of the boundary between mental illness and retardation corresponded to the space that deinstitutionalization opened up between professional jurisdictions. They became an integral part of the new institutional matrix of community treatment, special education, and early intervention.

So we had a hunch: what if "idiocy," "feeblemindedness," "mental retardation," "autism," "the spectrum," are all interpretations we superimpose over the *longue durée* of practices, and the real events take place not with the proliferation of this or that interpretation (such as the autism epidemic), but when a whole institutional matrix of practices gives way to another? This is precisely why we say that the question about the causes of the epidemic is simplistic, since it ignores this more subterranean change. The issue is not whether the rise in the number of diagnoses is due to vaccinations, pollution, or diagnostic substitution, whether it is "real" or fabricated. The issue is that our practices for representing and intervening in childhood disorders are no longer constrained by the opposition between retardation and illness, but proceed as if they can ignore it. What is the significance of this change? This is where the discursive link, the bridge between the autism world and its interlocutors, should be built.

So powerful, however, are the terms in which the current debate is joined, that we have no choice but to address them first, before we attempt to explore the significance of this blurred boundary between retardation and illness. Are we saying that there is no autism? That there is no epidemic? That autism is not real? That it's all "socially constructed"? Are we denying that autism is a real disorder, rooted in the neurochemistry of the brain? Or worse still, are we merely splitting philosophical hairs with no relevance to the actual suffering of children and their parents? The following section attempts to clarify the approach we are taking in this book and to indicate how it relates to existing explanations for the autism epidemic – why it is legitimate, we think, to emphasize the role played by therapies and institutional factors, and why it does not involve a denial of the reality of autism. Only once we have dealt with this issue and demonstrated that the terms of the current debate are imprecise and unproductive can we return in the concluding section of the introduction to drawing out the implications of our argument: what do we learn about autism and its history by connecting it with the deinstitutionalization of mental retardation?

Why focus on therapies?

To summarize our argument this far: the rise in the number of autism diagnoses is an indirect product of deinstitutionalization. The new institutional matrix of community treatment, special education, and early intervention that developed in its wake, and especially the very therapies that were meant to treat autism within this matrix, gave rise to a spectrum of autistic-type disorders that straddles an indeterminate terrain between mental illness and retardation, thereby laying the groundwork for the epidemic. The reader, quite justifiably, may suspect that this claim is another in a long series of "debunking" arguments made by social scientists, of which Szasz's *The Myth of Mental Illness* is perhaps the most notorious. Our contract with the reader, upon entering this section, is that we show that the focus on therapies is not a denial of the reality of autism. We would like to show, in fact, that the sociological approach we have crafted, with its focus on therapies, is better suited to accept without quotation marks the specific reality of autism and the autism epidemic, whereas the nonsociological approaches of medical researchers, what we call "naturalist explanations," inevitably lead to a controversy over the reality of autism and the autism epidemic.

By "naturalist" we mean arguments of the following type: "The rise in the number of autism diagnoses is an accurate reflection of an actual rise in the number of real autism cases out there, caused by . . ." There are different versions of this type of argument, and readers are invited to pick their poison. Some researchers have been looking for evidence of correlation between rising autism prevalence and environmental toxicity (Roberts et al. 2007). A group of parents has created a great deal of debate and controversy by linking new autism cases with a mercury-based preservative in vaccines (Bernard 2004). Other researchers have linked autism to TV watching (Waldman, Nicholson, and Adilov 2006). All of these explanations work on a "pollution" model, which some anthropologists characterize as an ancient moral narrative of accusation and blame (Douglas 1966, 1992). Conversely, other researchers and commentators assure us that the epidemic is "nobody's fault," by attributing the rising numbers to a genetic inheritance increasingly favorably selected in an age dominated by communications and information technology (Baron-Cohen 2006). It should be emphasized, however, that the bulk of naturalist research on autism does not touch at all on the question of rising prevalence, seeking merely to establish connections among autism, genes, and brain mechanisms. Those biologists and geneticists are content to endorse a social constructionist explanation for the epidemic, though vaguely and noncommittally insinuating that some combination of multiple genes in interaction with environmental factors or pollutants could have brought about some increase in prevalence.

No matter who or what they blame, or whether they avoid accusation altogether, all naturalist explanations face the same two problems, which cast doubt on their plausibility as explanations for rising prevalence:

First, the actual population of autism diagnoses is extremely heterogeneous. Until now we have been using the term "autism." We have neither been quite accurate, nor quite up to date. The correct term is "autism *spectrum* disorders." The DSM-IV classifies autism, or more precisely autistic disorder, as a "pervasive developmental disorder" together with Rett's disorder, childhood disintegrative disorder, Asperger's disorder, and pervasive developmental disorder-not otherwise specified (PDD-NOS). The latest word from the National Institute of Mental Health is that "all children with autism spectrum disorders demonstrate deficits in 1) social interaction, 2) verbal and nonverbal communication, and 3) repetitive behaviors or interests." That's quite broad. Admittedly, the numbers reported above were counts of autistic disorder by itself, without the other four conditions, but one should note, first, that the prevalence of Asperger's disorder and PDD-NOS has been rising in tandem with autistic disorder, and second, that the boundaries between autistic disorder, PDD-NOS, and Asperger's disorder are ill-defined and may change in accordance with pragmatic considerations.

Even if we look only at autistic disorder and exclude the other four, the heterogeneity remains enormous, because the diagnostic criteria are now organized in a way that reflects the idea of a "spectrum." The reader may consult Figure 1 below, which reproduces the DSM-IV-TR diagnostic criteria for autistic disorder. A child who meets six out of twelve criteria – that is, a child who is quite possibly verbal, affectionate, and friendly, but who does not engage in typical social play, and whose range of interests is rigid (1bc, 2bd, 3bd), would be diagnosed as autistic. The same holds, of course, for a child who meets all twelve criteria, struggles to communicate at all, and seems unaware of the presence of others. As a result, the spectrum includes children who do not speak and are profoundly disabled, together with semi-genius teenagers and the whole range of in-between cases. The spectrum includes many children who are concurrently diagnosed with mental retardation, but also many whose IQ scores are well above normal. Nobody really knows the true extent of co-morbidity with mental retardation.[6] Estimates vary widely, from 31 to 36 percent in a California study (Croen et al. 2002a; 2002b) to upwards of 89 percent reported by Dutch and Swedish researchers (Kraijer 1997, 40–42). Calling these "estimates" is misleading. They are more like prescriptive statements than descriptive ones. They reflect, in fact, a disagreement about the very nature of the disorder, what should count as autism, and what is to be understood by the metaphor of a "spectrum." The same heterogeneity is true for other co-morbid conditions as well. Many children with autistic disorder are also diagnosed with epilepsy, hyperactivity, emotional disorder, learning disability, or some combination thereof, but many are not.

As we shall see, a sociological explanation can coexist quite comfortably with such diversity. But the scientists, the medical researchers advancing naturalist explanations, cannot. If you conscientiously seek a naturalist explanation for autism and the autism epidemic, you must be deeply troubled by such mess, and indeed, many geneticists and brain researchers are deeply troubled. In their view, autism is not "a

psychiatryonline

⏏ **Print**   **Close Window**

DOI: 10.1176/appi.books.9780890423349.7585

DSM-IV-TR > Disorders Usually First Diagnosed in Infancy, Childhood, or Adolescence > Introduction > Pervasive Developmental Disorders >

299.00 Autistic Disorder

Diagnostic criteria for 299.00 Autistic Disorder

A. A total of six (or more) items from (1), (2), and (3), with at least two from (1), and one each from (2) and (3):

1. qualitative impairment in social interaction, as manifested by at least two of the following:
   a. marked impairment in the use of multiple nonverbal behaviors such as eye-to-eye gaze, facial expression, body postures, and gestures to regulate social interaction
   b. failure to develop peer relationships appropriate to developmental level
   c. a lack of spontaneous seeking to share enjoyment, interests, or achievements with other people (e.g., by a lack of showing, bringing, or pointing out objects of interest)
   d. lack of social or emotional reciprocity

2. qualitative impairments in communication as manifested by at least one of the following:
   a. delay in, or total lack of, the development of spoken language (not accompanied by an attempt to compensate through alternative modes of communication such as gesture or mime)
   b. in individuals with adequate speech, marked impairment in the ability to initiate or sustain a conversation with others
   c. stereotyped and repetitive use of language or idiosyncratic language
   d. lack of varied, spontaneous make-believe play or social imitative play appropriate to developmental level

3. restricted repetitive and stereotyped patterns of behavior, interests, and activities, as manifested by at least one of the following:
   a. encompassing preoccupation with one or more stereotyped and restricted patterns of interest that is abnormal either in intensity or focus
   b. apparently inflexible adherence to specific, nonfunctional routines or rituals
   c. stereotyped and repetitive motor mannerisms (e.g., hand or finger flapping or twisting, or complex whole-body movements)
   d. persistent preoccupation with parts of objects

B. Delays or abnormal functioning in at least one of the following areas, with onset prior to age 3 years: (1) social interaction, (2) language as used in social communication, or (3) symbolic or imaginative play.

C. The disturbance is not better accounted for by Rett's Disorder or Childhood Disintegrative Disorder.

Diagnostic Features

The essential features of Autistic Disorder are the presence of markedly abnormal or impaired development in social interaction and communication and a markedly restricted repertoire of activity and interests. Manifestations of the disorder vary greatly depending on the developmental level and chronological age of the individual. Autistic Disorder is sometimes referred to as *early infantile autism, childhood autism,* or *Kanner's autism.*

Figure 1: DSM-IV-TR Diagnostic Criteria for Autistic Disorder

single syndrome with highly variable severity (the autistic spectrum)," but "an aggregate of specific disorders that share some common [behavioral] features" because they involve the "dysfunction of one or more, probably widely distributed, brain systems" (Waterhouse et al. 2007, 308). To figure out "the patho-physiology of autism" – which brain systems are involved and through what causal pathways they are affected – "requires the development of a validated typology based on behavioral criteria." But, protest the scientists, there is no consensus on such a typology, and the spectrum is defined far too broadly to do the job (Rapin 1994). Consequently, the "inclusiveness" of the spectrum "has become a critical problem for genetic and brain research in autism" (Waterhouse et al. 2007, 308). Simply put, when they pick subjects for an autistic experimental group and a non-autistic control group, to determine if they differ in terms of genes, fMRI profiles, or what have you, they are never sure that experimental subjects in fact share the same condition. Now, our point is not to say that this makes medical research into autism necessarily impossible. This semi-vicious circle we describe is not unique to autism, but common to many psychiatric diagnoses, because they typically lack an objective biological marker (like trisomy-21 used to identify Down's syndrome), and yet there is no denying that research has produced great advances in the understanding and control of such conditions.[7] Our point, however, is to indicate that the logic guiding this research, the logic of naturalist explanation, of necessity pushes it in the direction of deeply distrusting the reality of the autistic spectrum and dissolving its unity. In the absence of a validated behavioral typology or a biological marker, and since any etiological typology "does not encompass the great majority of children in whom etiology remains unknown" (Rapin 1994), researchers of necessity "slice" the spectrum this way or that in order to get meaningful correlations with genes, brain structures, pollutants, and so on. As Harvard geneticist Christopher Walsh puts it: "I would like every child on the spectrum to have *not* 'autism,' but a more specific disorder" (Pettus 2008). This means that it is *they*, the scientists, not *us*, the sociologists, who must argue that some kinds of autism are not "really" autism, or that autism, as we heard above, is not a "single syndrome" but an "aggregate of specific disorders," which really means that they think that autism or the autistic spectrum is merely a provisional label, soon to be replaced by more specific and better specified knowledge.[8] For example, the *New York Times* reports that "with technology that can now scan each of an individual's forty-six chromosomes for minute aberrations, doctors are providing thousands of children lumped together as 'autistic' or 'developmentally delayed' with distinct genetic diagnoses." The article continued to report on six children, all with autistic symptoms, who have been knit together into a separate condition named "16p11.2" after the chromosomal address of their defective DNA (Harmon 2007). The quotation marks in the piece say it all. It is not some sociological mumbo-jumbo, but the very logic of scientific inquiry that is forcing a controversy over whether autism is really real or just a provisional label, whether the epidemic is real or socially constructed.

The genetics of autism

Is the argument of this book contradicted by the well-documented evidence concerning a genetic component in autism? Below we try to unpack the idea of autism as a genetic disorder and ask what it means. We try to show that while little is known at the moment about even the most basic questions, the thrust of genetic research is, if anything, supportive of an explanation of the rise in autism diagnoses due to a complex historical transformation that involved diagnostic expansion and substitution with mental retardation.

How much of autism is genetically inheritable?

Folstein and Rutter's 1977 monozygotic twins study established that autism is genetically inheritable, and led to subsequent studies that estimated the genetic heritability of autism to be very high, around 90 percent (Bailey et al. 1995). A heritability estimate is a population measure of the proportion of the overall phenotypic variance attributable to genotypic variance (typically by contrasting risks of monozygotic and dizygotic twin when the other twin has the phenotype). The problem is that all these studies were based on fairly small samples (21 in the original 1977 study) typically obtained through referrals, which made their estimates unreliable and biased upwards. A new study drawing on a much larger random population sample estimates heritability at 19 percent for males and 63 percent for females (Liu, Zerubavel and Bearman 2009). Ultimately, therefore, how much of autism is genetically heritable is simply unknown. It is possible, moreover, that there is no single number to be had, that the genetic heritability of autism is a moving target. In the time that elapsed between 1977 and now, as we show in this book, the autism spectrum has expanded, thereby likely making the autistic phenotype less specific and decreasing the genetic heritability of the condition.

Does genetic research resolve Waterhouse's question of whether autism is a single syndrome or an aggregate of specific disorders?

The short answer is no. The longer one is that on balance genetic research has come up with a great deal of evidence contrary to the idea that autism is a single syndrome of varying severity and instead has indicated that at the genomic level the boundary between autism and MR is blurred. What is this evidence?

14

Researchers trying to assess the genetic heritability of the three core deficits in autism spectrum disorders (social, communication, and repetitive behaviors / restricted interests), using a twin study design, found only modest co-variation between them. Individuals with extreme scores in one domain did not have extreme scores in others. Consequently, they now study each domain separately, finding each is traceable to a different quantitative trait locus (QTL)[9] with little overlap between domains or studies, underscoring "the importance of genetic and phenotypic heterogeneity in ASDs [autism spectrum disorders]" (Abrahams and Geschwind 2008, 342; Ronald et al. 2006; Alarcon et al. 2002; Schellenberg et al. 2006; Chen et al. 2006; Szatmari et al. 2007).

The search for QTLs is intimately connected with the attempt to specify endophenotypes that would put genetic research on autism on a more sound footing. Endophenotypes are a sort of intermediate phenotype. They underlie more overt symptoms; they are present in an individual whether or not the illness is expressed; they are found in non-affected family members at a higher rate than in the general population; and they have a clear genetic component. Up till now, the most common endophenotype found to be associated with autism is language delay, quantified as age at first word and associated with variation in the *CNTNAP2* gene. Language delay, however, is an endophenotype that obviously is not unique to autism but common to "other clinically distinct, but related, disorders," including intellectual disabilities, specific language disorder, and other conditions, thereby rendering autism *less* of a single well-bounded syndrome and leading researchers to suggest that "current clinical notions of boundaries between neuropsychiatric disorders need not be representative of the underlying genetic or biological etiologies" (Abrahams and Geschwind 2008, 350, 352–53; Alarcon et al. 2002; Bolton et al. 1994).

The genetic and phenotypic heterogeneity of autism spectrum disorders – which Abrahams and Geschwind (2008, 350) explain is due in part to aggregating samples from various groups throughout the world, as well as to differences in diagnostic criteria across both space and time[10] has led other geneticists to a slightly different research strategy that reduces this heterogeneity by subsetting the spectrum into smaller, more distinct phenotypes, for which a more specific genomic linkage may be sought. By thus splitting the spectrum into more cohesive clusters of children who, for example, experienced normal development before onset of autistic regression, or who suffer also from seizures, or who exhibit extreme rigid and repetitive behaviors, researchers were able to identify new loci on the genome associated with a cluster, but not with other autism spectrum cases (Abrahams and Geschwind 2008, 350; Cantor et al. 2005; Stone et al. 2004; Molloy et al. 2005; Buxbaum et al. 2001; 204; Shao et al. 2002).

A different though potentially complementary research strategy has been to look for rare mutations that are common to large groups of individuals on the spectrum. This approach has been productive – perhaps too productive. One authoritative survey found that "defined mutations, genetic syndromes and *de novo* CNV[11] account for about 10–20% of ASD cases." Yet, the authors hasten to add that "the striking finding" is "that none of these known causes accounts for more than 1–2% of cases," and that none of them "consistently results in autistic disorder, Asperger syndrome or any other defined spectrum disorders" (Abrahams and Geschwind 2008, 341, 350). In other words, any one of these mutations appears in only a very small proportion of the spectrum, yet they may also appear in the normal population, or in individuals with other diagnoses the most important of which is, unsurprisingly, mental retardation. Consequently, the authors say that there is an "absence of clarity surrounding the specifics of the relationship between the ASDs, MR and other neuropsychiatric conditions . . . such as specific language impairment . . . [or] attention deficit hyperactivity disorder" (352–53). What we know up till now about the genetics of autism, they say, paints a picture not unlike mental retardation, in the sense that the spectrum designates a whole domain of loosely related yet heterogeneous conditions "for which there is no single major genetic cause, but rather many relatively rare mutations" (341).

Indeed, at the genome level autism and intellectual disability are linked and overlapping, something that provides indirect support for the argument of this book. Recent studies demonstrate that "some types of autistic disorder and mental retardation may have common genetic origins" (Laummonier et al. 2004; Marshall et al. 2008). Two of the best known of these types are Rett's disorder and Fragile X. Both are very rare. Rett's prevalence is 1 to 10,000–15,000 of female births, Fragile X occurs in approximately 1 of 4,000 males and 1 in 8,000 females. Numerically speaking, these conditions are too rare to make a significant dent in the spectrum or the epidemic, but they demonstrate how uncertain and provisional are the distinctions we currently employ. Both Rett's and Fragile X cause intellectual disabilities as well as a range of autistic-like symptoms and both were often classified as either types or causes of autism. The genetic mechanisms of both conditions were recently identified – inherited in Fragile X, sporadic or *de novo* for Rett's – and consequently individuals who were in the past diagnosed as autistic may now, per Christopher Walsh's wish, have the single diagnosis of Rett's or Fragile X.[12] Additionally, many other mutations or regions implicated in autism spectrum disorders are also implicated in mental retardation (Abrahams and Geschwind 2008, 352–53).

Could change at the genetic level have caused the rise in autism diagnoses?

The Web is teeming with attempts to provide a genetic explanation for the epidemic, but this is speculative territory where few geneticists dare (or care) to tread.[13] The main sources for these speculations are the early *Wired* article that claimed there was an autism pocket in Silicon Valley (Silberman 2001) and Baron-Cohen's (2006) theory of "assortative mating" according to which autism risk is elevated by having two parents who are, in his terms, "high systematizers." The problem with any such theory, in which the mechanism of change is inheritance of a trait or a mutation, is that it works only for long secular trends (Mingroni 2004). It is simply ill-equipped to explain large short-term spikes like the huge rise in autism rates from the early 1990s to roughly 2004. Additionally, if Liu et al. (2009) are correct and the heritability of autism is lower than previously estimated, such explanations would only capture a small portion of the increase. *De novo* mutations and deletions, on the other hand, could potentially provide a better mechanism to explain short-term change, but they of course must be combined with other mechanisms: either environmental pollution or demographic change. For example, Liu et al. (2009) demonstrate that a small but significant proportion of the rising autism caseload is caused by an increase in *de novo* genetic deletions due to rising parental age and the increased use of assisted reproduction technologies by older parents. The case for environmental factors, by comparison, is more speculative, though it has a lot of adherents. Supporters point to the large unexplained variance left over after estimating the effects of changes in diagnostic practices and argue that it must be due to environmental factors (Cone 2009). Both demographic and environmental accounts, however, suffer from the same problem. They identify mechanisms that change the actual genetic makeup of the population, but which would lead one to expect not a steep rise in autism per se, but a steady upward trend in developmental disorders across the board. Why would rising parental age or environmental pollution not increase also the rate of mental retardation? And yet, as we shall see in the following chapter, there is evidence that as autism rates were rising, the rate of MR diagnoses was decreasing. The explanation we develop in this book (which points to diagnostic substitution as a proximate cause of the rise in the number of autism diagnoses), by comparison, is more parsimonious and targeted, and it does not require one to deny the incontrovertible evidence of the role of genetic mutations, whether inherited or *de novo*. On the contrary, it makes use of the evidence cited earlier about the genomic overlap between autism and MR (and possibly other developmental disorders). We do not need two or three mechanisms – one that explains change in the actual genetic makeup of the population, another that explains why this change is expressed as autism and not as other developmental disorders, and yet another that explains how and when these changes were recognized and diagnosed as autism – but only one: as diagnostic criteria change and as diagnostic substitution from mental retardation to autism takes place, these factors increase the genetic pool from which autism cases are drawn. The proportion of autism cases attributable to various (and unrelated) rare mutations, as well as the proportion of *de novo* mutations relative to genetic heritability, thus also increase. Stated in terms of genetics, diagnostic substitution allows us to make sense of how a population that must be relatively genetically stable could have experienced an "epidemic" of a genetic disease. It allows us to see that autism encompasses more of the population's genetic variance than it once did, not because the population's genetic makeup changed over a generation, but because the category of autism changed. It became a spectrum that captured a greater proportion of genetic endowments. Thus, the more of a realist one is about the impact of genes, the more one is obliged to adopt a sociological explanation for the rise in autism diagnoses.

Diagnostic change

Let us now turn to the second problem facing naturalist explanations: not only are diagnostic criteria overly broad, but over the last thirty years they have been continuously modified to reflect an increasingly broad understanding of autism. To begin with, in the DSM-II, autism was included within the diagnosis of "child schizophrenia," which almost by definition made it a rare condition. In 1980, the diagnostic criteria were considerably relaxed by the publication of DSM-III, which separated autism from the diagnosis of childhood schizophrenia and included it within the newly created category of Pervasive Developmental Disorders. This meant that the diagnosis of autism became independent of considerations of etiology, deep interpretation of symptoms, presence of delusions and prognosis, and was based strictly on the observation of "surface" behavior. But the diagnostic criteria were relaxed even more in 1987, with the publication of the revised edition of the DSM-III (DSM-III-R). The early onset (before thirty months) requirement was dropped. The diagnostic criterion of complete lack of social responsiveness was changed to simply abnormal social responsiveness. More important, the internal structure of the three main diagnostic criteria was changed in accordance with the idea of a spectrum. The symptoms in each of the three domains were arranged in decreasing order of severity, such that lack of social play, adequate speech but incapacity to engage in sustained conversations with others, plus a restricted range of interests, were enough to diagnose a child as autistic. The exponential rise in the number of autism diagnoses followed hard on the heels of these changes. If you are a firm believer in naturalist explanations, you can still try to claim that these changes in diagnostic criteria reflected a better understanding of autism, but you would be hard pressed to tell your skeptical listeners what might refute this assertion of belief, since the only way to diagnose autism is using the very same behavioral criteria that have changed, and there is no "objective" marker (no known brain lesion, no single gene mutation) to use in order to check their validity.

It is for this reason that many medical researchers have suddenly become sociologists and espoused a "social constructionist" explanation for the epidemic. Over and over again one finds them arguing that the rise in autism diagnoses does not reflect a real, natural rise in the number of cases out there, but is an artifact produced by the confluence of supply and demand forces (Prior 2003; Yeargin-Allsopp et al. 2003; Fombonne 1999; Croen et al. 2002a). On the supply side there was this relaxation of diagnostic criteria, and on the demand side, a heightened awareness of autism among parents, teachers and experts, which therefore led to increased detection (once people no longer think of autism as a rare condition – as it was under the guise of "childhood schizophrenia" – they begin to see it where they did not do so before), and a greater availability of services from 1991 onwards when autism was added to the Individuals with Disabilities in Education Act (IDEA) (once there are concrete benefits to getting the diagnosis, parents demand it and clinicians are happy to make it).

Does that mean that autism is not "real"? As Ian Hacking (1999) says, the question is meaningless unless we specify a real "what." A real "disease entity"? Probably not, but not even the DSM assumes that it is. Real behaviors and brain processes that are nonetheless dependent on social experiences, habits and institutional processes? Why not? Thus, we are brought back to the statement made by the scientists: autism is not a single syndrome, they say, but a collection of specific disorders that share some behavioral manifestations because similar brain systems are affected. What do they mean by that? A term that has been used with respect to schizophrenia might be useful to clarify the point: "final common pathway" for distinctly different pathological processes, something like a "funnel" into which spill different chains of cause and effect (Jablensky 1999). The causes are antecedent and independent, as we were taught in Scientific Method 101, and so the causal chains lead one back to genes, prenatal trauma, infection, and pollution. But it would be meaningless to ask which is more "real" – the uncaused, primeval causes, or the final common pathway? Certainly the sociologist has no prejudice in this respect. One can ask which is more important, which is the weakest link in the chain, which provides the most efficient target for intervention. Yet it is very clear that for the scientists the first, and random, terms in the causal chain somehow possess more reality, or more accurately, that the final common pathway, the behavioral syndrome, possesses the least reality. Why? Because scientists think the former are "natural kinds" and that they can be isolated and studied as such, while the latter hopelessly mixes together the natural and the artificial, since it brings into play, at the very least, the judgment of clinicians, conventions of behavior (what we think we know about how "normal" children behave), childrearing practices, retrospective parental reports, and the agency of children.

Does that mean that the epidemic is not "real"? Here the sociologist is on even firmer ground. Unlike the geneticists and brain researchers, who in order to possess a proper object of study are forced to enter a dispute about which part of the epidemic is "really" autism, we can take as our object the total population of actual autism diagnoses, treating it as a real phenomenon in need of explanation. Unlike the scientists who are forced to exclude the changes in diagnostic criteria, the increased awareness, the inclusion in legislation, or the increased availability of services, as "artificial" factors, not really germane to the question at hand, we need make no such distinctions as we seek the actual processes that produce the actual population of autism diagnoses. Unlike the medical researchers, who are therefore forced, almost unanimously, to dispute, or at least downgrade, the reality of the epidemic, we need not enter such a dispute, but simply observe that no epidemic has ever existed outside an institutional matrix that determined how cases were detected (or not), identified, named, enumerated and treated.

Sociologists have their own notion of mental illness as a "final common pathway," as developed in Erving Goffman's (1961) analysis of "the moral career of the mental patient." To be a mental patient, explains Goffman, it is neither sufficient nor necessary to be mentally ill in the psychiatric sense. There are many people who never come under psychiatric scrutiny, "who would be judged 'sick' by psychiatric standards but who never come to be viewed as such by themselves or others, although they may cause everyone a great deal of trouble." Conversely, there are many people, "however robust in temperament, who somehow get caught up in the heavy machinery of mental-hospital servicing" (120). What decides, therefore, whether one is a mental patient or not? Goffman's answer is "career contingencies": any factor, however accidental or artificial, that serves to move one along the steps of the predetermined career in a given institutional matrix. For example, at the time when Goffman did his research, when the career of the adult mental patient crucially involved long-term hospitalization in a residential facility, it was no doubt important that one suddenly began to hear voices, but it was only one contingency among many others no less consequential, such as one's socioeconomic status, how visible were one's offenses, how tolerant one's family, and most astoundingly, whether one lived in proximity to a mental hospital. Hence Goffman's memorable aphorism: "One could say that mental patients suffer not from mental illness, but from contingencies" (124–26). Note that the status of being a mental patient is thus an achieved status, similar to an occupational status. It is the end point of a career, within a given institutional matrix that provides the "final common pathway," the funnel, for distinctly different career contingencies. Once achieved, however, it comes to retrospectively determine and color all the preceding steps in the career; one comes to see that it was one's mental illness that caused one's institutionalization, and if one refuses to see this (a clear symptom of being ill), others will make sure the point is not lost, as in the memorable comment made by one inmate to another, and recorded by Goffman (142): "If you're so smart, how come you got your ass in here?"

Just as the behavioral syndrome of autism may be the "final common pathway" of diverse pathological processes, the autism diagnosis and assignment to intensive therapy may be the final step in a moral career determined by contingencies, and it matters a great deal, therefore, within what institutional matrix such a career unfolds. This is the meaning of our earlier claim that the new institutional matrix replacing custodial institutions – community treatment, special education, and early intervention programs – and the therapies that populate it, gave rise to the autism epidemic. Just as the significance of the moral career of the mental patient was determined by a finality – institutionalization confirmed that one was mad all along – so does the moral career of the autistic child. Why does it matter that a child is diagnosed with autism, PDD, mental retardation, or emotional disturbance? Within a custodial institutional matrix the difference would have been minimal, since all these diagnoses would have been greeted with the same gesture of institutionalization. If we think of an institutional matrix as a sieve, it is clear that the holes in the custodial sieve were too large to be sensitive to these differences. Not so for the institutional matrix of community treatment, special education, and early intervention. As it tailors an early intervention plan or an Individualized Educational Program (IEP) to the specific disability profile of each child, it seems to act more like a silk-thin micro-sieve, and it differentiates autism as never before. Here too the finality of intensive therapy – ideally with a one-on-one teaching ratio, forty hours of speech, occupational, ABA therapies a week, individual aides or "shadows" in the classroom – comes to determine the moral career of the autistic child, so that being in intensive therapy confirms that one is "on the spectrum."

Here, as in many other cases, it is useful to analyze utopian projects because they manifest in sharp relief the ideal toward which an institutional matrix tends, but which remains somewhat obscure because of the practical everyday compromises that need to be made. "All Kinds of Minds" is the name of a "non-profit institute for the understanding of differences in learning." As the title testifies, the premise is that the wiring of each child's brain is unique, and that effective intervention is ultimately individualized. For each child, the project aims to create a unique "neuro-developmental profile – a kind of balance sheet that accounts for the student's strengths and weaknesses. Once this is identified, a highly individualized plan can be developed." The governing ideal here is to do away with classification, to deploy a micro-sieve where each hole corresponds to the unique profile of a single individual.[14] If you can't do away with diagnostic classifications altogether, you need them to be flexible enough to accommodate a great many gradations and distinctions, so they can sanction tailoring a highly individualized intervention plan to each child. The spectrum of autistic disorders, with its fuzzy margins, seems to be ideally suited for this purpose.

So where do we fall in the debate between naturalist and social constructionist approaches? We attempt to walk a tightrope between them, following in the footsteps of Ian Hacking (1995, 1999, 2007) – though it's probably never advisable to follow someone on a tightrope! The key concept is "looping." Certain human conditions, says Hacking, are interactive in the sense that the very act of naming, classifying, diagnosing, and assigning them to treatment loops back to modify the condition thus named. Often this happens because the condition becomes an identity, a particular way of relating to oneself, working on oneself (alone or with therapists), and also a focal point for individuals to meet, recognize each other, organize and develop a shared language that gives shape and meaning to their experiences. We suggest thinking of the autism epidemic, therefore, neither as a naturally occurring event, nor as a socially constructed fiction, but as a final spiral in an increasingly widening vortex of looping processes.

As we argue in Chapter 8, the first spiral of looping was initiated because the newly invented autism diagnosis became a focal point for *parents* to organize around the identity of "autism parents." The parents found themselves in a difficult position. Not only were they accused of having caused their children's condition, but their testimony was discredited, even as clinicians used parental reports as the main source of evidence for their diagnoses. The parents responded by forming NSAC and forming a coalition with therapists to weave a new and alternative network of expertise, in which parents were recognized as credible experts. At this point in the history of autism, it was a rare illness, but as the new network of expertise began gradually to spread out and recruit new members, the scope of the condition began to change, to include many who in the judgment of at least one of NSAC's original founders were less clear-cut cases of autism.

The second spiral of looping came with deinstitutionalization. It was a moment of convergence. Deinstitutionalization created the need for a new type of expertise, capable of sorting and differentiating the "atypical children." The new network of expertise, with parents and therapists at its core, provided a model for how this task could be legitimately performed. This meant that the register upon which autism was inscribed and differentiated shifted. From being a rare syndrome, the object of clinical observation, it became a set of thresholds on a list of "items of autistic behavior" aggregated and differentiated on the basis of pragmatic considerations, especially response to therapy (Wing and Gould 1979; Wing 1981).

The looping dynamic continued within the new institutional matrix, especially because of its relative openness and permeability, which presented a low barrier for the entry of new therapies. The combined effect of old and new therapies was to change the autism prototype – what clinicians and diagnosticians were most likely to see in their offices, what they recognized as typical and clear-cut clinical pictures – as well as the experience of autism.[15] Some behaviors that in the past were central to the diagnosis, such as self-mutilation, became marginal because they were controlled by behavior modification. Even a core clinical syndrome – and presumably a core experience – such as "autistic aloneness" lost its coherence and central diagnostic significance because all therapies practiced what Schopler and Reichler (1971) called "non-specific impingement on the child" and forced him or her to engage in – however halting – social interaction. Autism became a continuum of "impairment of social interaction" rather than aloneness and flat affect. By the same token, Sensory Integration Therapy and similar approaches established both sensory hypo- and hyper-sensitivity firmly as a core feature of the autistic prototype, and arguably provided language and practices to give meaning and shape to autistic experience not as aloneness but as neurodiversity.

This looping spiral was reinforced by the fact that as the prototype changed, the population captured by the diagnosis became more heterogeneous, extended to become concurrent with mental retardation *and* to include Asperger's disorder within it. As we will see in Chapter 10, the extension of the spectrum to include "higher-functioning" people brought to the fore autistic individuals who were capable of representing themselves in public media, and who elaborated a language of neurodiversity with which to represent a thick autistic person (that is, one with emotional and cognitive depth, whose actions are meaningful and intentional if also hard to decipher [Hacking 2009b]). The extension to people labeled mentally retarded, especially with therapies such as ABA, provided language and practices with which to represent a thin autistic person (that is, one lacking depth, whose actions are behaviors to be controlled or reinforced). Further, these two images were by no means sealed off from one another but combined and hybridized in therapeutic practice and domestic life. Autism thus has become protean, a vast spectrum encompassing multiple forms and degrees of severity, a "free-floating signifier" that could be many things at once, that could mean one thing and its opposite at one and the same time: profound mental retardation and near-genius

24

abilities, hyper-sensitivity and hypo-sensitivity, aloofness and over-attachment, flat affect and combustible tantrums.[16]

Between mental illness and mental retardation

Let us forgo, therefore, as much as we can, the language of epidemic. Let us pose the matter in stark and simple terms. In the past, autism was rare. Now it is increasingly no longer so. Is this change due to an improvement in knowledge? It is clear that we have more autism diagnoses today because diagnostic criteria have changed, but this merely begs the question of why they have changed. Why now? It is possible, however, that we – and practically all others who have written about this matter – have been going about it the wrong way. We all have been asking: "Why is autism more prevalent today?" But a more profitable question may be: "Why was autism rare in the past?" In Chapter 6 we shall see that this is no idle question, and that in fact Kanner and others were warning of an impending epidemic of autism already in the 1960s. Obviously, the scarcity of autism in the past had to do, as we noted earlier, with the insensitivity of the custodial sieve, but this answer merely raises even more questions, specifically about the interrelations between medical knowledge – which was refined enough to make the necessary distinctions – and therapeutic practice – which was not.

So we would like to delve a little bit deeper into this question. Why was autism rare in the past? Because it was *unthinkable*, unless along the models of mental illness (hence the attempt to assimilate it to childhood schizophrenia, to characterize it as "the one psychosis unique to childhood" [Eisenberg 1973, xii]) or mental retardation, and these two were mutually exclusive, especially at the level of what we will analyze as ethical programs for intervention.

What are mental illness and mental retardation, and how do they differ? But let us ask an even more preliminary question: why compare the two at all? How are they similar? This requires dealing with the notoriously elusive idea of the "mental" and asking whether mental illness and physical illness differ, and if so, how? We do not intend to enter the philosophical or scientific debate about this question, which is very old, complex, and nuanced, and which is currently tearing American psychiatry apart (Luhrmann 2000). Instead, we would like to propose a simplistic, descriptive sociological criterion of differentiation, merely as a point of departure: the structure of the referral process, and how it affects the ethical dimension of medical intervention. A physical illness usually begins with a *subjective* complaint addressed by the patient to the doctor. We feel pain, shortness of breath, dizziness. We go to the doctor of our own accord seeking an explanation and a treatment. The doctor need not use legal authority, as commonly understood, to subject us to treatment, since we came of our own free will. Being ill, as Talcott Parsons pointed out long ago, may release us from certain normative expectations, but only on condition that we recognize ourselves as "ill" by the very fact that we come, of our own free will, to consult the doctor, and therefore authorize the doctor to intervene. Intervention, the doctor's task, is thus tantamount to localization – to our complaint, the doctor responds, "Where does it hurt?" She feels the place, seeking to draw out the pain, or orders a test that may confirm a localizing hypothesis. The task is to translate the diffuse complaint into spatial coordinates where intervention may take place (Gadamer 1996).

But what if we do not recognize ourselves as "ill" and do not authorize the doctor to intervene? It is likely that our recalcitrance will conjure the entrance of a new player on stage – the term "mental," in whatever conjugation, since it serves as a resource for making sense of our behavior as well as potentially authorizing intervention under a different ethical regime. Physical illness is not clearly demarcated from mental illness, but shades into it. At the other extreme, mental illness begins with the *objective* fact of complaint. Somebody else – a neighbor, a family member (very often), a coworker, a passerby, the police – has voiced a complaint against us and has brought us – through pressure, coercion, or false pretenses – to see the doctor (Goffman 124–25). Some form of legal authority, however rudimentary and limited it may have become (Luhrmann 2000), must come into play at this moment, because we have not come of our own free will. We may not recognize ourselves as ill and in need of treatment. As a result, mental illness involves the strange and possibly untenable combination of objective ailment and moral fault (Foucault [1961] 2006, [1962] 1987). The moral fault, which consists of nonrecognition of one's illness, must first be subdued, by legal means if necessary, or by guilt or persuasion, in order for the localization procedure to begin. This places the patient in a "Catch-22," which many authors have noticed: the only way to be treated as a rational person, that is, not sick, is to admit that one is sick (Estroff 1981; Luhrmann 2000; Martin 2007). Then one graduates from child to adult, from an illness with a body to a person with an illness. At this point, mental illness begins to shade into physical illness, as in the case of the psychiatrist, Luhrmann reports, who used to ask patients on his round: "So, how is your depression doing today, Mrs. So-and-So?" But even he was stumped when a patient would reply "I am fine, can I go home now? Don't I know myself best?" To which he replied, "That's a complicated question" (Luhrmann 2000, 136–40). This incident demonstrates the extent to which the referral process and the ethical regime of intervention we commonly invoke with the term "mental" differ from those one associated with physical illness. Not only do they bring into play legal authority, but they proceed within a peculiar type of negotiation. It does not make sense here to translate subjective complaint into a location, because it is precisely the subjective report that cannot be trusted (the patient may be saying she is fine so she can go home and commit suicide) and the doctor endeavors to prove to the patient, as a condition of cure, the falsity of that very report. Everything takes place as ongoing negotiation about the ethical status of the patient's intentions. Which ones are symptoms of the disease, and which ones are expressions of rational personhood? The intentions themselves determine the ethical status of medical intervention, from pure localization to the invoking of legal authority to keep the patient safe from herself / her illness.[17]

Obviously, this is a very limited distinction. Many who suffer from what are commonly understood as "mental" illnesses such as depression go to the doctor of their own accord. In the case of an epidemic such as tuberculosis, many who suffer from what are commonly understood as "physical" illnesses may be referred by others on the basis of external criteria and compelled by legal authority, exercised by doctors in their capacity as public hygienists, to undergo treatment. For many "physical" illnesses the initial complaint is not subjective, but an objective finding in a test of which the patient is unaware. And we still have not touched on the vexed problem of childhood disorders, where by definition somebody else – a parent or a frontline worker – articulates the complaint on the basis of objective behaviors and subjective reports. Nonetheless, it is possible to treat this distinction, on the basis of the referral process, as a continuum, although one no doubt crosscut by many other distinctions, along which illnesses and conditions are arranged in order from the most physical, that is, least demanding of the exercise of legal authority because the patient recognizes herself as ill by the very act of consulting a doctor, to the most "mental," that is, where the patient refuses to recognize herself as ill, and must first be legally defined as ill in order to undergo treatment. We are not troubled by the exceptions noted above – depression, epidemic – because our point is not to resurrect the distinction between the mental and the physical, but on the contrary to describe it as a dimension along which many characteristic movements are possible.[18]

Here we find the main similarity between mental illness and mental retardation, at least as the latter condition was understood up to the moment of deinstitutionalization. What was the meaning of mental retardation during this period? Alfred Frank Tredgold, the notorious eugenicist, is a good source to consult ([1908] 1947, 3). Maybe because he was free of any human sympathy for the mentally retarded, and so free of liberal or medical self-delusion, we think he was also very clear-sighted about the actual significance of the practice of institutionalization. What was common to the individuals institutionalized as "mentally retarded"? Tredgold said IQ had nothing to do with it. "Actually there are many persons in institutions for defectives, whom no one doubts to be in need of care and control, but whose IQ is considerably higher than that of others fending for themselves satisfactorily in the general community." His point was that "mental deficiency is, in fact, mainly a legal and social concept." Mental deficiency, to be precise, was a legal interpretation of the practice of locking up those who were "socially incapable," to use his phrase. Here the legal definition of "socially incapable" precedes and determines any specifically medical conception of ailment.

From this point of view, the distinction between mental retardation and mental illness is fairly straightforward. Tredgold explained the difference this way: the mentally ill are like a person in temporary financial embarrassment, while the mentally deficient are simply poor, like a person who never possessed a bank account. Note the idea of restorative (as opposed to distributive) justice embedded in this distinction: to avoid these situations of financial embarrassment, prudent people insure themselves. Prudent liberal societies legislate limited liability and institutionalize bankruptcy. The treatment of mental illness is analogous to these devices. It is legitimate, and cannot be hindered simply on the basis of the expense involved, because it is merely restoring sanity to those who rightfully possess it. By contrast, prudent liberal societies cannot undertake to raise the station of all the poor, all those who never possessed a bank account, or they risk economic ruin – which would be unjust for the rest of the prosperous population. The treatment of mental retardation, therefore, is inherently limited by considerations of legitimate expenditure. This is precisely the same image that insurance companies today use in order to deny coverage for interventions that, in their language, are not "restorative," not amending a previously normal state of affairs. We should note, however, that in a recent case in New Jersey, when the insurance company used this justification to deny coverage for Applied Behavior Analysis provided to an autistic child, the court ruled in favor of the child and forced the insurance company to pay (Abramson 2007). This is already an indication that with autism the neat distinction between mental retardation and mental illness has been disrupted.

In fact, there are other ways today in which this distinction has been disrupted, all inherited from deinstitutionalization, especially through the category of "developmental disability." We will have more to say about these below, but for the moment let us remain with the distinction between mental illness and retardation a little bit longer, since it is the background against which to grasp the significance of autism and related categories. A mid-1970s psychiatry textbook (Langone 1974) articulated a different dimension of this distinction. Mental retardation is not illness, the author explained, it is simply slowness, like a bottle that is filled through a clogged funnel. This is an interesting distinction, because it tells us that our notion of illness and cure, of what belongs to medicine and what does not, is implicitly reliant on a calculation of economy of effort. The mentally retarded are not ill, says the textbook, because how much they will learn depends only on the amount of effort that is made. If the amount of improvement is exactly the same as the time and effort of intervention (or sometimes even less, when you put a lot of effort and see very little improvement), if there are no "multiplier effects," there is nothing economic about it, and therefore it is not a medical cure. Ultimately, custody alone would be economic.

This economic distinction is intimately connected with another one, according to which *teaching* the retarded is opposed to medical *cure* as artifice is opposed to nature. A medical cure is economical because, even though it is administered from the outside, it sets in motion an internal natural process. This is an intimately related meaning of the term "restorative treatment." The slowness that is mental retardation, on the other hand, cannot be put in motion. It can only be fed slowly from the outside, and it remains completely dependent on this artifice. We still make this distinction, even in this age of bio-enhancement, a distinction that harks back to the original Greek meaning of "therapy," that is, "service." To treat medically is to stand in the service of nature, let it do its work, and not to impose on it so as to create something wholly new, wholly artificial. The opposition is between something "grown" and something "made" (Gadamer 1996, 110; Habermas 2003, 44–53).

We hope the reader can appreciate now to what extent the

distinctions between physical and mental illness and between mental illness and mental retardation are neither simple differences given in the nature of things, nor questions that one can hope to settle with the proper scientific knowledge or philosophical reflection. The distinctions determine what we think we can legitimately do about these conditions. They can never be clearly defined from within medical science, because where they shade into one another they bring into play the force of law, the weight of economic considerations, the delicacy of moral and ethical judgment, the fury of politics. Rather than clearly demarcated regions of medical expertise, they are fuzzy intersections of the forces impinging on medicine and traversing it.[19] To sum up, if the distinction between mental and physical illnesses as ethical regimes of intervention revolves around the legal question of the rationality of speech, then the distinction between mental illness and mental retardation as ethical regimes of intervention revolves around the economy of the cure, around the question of *therapy*.

The ways in which we diagnose, understand and *treat* autism nowadays scramble this distinction, this fuzzy boundary between mental illness and mental retardation, and thus make autism a legal, economic, and ethical challenge. This is why one cannot provide a simple answer to the question of whether an autism epidemic exists. This is also why the fact that autism is no longer rare cannot be due to a simple increase in our knowledge about the condition. The very structure of our knowledge – how we make distinctions – is what has changed.

To begin with, we may notice that the nominators and classifiers of autism seem to have been undecided about its status, giving it names that signified very little, or which gestured vaguely toward either illness or retardation, only to retreat and retract the gesture abruptly. Kanner's (1943) original term – "disturbance of affective contact" – said very little and would not commit on the medical status of the condition. A few years later, however, he included autism among what he called "apparent" or "pseudo-feeblemindedness" (Kanner 1949). We will analyze his move in Chapter 3, where we will argue that it must be understood within an emerging project for early monitoring and surveillance of childhood. If autism underlay many forms of retardation, Kanner reasoned, then there was urgent need for earliest possible diagnosis and intervention. Incidentally, this is why the explanation centering on diagnostic substitution alone is ultimately unsatisfying and inconclusive. Already in 1949 Kanner positioned autism between illness and retardation, or more precisely as an illness masquerading as retardation. Why would it take 42 years for substitution to begin?

Indeed, Kanner's followers took this point about autism being "apparent feeblemindedness" and connected it with his few vague speculations about the relation between autism and childhood schizophrenia to attach the condition firmly to the model of illness – remember Eisenberg's (1973, xii) attribution to Kanner of the discovery of "the one psychosis unique to childhood." But this was a very short-lived period in the career of the concept. Most often, autism is termed a "disorder," following the DSM-III's (1980) invention of a category of "Pervasive Developmental Disorders." There is "autistic disorder" or "Asperger's disorder" or there are "autistic spectrum disorders" more generally. The metaphor of "disorder" certainly is semantically connected with "disease," but in reality admits inability to classify a problem as "illness," and unwillingness to classify it as "retardation." What Jablensky (2007) and Jaspers say about "illness in general" (see n. 13 above) is doubly true of "disorder in general," which is almost an empty term. The ICD-10 definition of "disorder" is "a clinically recognizable set of symptoms or behaviors associated in most cases with distress and with interference with personal function." This is so broad as to encompass mental illness, mental retardation, alcoholism, or grief. Clearly, terming something a "disorder" is merely a way of flagging it as a problem.

How did autism become a "disorder"? A confluence of forces colluded in wresting autism away from among mental illnesses and balanced it somewhere closer to retardation. As we shall see in Chapters 6 and 8, the struggles and interests of the parents of autistic children organized in NSAC played a role. To accept that autism was mental illness, as things stood with 1960s American psychiatry, was to accept the "psychogenic hypothesis," that is, their own culpability. To accept that it was retardation was to disappear within a much larger and dominant movement – NARC. So NSAC sought a middle ground between these two. Chapter 9 lays out a complementary cause: the determination of the reformers of the DSM-III to keep the manual in its new incarnation away from speculative etiological categories, and instead create validated behavioral typologies as bases for future research, hence the category of "pervasive developmental disorders." These two forces came together in the work of Lorna Wing (Wing and Gould 1979; Wing 1981): mother of an autistic child, active in the British National Autistic Society, interlocutor with the American NSAC, and the key person in the DSM-III-R committee that rewrote the diagnostic criteria for autism. She held that "classical autism" was only one subtype of a larger spectrum of impairments in social interaction and communication, that retardation was an ill-defined blanket category and was often concurrent with autism, and finally that Asperger's syndrome was also part of this spectrum. All this contributed to positioning autism between mental illness and retardation, with the term "disorder" merely signaling that the behavioral syndrome had underlying and unknown biological causes, most likely genetic. Asperger's ([1944] 1991) original formulation – "autistic psychopathy" – drew on a current in German-language psychology that postulated the existence of inherited "personality disorders," distinct from mental illness, and thus somewhat akin to Freudian "neuroses" (Nadesan 2005). By the 1980s, however, "personality" had become a distinct "axis" of the DSM, and there was no logical way to apply it to childhood. "Disorder," therefore, was and is an inherently unstable designation, a placeholder marking where the new conception of genetic illness – so different from earlier conceptions of illness, as it designates the *potential* to be ill – may come into its own.

The opposite gesture is sometimes encountered when autism is understood as "developmental delay."[20] The notion of "delay" clearly is semantically connected with "retardation" and both are different ways of saying "slow." Delay, however, is not a euphemism, but a downgraded version of retardation in two ways: first, "delay" is more readily understood as temporary; second, "delay" is typically understood as specific to a particular sphere of functioning that is out of synch, rather than designating a global, across-the-board equilibrium. Children with mental retardation are thought to lag equally in language, cognition, motor abilities, auditory processing, and visual-spatial processing, while autistic children are typically described as children with uneven abilities, delayed in some areas, normal or even advanced in others. Indeed, the comparison between retardation and autism-cum-developmental-delay shows very clearly what is so new and challenging about the ethical mode of intervention underlying the rise in autism diagnoses: on the one hand, the structure of the referral process for both retardation and autism is strictly equivalent. It typically hinges on neither subjective nor objective complaint, but on the assessment of "delay" in comparison with peers, siblings, milestones found in books or on the internet, and so on. Parents typically bring the child to the doctor of their own accord. It is also true, however, that the official designation of "delay" triggers legal mechanisms such as entitlement to early intervention services; the jurisdiction of a Committee on Special Education or a similar body; mandatory IEP meetings; and, most important, guarantee of "free and appropriate education in the least restrictive environment" – none of which are conditional on the patients recognizing themselves as "ill" (though parents have significant discretion in this regard).

Yet there is a clear divergence in the fortunes of retardation and autism, even though a "delay" is implicated in both. The interventions that in the case of retardation were excluded from medical cure as uneconomical we find implicated within the economy of medical cure with regard to autism. Autism differs from retardation to the extent that the diagnosis of autism typically comes packaged together with the idea of a "critical window of opportunity," a period of time during early childhood during which it is still possible to influence neural pathways and which therefore calls for intensive intervention. Precisely this idea differentiates it from retardation and makes the diagnosis of autism more appealing to parents. It holds up the hope for a "cure"[21] – and of course, these are illnesses that are "cured," never retardation – yet within a completely different economy of effort than mental illness. The faint outline of the economy of "cure" is still discernible – intensive early intervention is said to pay dividends in the future in the form of more spontaneous improvement or "incidental learning" – but since nobody knows the critical period's length or when it is time to call it quits, and everybody remains vague about how much improvement can be expected, the content of this economy is precisely what appears uneconomical in the case of retardation: the amount of improvement is strictly equivalent to the "intensity" of intervention, which ideally can involve one-on-one teaching and forty hours of speech, occupational, and ABA therapies a week, individual aides or "shadows" in the classroom, and so on. While from the point of view of practitioners and researchers ABA treatment is prescribed for intellectual disability just as much as it is for autism (Matson, Mahan and Lovullo 2009; Matson and LoVullo 2008), in the *actual practice* of special education, given limited budgets, only autistic children and their parents are able to make a legitimate claim to the considerable resources and investments that ABA requires (Katz 2006; Fairbanks 2009). A quick, albeit inconclusive, test can demonstrate this point. Of 244 decisions involving autism in the special education decisions database of the California Administrative Hearings Office, 92 (38 percent) refer to ABA. Of the 150 involving retardation, only 29 (19 percent) refer to ABA, and upon closer scrutiny *all* 29 cases turn out to be a concurrent diagnosis of autism with MR.[22] This discrepancy, despite the recommendations of researchers, testifies to the way autism is able to blur the distinction between the economies of effort associated with illness and retardation.

33

Moreover, autism also scrambles the very distinction between inside and outside that constituted the naturalness of medical cure, its standing in service of nature, as against the artificiality associated with teaching the mentally retarded, because autism is imagined as a disruption of precisely the connection between inside and outside. The Dutch have an apt term for it: they call it "contactual disorder" (Kraijer 1997) after Kanner's original term – "disturbance of affective contact." The intervention, therefore, has to be external and artificial, precisely because it aims at establishing the natural rapport with the environment. Further, the image of a critical window of opportunity comes with the hope that externally applied therapies can kick-start internal processes that will eventually lead to "recovery."

Ultimately this discussion brings us to the third D-word – disorder, delay, *disability*. In outlining this middle position between illness and retardation, are we really telling the story of autism or of the new category of "disability," specifically "developmental disability"? More pointedly, isn't our discussion anachronistic and irrelevant because retardation is a thing of the past and has been replaced by the more humane and enlightened category of "developmental disability"? We answer a qualified "yes" for the first question, and a resounding "no" for the second. Sociologically speaking, autism no doubt is a "developmental disability," in the sense that this category stands for the intermediate space opened up by deinstitutionalization. Autism was rare in the past but is no longer, because it became thinkable within the horizon of "developmental disability." Yet the opposition between the ethical economies of retardation and mental illness has not been overcome and superseded in this space; it remains as a contradiction and tension within it. In many respects, the autism epidemic is nothing but a symptom of this tension, a resolution-by-other-means of the underlying contradiction.

What is a "disability"? Just as Tredgold's distinction between mental illness and retardation reflected a mode of governance characteristic of early liberal states, so the origins of "disability" take us back to the building of postwar welfare states. Individuals who in early liberal polities were excluded because they could not approximate the bourgeois norm of rational autonomy, or whose lives would have been deemed "not worth living" and thus subject to abortion, sterilization, or euthanasia, were transformed into citizens with a "handicap," or as the Scandinavians preferred to call them, "partially able-bodied." Disability expresses a revision of the social contract between citizen and state: provided they are equipped with the necessary prosthetic devices and accommodations that are, at bottom, their legal right, no different from any other right to equal treatment and equal opportunity, all individuals should be able to govern themselves and contribute to collective welfare. It outlines a new ethical goal between cure and custody: habilitation, making able (Shapiro 1993; Ericsson 2000; Esping Andersen 1990; Wagner 1994).

The language of "rights," however, does not resolve the core ethico-economic question – how much accommodation and effort is justified? Making able to do what? At what price and by what means? "Partially able-bodied" conveys a precise image. Intervention should turn the partial into the equivalent of fully able-bodied, capable of working, and the resulting benefits in terms of contribution to societal values would vastly outweigh the expense on prostheses. This formula fits neatly cases of missing limbs, blindness, deafness, and so on.[23] It is far more ambiguous with chronic degenerative diseases, where the prospects for restoration to equilibrium are dim,[24] or with what we may call for want of a better term the "partially able-to-develop" – where the notion of prosthesis is stretched thin. At the level of economy of effort, therefore, making able differs from both cure and custody as differential equations differ from simple calculation. Different disabilities at different levels of severity are to be fitted with different goals of making able, with differential expenditure on prostheses and accommodations, such as to minimize the risks they involve and maximize their potential for contribution (Castel 1991). As we shall see in Chapters 3 and 5, on this point there was in fact direct continuity and agreement between the institutionalization of children in the 1950s and the ideal of normalization that animated deinstitutionalization two decades later. We dedicate all of Chapter 5 to normalization. Here, suffice it to say that normalization is an overall principle guiding policy and services for the mentally retarded. Its most succinct formulation is "letting the mentally retarded obtain an existence as close to the normal as possible," with all that this entails regarding residential and educational services. It was introduced into legislation first by Denmark in 1959, then by Sweden in 1967, from where it migrated to the US in 1969 due to the advocacy of Bengt Nirje, executive director of the Swedish association for mentally retarded children, and Wolf Wolfensberger, who served on the President's Committee on Mental Retardation (Wolfensberger 1972; Nirje 1969). Making able to obtain "an existence as close to the normal as possible" meant a set of differential "tracks" composed of sequentially ordered residential, educational, and work arrangements, each going only as far as reasonable, each perfectly adjusted to the potential of the individuals involved, providing just as much integration as they could tolerate (Wolfensberger 1972). This vision was enshrined in the language of the law that Americans inherited from deinstitutionalization, currently called the Individuals with Disabilities in Education Act (IDEA). The law mandates that each child will receive a "free and appropriate education" (FAPE) in the "least restrictive environment" (LRE) suitable for his or her individual needs and abilities.

We can explore the tensions within the domain of disability from another angle. What is a prosthesis? Is it natural or artificial? Does it set in motion a natural process, or is it an intervention imposed from without? On the one hand, it is clearly artificial. "Prosthesis" is defined as "an artificial extension that replaces a missing body part or faculty." It is clearly something "made," not "grown." On the other hand, a prosthesis is something that is meant to be *grafted on to nature*, to complete it by means of imitating it, and then to function as an integral part within an intact whole. A prosthesis, therefore, defies the neat opposition between the naturalness of medical cure and the artifice of teaching the retarded. Again, this is easy to imagine with missing limbs and sensory deficits, much less so with cognitive and developmental disabilities. The term "prosthesis" conveys the image of something that mediates the environment for the organism in the same or functionally equivalent way that a missing limb or sense organ would have done, requiring therefore fairly limited modifications to the environment. The opposite of a prosthesis, therefore, is *custody*, an artificial and sheltered environment. Again, it is not the case that one replaces the other, but that between them stretches a whole range of hybrid and ambivalent arrangements, a dimension along which "prosthesis" gradually becomes metaphoric. It is significant, therefore, that one of the best known schools for autistic children defined its mission with an expression that seems to merge these opposites – "prosthetic environment" (Holmes 1990). How could an environment be prosthetic? Only, it would seem, if the object of intervention is no longer the individual per se, but the individual-within-an-environment, or the individual's contact with the environment. One works simultaneously on both individual and environment, seeking not only to make the individual able to function in a given environment, but also to extend the perimeter of the prosthetic environment so it gradually comes to overlay more and more of the "normal" everyday one.

We can see why, despite the fact that retardation is now included along with autism (and blindness) in the intermediate zone of disabilities, there would be such a divergence in fortunes between autism

36

and mental retardation. The vision of a multitrack system, the range between prosthesis and custody, permits such divergence and pre- serves the opposition between illness and retardation as one between upper (faster, longer) and lower (slower, shorter) tracks. Clearly, the proximate cause for the divergence of fortunes lies in how the law treats autism and retardation. But the law cannot be the origin of this distinction, nor its arbiter. The law is ill-fitting and sits awkwardly with such a distinction, which could hardly be deduced from the phrase "free and appropriate education in least restrictive environ- ment." How do you know whether the education provided is free and appropriate? According to hearing officers presiding over due process hearings, education is appropriate if it provides "sufficient support services to permit the child to benefit educationally from . . . instruction." How can you know how much is sufficient? "The quantum of educational benefit necessary to satisfy IDEA varies with the potential of each pupil." How can you know what this potential is? In some cases, such as those of deaf or blind children, it is obvious that there are no inherent limits to their potential, only external ones. In this case, the support services are strictly equivalent to prostheses, and education operates with the logic of restorative treatment, as in illness. But what do the hearing officers have to say about the men- tally retarded? "For a severely retarded pupil, IDEA requires more than a trivial or *de minimis* educational benefit but rather mandates meaningful benefit which generally implies progress as opposed to regression. However, the State is not required by IDEA to maximize the child's potential."[25] This means that the goals annually set must show only some incremental gain or, put differently, that the only potential ascribed to the severely retarded is the potential to have a potential at all, that is, not to regress or stay the same from year to year. There is nothing restorative about it, and in reality, as the years pass, the IEP goals do not go much beyond the attainment of "self-care" skills. Between these two clear poles, however, there are no signposts. With autism, and especially with the idea of a "critical window of opportunity," the very basis for distinguishing what is restorative intervention is disrupted, since what is to be restored is an unknown quotient of *potential* for development. The distinction between custody and prosthesis becomes fuzzy, as we saw with the notion that support services constitute a "prosthetic environment." The law, in this respect, clearly declares itself unequipped to deal with these questions, and delegates authority to experts: "A determination as to the adequacy of an IEP is a matter of expert opinion."[26]

But what kind of experts? No doubt the idea of "critical window of opportunity" comes out of biological and psychological research. It has a long pedigree, going back at least to 1952 and John Bowlby's *Maternal Care and Mental Health*, and even before that to the idea of "sensitive periods" and "imprinting" formulated in ethology (Nadesan 2005). But how could this idea, which was at the core of the "mother blaming" of an earlier age, so derided and despised by virtually everybody in the autism field today, provide the basis for the new ethical mode of intervention now synonymous with autism? Psychiatry, even armed with the findings of science, could not have wrought this by itself. First, contrary to what is now the received wisdom in the autism field, twentieth-century child psychiatry has been reluctant to resort to parent blaming (Ong-Dean 2005, 148–50). By the time he named autism, for example, Kanner (1941) was already the author of *In Defense of Mothers* (though the title is more emphatic than the actual "defense"). Second, late twentieth-century psychiatry, especially in its biomedical reincarnation, has been moving decidedly away from blaming anybody, declaring boldly with Koplewicz (1996) that *It's Nobody's Fault* (see also Siegel 1996 and Luhrmann 2000). Third, after the attacks it sustained during the upheavals of the late 1960s and early 1970s, especially after its role in the mistreatment of mental retardation had been exposed by the deinstitutionalization movement, psychiatry as a discipline was reluctant to take upon itself a charge as fraught as the medical diagnosis of social destiny.

This is the crux of the matter: deinstitutionalization and the reforms that followed it, especially IDEA, have created the *need* for medical diagnosis of social destiny, a synthesis of psychiatric and special-education expertise capable of justifying the assignment of atypical children into distinct tracks going different ways at markedly different speeds. Siegel (1996, 274–300) talks about "forks in the road," the first at the transition to kindergarten and the most significant one at about fifth grade, and they all involve the assessment of "overall degree of mental retardation." Contrary to sociological theories of professional imperialism (Sarfatti-Larson 1977; Freidson 1986; Abbott 1988), however, the strongest contender for such a diagnostic position – the psychiatric profession – is also reluctant to step into it, while the normal executors of this function – the special education bureaucracy – lack the legitimacy to perform it. The reforms have created a position for an expert whose diagnostic decisions are necessary for the functioning of the whole machinery. This expert would diagnose not simply a condition but a whole social destiny. Yet, no one dares to step into the role. In Chapters 2 through 5, we will tell the story of how this position was created. Instead of the slot being filled by a bold new profession, laying imperial claims to jurisdiction over the medical diagnosis of social destiny, something else happened: the slot remains empty, but it has been surrounded by a whole new network of expertise that orbits it, so to speak, peopled by less assuming actors – occupational therapists, speech therapists, ABA specialists, behavioral psychologists, other "therapists" of various kinds, child psychiatrists, and the parents themselves. That the diagnostic function is no longer the monopoly of psychiatry is evident, for example, in psychiatrist and expert autism diagnostician Bryna Siegel's advice book for parents (1996, 124–25). In a chapter dedicated to how parents cope with the diagnosis, she concedes that the clinician's diagnosis is just a description, "a best guess," and that it is important for the clinician to communicate the ambiguity and provisional nature of their diagnosis, otherwise parents will not trust it: "parents are experts on their own children too, and are in an excellent position to detect rubbish." The introduction to this book, written by another expert, Lorna Wing, herself the mother of an autistic child, makes plain the new balance of power and the shared nature of expertise:

> Parents of children with autistic spectrum disorders do not, in general, have a high opinion of professionals. Parents rapidly recognize whether a professional worker really knows anything about autism – and they tend to find that most do not. There are only two ways of acquiring a depth of knowledge on the subject that earns the parents' respect. One is to be a parent oneself. The other is to work closely with the children over many years, observing and interacting with them and listening with great attention to the parents' descriptions of their children's development from infancy. This cannot be done sitting comfortably on the other side of a desk in a consulting room. You have to be part of the action to see it for yourself. (ibid., vii-viii)

In Chapters 6 through 8, we tell the story of how the model for this form of expertise was provided by the research-advocacy-therapy network innovated by autism parents and therapists. The function of medical diagnosis of social destiny is not so much outsourced to these actors as postponed into an indefinite future, fragmented into multiple concrete decision points (spelled out in an IEP), interiorized in the unfolding of a practice. In a pragmatic sort of way, the therapies they wield sidestep, ignore, neutralize, the antinomies of medical discourse, the opposition between physical and mental, between illness and retardation, between the economy of "cure" and the diseconomy of educating the retarded, between the natural and the artificial, between prosthesis and custody. It is as if the in-betweenness of the space they inhabit provided them with the flexibility necessary to develop a different ethical model of intervention, of which autism is the necessary object. Indeed, the diagnosis of autism permits this network of expertise maximum flexibility to dodge and postpone into the future the function of diagnosing social destiny. Perhaps this is why it is so popular now, why child psychiatrists, pediatricians and early intervention workers do not hesitate to "make the call," because it merely functions to postpone later, more fateful, calls. As Siegel says, parents fear a diagnosis of MR more than autism (and they often resist IQ testing, the putative arbiter of social destiny), because MR is understood as something fixed, something that will not go away (1996, 97). Autism is more ambiguous and leaves space for vague hopes. As the adolescent years draw to a close, however, the space between illness and retardation begins to narrow down once more, and the situation is inverted. Many parents find themselves advocating for the diagnosis of intellectual disability, the opposite of what they advocated in the past.[27] Once high school is over (it can be extended until age 21 and no more) and social destiny has been decided by default, perhaps it is the category of intellectual disability and not autism that would provide access to services, however meager and paltry they might be.

— 1 —

THE PUZZLE OF VARIATION IN AUTISM RATES

Autism may be everywhere, but it is not found everywhere at the same rate. When it comes to the autism epidemic, all U.S. states were *not* created equal. American readers should know that the chances their own children will be categorized and served as "autistic" by school boards are about twenty-two times higher if they live in Maine than if they live in Oklahoma. As the readers can see in Table 1, some states – Maine, Massachusetts, Minnesota, Oregon – diagnose children between the ages of 3 and 5 as autistic, and provide them with special education services, at rates that are much higher than the national average of 29 in 10,000 (for this age group in 2006) while other states – Mississippi, Iowa, Oklahoma, West Virginia – are well below it.[1]

The same holds around the globe. For some reason, Swedish children have a much greater chance of being diagnosed as autistic than children in any other country. A 1997 epidemiological survey on the west coast of Sweden found a prevalence rate of 46.4 in 10,000, but the following year, across the well-traveled border with Norway, a survey using the same ICD-10 diagnostic criteria found a prevalence rate of only 5.2 in 10,000. One more year passed, and on the south coast of Sweden, only a short ferry ride from Denmark or Norway, an epidemiological survey using somewhat different diagnostic criteria found a rate of 72.6 in 10,000 (Fombonne 2003).[2]

Scant attention has been paid to these differences, for an obvious reason. While both sides in the debate about the autism epidemic play the numbers game with relish, ultimately they do not trust the numbers and at the slightest discrepancy are ready to sweep them aside. The underlying, scarcely articulated, article of faith they share is that at bottom the real rate of autism should not differ between states or countries, because it is determined by biological factors that,

Table 1: Rates of Children ages 3 through 5 served under IDEA, disability category "autism" as a percentage of state population[a]

State	Autism rate
Maine	0.89
Massachusetts	0.67
Minnesota	0.61
Oregon	0.61
Pennsylvania	0.56
California	0.54
Nevada	0.46
Delaware	0.41
Connecticut	0.35
Rhode Island	0.35
Michigan	0.33
District of Columbia	0.31
Hawaii	0.31
Indiana	0.31
New Hampshire	0.31
Vermont	0.29
Wisconsin	0.29
Maryland	0.28
South Dakota	0.28
Florida	0.27
New Jersey	0.25
North Carolina	0.25
Illinois	0.23
South Carolina	0.23
Nebraska	0.22
Texas	0.22
New York	0.21
Washington	0.21
Tennessee	0.20
Virginia	0.19
Kentucky	0.18
Louisiana	0.18
North Dakota	0.18
Wyoming	0.18
Arkansas	0.17
Montana	0.17
Utah	0.17
Georgia	0.15
Kansas	0.15
New Mexico	0.14
Arizona	0.13

Table 1:   (continued)

State	Autism rate
Missouri	0.13
Colorado	0.12
Idaho	0.12
Alabama	0.11
Mississippi	0.08
West Virginia	0.06
Oklahoma	0.04
Alaska	N/A

[a] The number of disabled children divided by the total number of children 3 to 5 years old in the state's population, and multiplied by 100.

barring concentrations due to pollution or assortative mating, should be the same everywhere. This belief empowers them to dismiss the differences in numbers as artificial and temporary, merely reflecting the peculiarities of how each state (or country) defines autism, the effort and resources it dedicates to detecting it, or how deep epidemiologists have dug for it. In particular, researchers treat the U.S. Department of Education data, which we used in Table 1 above, as "not reliable for tracking autism prevalence," essentially because the guidelines for educational assessment and administrative categorization differ a great deal between states. No wonder the rate of autism is very high in Oregon, since all that Oregonian children require to qualify as autistic for special education services is to demonstrate "impairments in social interaction" (Laidler 2005).

The sociologist, however, need not assume that there is a single, real rate of autism everywhere underlying the different survey results, and therefore can pay more attention to what may be learned from these differences. We take the total population of *actual* autism diagnoses as our object. Unlike the epidemiologists, the scientists, and the activists on both sides of the debate, we do not treat these actual rates as merely imperfect reflections of some real though unknown and hence hypothetical rate, which must somehow be true everywhere. We do not consider the differences in diagnostic criteria, in awareness, in legislation, in the availability of services or the effort expended at detection, to be "artificial" factors masking the underlying natural reality. We are interested in identifying and explaining the looping processes that produce the actual population of autism diagnoses, and there is no better way of doing this than looking at factors that produce variation in this population.

43

There have been few efforts to date to explain state or international variation in the prevalence of autism. A promising start for the U.S. was made by Mandell and Palmer (2005), who found positive associations between state variance in the administrative prevalence of autism and the state's education-related spending, the number of pediatricians in the state, and the number of school-based health centers (though the latter was not significant). This can be characterized as a "supply-side" argument. Where there are more spaces available because more dollars went into special education, more children with autism will appear to take these spaces;[3] where there are more pediatricians and school health centers, this wider net of detection and screening would bring up more children with autism.

It's a good start, because it shows that variation in the administrative prevalence of autism is neither random nor arbitrary. It is not simply a matter of how obscure bureaucrats at a state's department of education chose to define autism, but varies systematically with certain variables that measure the effort of detection, or the relative probability of being diagnosed and serviced. We see problems, however, both with the logic of Mandell and Palmer's argument, and with their results. The logic of the supply-side argument is ad hoc. Substitute for autism another developmental disorder – for example, learning disability – and the theory would predict the same result, despite the fact that variance in the administrative prevalence of learning disability is very different from autism. Only four of the seventeen states that are at or above the national mean in autism rates are also at or above the national mean in learning disabilities. Obviously, one would be entirely correct to argue that such a comparison is spurious because special education spaces, dollars, and other resources are finite and increases or decreases in one category are not independent of increases or decreases in another. This is, however, precisely the point, precisely why we said above that the supply-side argument is ad hoc. It is merely "glued" to the empirical case of autism, and one would require an additional and unrelated argument to explain why it is specifically *autism* that is increasing while other diagnoses are decreasing.

Mandell and Palmer's results are elegant – each additional 1 million dollars spent increased the administrative prevalence of autism by 0.02 percent, each additional pediatrician was worth a 0.06 percent increase – but using an ad hoc logic of our own we can easily produce much better results. We invite the reader to re-examine Table 1. Is there something familiar about the distribution of states above and below the national mean? Of course there is! It is almost identical

Maine	0.89
Massachusetts	0.67
Minnesota	0.61
Oregon	0.61
Pennsylvania	0.56
California	0.54
Nevada	**0.46**
Delaware	0.41
Connecticut	0.35
Rhode Island	0.35
Michigan	0.33
District of Columbia	0.31
Hawaii	0.31
Indiana	**0.31**
New Hampshire	0.31
Vermont	0.29
Wisconsin	0.29
Maryland	0.20
South Dakota	**0.28**
Florida	**0.27**
New Jersey	0.25
North Carolina	**0.25**
Illinois	0.23
South Carolina	**0.23**
Nebraska	**0.22**
Texas	**0.22**
New York	0.21
Washington	0.21
Tennessee	**0.20**
Virginia	**0.19**
Kentucky	**0.18**
Louisiana	**0.18**
North Dakota	**0.18**
Wyoming	**0.18**
Arkansas	**0.17**
Montana	**0.17**
Utah	**0.17**
Georgia	**0.15**
Kansas	**0.15**
New Mexico	**0.14**
Arizona	**0.13**
Missouri	**0.13**
Colorado	**0.12**
Idaho	**0.12**
Alabama	**0.11**
Ohio	**0.09**
Iowa	**0.08**
Mississippi	**0.08**
West Virginia	**0.06**
Oklahoma	**0.04**

Figure 2: Red and Blue states (2004 elections) sorted by rates of children ages 3 through 5 served under IDEA, disability category "autism" as percentage of state population

with the distinction between "red" and "blue" states (as you can see in Figure 2), at least as they divided during the 2004 presidential elections. The correlation is unbelievably neat. Of the 17 states above the national mean, a full 15 voted for the Democratic presidential candidate in 2004. Only 5 blue states were below the national mean, and none too far below it. The 22 states with the lowest administrative prevalence of autism were all red: they all voted for George W. Bush.[4]

Of course we do not mean to argue that a state's political affiliation, whether it reliably polls Democratic or Republican, directly determines autism rates. The variable of political affiliation packs a lot of punch, to be sure, but it also packs a lot of different processes within it. It almost certainly stands for a whole package of supply-side factors such as a state's GDP (reliably blue states are richer than reliably red states) and therefore the level of education-related spending, or the degree of urbanization (red states tend to be rural) and therefore the number of pediatricians and easily accessible diagnostic facilities. Almost certainly it stands also for demand-side factors such as the relative proportion of the highly educated in the population – blue states are more educated – which translates into more educated parents' greater awareness and initiative in securing the diagnosis, such parents' clout against special-education bureaucracies, or their tendency to form advocacy organizations.[5] Finally, it measures something a little bit less tangible, such as a state's political culture, the relative sensitivity of legislators to the rights of the disabled, their commitment to ideals of normalization and mainstreaming, or their electoral vulnerability to issues relating to early childhood education (Sigelman et al. 1981; Parish 2005). The distinction between "blue" and "red" is shorthand for an assemblage of social and political differences. It is instructive to see how neatly the administrative prevalence of autism varies with it. It certainly should give pause to those who argue that the rise in the number of autism diagnoses is caused by vaccines, or by environmental pollution, or by any other naturalist mechanism. We believe it is good evidence that "autism" is not simply a medical diagnostic label but also a charged *political* category. But to try to deduce an explanation from this finding would be completely ad hoc.

So let us lay the ground rules for what is to follow in the rest of this book. Any explanation for state variation in the administrative prevalence of autism must also be at the same time an explanation for the autism epidemic, which means it must answer two questions: "Why autism?" – that is, why is it specifically autism that is increasing and not learning disabilities or other disorders (something that supply-side arguments find difficult to do), and "Why now?" – since autism was named in 1943, why did it take 48 years for the number of diagnoses to begin to rise (something that demand-side arguments find difficult to do)?

Diagnostic substitution

Let us see how these ground rules work with what we believe is the strongest and most plausible account to date for the autism epidemic: the argument that it is driven by diagnostic substitution with mental retardation, that children who in the past would have been diagnosed as mentally retarded are now given the diagnosis of autism at increasing rates.

Two recent American studies provide strong evidence that diagnostic substitution has taken place and that it accounts for a significant portion of the rise in the number of autism diagnoses. First, Paul Shattuck (2006) used state data on special education enrollments – the same data we used in Table 1 and Figure 2 – to show that from 1994 to 2003, just as enrollments as either autistic or "developmentally delayed" increased across states, there was a corresponding decrease across states in special education enrollments as either mentally retarded or learning disabled. These were not two independent trends, but a single process of substitution. When Shattuck examined the two trends *within* each state there was a significant inverse correlation between the increase in the rate of autism enrollments and the decrease in mental retardation enrollments. Moreover, minus the rise of autism, there would have been no reason to assume that mental retardation and learning disability enrollments would decline. Before 1994, that is, before autism's addition to IDEA legislation finally began to be implemented nationwide, the trend was of steady, albeit small increases in mental retardation and learning disability enrollments. Then in 1994 the curve turned downward. Shattuck interpreted his findings to indicate, albeit indirectly, that children who in the past would have been enrolled in special education as mentally retarded are now enrolled as autistic.

By no means is diagnostic substitution unique to the U.S. Numbers from the Israeli Ministry of Education paint a roughly similar picture. The proportion of children classified as autistic among all kindergartners with special needs increased from 7.6 percent in 2001 to 10.3 percent in 2008. There were even bigger increases in the proportion of children diagnosed with developmental delay and language delay, while the proportion of children diagnosed with mental retardation (of all degrees) and learning disability decreased from 16.3 percent to 9.4 percent, and from 8.3 percent to 1.3 percent respectively.[6]

Why would there also be a decrease in enrollments of learning disabilities associated with the rise of autism diagnoses? Earlier studies (MacMillan and Speece 1999; Macmillan et al. 1996) have shown that from 1976 to 1992, learning disabilities enrollments in the U.S. increased in association with decreases in mild mental retardation enrollments; that is, there was an earlier diagnostic substitution between the two. This makes it possible to speculate that the contemporary decrease in learning disabilities enrollments is, at bottom, also a form of diagnostic substitution from mental retardation to autism, albeit one that went through the circuitous route of learning disabilities, during a long period in which they were a more "popular" diagnosis.

Why would there also be significant increases in the diagnosis of "developmental delay"? This is an even more recent category. It was added to IDEA in 1997, and can be applied only to children between three to nine years of age. Thus it is a temporary designation, a placeholder. This diagnosis is a polite way of saying that mental retardation or autism or some other problem is suspected, but that the suspicion is not going to govern the assignment or treatment of the child, because it's too early to call. As we argued in the introduction, there are strong connections between the diagnosis of autism and the designation of a child as "developmentally delayed," as both categories encode the same kind of move away from the image of a fixed and global mental retardation. To the extent that autism, or the autism spectrum, is not really a thing but a domain of intervention composed of similarly structured objects of discourse, "developmental delay" no doubt is an integral part of this domain. One may add to it also the diagnosis of "language delay" or "language disorders," since in the Israeli case, at least, they have experienced marked increase over time along with autism and developmental delay, but only among kindergartners, since after age six the same children tend to be switched to the category of "learning disabled" or to more specific diagnoses.

Shattuck's evidence (or the evidence we gleaned from the reports of the Israel Ministry of Education) is indirect. He looks at global population trends and infers information about individuals. Using data from the California Department of Developmental Services on the actual diagnostic career of children from 1991 to 2004, Peter Bearman and Marissa King (2009; see also King 2008) were able to provide direct evidence of a rapidly rising rate of diagnostic substitution from mental retardation to autism in this state. They estimate that about a quarter of the rise in the autism caseload was due to this diagnostic substitution. A Canadian study, incidentally, reached a similar conclusion, estimating that diagnostic substitution from mental retardation accounts for a third of the increase in autism prevalence in British Columbia (Coo et al. 2007). There are good reasons, however, to assume that these are underestimates. Bearman and King use the known cases of actual diagnostic substitution, in children who were six or older by 1992, to estimate the probability that children born later and given the diagnosis of autism only would have been diagnosed as mentally retarded if there were no change in diagnostic criteria. Yet this assumes that the probability of getting a diagnosis of autism rather than mental retardation at age six is the same as at age two or three. This assumption is clearly untenable. Everything we know about how autism is diagnosed leads us to predict that the probability of being diagnosed as autistic rather than retarded decreases with age. There is also substantial evidence that the modal age of diagnosis has been going down significantly over the last two decades (Yeargin-Allsopp et al. 2003, 54; Fombonne 2003; Hertz-Picciotto and Delwiche 2009). This would lead one to estimate that diagnostic substitution from mental retardation accounts for a great deal more than a quarter or even a third of the increase in the autism caseload.

Yet it is probably the case that diagnostic substitution from mental retardation is only one pathway by which diagnostic change leads to increases in the number of autism diagnoses. As was evident in the much earlier "epidemic" of learning disabilities, there usually are several different pathways into a newly popular diagnosis (Ong-Dean 2005; 2006). One pathway leads from mental retardation presumably into the "low-functioning" pole of the autism spectrum, as it did with learning disabilities in the past; another pathway leads from "borderline" cases that may have been undiagnosed in the past, or from less severe disorders, like "specific developmental language disorder" (Bishop et al. 2008), into the "high-functioning" pole of the spectrum.

Supply-side and demand-side explanations for diagnostic substitution

Demonstrating the occurrence of diagnostic substitution, however, is hardly the final word in explaining the autism epidemic or the variation in autism prevalence. It raises other questions. Why is diagnostic substitution taking place? Why would it vary so markedly between states and countries? Pointing to the change in diagnostic criteria, as we noted in the introduction, again constitutes no answer at all. Why have these been changed? The reader may feel that we are unfairly and arbitrarily pushing the burden of explanation backwards, perhaps because we are partial to historical explanations. "One cannot explain everything," the reader could protest, "it is well known that one can extend causal chains all the way back to Cleopatra's nose, but at a certain point it becomes a futile and unproductive exercise." We beg this reader's patience. We think that there are excellent reasons to push the burden of explanation further back, so to speak, but it will take a few pages to demonstrate these reasons. The main point is that what diagnostic substitution means is not self-evident, and so what should be done about it is also not yet clear. At least several competing explanations are possible, and the best way to decide among them is to submit them to the test of answering "Why autism?" and "Why now?"

Why would there be diagnostic substitution from mental retardation to autism? Not much has been written about this, but everybody in the field of autism has an opinion about it, and the answers and speculations we heard fell predictably into either supply-side or demand-side accounts, or some combination thereof.

Supply-siders typically argue that diagnostic substitution is taking place because the science of autism has progressed. We know more about autism now than ever before and consequently we are able to identify autism and distinguish it from mental retardation much better than in the past. It would follow that state variation in the administrative prevalence of autism reflects the variable extent to which scientific knowledge about autism has diffused to states' educational bureaucracy. Red and blue states would map, therefore, onto a distinction between "backward" and "progressive" states. The global distribution of autism prevalence, too, would map onto the distinction between the advanced Western countries at the core of the global world system, the G-7 or G-8, and countries at the underdeveloped periphery. This sounds plausible, but upon the briefest examination appears to be an empty claim, impossible to verify. First, as noted in the introduction, there is no biological marker with which to verify whether diagnoses made on the basis of one strictly behavioral definition of autism are more or less accurate than those made on the basis of another. Second, as we shall see in Chapter 9, the main change that "opened the floodgates" and permitted autism to become a spectrum disorder was not the capacity clearly to distinguish it from mental retardation, but on the contrary the possibility of considering it as *concurrent* with mental retardation; to think of them as coexisting and not mutually exclusive conditions. Third, if we read carefully what the researchers who formulated the new diagnostic criteria say about them, we see that when pressed to the wall they are forced to defend them not as more accurate, but on the basis of pragmatic considerations. Other labels are possible, they say, but this one – autism – is more useful than others (Rutter 1978; Wing 1981). Finally, the correlation between the prevalence of autism and the advancement of medicine and science is by no means universal, as proven by the

French case. France bucks the autism trend, with relatively low and steady levels of prevalence – 4.5 per 10,000 in 1989, 4.9 in 1992, and 5.35 in 1997. If we look at the last two decades, France has the lowest rate of autism among the few "advanced" countries that actually conduct prevalence studies (Fombonne 2003). No doubt this has to do with the unique prestige that psychoanalysis continues to enjoy in France (Grinker 2007; Chamak 2008), and consequently the different way in which the CFTMEA[7] classifies autism and specifies diagnostic criteria (Burstejn and Jeammet 2002). To say, with Grinker, that this is due to French atavism and the resistance of vested professional interests, is illegitimate. It is a case of shooting the messenger who is bringing the bad news – evidence contrary to the hypothesis – instead of attending to the news itself.

Indeed, the biggest objection we have to this supply-side account is that it is simply untrue. There is no new knowledge about the relations between mental retardation and autism. As we will show in Chapter 2, from the very moment, more than sixty years ago, that autism was named, it was speculated, suspected, asserted that it underlay mental retardation. Kanner himself regarded autism as "apparent" or "pseudo feeblemindedness" and speculated that many children institutionalized as mentally retarded were, in fact, autistic. Put differently, the supply-side account of diagnostic substitution completely fails the "Why now?" test. Diagnostic substitution and with it the autism epidemic were long foretold, long in coming, one could say they were built into the very concept of autism. The slot or ecological niche for a spectrum running from the most severely disabled all the way to the high-functioning was already prepared in Kanner's original account. Over the years there were many smaller and abortive epidemics, as we shall see in Chapter 6, yet the conditions for autism to be generalized to the point that, with the spectrum, it covers an ever-increasing range of childhood disorders, did not exist until the institutional matrix of custody was dismantled by deinstitutionalization, and a coalition of parents, clinicians and therapists was able to occupy the niche and develop its inherent possibilities.

"Aha!" exclaims the reader, or the medical researcher with sociological inclinations, or the rare sociologist who strays into this field, "isn't this an indication that diagnostic substitution is really driven not by supply factors – such as better scientific knowledge – but by consumer demand?! Forget about deinstitutionalization! Forget about the clinicians and their diagnostic sophistry! There is no need to look far back into history! It's the parents, stupid! Diagnostic substitution is taking place because the autism diagnosis removes the stigma of mental retardation, gives hope to parents (which con-therapists can exploit) that behind the veil there is an intact child they may win back, and most important, it provides access to services, ten to twenty weekly hours of intensive therapies, that mentally retarded children have no chance of obtaining. Do you really need any other explanation?"

We are certainly more partial to this line of argument, and it is certainly not as empty or circular as the comfortable assumptions of supply-siders. In a brilliant unpublished paper based on the California Department of Developmental Services data, Bearman and King demonstrate that, net of other factors, living in very close proximity to a child previously diagnosed with autism significantly increases another child's risk of being diagnosed with autism, and significantly lowers their risk of being diagnosed with mental retardation. Behind diagnostic substitution, therefore, there is a dynamic of social influ-ence and diffusion of information among parents who are no doubt interested in lessening the stigma and obtaining more services. But this argument too is ad hoc. With some charity, we may let it pass the "Why now?" test. Things did not come easy to the parents of autistic children in earlier years. They have fought a long struggle, beginning in the mid-1960s, first to destigmatize the condition, to remove the implication that it was caused by parental coldness and mistreatment, the famous "refrigerator mother" accusation, and then to obtain recognition of autism as a "developmental disability" (akin, in fact, to mental retardation) or a vaguely defined "neurological disorder." Only after they had won a seat at the table and federal legislation made autism part of the Individuals with Disabilities in Education (IDEA) act, did the diagnosis become relatively advantageous to parents over the designation of their children as mentally retarded or "intellectually disabled" (King 2008).

Yet even this more historical demand-side explanation is ad hoc, because it fails the "Why autism?" test. Like Mandell and Palmer's account for state variation, this explanation could be applied to any condition or diagnosis. It could explain an epidemic of bipolar disorder in children, as some are predicting will shortly be upon us (Groopman 2007); it certainly could be, and has been, applied to explain the earlier epidemic of learning disorders just as well as it could explain the autism epidemic (Ong-Dean 2005; 2006). It pro-vides no account of conditions of existence nor of limits and obsta-cles. It makes it seem that if parents just fought hard enough, they could simply change diagnoses at will and produce an epidemic out

of thin air (but what about the parents of children with other conditions?). Social influence and advocacy, destigmatization and demand
for services, are definitely crucial ingredients in the looping process
that produces diagnostic substitution, but they would have been futile
without deinstitutionalization, and of markedly different significance
if autism did not occupy a niche between mental illness and mental
retardation.

Comparison demonstrates the blind side of such demand-side
explanations. In this chapter, we use information not only from the
U.S. and the U.K., but also from several other countries – France,
Israel, Turkey, Canada, Japan, Sweden, and South Africa – chosen
for no special reason other than that we had access to informants
and data sources in these countries, and because they seem to represent a wide enough variation, from the core of the "old world" to
developing "third world" countries and others. Almost invariably, in
all these countries there are strong parent organizations, some quite
old, advocating on behalf of autistic children. Everywhere we looked
there were parents tuned to autism web sites propagating the Anglo-
American gospel, who spoke the same language of disability rights,
neurodiversity, fast-closing windows of opportunity, or what have
you, and who advocated forcefully on behalf of their children. But in
many of these cases (Israel, Turkey, France, South Africa) the rates of
autism – if they were known at all – were well below those found in
the U.S. and the U.K.

The French organization ASITP – Association au Service des
Inadaptes ayant des Troubles de la Personnalité – dates from the
mid-1960s. A later organization – Autisme France – is very active and
modeled after similar American and British societies, with which it
collaborates (Chamak 2008; Roge 1997).[8] Yet we have seen how low
is the autism rate in France.

The Israeli organization representing parents of autistic children –
ALUT – dates from 1974. It is very active in providing treatment and
assessment services in collaboration with the Ministry of Education.
Its founders reported being strongly influenced by similar American
organizations.[9] Yet the autism rate in Israel, measured as the number
of recipients of disabled child payments from the National Insurance
Institute who are categorized as autistic, is 18 in 10,000 in 2007,
inching up from 7 in 10,000 in 2001, but still well below the comparable American estimates, though much higher than in France.[10]

In Turkey, as well, sixteen parent-run autism organizations have
recently formed a collective called the Autism Platform, no doubt
following the banding together of American organizations in Autism

Speaks. They provide support for families and advocate for early diagnosis, early intervention, and improvement of special education services.[11] One of the parent advocacy organizations – Tohum Otizm Vakfı – has joined forces with the Ministry of Health and organized autism screenings in several major areas.[12] The language adopted by these groups is very similar to American advocacy organizations. There are no reliable estimates of autism rates in Turkey, but in the 2006–2007 school year, there were 2,114 students who were diagnosed with autism in the special education system, roughly 2 percent of all students receiving special education in Turkey (Kırcaali İftar 2007). For a population of 72 million this is extremely low (in Israel, with a population of 7 million, the comparable number was 2,187, 5.8 percent of children in special education).[13]

In South Africa, finally, the nonprofit organization Autism Western Cape was already established in 1967 and the Vera School for autistic learners and the Alpha School have been operating in Cape Town since 1970 and 1974, respectively. There are also parent-run schools, therapy centers, and public awareness campaigns. There are no reliable estimates of the autism rate in South Africa.

To sum up, parents may be mobilized and organized, and may advocate on behalf of their children, yet the rates of autism may still be low and there would be very little diagnostic substitution, absent other factors. International comparison clearly demonstrates that the demand-side explanation fails to take into account the institutional conditions that turn parental demand into "effective demand," as the economists would say.

As we shall see in Chapter 6, this is not an idle line of criticism, because during the early career of the autism diagnosis it was locked into intense competition with other diagnostic labels (which had their own clinicians-champions, and also offered distinct advantages to parents) that sought to occupy the same terrain, the same ecological niche of childhood disorders. In fact, during the 1950s and 1960s, autism was outmatched and dominated by the diagnosis of childhood schizophrenia. Childhood schizophrenia was proposed as a comprehensive diagnosis, a spectrum that included autism and other disorders within it, and which underlay a large, though unknown percentage of cases of mental retardation. In response to this situation, the clinicians and parent-advocates who spoke for autism chose to radically limit its scope, to argue that it was an extremely rare disorder, and in fact had nothing to do with mental retardation. The point we are making is that under different institutional conditions, the same factors that make up demand-side explanations – i.e.

parents' interests and agency – could lead to opposite results, to lower numbers and flight away from diagnostic substitution. If any condition, in the mid-1960s, was ripe to become an epidemic through diagnostic substitution with mental retardation, it was childhood schizophrenia and most certainly not autism. Why is it, therefore, that thirty years later precisely the opposite took place and childhood schizophrenia in fact is extinct?

Deinstitutionalization as key to explaining diagnostic substitution

The following chapters provide an answer to this question, which centers indeed on diagnostic substitution with mental retardation and through other pathways, which takes into account the struggles and interests of parents, which indeed combines supply and demand forces, but which also highlights the institutional underpinnings that give rise to these forces and orchestrate their meeting. Autism, we suggest, is neither simply a condition that exists out there as in supply-side accounts, nor a mere label as in demand-side accounts, but a *domain of intervention*, a domain of similarly structured objects of discourse for which there are fairly specific historical conditions of existence. The main characteristic of this domain, as we signaled in the introduction, is that it lies between illness and retardation, links them, yet can resist being assimilated to either side. This is what we meant when we spoke of something like an "ecological niche" prepared in advance in Kanner's original account, or becoming an object of contention between different diagnoses and their champions. Kanner's account of autism (or Bender's [1953] account of childhood schizophrenia) identified a new domain of intervention for a new type of expertise. If autism, or for that matter childhood schizophrenia, was a very early (possibly inborn) condition that gave rise to various forms of mental retardation and mental illness, it would justify the utility of a system for the comprehensive surveillance of childhood, a system that would screen infants and toddlers in the very early years of life, track their progress and assign them with correct interventions and appropriate milieu, thereby minimizing the risks posed by the whole gamut of childhood ailments, from problem behaviors to feeblemindedness. It would also justify the form of expertise which we called "medical diagnosis of social destiny."

This domain of intervention was identified, but the possibilities inherent in it could not be exploited, however, within the institutional matrix of custody. Within the institution, autism was completely below the radar, undifferentiated from an inchoate mass of institutional residents. Childhood schizophrenia was able to thrive during this period, as we shall see in Chapter 6, precisely because it lost the delicate balance and swung all the way into the domain of mental illness, the domain of the psychiatric hospital and electroconvulsive treatment. This meant, however, that it could not secure the crucial alliance with middle-class parents. We do agree in this with the demand-side accounts, that new diagnostic labels and new conditions do not become widespread without securing the cooperation of the individuals so labeled, and in this case parents. But what the demand-side account misses is that usually such alliances are secured by *therapy*, and that there are institutional and discursive conditions for the proliferation and circulation of therapies. In the case of autism, an incipient alliance, a network of expertise connecting parents, therapists and clinicians did form in the 1960s, as we shall see in Chapters 7 and 8, but in the absence of the institutional context in which socially innovative therapies could thrive, this alliance was premised on a radical restriction of autism into a rare condition, having nothing to do with mental retardation.

This state of affairs was completely upended by the deinstitutionalization of mental retardation. Not only did it mean that a large number of children, who previously would have been institutionalized as mentally retarded, were now to be treated in the community at the earliest age possible, it also meant that the categories employed by the institutions to distinguish and diagnose children became meaningless and blended together into an ill-defined mass of "atypical children" (see Chapter 9). Here the ideology of "normalization" that guided much of the deinstitutionalization movement played an important role. It involved a thoroughgoing reorganization and democratization of the relations of expertise, by breaking the monopoly enjoyed by psychiatry over administrative power in the field of retardation, and by empowering more peripheral professions as well as patients and parents. It thus opened up a domain of intervention between illness and retardation, where children who were simply "developmentally disabled" were to be "habilitated" (i.e. neither cured nor merely kept in custody) by a new set of socially innovative therapies. These socially innovative therapies involved parents and autistics themselves in active roles and accorded them a significant measure of expertise, something that could only happen once the administrative monopoly of psychiatry was broken. As we suggested in the introduction, deinstitutionalization generated an empty slot, the impossible-yet-unavoidable need for medical diagnosis of social destiny, and the network of expertise developed by autism parents and therapists became the model for the set of institutions and actors that surrounded this slot. Gradually, within the new institutional matrix that replaced custodial institutions – a matrix composed of early intervention, socially innovative therapies, special education, and community treatment – autism became differentiated from mental retardation and generalized into a spectrum, laying the groundwork for diagnostic substitution in the 1990s.

Kanner's gambit has finally come to fruition, but in a very different way than he reckoned. The new domain of intervention and the power to offer medical diagnosis of social destiny did not become the jurisdiction of child psychiatry, but had to be shared with parents, more peripheral professions, and a host of fast-growing therapies. Similarly, autism is no longer what Kanner saw and described. Kanner identified cardinal symptoms – autistic aloofness and utter lack of interest in people, insistence on sameness – that differentiated autism as a unique clinical syndrome. In the new institutional matrix, however, autism no longer needed to be differentiated in this way. Against the background of therapies that sought to establish communicative rapport with the child, a certain set of behaviors, "items of autistic behavior," would become particularly visible and differentiable as the recalcitrant material requiring an intensification of the efforts of the therapists and the mobilization of all available agents, especially the parents. Autistic aloofness became a continuum of behaviors ranging from radical indifference, through instrumental attitude toward other people, indifference only toward other children but not toward adults, passivity, or at the end, social inappropriateness and naiveté. These behaviors were grouped together not by the sort of autistic essence that underlay the "cardinal" clinical symptom, but by the pragmatic criterion of the resistance they offered to the sociability demands of the new institutional matrix, and the prospect that they could all be treated by an identical set of therapies. The therapies themselves represented mostly an intensification of existing features of the institutional matrix. They broke the syndrome down to a list of "items of autistic behavior" and arrayed these on the same register as the behaviors exhibited by the mentally retarded, so that one no longer needed to choose between illness or retardation. Autistic aloofness had become "impairment of social interaction."

Deinstitutionalization and the variation in autism rates

Before we embark on the story of how the autism spectrum was made, before we set out to show that this explanation withstands the tests of "Why autism?" and "Why now?," let us return one more time to the question of the variation in the administrative prevalence of autism with which we started. Can the explanation for diagnostic substitution sketched above also account for this variation? We think so. We do not propose it as an alternative hypothesis to be tested against other hypotheses – Mandell and Palmer's supply factors, the demand factors of social influence and destigmatization that supposedly drive diagnostic substitution, or the set of political determinants packaged by the distinction between red and blue states. We are determined not to produce one more ad hoc hypothesis that prides itself on being independent of its competitors. Instead, we would like to propose an explanatory narrative that can comprehend the other hypotheses, stitch them together, demonstrate their connections, and rescue them from the "ad-hockery" that according to Waterhouse (2008) pervades the whole research program on the causes of autism and of the autism epidemic.

We begin by demonstrating, albeit inconclusively, a probable correlation between the extent of deinstitutionalization in a particular state or country and the rate of autism there. With U.S. states this is fairly easy to do, using the same data we used earlier. The administrative prevalence of autism – measured as special-education enrollments – correlates, somewhat imperfectly, with state variation in the rate of deinstitutionalization of mental retardation. Figure 3 provides a color-coded map and tabulation of the relationship between deinstitutionalization and autism rates. Dark gray states are where the rate of deinstitutionalization of the young mentally retarded (< 21 years old) from 1977 to 2000 was above the national average, while light gray states are where it was below this average.[14] The reader can see, in comparison with Table 1, that 11 of the 17 states with autism rates above the national mean are dark gray. The correlation, while statistically significant, is not as strong as with red/blue states.

It is much harder to investigate this correlation systematically at the international level, because there are no credible estimates of the international variation in autism prevalence, no World Health Organization (WHO) surveillance program to monitor its global spread. One has to settle, instead, for comparing quite heterogeneous data sources, like the national insurance disability payments and special-education enrollments, as we did earlier, or a patchwork of

States	Change in Institutionalization
Maine	–0.0155763
Massachusetts	–0.0079898
Minnesota	–0.0071654
Oregon	–0.0120969
Pennsylvania	–0.0085475
California	–0.0125073
Nevada	–0.0051577
Delaware	–0.0124775
Connecticut	–0.0131403
Rhode Island	–0.0163713
Michigan	–0.0086833
District of Columbia	–0.0124775
Hawaii	–0.017734
New Hampshire	–0.0155966
Indiana	–0.0123642
Vermont	–0.0194163
Wisconsin	–0.0190082
Maryland	–0.0146622
South Dakota	–0.0055726
Florida	–0.0193671
New Jersey	–0.0174588
North Carolina	–0.011033
Illinois	–0.016434
South Carolina	–0.0113739
Nebraska	–0.0179195
Texas	–0.0154534
New York	–0.0121447
Washington	–0.0181135
Tennessee	–0.0150218
Virginia	–0.0121169
Kentucky	–0.0243909
Louisiana	–0.0166756
North Dakota	–0.0060451
Wyoming	–0.0108435
Arkansas	–0.0213264
Montana	–0.0111937
Utah	–0.0189306
Georgia	–0.0121314
Kansas	–0.0198229
New Mexico	–0.0.137476
Arizona	–0.0262759
Missouri	–0.0113739
Colorado	–0.0179279
Idaho	–0.0063967
Alabama	–0.0064234
Ohio	–0.0265495
Iowa	–0.0095247
Mississippi	–0.0079442
West Virginia	–0.0282609
Oklahoma	–0.0241562
Alaska	–0.0562536

Figure 3: Change in Institutionalization of 0–21 year olds as precentage of State Institutions Residents, 1977–2000, sorted by autism rates among 3–5 years old

epidemiological surveys conducted at different times, by different researchers, utilizing different diagnostic criteria and methods. If one believes in a real rate of autism waiting to be discovered, then such a comparison is either impossible, or it would require heroic efforts (with judicious use of assumptions) to construct. If one is interested, on the other hand, in explaining the actual global population of autism diagnoses, there is no other place to look. Fombonne (2003) provides an authoritative summary of autism epidemiological surveys, and we added to it some more recent studies. From 1966 to 2009, as can be seen in Table 2, such surveys were conducted in comparatively few countries – the U.S., U.K., Japan, Sweden, Denmark, Canada,

Table 2:   Epidemiological Surveys of Autism, 1966–2001
(Based on: Eric Fombonne, "Epidemiological Surveys of Autism and Other
Pervasive Developmental Disorders: An Update," *Journal of Autism and
Developmental Disorders*, 33, 4 (2003), 365–382. Additional sources listed
below.)

Country	Number of surveys	Survey years	Autism rates (per 10,000) excluding Asperger and PDD-NOS
UK	9	1966; 1976; 1997; 1999; 2000; 2000; 2001; 2001; 2006[b]	4.1 -> 38.9[b]
Japan	5	1982; 1987; 1988; 1989; 1996	2.33 -> 21.8
USA	5	1970; 1987; 1989; 2001; 2006[c]	0.7 -> 55–57[c]
Sweden	4	1983; 1991; 1997; 1999	5.6 -> 72.6
France	3	1989; 1992; 1997	4.5 -> 5.35
Canada	3	1988; 2006[h]; 2006[e]	10.1->28.4–35.2[e]
China	2	2005[j]; 2009[i]	11[j] ->16.1[i]
Denmark	2	1970; 2004[a]	4.3 ->15.1[a]
Faroe Islands (Denmark)	1	2007[d]	56[d]
Norway	1	1998	5.2
Finland	1	2000	12.2
Iceland	1	2001	13.2
Germany	1	1986	1.9
Ireland	1	1984	4.3
Indonesia	1	1992	11.7
Australia	1	2004[f]	39[f]
Portugal	1	2007[g]	9.1[g]

[a] Lauritsen, M. B., Pedersen, C. B and; Mortensen, P. B. 2004. The incidence and prevalence of pervasive developmental disorders: a Danish population-based study. *Psychological Medicine* 34(7): 1339–1346.

[b] Baird, G. et al. (2006). Prevalence of disorders of the autism spectrum in a population cohort of children in South Thames: the Special Needs and Autism Project (SNAP). Lancet, 368(9531), pp. 210–215.

[c] Centers for Disease Control and Prevention (CDC). (2006). Mental health in the United States: parental report of diagnosed autism in children aged 4–17 years – United States, 2003–2004. MMWR Morb Mortal Wkly Rep, 55(17), pp. 481–486.

[d] Ellefsen, A. et al. (2007). Autism in the Faroe Islands: an epidemiological study. J Autism Dev Disord, 37(3), pp. 437–444.

Table 2:   (continued)

e Ouellette-Kuntz, H. et al. (2006). Prevalence of pervasive developmental disorders in two Canadian provinces. Journal of Policy and Practice in Intellectual Disabilities, 3(3), 164–172.
f Icasiano, F. et al. (2004). Childhood autism spectrum disorder in the Barwon region: a community based study. J Paediatr Child Health, 40(12), pp. 696–701.
g Oliveira, G. et al. (2007). Epidemiology of autism spectrum disorder in Portugal: prevalence, clinical characterization, and medical conditions. Dev Med Child Neurol, 49(10), pp. 726–733.
h Fombonne, E. et al. (2006). Pervasive developmental disorders in Montreal, Quebec, Canada: prevalence and links with immunizations. Pediatrics, 118(1), e139–150.
i Wong, V.C.N. and Hui, S.L.H. 2009. Epidemiological study of autism spectrum disorder in China. J Child Neurol. Forthcoming.
j Zhang X, Ji CY. (2005). Autism and mental retardation of young children in China. Biomed Environ Sci, 18(5), pp. 334–340.

and France, in fact, account for 75 percent of all surveys, yet France should be dropped from this list since by 2001 the epidemic clearly had yet to register even a tremor in its epidemiological surveillance net. The epicenters of the epidemic, one could say, are in Scandinavia, the U.K., North America, and Japan. Putting Japan to the side for the time being, these epicenters neatly correspond to where the deinstitutionalization and normalization of mental retardation has proceeded most fully. The arc of normalization begins in Scandinavia as early as 1946, from which it spreads to the American northern Midwest in the 1960s, and then to the Northeast, across the Atlantic to the U.K. and across the border to Canada. Sweden, Norway, Minnesota – this is also where deinstitutionalization has reached its logical conclusion in the "non-institutional society," that is, the complete closure of all public institutions and a legal mandate that all services for individuals with intellectual disability be provided in the community (Hatton et al. 1995; Ericsson 2000; Sigelman et al. 1981; Meyer 2003).

Thus the rise in prevalence in Canada, for example, is probably even more dramatic than what Table 2 documents. Fombonne et al. (2006) found the prevalence of pervasive developmental disorders to be 65 in 10,000 in a sample of children in Montreal, Quebec, born between 1987 and 1998. In 2001, the Canadian Institutes for Health Research launched a National Epidemiologic Database for the Study of Autism in Canada (NEDSAC), and studies associated with this initiative found not only the numbers of 28 and 35 in 10,000 reported in Table 2 (Ouellette-Kuntz et al. 2006), but generally a rise of prevalence in all areas studied between 2002 and 2006 (2008 Family Update[15]), and prevalence estimates in various regions ranging from

61

44 in 10,000 to 80 in 10,000 in Manitoba and Ontario, respectively. These relatively high rates correspond, indeed, to a high degree of deinstitutionalization, comparable to what happened in the U.S. at roughly the same early period (Sealy and Whitehead 2004; Braddock et al. 2001; Pedlar et al. 2000). In 1965, at the high point of the institutionalization of children, when children five years and younger were institutionalized in Canada at a rate 2.5 times the comparable British rate (Richards 1963), 56 percent of first admissions to Canadian institutions for the mentally retarded were nine years old or younger. By 1976, however, it was already down to 40 percent and the median age at admission went up from nine to twelve.[16] By 2006, there were only 815 children younger than fifteen years old institutionalized in Canadian institutions for children with psychiatric disorders or developmental disabilities.[17] The rate of institutionalization, therefore, is probably lower than even the low U.K. rate (see below).

By the same token, it is also possible to show – albeit unsystematically – that where deinstitutionalization never happened or was delayed, autism rates tend to be low. The most spectacular and convincing case is the French one. Even though France was an important center of the antipsychiatry movement, it never really took the step of reducing institutionalized populations. The number of psychiatric beds in France was 93.9 per 10,000 in 2005, which is well above the European Union average of 59.4 (Eurostat 2008). More significant, children are still institutionalized at a rate much higher than elsewhere in Europe. In 2007, more than 108,000 French children with disabilities were in residential institutions, while in the similarly populous Great Britain, only 2,245 children lived in similar arrangements! The majority of these children were classified with intellectual disability, and an important segment was diagnosed with autism. Indeed, the parent group Léa Pour Samy has taken French authorities to court for institutionalizing children with autism instead of providing them with educational programs.[18] The lower rate of autism in France thus corresponds to the fact that deinstitutionalization never happened there.

The rate of institutionalization in Turkey and South Africa, by comparison, is very low. Turkey's is the lowest in the European Union (World Mental Health Atlas 2005; Eurostat 2008). This is not, however, due to deinstitutionalization, but simply to the underdevelopment of the mental health system in both countries, evidenced by the fact that Turkey's low rate of institutionalization remained fairly stable over the last ten years. In both countries, the custodial institutional matrix simply has not been dismantled yet. The largest psychiatric hospital in Turkey – Bakırkoy Psychiatric Hospital – is commonly described as a warehouse where patients who suffer from a variety of disorders are dumped together. Many with indeterminate diagnoses are kept for years, including many who are likely to be autistic (Munir 2006; Tek 2008; Yazgan 2008). Similarly, Molteno et al. report that "most children in Cape Town diagnosed as having ID [intellectual disability] attend 'segregated' special schools" (2001). Grinker adds that many people who could be diagnosed as autistic are institutionalized in a Cape Town facility (2007). To the extent that some deinstitutionalization has begun, it is a phenomenon of the last decade and mostly rhetorical. In 1997, a White Paper issued by the Office of the President of South Africa announced the beginning of a "transition from institutionalization towards community-based services" for individuals with intellectual disabilities and warned of the difficulties ahead.[19] Likewise, it was not until the late 1990s that individualized special education, early intervention, and inclusion gained significance in Turkish law (Akkök 2000).

Here we have an answer as to why the rates of autism were relatively low in France, Turkey, and South Africa even though parents' advocacy organizations were quite developed. In these countries only one of the two necessary components – namely, the parent-therapist-researcher-advocate network of expertise – was present, but not the other, deinstitutionalization. None of these countries had undertaken the deinstitutionalization of mental retardation to the same extent, or as early, as in the U.S., U.K., Canada, and Scandinavia.

Obviously, these findings, together with the very sketchy international comparison above, should not be interpreted as a test for an alternative hypothesis. To begin with, the correlation between autism rates and deinstitutionalization is far from perfect. There are U.S. states – Mississippi or Alabama, for example, as can be seen in Figure 3 – that rank quite high on measures of deinstitutionalization, but their autism rates are among the lowest in the U.S. There are countries, on the other hand, such as Japan, and to a lesser extent Israel, where deinstitutionalization does not seem to have proceeded very far, yet their autism rates begin to approach those in the epicenters of the epidemic. As can be seen in Table 2, the estimated prevalence of autism in Japan since 1982 has risen to levels just below the U.K. by 1996. Yet in terms of deinstitutionalization, Japan is a laggard. Between 1990 and 2002, in fact, institutionalized populations *grew* by 45 percent, and only in 2002 did the government commit to no longer building new institutions (Tsuda 2006). The Israeli case is complicated, but is more similar to Japan than to any of the other cases surveyed thus far. The 2007 autism rate of 18 in 10,000 cited earlier would put it just below the Japanese case, and there is a clear upward trend. Yet deinstitutionalization in Israel has not proceeded very far. The rate of Israeli children with intellectual disability in out-of-home placements is relatively high, and typically they are to be found in fairly large institutions and boarding schools. Currently there are 6,500 persons with mental retardation who live in 56 institutions, usually midsize institutions with about 100 residents. Almost 25 percent (n=1,600) of inmates are children; there are eight institutions specifically for children. This rate is essentially identical to the situation in 1965 (1,934 residents in nineteen institutions), and significantly higher than in the U.S. Deinstitutionalization in Israel started late and has not proceeded very far. In fact, during the mid-1990s the rate of institutionalization increased by 42 percent due to the actions of a particularly powerful and ambitious Minister of Labor and Welfare, and in response to long waiting lists. Four new institutions for children with mental retardation were built in the last 25 years (Aviram 1981; Don and Amir 1968).[20]

We said above that we do not aim to produce another alternative and ad hoc hypothesis, to be tested against others. By the same token, we do not expect to obtain a mechanical correlation between autism and deinstitutionalization in all cases. Deinstitutionalization is short-hand for a complex multisided, multicausal process, and its relation to the autism epidemic two decades later is no less complex. Though we test it – for want of better measures – in quantitative fashion, we do *not* mean to suggest that this relationship is a simple numerical one, such as "the more children are deinstitutionalized, the more can be diagnosed with autism." If we typically see higher rates of autism where deinstitutionalization has proceeded the furthest, it is not because the latter directly "dumps" into the former, but because the extent of deinstitutionalization typically – but not universally – correlates with intensification of the surveillance of childhood, with democratization of the relations of expertise, with de-differentiation of the domain of "atypical children" between illness and retardation, with the proliferation of socially innovative therapies, and with commitment to normalization and the rights of the disabled. All of these together are likely to produce a rise in autism diagnoses.

From this point of view it is easy to understand the anomaly of Mississippi and Alabama. That Alabama, quantitatively speaking, had the same rate of deinstitutionalization as Minnesota obscures the fact that we are dealing here with two fundamentally different processes. We will have occasion in Chapter 4 to refute the argument that deinstitutionalization was merely a cynical response to the fiscal crisis of the state (Scull 1983). Yet there is no denying that in some southern U.S. states this was the main impetus behind deinstitutionalization. Alabama, for example, may have reduced its institutionalized population just as much as Minnesota, but it did so for fiscal reasons, without replacing institutions with anything similar to Minnesota's network of community residences and group homes, or commitment to early intervention. Consequently, its autism rate is one of the lowest in the nation. Significantly, the states where deinstitutionalization was coupled with the creation of an alternative institutional matrix of community treatment, early intervention, and socially innovative therapies (and where autism rates are now the highest), were also the states that led the U.S., two decades earlier, in the rate at which young children were institutionalized. We shall see in Chapter 3 that in the U.S., Britain, and Scandinavia deinstitutionalization was preceded by, and responded to, an earlier and massive rise in the institutionalization of children as part of a new project for the surveillance of childhood. We will develop this point further in Chapter 4, arguing that deinstitutionalization should not be seen as the complete opposite of what preceded it, but as a tactical reversal within the surveillance of childhood, a project that for a long while gained very little traction in southern states such as Alabama or Mississippi (Sigelman 1981).

Anomalies can be utilized to sharpen the theory and the explanatory narrative. What we learn from the anomalous cases of Mississippi and Alabama is that deinstitutionalization was a politically determined process – so is, ultimately, the autism epidemic. There are political conditions of possibility for the epidemic having to do mostly with the type of welfare state and the mode of governing individuals. Alabama's drive to empty institutions, after all, began under the watch of George Wallace, and was justified not simply in fiscal terms, but also in libertarian terms as limiting state intervention into the private sphere of the family. The normalization principle, on the other hand, which imbues the type of deinstitutionalization with which we are concerned in this book, was formulated as part of the postwar reorganization of the Scandinavian welfare state. It took its first halting steps in Sweden, which now reports some of the highest rates of autism in the world. Normalization was an integral part of the new social contract between citizen and state envisioned by Swedish reformers and advocacy groups immediately after the war: as social services became a universal civic right, individuals who previously were excluded because they could not approximate the bourgeois norm of rational autonomy, were transformed into "partially able-bodied" citizens who, provided they were equipped with the correct prosthetic devices, could govern themselves and contribute to collective welfare. The welfare state was entrusted with the duty – as a citizenship right but also as a principle of economy – of empowering the self-governing faculties of individuals. The normalization of mental retardation – begun in Sweden scarcely a decade after the war – simply extended this principle from the "partially able-bodied" to the "partially able-minded" (Ericsson 2000; Esping Andersen 1990; Wagner 1994).

Here we have an account that can make sense of the correlation between autism rates and the blue state / red state division, while also accommodating the less-than-perfect correlation between deinstitutionalization and autism rates among U.S. states. The arc of normalization, as we noted earlier, began in Scandinavia and spread to the American northern Midwest (Minnesota, Michigan, Nebraska) in the 1960s and thence to the Northeastern states of the Atlantic seaboard. As the first wave of deinstitutionalization of the mentally retarded swept over American states, Sigelman et al. (1981) had no difficulty demonstrating that it went the furthest in affluent states with a pluralist, reformist, and liberal political culture and a high degree of legislative professionalism – the states that were likely to be "blue" in the 2004 elections, the states where the surveillance of childhood (and institutionalization) was the most developed. Deinstitutionalization, therefore, should be seen as a mediating variable. It transmitted the effects of political culture and the welfare state model by giving rise to a new domain of intervention between retardation and illness – the domain that could be called the "partially able-to-develop," emerging out of the meeting between normalization and the surveillance of childhood – within which autism became a spectrum.

Yet the arrow of causation could also swing the other way. Deinstitutionalization was not a passive transmitter of effects but an active filter, a crucial historical contingency. The struggle over deinstitutionalization was a *political* struggle; occasionally it shaped the political trajectory of a state. Its resolution certainly shaped future healthcare policy, that is, the sort of supply-side factors identified by Mandell and Palmer. It also likely shaped demand factors by privileging a particular model of parental activism. Parish (2005) compares the uneven progress of deinstitutionalization in two states – Michigan and Illinois – with initially similar points of departure. In Sigelman et al.'s assessment (1981), Illinois was among the early leaders in deinstitutionalization. Michigan, for its part, participated in the regional spread of deinstitutionalization from the Northwest to the Northeast. Yet in the decade that followed, Michigan rapidly transformed its system from institutional to community-based, while in Illinois a powerful coalition of unions, parents of institutionalized children, and private service providers worked for retention of institutions and against development of community residential services. A crucial contingency was the role played by the parents' organization, the Association for Retarded Children (later Association for Retarded Citizens, or ARC), in the two states. The national association (NARC) typically advised state organizations against becoming service providers themselves. Day schools were okay – in fact, many state ARCs began this way – but residential schools and nursing homes were ill-advised, as they would discourage the state from upholding its side of the social contract between citizen and state and would represent a dangerous conflict of interests. State ARCs, however, were independent organizations and set their own policy. The Michigan ARC avoided the service-provider role like the plague; the Illinois ARC enthusiastically assumed it. In the 1960s NARC became a formidable lobby and played a major role in pushing forward the radical agenda of deinstitutionalization and normalization. Yet in states like Illinois, where the state ARC ran residential schools and institutions, it became an enemy of deinstitutionalization as it stood to lose, both materially and symbolically, from it (Parish 2005). The reader would not be surprised to consult Table 1 once more and discover that, 25 years later, the administrative prevalence of autism in Michigan was the eleventh highest in the nation, well above the national mean, while Illinois's was twenty-third and well below it.

By focusing on the role of deinstitutionalization we do not intend to exclude other explanations, but to comprehend them. Supply factors such as spending on special education and early intervention programs can explain a great deal of the variation in the administrative prevalence of autism, but they are not independent of deinstitutionalization. The same goes for demand factors such as parental activism and advocacy organizations. They no doubt played a major role in diagnostic substitution, but they themselves were created or at least shaped in the crucible of deinstitutionalization. Neither do we intend to present deinstitutionalization as the ultimate, uncaused cause. Deinstitutionalization was one event in a series, one battle in an ongoing political conflict over welfare policy and citizenship rights. Its status in our story is not as the origin of this series, but as a crucial contingency, a juncture at which the series could develop in several possible directions.

We feel better equipped now to deal with the anomalous cases of Israel and Japan: exact inverses of Alabama and Mississippi. While

67

in these two American states one finds deinstitutionalization without autism, in Israel and Japan one finds significant and rising rates of autism in the absence of deinstitutionalization. Indeed, Israeli legislation still reflects the reasoning of the custodial institutional matrix. It grants welfare authorities the power to impose therapeutic frameworks (including out-of-home placement) on persons with retardation when they do not receive appropriate care from their families (Welfare Treatment of Retarded Persons Law 1069, 23, LSI, 144). Significantly, it defines retardation as social inadequacy, which as we shall see in the next chapter was the *raison d'être* of the custodial matrix (Welfare Law; Treatment of the Retarded Person; 1969). By comparison, the right to receive care and services at home in the community is not mandated by Israeli law (Shnit, 2003; Rimmerman 2003, 425).

Why has deinstitutionalization in Israel been delayed and half-hearted? Normalization and community treatment ideology made its way to Israel in the mid-1970s and was espoused by nonprofits, municipal authorities, and the Welfare Ministry. It encountered an already well-developed system for the surveillance of childhood. Preventive maternal and child health services have been provided in Family Health Centers (known as "drops of milk" טיפות חלב) throughout Israel beginning with the state's establishment in 1948. A recent study found that a very high percentage of mothers in Israel report that their infants received the basic core services including developmental tests in Family Health Centers (Rosen, Elroy and Nirel, 2007). Another study shows that the Family Health Centers play an important role in the identification of children in the community with developmental problems (Naon, Sandler-Loeff and Strosberg, 2000). At the same time, however, in the Israeli context the meanings of "institutions," "community," or "normalization" were not necessarily the same as in Scandinavia or the U.S. Institutions, to begin with, were midsized and, since this is a small country, typically located close to large population centers. There were significant sectors of the population, moreover, for whom sending children to boarding schools was "normal" – the religious, immigrants, and of course the kibbutzim. Institutions were thus able to present themselves – in accordance with the overall collectivistic ideology of the state – as a "community," a normal way of life in continuity with the society at large. Finally, as in Illinois, the parents' organizations representing children with mental retardation or cerebral palsy were themselves service providers and operated residential institutions. They, therefore, opposed wholesale deinstitutionalization.[21] All of these specificities of the Israeli case, moreover, are connected with the fact that the Israeli welfare state was "republican" or "continental" (Shafir and Peled 2002; Esping Andersen 1990) – it stratified the population into sectors on the basis of their putative contribution to the collectivity. Its chief aim was to organize these sectors, rather than empower the individual. It was not until the early 1990s, when the Israeli welfare state had begun transitioning into a model of universal individual rights – with the passage, for example, of the National Health Insurance Law guaranteeing universal coverage – that significant attempts at deinstitutionalization, especially of children, gained momentum (Baruch et al. 2005).[22] A law passed in 2001 allocated resources and led to a wave of programs for community treatment and integration. In the context of an already highly developed system for the surveillance of childhood, and of increased activism and advocacy by autism parents' organizations inspired by developments in the U.S., this led to a spike in autism rates between 2001 and 2007.

The Japanese lack of appetite for deinstitutionalization was probably due to some of the same causes operating in Illinois and in Israel – the role played by Inclusion Japan, the organization representing parents of mentally retarded children. Created in 1952, practically at the same time as the American NARC, it became highly influential. It lobbied for the passage of a 1960 law on the welfare of the mentally retarded. It advises the government on relevant matters of policy, and it sponsors numerous self-advocacy groups. Early on, it assumed the role of service provider, establishing and managing institutions. Therefore, until quite recently it opposed and impeded deinstitutionalization. Yet since Japan did not experience anything similar to America's massive 1950s institutionalization of children, and since the organization of welfare provision in Japan is very different from the U.S., U.K., or Scandinavia, once again, as in Israel, the meanings of institutions or normalization in the Japanese context are quite distinctive. The structure of welfare provision is still dominated by the local community as a structure of mutual dependence (owing its origins to the system of traditional organizations created in the seventeenth century). The community provides many traditional supports to disabled individuals and is much more conducive to action by parents, especially mothers. There is a much greater tolerance for young adults living at home with parents, even for "normal" adults and couples in their thirties. In this context, the American or Scandinavian focus on transition from institutions to group homes to independent living, or the understanding of normalization as the achievement of self-sufficiency and self-advocacy, makes much less sense. Children with intellectual disabilities were typically cared for at home, or in a differentiated system of day preschools and day schools dating from the period of reconstruction after WWII. Among these is the celebrated Higashi day school, opened in 1964, where normal, retarded, and autistic children studied together in a mixed setting. It later opened a branch in Boston.[23] For these reasons Japanese parents' activism was not directed at emptying institutions holding their young children, but at establishing institutions to care for their adult, even middle-aged, children after their passing. It was not the residential location of young children that was problematized, but of middle-aged people with developmental disabilities. Even institutions originally created to hold children gradually shifted their purpose. By 2004, half of the users of the institutions for mentally handicapped children were adults (Takeshi 2004; Tsuda 2006; Kurita et al. 1994). There are similar developments in Israel, where a colony-type residential setting for autistic children and adolescents has been transformed over the years into a residence for adults, even aged individuals, with autism.[24]

It is not surprising, therefore, that the autism epidemic began in Japan. Three Japanese studies during 1986–1988 were the first to report elevated estimates of autism prevalence, ranging from 13 to 15.5 per 10,000. Higher American and European estimates followed a few years later (Kurita 2006). Japanese clinicians may claim that they are simply better than others at diagnosing autism (but if so, why are they now lagging behind the U.S., U.K. and Sweden?),[25] but we would tend to emphasize the fact that in the Japanese case there was a highly developed system for the surveillance of childhood which was already seeking to provide differentiated care for young children with intellectual disabilities in the family and the community.

As the Japanese case demonstrates, autism is a truly global phenomenon. While much of the following narrative will focus on the United States, with only scattered references to other countries, this is due to limitations of our research, and should not be taken as characteristic of the autism epidemic. The crucial distinction to be drawn here is between "diffusion" and "translation" models (Latour 1987; Bockman and Eyal 2002). While it is tempting to see the autism epidemic as an American phenomenon exported to other countries through some form of imitative isomorphism, we think there are several reasons why this image is ultimately false. Thinking of it as the spread of a network of expertise seems more productive.

First, the making of the autism epidemic involved not one-way but two-way transfers. Various programs and innovations traveled not from the American "core" to the "periphery," but in the opposite direction. The ingredients that went into making the autism epidemic *in the U.S.* included Swedish normalization (which also informed the perspective of Norwegian-American Ivar Lovaas, founder of Applied Behavioral Analysis, the most influential autism therapy), the work of British psychologist Lorna Wing, the findings of Japanese epidemiologists, and the export of Higashi Daily Life Therapy from Japan to the U.S. after American psychologist Bernard Rimland and a team of colleagues gave a glowing report to the Boston parent group that sent them to investigate it (Rimland 1987).[26] In another transnational example, HANDLE therapy's founder Judith Bluestone moved back and forth between Israel and the US.[27]

These two-way transfers were not later developments that took place after the American network of autism expertise was already put together. They were crucial to the network's development from its beginnings. In 1970, Rimland – sometimes called the "father of autism research" in the U.S. – already possessed data on children from twelve countries (see Chapter 8 for more on this). By the same token, in 1972 Rimland could proudly report that one of his articles had made its way to nearly all English-speaking countries and was in translation in six other nations. Further, beginning in the late 1960s, parents in the U.S. National Society for Autistic Children (NSAC), the central node of the emerging network of expertise, were working to forge links with parents and professionals from the U.K., France, Denmark, Norway, Ireland, Australia, New Zealand, and South Africa, to name a few. They invited representatives from foreign parent societies to their conferences and urged their own members, if they were traveling abroad, to contact those societies in order to exchange information about treatment strategies and services. In this way, for example, connection was made with the Brauners, a French couple running a school for retarded and psychotic children, who sent films and letters to NSAC, sharing their work and hoping to exchange insights. In short, the autism epidemic is, and was from the very start, a global assemblage, not a neatly packaged model exported from the core to the periphery.

Second, and no less important, these two-way transfers are constitutive of the autism epidemic in the sense that they endow it with reality, extension, depth. Whatever happens in the "periphery," even if it seems to be merely copying or imitating the Anglo-American model, comes back to play a role in the "core" as *proof* of the epidemic. With the causes for the rise in autism diagnoses in dispute in the U.S. or the U.K., evidence that the number of diagnoses is rising in Japan, Israel, or South Africa (even if the "evidence" turns out to be merely an extrapolation from the American numbers, as in the South African case) serves to lend factuality to the epidemic, make it stronger and more capable of withstanding critical scrutiny, simply by virtue of accumulating more "cases."[28] Again, the utility of international connections and comparisons was not an afterthought once the epidemic took shape in the U.S., but was recognized very early on by American parents-advocates. They interpreted what they saw on their trips abroad as evidence supporting their central claim that autism had biological, rather than psychological, roots. In 1970, Clara Claiborne Park (parent, editor of NSAC's newsletter, and author of one of the earliest and most successful parent memoirs, *The Siege*) wrote, "mental illness knows no frontiers; your editor . . . has been astonished to see French children so like ours at home, the similarity of their symptoms overriding all differences of language and upbringing – massive evidence for the biological causation of these afflictions." She even harnessed the new global reach of autism to NSAC's attempts to mobilize American parents and convince them of the broader ethical dimension of their work: "So many children . . . needing so much . . . all over the world . . . When the hours (or the money) you devote to NSAC seem too much, reflect that the waves you make may wash shores thousands of miles away, bringing hope to families you will never see" (Park 1970). This is why we suggest it is more useful to think of the autism epidemic in terms of the extension of a network. The more actors that are enrolled by the network, the stronger the ties between them, the more is the whole network "black-boxed" as a fact.

Contemporary autism advocacy organizations in the U.S. have certainly recognized the opportunities and advantages of transnational collaboration. As they banded together in 2005 into the formidable group Autism Speaks, they immediately formed alliances and connections across the globe to give the organization truly global reach. Autism Speaks organized an International Meeting for Autism Research, with attendees from thirty countries; it collaborates with an international consortium of researchers, philanthropists, government funding agencies, and participating families to launch the Autism Genome Project (AGP), "a global scientific effort to discover the genes responsible for causing autism"; it co-sponsored "Autism Speaks to the World," the International Congress for Autism Research held in Mexico City, and initiated collaboration between leading U.S. and Mexican autism researchers; and it has joined forces with the Centers for Disease Control and Prevention to establish an International

Autism Epidemiology Network that meets annually in order to foster global collaborations.[29]

By the same token, parents and autism advocacy organizations outside the U.S. have found that adopting the language of epidemic, and forging connections with their American counterparts, could be advantageous. In the Canadian case, for example, the notion of an "epidemic" is extremely useful for parents and advocates. Typically, autism therapies are not provided by physicians and so are not considered a "core" health service to be publicly funded. Within the educational system, the policies of all provinces and territories place a strong emphasis on inclusion of children with disabilities within the regular classroom (Dworet and Bennett 2002), and consequently there are very few spaces in special classes for autistic children.[30] What could Canadian parents do? A reasonable strategy has been to count on the progressive reputation of Canadian courts, to raise public outcry over the government's lack of an adequate response to an "epidemic" and use it as a basis for lawsuits.[31] Similarly, we saw that many autism advocacy organizations in Israel, Turkey, and South Africa, in fact, are quite different from the American "model" – especially if Autism Speaks is taken to represent it – because they are first and foremost service providers. Yet they too can leverage the language of "epidemic" and their connections with authoritative American organizations to make more demands on the government, to obtain government funding and collaboration for existing services and new initiatives, to raise public awareness and enroll new members. For instance, in Turkey the epidemic trope has been a crucial factor in putting autism on the public agenda, exemplified in part by recent public awareness campaigns.[32] In an effort to demonstrate that domestic prevalence rates for autism are similar to those found elsewhere (and hence require urgent attention), one advocacy organization has strategically deployed the language of a worldwide epidemic in order to secure funds for large-scale screening projects from the federal government as well as the European Union.[33] In South Africa, where the lion's share of health care dollars are targeted at HIV/AIDS, the cries of autism advocates might fall on deaf ears were it not for the language of "epidemic." Accordingly, Autism South Africa cites international prevalence rates to stress the importance of its cause,[34] and its newsletter is frequently interspersed with reprints of interviews and articles from American and British publications.[35] Autism Western Cape is even more explicit, boldly declaring that its estimate of the prevalence of autism in South Africa – based solely on extrapolations from international data – is a staggering 1 in

86 for children under six years of age, having increased 500 percent in the last five years.[36]

In short, the global spread of the autism epidemic is conditioned on translating and aligning local interests formed in differing institutional matrices. This is another reason why the model of translation, of the extension of a network, is preferable to a diffusion model. Local actors do not imitate blindly, they do not become identical to "core" models. They strategically attach themselves to the network by various means, and they have done so from the moment this network began to form in the late 1960s. In the past, the dominant idiom that served to connect far-flung parts of the network, as we saw earlier, equated the universality of autism with its biological nature and thus provided everybody with ammunition against the psychogenic theory. Currently, it is the language of "epidemic" that has become a dominant idiom. It translates and aligns the interests of local actors with others in the network. In the process, in the profitable exchanges within the network, the phenomenon of the autism epidemic itself is hardened, stabilized, factualized, and it becomes easier to attach it to local conditions, which is why, over time, it would correlate less and less with the extent of deinstitutionalization in a given country.

Now that we have laid the groundwork of a sociological-historical perspective from which to see the significance of autism's rise in the U.S., Europe, and other parts of the globe, we are ready to begin our historical exploration of the multiple processes that made autism's increasing importance possible and practical. In order for children to be diagnosed at the astounding rates that we read in today's headlines many institutional, discursive, and political conditions needed to be put into place. Laws needed to be passed. Diagnostic criteria had to be standardized. It was necessary for parents and therapists to organize. Schools needed to be built, teachers and their assistants trained. A whole institutional matrix, with autism eventually at its center, had to come into being. In the chapters that follow, we will tell a set of stories that give an account of that coming-into-being of this matrix and the myriad actors – parents, physicians, researchers, activists – who contributed to it. The order of the chapters will be thematic rather than chronological. In Chapters 2 and 3 we will consider the reasons that the practice of institutionalizing certain groups of children became common in the first place. Chapter 2 focuses on the period of the "menace of the feeble-minded" (1920–1950) and the meaning of categories like "feeblemindedness." Chapter 3 deals with the program of child surveillance of the 1950s and 1960s. It follows the process of the problematization of the middle-class child, and the changes of the population in institutions for the mentally retarded. More important, it shows how the institutionalization wave of the early 1950s must be understood as one tactical aspect in the new vision of a comprehensive surveillance and placement system. Chapter 4 tells the story of deinstitutionalization of the mentally retarded during the 1970s and 1980s and revises existing interpretations of this phenomenon. Next, in Chapter 5, we will consider the philosophy of normalization that guided deinstitutionalization and the ways in which it contributed to a reconfiguration of the relations of expertise. In Chapters 6–8 we go back in time, before deinstitutionalization, to consider first in Chapter 6 the remaking of the classificatory space during the 1940s, 1950s and 1960s due to the emergence, brief popularity, and then abandonment of the diagnosis of childhood schizophrenia. In Chapter 7 we will identify the origins of contemporary therapies for autism. We will consider especially the trajectories of perceptual-motor therapy for "brain-injured" children and behavioral therapy for "emotionally disturbed" children to show how they converged and complemented each other and how their combined movement blurred the boundary between mental illness and retardation and created a large indeterminate zone between them. Chapter 8 is dedicated to the story of the establishment of NSAC during the 1960s and how parents of autistic children upended the relations of expertise, acquired credibility as experts on their own children, and struck alliances with therapeutic practitioners and researchers. In the final three chapters, before offering some concluding remarks, we will consider mostly changes that took place in deinstitutionalization's aftermath. Chapter 9 reviews changes in diagnostic criteria and special education legislation during the 1970s and 1980s. Chapter 10 tells the story of how Asperger's disorder became connected to the autism spectrum. Finally, Chapter 11 will bring us to the present with a closer look at some of the most common contemporary therapies for autism and how they continually upset the boundaries between established and alternative medicine, between illness and retardation, and between expert and layperson.

— 2 —

THE FEEBLEMINDED

If the current autism epidemic is an aftershock of deinstitution-alization, then it follows that in the past some children were insti-tutionalized as mentally retarded who today would be diagnosed as autistic. Is there evidence to support this contention? We do not intend to engage in retroactive diagnosis, which is quite common in the autism world (Grandin 1995, 207–18; Houston and Frith 2000; Grinker 2007, 39–42, 57; Bottomer 2009; Farmelo 2009).[1] Besides being problematic from an epistemological point of view (Hacking 1998; 2009), and definitely beyond our expertise as sociologists, it is simply contrary to the argument of this book – which traces how the understanding and treatment of autism changed over time – to apply backwards one contemporary version of what we show was a highly mutable and significantly transformed prototype. Yet it is possible to translate this question into two less anachronistic ones. First, did *contemporaries* think that autistic children were being institutionalized as mentally retarded? If they did – which is easy to find out – then not only is this indirect evidence for the presence of autistic children in the residential schools for the mentally retarded (contemporaries would know about this better than us), but it may indicate a certain dissatis-faction with institutional intake policies, an interest in a more detailed and fine-grained surveillance of childhood disorders. As we said, this question is easy to answer. Two of the most influential contemporary observers – Leo Kanner and Bernard Rimland – thought it likely that autistic children were institutionalized as mentally retarded. The first reported he knew of a "few" such cases and wondered if there weren't many more; the second, 15 years later, simply stated as a fact that "many" eventually become institutionalized (Kanner 1949; Rimland 1964).

The second question is more complicated. We can ask, what was the meaning of the institutionalization of mental retardation? Was it likely to be insensitive to the distinction between autism and mental retardation? If so, then coupled with the testimony of contemporaries, we do not need to engage in retroactive diagnosis, but simply note that for contemporaries it was plain that autistic children passed undetected through the custodial sieve and disappeared among residential populations.

Let us begin with the second point and with the period preceding 1950. What was common to the individuals institutionalized as mentally retarded during this period? As we heard earlier from Tredgold, it was not the fact that their IQ was low. How could it have been? When the U.S. Army first began experimenting with IQ tests during WWI, more than 50 percent of Southern male recruits tested as "imbeciles" (apart from Virginians, who excelled and tested only as "morons" according to the then-current taxonomy).[2] There was no question of institutionalizing all of them, and social commentators as well as psychologists were quick to point out that the tests were biased and untrustworthy. While there is no doubt that Goddard's invention of the category of "moron" contributed mightily to the steady rise in the rate of institutionalization during these years, it is equally certain that IQ testing itself played only a marginal role in the actual procedure of commitment. By the time trust in the IQ tests was sufficiently restored, with the new version of the Simon-Binet test in 1939, the rise in the proportion of those institutionalized as mentally retarded had already crested (to resume again after 1950, but for completely different reasons, as we shall see in the next chapter). Moreover, as Kanner and others have noted, IQ testing by itself could not determine who should be institutionalized. The effect of IQ testing was, in fact, to construct intellectual inadequacy as a continuum, "not an absolute, all-or-none attribute" (Kanner 1964, 122–23; Kanner 1949, 3; Norsworthy 1906, 77; Clausen 1966, 731, 741–42; Wallin 1949, 43–62).

By that time, moreover, the American Association on Mental Deficiency had already settled on a method of identification which, like the influential British definition, privileged the fact of "social inadequacy, due to low intelligence, which has been developmentally arrested." Tredgold was thus quite representative of British and American practices when he declared that mental deficiency was a social and legal concept identifying those who were *socially incapable*, rather than a precise medical or psychological diagnosis measured by IQ (Tredgold [1908] 1947, 1–6; Noll 1995, 30–33; Wallin

1949, 20–36). Tredgold's textbook went through seven editions from 1908 to 1947 and "has had most profound influence in the field" (Clausen 1966, 729). Psychiatrists, in their role as superintendents of state institutions and directors of state departments of mental health, dominated the field of mental deficiency, and they looked with suspicion at upstart psychologists and their IQ tests.

It is patently clear that from the point of view of the actual practice of institutionalizing the mentally deficient, the distinction between mental retardation and autism (which of course did not exist before 1943) would have been meaningless. The above threefold definition clearly privileges the initial objective complaint, typically from the family or local authorities, that one is "socially inadequate," while assigning psychological testing or medical diagnosis the secondary role of verifying this complaint if necessary. In reality, medical or psychological expertise was called upon mostly to provide a seal of approval for a pre-existing social mechanism of exclusion. Any relative or even "any reputable citizen" could apply to the court to have somebody committed (especially if they were under twenty-one, or for women in some states, even under thirty). The application would typically need to be verified by a three-person panel, only one of whom was a medical doctor or a psychologist. Typically, the panel's examination was brief and the whole procedure took only one day.[3] Some states – Kentucky, Louisiana, Mississippi, and Wyoming – didn't even require a doctor; any jury could do it. And many states did not require a psychologist or mental examiner (Noll 1995, 33–34, 171, n.27). This is completely in accordance with Tredgold. You hardly need a doctor or a psychologist to judge that someone is *socially* incapable.

You might need them if you wanted to determine the cause for a person's social inadequacy. Besides being feebleminded, such a person could have been criminally inclined, psychotic, physically disabled, too young, demented (Wallin 1949, 30–31). But such differentiation was not, in fact, germane to the practice of institutionalization at this period. This interpretation of the practice of institutionalization is borne out by the character of those institutionalized as mentally retarded. Who were these "socially incapable" individuals? It is hardly a secret that they were disproportionately likely to come from the lower rungs of society: immigrants, African Americans, or lower-class whites (Castles 2004, 352–53; Jones 2004, 322–23, 348, n.41; Trent 1994, 141–81). From 1904 to 1945 the prototypical first admission to state institutions for the mentally retarded was a lower-class or immigrant "moron" adolescent. As can be seen in Table 3,

Table 3: Age group as percentage of first admissions at US institutions for the mentally deficient, 1904–1951

Age at first admission	1904	1923	1938	1945	1951
Under 5	3	5.5	6	9	18
5–9	23	20	17	21	24
10–14	34	28.5	27	26	23
15–19	22	24	27	23	17
20–	18	22	23	21	18

(Source: Goldstein, H. (1959). "Population Trends in US Public Institutions for the Mentally Deficient." *American Journal of Mental Deficiency* 63(4): 599–604.)

older children and adolescents between the ages of 10 and 19 consistently constituted more than half of first admissions during these years. Additionally, "morons" constituted the largest category of first admissions throughout this period, hovering around 44 percent (Goldstein 1959). In 1951, for example, 16.1 percent of first admissions to New York institutions for the mentally retarded were black, while they constituted only 6 percent of the general New York population. Almost 58 percent of black first admissions were "morons," and 35 percent were between the ages of 10 and 14. The corresponding numbers for Jews and Irish, for example, while higher than for WASPs, were only 26–28 percent morons and only 10–12 percent between the ages of 10 and 14 (Malzberg 1952, 35).

Moreover, the causes for and the character of institutionalization reflected the prevailing identifications between feeblemindedness, degeneracy, and crime, which is why differentiation by etiology was not really germane to the practice of institutionalizing the feebleminded. This was the age of – as Trent put it – "the menace of the feebleminded" (Trent 1994). Truancy, delinquency, epilepsy, alcoholism, sexual promiscuity, even masturbation, all served as pretexts for commitment as mentally deficient, and the category of "defective delinquent" was the main prism through which the problem of feeblemindedness was viewed. As compared with other groups, many more blacks in New York were admitted to institutions for the mentally retarded because of "severe behavior disorder" and aggressiveness. Many states created institutions specifically for this purpose, such as the Virginia State Prison Farm for Defective Misdemeanants (Noll 1995, 33–35; Goddard 1915; Fernald 1909; Kline 2001; Malzberg 1952, 35). At this point in the history of mental retardation, the category was part and parcel of the domain of "abnormal individuals" associated with danger and criminality, which formed the main jurisdiction of psychiatry in its role as a supervisor of public hygiene (Foucault [1975] 2003).

This means that the institutionalization of mental retardation during this period served as a major barrier to the identification and differentiation of autism, which could only develop on its margins as a residual and rare category. The initial complaint about "social inadequacy" and the association with danger and disorder could hardly differentiate between autism and mental retardation. Indeed, as we saw above, it hardly bothered to differentiate between mental retardation and a variety of other "abnormalities." Autism, of course, was only "discovered" in 1943, as this era in the history of mental retardation treatment was coming to an end. But it was discovered or invented precisely on the margins of the institution, as a residual category of the mechanisms of class and racial control that served as the "surfaces of emergence" (Foucault 1972, 41) for the category of mental deficiency during these years. All eleven children whom Kanner reported in his seminal article were white (two were Jewish, the rest "Anglo-Saxon") and of upper- or middle-class families. Quite a few, in fact, were the sons and daughters of psychologists, psychiatrists, and medical doctors. Crucially, many of them arrived at the clinic because their parents challenged the diagnosis of "feeblemindedness" given to their children (Kanner 1943). As we noted earlier, feeblemindedness in this period was considered to be a problem of the "lower classes" and "lower races." It was an "organic defect," which therefore potentially implicated the parents and their pedigree. Middle- or upper-class parents, therefore, were likely to vigorously resist it, as well as the recourse to institutionalization.[4]

Right from its inception, therefore, the identification of autism, its differentiation from mental retardation, was limited by social factors, by the sometimes explicit and more often implicit assumption that mental retardation was a widespread phenomenon among lower classes, while autism was a middle- or upper-class condition, and quite rare. A small cottage industry of studies developed in order to try to tease out the connection between autism and class, how much of it was real, and how much due to "selection bias" (Lotter 1966; Schopler, Andrews, and Strupp 1979; Wing 1980). But when the numbers of diagnoses began to rise in the late 1980s, epidemiologists reported that the correlation between class, race, and autism disappeared (Fombonne 1999; 2003).[5] It stands to reason, therefore, that for a long time lower-class or African American children, who today would be diagnosed as "autistic," were in the past institutionalized as mentally retarded. If four of the eleven children on whom Kanner reported ended up institutionalized for the rest of their lives with the severely retarded or the psychotic (Kanner 1971, 144), even though they were diagnosed with autism and had middle-class parents, what chance in hell was there that African-American[6] or poor children, who saw nobody of Kanner's caliber, would escape institutionalization?[7]

From the point of view of custody as an institutionalized practice, autism was simply meaningless, below the radar, because the institution produced something like autism on a massive scale – withdrawal, detachment, and indifference, these were reactions to the institutional environment that already in 1945 Rene Spitz identified as "hospitalism," and as akin to autism. This situation was not changed by the "discovery" of autism, only by deinstitutionalization. In his follow-up study, Kanner (1971, 144) noted that the four children who "spent most of their lives in institutional care, have lost their luster early after their admission. Originally fighting for their aloneness and basking in the contentment it gave them, originally alert to unwelcome changes and, in their own way, struggling for the status quo, originally astounding the observer with their phenomenal feats of memory, they yielded readily to the uninterrupted self-isolation and soon settled down in a life not too remote from a nirvana-like existence. If at all responsive to psychological testing, their IQ's dropped down to figures usually referred to as low-grade moron or imbecile . . . One cannot help but gain the impression that State Hospital admission was tantamount to a life sentence . . . a total retreat into near nothingness."

In fact, as part of their case for deinstitutionalization, the reformers pointed to the problem of children whom they called "clinically homeless," who fell between the cracks of mental illness and mental retardation. Anecdotally, we know that at least a few of these children were diagnosed with "infantile autism," or with "childhood schizophrenia" (recall that in DSM-II, autism was classified as a subtype of childhood schizophrenia), or with "schizoid reaction, childhood type" and were referred to the child or adolescent units of state mental hospitals or to residential centers for emotionally disturbed children. Oftentimes, however, they would be evaluated as "retarded," or as "severe mental defective with behavioral reaction," and refused admittance or pushed out. They would be sent to state schools for the mentally retarded, but there they were considered "emotionally disturbed" and transferred to back wards and isolation rooms. Or they would be refused admittance, and sent once more to the state hospital, where they would be kept in seclusion until they were capable of fending for themselves in an adult dormitory for the mentally ill (Blatt 1970, 82–84). In 1976, when deinstitutionalization was beginning to gather steam in Canada, it was still the case that of 1,152 first admissions to institutions for the mentally retarded, only 75 percent carried a diagnosis of mental retardation, while the remaining 25 percent were classified with diagnoses falling under the categories of psychoses (about 3 percent), neuroses / personality disorders / other non-psychotic disorders (18 percent), or other conditions (4 percent).[8] While the sieve constructed by child psychiatry was becoming fine enough to capture autism within it – though still dependent on the residual stream of middle-class self-referral on the margins of the institutions – the practice of institutionalization only offered two main slots, "emotionally disturbed" or "mentally retarded." How many children must have disappeared into these gaping holes without even registering a tremor in the net! Kanner suspected as much. In 1949 he suggested that a good portion of feeblemindedness was only "apparent" or "pseudo feeblemindedness" – that is, individuals who only appeared to be "feebleminded" because various conditions prevented them from realizing their potential. Autism was among these conditions. He wrote: "I wonder if some persons who are harbored in institutions for the feebleminded are not in reality individuals whose early infantile autism had not been recognized and who abandoned themselves uncompromisingly to idiotic-like dysfunction. A few such children have come to my attention in the past few years" (Kanner 1949, 11, 27–28). Rimland (1964, 13) simply stated that "many autistic children do eventually become institutionalized as mentally deficient."

But we are getting ahead of ourselves. The very fact that young children were institutionalized *en masse* in the 1950s and 1960s was itself historically unprecedented. We must first register its meaning and attempt to explain it, for it will contain important clues to the role played by the diagnosis of autism in this period, and why deinstitutionalization was likely to increase its salience.

— 3 —

THE SURVEILLANCE OF CHILDHOOD

To grasp how historically unprecedented the 1950s institutionalization of children was, we invite the reader to re-examine Table 3 and note the radical change in the rate at which very young children, 5 years old or younger, were institutionalized in the post-WWII era. Until the end of WWII, roughly 75 percent of first admissions to state institutions for the mentally defective were older than 9, and hardly any were very young children, 5 years old or younger. This fits well with Tredgold. Children that young are by definition "socially incapable," so what's the point of institutionalizing just some of them? But after the war, the proportion of first admissions 5 years of age or younger increased dramatically to 18 percent, while the proportion of first admissions at 10 years or older decreased. Moreover, as can be seen in Table 4, from 1953 to 1968 these trends remained remarkably consistent. In 1965, children 14 years old or younger constituted the largest category of first admissions to large state institutions. Then, with deinstitutionalization, the trend changed dramatically (see Chapter 4 for more on this).

But for the moment let us stay with this astounding change in the fate of young children. What happened in the wake of WWII is hard to understand, since it was historically unprecedented: children younger than 5 were *never* institutionalized at a high rate. Up until 1945, for example, New York State institutions for the mentally retarded were prohibited from admitting children younger than 5 (Malzberg 1952, 30). These were of course the years of the baby boom, so one may argue that the rise in the proportion of young children institutionalized simply reflected overall demographic changes, but this is, at best, a very partial explanation. As can be seen in Table 5, while the baby boom registered a significant change from pre-WWII years, the age

Table 4:   Mean Age at First Admission and Percentage of First Admissions between Ages 0–19 at US Institutions for the Mentally Retarded, 1953–1977

	1953	1956	1959	1962	1965	1968	1971	1974	1977
Mean age of first admission	13	12.6	13.6	12.2	12.4	13.3	14	16.3	18
Percentage of first admissions between ages 0–19	83.6	86.3	83.2	88.9	88.5	84.1	79.5	74.8	65.4

(Source: Lakin, K. Charlie., B. K. Hill, F. A. Hauber and R. H. Bruininks, 1982. "Changes in Age at First Admission to Residential Care for Mentally Retarded People," *Mental Retardation* 20(5): 216–219.)

Table 5:   Changes in the Proportion of Children 0–9 years old in the total US population

Census Year	Proportion of children 0–9 Years old
1920	22
1930	19
1940	16
1950	20
1960	22
1970	18

(Source: http://www.census.gov/prod/2002pubs/censr-4.pdf)

distribution to which it gave rise was hardly unprecedented. The proportion of children younger than 10 years old in the total U.S. population reached 20 percent in 1950, and climbed to 22 percent in 1960. Then it would decline again. Thus, it never increased beyond the level already registered in 1920. No doubt, the proportion of young children in the 1920 U.S. population reflected different demographic processes than 1950 – greater mortality, higher fertility among immigrants, and so on – but the crucial point is that 1920 was already a high point in the institutionalization of the "feebleminded," yet only 5.5 percent of first admissions were young children. If the proportion of children institutionalized merely tracked demographic changes, then we would expect to see it rising, falling, then rising again – not relatively flat until it suddenly doubles between 1945 and 1950.

Nonetheless, the baby boom is significant not as demographic change but as shorthand for a sea change in the perception and government of childhood, in the roles and responsibilities of parents (especially mothers), and in the position of medicine vis-à-vis both children and parents. Trent (1994, 238–39) calls this the period of "reproductive consensus," when having healthy and normal children became an ethical goal, and adult life fulfillment became a matter of successful parenting. Kline (2001) calls it "positive eugenics." Regardless of the terms, the main point is that the "consensus" involved a bargain between the middle-class family and the state, brokered by medicine. Producing healthy and normal children as a "contribution" to society required that the state relieve the family of the burden of caring for those who were not likely to be healthy or normal. It also required that someone possess the expertise necessary to determine this likelihood.

Another way of saying this is that in the years between 1945 and 1950, two histories converged that could not converge before: the history of care and research on the "feebleminded" on the one hand, and the history of problematizing the middle-class child, on the other. The institution meets the child guidance clinic; eugenics meets mental hygiene; and the linchpin, the hinge that connected these two histories, was the middle-class family.

The unification of mental deficiency and mental hygiene under child psychiatry

From the beginning of the twentieth century and up until 1945, there was a fairly clear division of labor between specialists in retardation and child guidance clinics dealing with behavior problems. Feeblemindedness, as we have seen, was construed as a problem of the lower classes and lower races. Particularly with the figure of the adolescent moron, feeblemindedness was construed as an organic and heritable cause of delinquency and social inadequacy among the lower classes, which explains why the custodial institution provided the chief reaction to the "menace of the feebleminded" (Trent 1994) and why there was frequent resort to the extreme measure of sterilization (Kline 2001). The arrow of harm, so to speak, especially under the influence of eugenics, went from the parents to the child. It was the parents' "organic defect" that was evident in the adolescent's retardation, and which called for interventions at the level of reproduction.

The child guidance clinics, by contrast, had very little to do with

85

mental retardation. They considered it uninteresting and refused to be bothered with it. Over time, their initial focus on "saving" immigrant and lower-class children at risk for delinquency changed into an emphasis on the behavior problems of the mostly normal middle-class child, considered to be caused by emotional conflict and treatable by dynamic therapy. The focus, therefore, in the spirit of the mental hygiene movement, was on prevention, on identifying and treating these problems early on, before they overwhelmed the parents' attempts at control and education, or before they turned into adult forms of mental illness and delinquency. The arrow of harm was pointed in the inverse direction, from the child to the parents, since the young child's behavioral problems threatened the functioning and stability of the family. Over time, however, the child's behavior problems came to be viewed as themselves symptoms of inadequate mothering, either too indulgent or too cold and rejecting, and both parents and child came under the purview of the clinic to undergo therapy. "By 1940," says Jones, "child guidance became synonymous with mother-blaming" (Nadesan 2005, 44–45, 58–73; Jones 1999, 7–8; Nehring 2004, 371–72; Kanner [1941] 1964, 141–42).

For scientific entrepreneurs like Kanner, this division of labor was a major obstacle. He wrote in 1941 that the child guidance clinics did not see "retardation as worthy of full inclusion in their scientific concerns. This was left almost entirely to the specialists, mostly connected with institutions in more or less splendid isolation" (141–42). Kanner, the founder of child psychiatry in the U.S., was uniquely located between these two mechanisms, and expended a great deal of energy and rhetoric into unifying them in his practice. He was director of the Child Psychiatry Clinic at the Johns Hopkins Hospital, established in 1930, the first of its kind in the U.S. His mentor was Adolph Meyer, founder of the mental hygiene movement, and the new clinic, therefore, was continuous with the work of child guidance clinics. In this vein, Kanner saw his fair share of self-referred middle-class children and their behavior problems. Likewise, he did his own fair share of advising, "defending," and blaming middle-class mothers. Yet he also insisted that the new clinic's mandate include the mentally deficient. "It's a luxury," he wrote, "to give child guidance only to intelligent children . . . The behavior problems of the intelligent, less intelligent and unintelligent cannot possibly be assigned to separate categories. Occupation with mental deficiency is a legitimate part of child . . . psychiatry – not merely an appendix but one of its integral functions" (Kanner [1941] 1964, 142–43). In a corresponding movement, he strove mightily against the self-imposed isolation of the field of feeblemindedness. In 1949, he claimed the field was on the cusp of a major transformation. It has become clearer, he said, that the feebleminded are not a homogenous group, and that feeblemindedness as such is not a hereditary unit trait. It followed that one could take toward them the same approach as the mental hygiene movement and the child guidance clinics did with respect to the mentally ill and the problem child. That is, one could classify them on the basis of "pragmatic considerations . . . the different adjustment and treatment possibilities" with a view not "backward to origin or cause . . . [but] rather . . . forward toward practical communal, educational, and clinical possibilities for human engineering" (Kanner 1941; Kanner [1941] 1964, 142–43; Kanner 1949, 6–11; Wallin 1949, 67–69; Clausen 1966, 736–39).

Clearly, Kanner was trying to *unify a field of intervention* for the new discipline of child psychiatry, and achieve control over the referral streams into it (partially siphoned off by the institution) with the promise if not of prevention, then of a universal surveillance and placement system that could minimize the risks posed by all childhood ailments – the whole field running from problem behaviors to feeblemindedness – and maximize each child's potential. To achieve this aim it was crucial to demonstrate that retardation was not the cause of all other afflictions of the retarded child. A corollary point was that retardation itself could be caused by these other afflictions: "parental overprotection, rejection, perfectionistic disapproval, and neglect tend to warp the personalities of children regardless of their intellectual endowment" (Kanner 1949, 4). Thus there were two complementary movements: first, to show that the behavior problems of the feebleminded were not different from those of normal children and were amenable to the same treatments; and second, that feeblemindedness was protean enough to shade into the area claimed as the jurisdiction of the child guidance clinics: the problem behaviors of the middle-class child. This was the function of his distinction between "absolute," "relative," and "apparent" feeblemindedness. The absolutely feebleminded were those who in any civilization would be recognized as nonfunctional, and who stood in need of permanent enlightened custody. They were "institutional material" (17). The relatively feebleminded were those whose impairment was culturally specific: that is, they were merely "intellectually inadequate" and in any civilization but the modern one would have been indistinguishable from the rest of the population. Only modern universal education, scholastic competition, and the unrealistic expectations of middle-class parents have constituted them as impaired. They are in need of "adjustment and guidance," typically toward a menial, less intellectually demanding vocation. The solution, then, was vocational education and downward mobility. Finally, the pseudo or apparent feebleminded were those who suffered from a specific delay or disability, such as infantile autism or speech delay, which masked their otherwise considerable intellectual potential. Rather than being absolutely or relatively deficient, they were only apparently so. They have "removed themselves" from the world, and so their intellectual development was warped. They were in need of careful diagnosis and therapy, which would help them "reenter the world" and which would "not only bring hidden potentialities to light but can also do something to turn the discovered potentialities into realized actualities." They were not, therefore, "institutional material" but "clinical material" (Kanner 1949, 4, 10–11, 17, 20).

The reader can appreciate, therefore, the crucial role, the demonstrative value, of autism in the establishment of modern child psychiatry. It permitted child psychiatry to lay claim at once to the lower-class feebleminded and the middle-class "problem child" and to unify them within a single observational field.

And not a moment too soon. Kanner's acid remark about the "splendid isolation" of the institutions signaled his recognition that the jurisdictional arrangement underlying psychiatric dominance in the field of feeblemindedness was crumbling. Psychiatrists used to rule the roost in their role as institutions' superintendents, but by 1947, psychologists and educators outnumbered medical doctors almost three to one as members of the American Association of Mental Deficiency, and they were also becoming more visible on the editorial board of the *American Journal of Mental Deficiency*. The year 1948 was to be the last that a psychiatrist, an institution superintendent, served as the editor of the journal. The following editors were all educators and psychologists. Most research was still carried out in institutions, but in 1946 funding became available through the National Institute of Mental Health and university-based research had begun to threaten the monopoly of the institution. The child guidance clinics, on the other hand, embodied a different jurisdictional arrangement, with multidisciplinary teams led by psychiatrists. Kanner envisioned a similar interdisciplinary future for the unified field presided over by child psychiatry. Approvingly, he quoted George S. Stevenson, medical director of the National Committee for Mental Hygiene: The "system must be designed to serve all of the mentally deficient, not only those that bother us the most." This one sentence, Kanner said, contained a program that would elevate the specialty "to a rank equal to the other disciplines which have human engineering as their goal . . . Institutions could become active community centers with outpatient departments which, in collaboration with schools, social agencies, the physicians of the district, and the industries, would make themselves responsible for the best mental hygiene for the absolutely, relatively and apparently feebleminded" (Trent 1994, 244–47; Kanner 1949, 29–31).

The role of the middle-class family

Kanner was acutely aware that none of this would have been possible without the crucial role played by middle-class parents. To bring feeblemindedness within the orbit of mental hygiene could only be done by providing services to those "mental deficients" who, as Stevenson put it, did not "bother us the most." That is, they did not threaten public order and were not (yet) "socially inadequate." They did pose a risk to society to the extent that they, as the child guidance movement taught, threatened the stability and functioning of the middle-class family, drained its resources, and prevented it from making its promised contributions to societal health and wealth. Put differently, the problematization of the middle-class child pioneered by the child guidance movement was being transferred to the sphere of feeblemindedness, thus linking the two, but the only agents who could accomplish such a transfer were the middle-class parents themselves. One needed these parents, who previously hid from public view because of the stigma of "organic defect," to issue the complaint and invite the psychiatrists and the state into the middle-class family (Schumacher 1952, 55).

Thus the middle-class family served as the linchpin that unified the field of intervention presided over by child psychiatry. This unification, by the same token, also led to the increased institutionalization of very young children. We should remember that Kanner made his "discovery" of autism, and also came to recognize what he called "pseudo-feeblemindedness," by way of the middle-class parents who brought their children to him. It was parental pressure, though significantly in the name of the war effort, that in 1945 repealed New York State's ban on institutional placement of children younger than 5, in order "to alleviate difficult circumstances in certain family groups" (Malzberg 1952, 30). This was the period when the first associations of parents of retarded children were formed. By 1950 there were already 88 local parent groups in 19 states, 77 of which were formed between 1946 and 1950, including the highly influential state associations in New York, New Jersey, and Rhode Island. Typically, these associations were mobilized to demand the inclusion of their children in public schools, but they also advocated strongly for shortening waiting lists for institutionalization, providing more funds to existing state institutions, building new institutions, and admitting very young children. And they did so in the name of protecting the family from the burden, especially the emotional burden, posed by the retarded child (Trent 1994, 236–41; Jones 2004, 131–33; Castles 2004, 351–52, 358). Clearly, as feeblemindedness came within the magnetic field of mental hygiene, the arrow of harm was bent in the inverse direction; no longer an organic defect that implicated the family, feeblemindedness now began to be something from which the middle-class family itself demanded to be protected.

No doubt this was partly due to the very elastic nature of this category – "middle class" – which precisely in those years was stretched once more to include many who would have not qualified in the past. Significantly, the newcomers, while held to the same standards of normalcy and respectability that being "middle class" connoted, did not have the means to place their children in a private institution, or to surround them with a sort of social and familial protective environment, as did better-endowed members of the "middle class." Jacques May, for example, moved deeper into Long Island, and bought a house with several acres around it, to provide his autistic twins with a suitable protective environment (May 1958). Readers of Faulkner's *The Sound and the Fury* recall that Benji's fate was sealed once the Compson family estate that sheltered him was sold. The burden of caring for a disabled child, therefore, became evident specifically in the post-war era's new suburban life, with each nuclear family isolated in its own little plot, surrounded not by a protective environment but by fear of stigma and shame (Trent 1994). We became acutely aware of this predicament reading a contemporary listserv for autistic parents. A mother fired rapid messages one after the other, pleading with everyone for help and advice. Her problem: how to stop her autistic son from going over across the yard to see the neighbors. Many who responded told her they were grappling with similar issues and provided pragmatic advice (locks, fences, cookies). She reported that half of her day was spent dealing with this issue, and almost all of her emotional energy. Yet the Compsons and the Mays in their day could deploy money and social power to completely blunt the edge of this sort of problem.

The institutionalization of children and the comprehensive surveillance system

As parents began to appeal for institutionalization, special education, and therapy as relief from the physical and emotional burden of the retarded child, this burden also became a dominant concern of the medical profession. After 1945, the medical profession's involvement in mental retardation no longer meant simply affixing a seal of approval on a pre-existing social mechanism of exclusion. Doctors began to assume a different role, encouraging parents to commit their very young children to institutions for the mentally retarded. A state mental health official opined that "mental hygiene education has been sufficiently widespread to create a greater demand for the removal of young idiot children from the home. Social workers recognizing them are prone to advise institutionalization . . . Physicians, who now receive more psychiatric training, are also alert to the social implications of an idiot child in the home" (Castles 2004, 362). A survey of parents from the late 1950s found that about half of all respondents had been instructed by their doctors to immediately institutionalize their young retarded child. Typically, the doctors justified institutionalization in the name of concern for the well-being of the family. In particular, they worried that mothers of young retarded children would exhaust themselves and consequently neglect the rest of the family (Brockley 2004, 144–45; Castles 2004, 352–53, 361–63; Trent 1994, 232–33).

A great deal has been written about this medical zeal for institutionalization, which, because it offends our sensibilities, seems outlandish, arrogant, cruel. No doubt it was one of the main causes for the sharp increase in the proportion of young children institutionalized. But we must overcome our indignation in order to grasp what happened in these years, because in fact it is continuous with our own practices, it is their point of origin. The institutionalization of young children is probably the most visible and impressive aspect of the complex transformation that took place in these years, but in retrospect it strikes us as more incidental than essential. It seems a specific and provisional tactical component within an overall strategic ensemble, the main aspect of which was the unification of the fields of mental deficiency and mental hygiene, under the aegis of child psychiatry, through the crucial role played by the middle-class family, and with the prospect of installing a comprehensive surveillance and placement system for early childhood. This is easy to demonstrate. First, the medical zeal for institutionalization would have come to naught, if it did not meet with and respond to the growing demand for institutionalization coming from middle-class parents. Donald Jolly, the chief physician of a Massachusetts State school for mentally retarded children, noted the fivefold increase in the institutionalization of young children from 1936 to 1950 (1952, 632–33). He attributed it to the building of new facilities (when Willowbrook opened in 1948, there was an immediate spike in the proportion of young children institutionalized in New York State [Malzberg 1952, 28, 31]), to the increased emphasis on developmental diagnosis at an early age, and to increased recommendations for the institutionalization of children by pediatricians and obstetricians. But the most important cause, he said, was the strong pressure from parents. Second, the main focus of child psychiatry was protecting the middle-class family and assisting in its functioning, and just as this focus led to recommending institutionalization, it could also justify the opposite. Jolly was highly critical of the physicians who recommended immediate institutionalization (1952, 633–35). They completely misunderstood, he said, the emotional conflict of the parents. Instead of relieving them of the emotional burden, institutionalization at too early an age would in fact increase guilt and emotional conflict. Solving these parental problems, he argued, is more important for the total situation than any effects that earlier institutionalization may have on the child himself. He recommended waiting until the parents work out their emotional conflicts, reach "complete acceptance," and come asking for institutionalization of their own accord. The doctor's role was not to pressure parents, but to guide them slowly and carefully toward recognizing that institutionalization may be the "proper positive action in planning for the future of the[ir] exceptional child."

Doctors repeat this point over and over again. One is not treating the child alone, but the family as a whole, because it is the functioning of the family unit that is the best predictor of the child's prognosis. Hence, the arrow of harm could swing back, and the apparatus of child guidance could be brought to bear on the mother of the retarded child, analyzing, first, how her overindulgence of the retarded child may harm the rest of the family, spouse, and siblings (and many times mothers tearfully concurred with this diagnosis); then second, how denial, overindulgence, rejection or some combination thereof (some psychiatrists claimed the mother's overprotectiveness was rejection in disguise), may harm the retarded child and compound her already precarious situation with additional emotional and behavioral disturbances (Brockley 1004, 148–49; Schumacher 1946, 53); finally, with Kanner, one gets the logical conclusion of this analysis: an account of how the parents' coldness has caused a form of "pseudo-feeblemindedness," namely autism: "we find almost invariably that the children have been brought up in emotional refrigerators in which there was extremely little fondling and cuddling, in which the infants have been treated more as coldly watched and preserved experiments than as human beings enveloped in the warmth of genuine parental affection . . . Many of the autistic children are functional idiots when they are brought for examination at three or four years of age. They do not talk, do not respond to other people . . . not accessible to any kind of testing. Some remain so for the rest of their lives . . . For all practical purposes, they function at the level of absolute feeblemind-edness. Yet some of them, with permissiveness and affectionate stim-ulation, are able to make sufficient compromise with reality to reenter the world from which they have removed themselves so completely" (Kanner 1949, 27; see also Neuer 1947; Wallin 1949, 70–83).

If we were playing the blame game, then we should have now exon-erated Bruno Bettelheim, whose name today stands for everything that was wrongheaded, arrogant, and cruel in early autism treat-ment. Bettelheim served as Director of the University of Chicago's Sonia Shankman Orthogenic School, where he treated autistic chil-dren in out-of-home placement using a form of milieu therapy, in which children could form strong attachments with adults within a structured but caring environment. As we shall see in Chapter 7, for its time there was nothing exceptional about this choice of therapy outside the home, and it was the norm even in parent-run establish-ments. The therapy preceded the theory, which was propounded in his 1967 classic *The Empty Fortress*, and which followed in many respects Kanner's imagery of the "refrigerator mother." In subse-quent years, Bettelheim became the most vilified figure in the autism world, especially after his suicide in 1990 when former students of the Orthogenic School accused him of being a cruel tyrant who abused students. Yet his indictment of parents was much more muted than Kanner's in some ways, and his choice of therapy merely followed Kanner's account, from which it is clear that Kanner thought autistic children should neither stay at home nor be institutionalized, but should be immersed in a milieu of "permissiveness and affectionate stimulation," not a bad description of what Bettelheim did. But we are not playing the blame game,[1] and the significance of Kanner's analysis of autism lies elsewhere. It was merely part of an (admittedly crude) attempt to organize the newly unified field of child psychiatry according to, as he put it, "forward practical possibilities for human engineering," taking into account the total family situation. Children with autism and other forms of pseudo-feeblemindedness required therapy. The parents likely would need therapy as well. The relatively feebleminded and their families would be well served by special education and vocational training. Institutionalization would solve the specific plight of families with the "absolutely feebleminded," for example, the "Mongolians" (Kanner 1949, 19). Malzberg (1952, 33) claimed that the increase in the proportion of very young children institutionalized in New York State was "in large part" due to the increase in admissions of "Mongols," and of those with "cranial abnormalities," since they are typically identified at birth, and they are without exception of very low intelligence. Indeed, we know that parents of children with Down's syndrome were encouraged to immediately institutionalize their children at rates much higher than the 50 percent reported earlier for parents of children with all types of mental retardation (Castles 2004, 363).

The distinctions Kanner employed may have been crude, but the system he envisioned was already our own. It was a system for the comprehensive surveillance of childhood, which aimed to identify, as early as possible, the differential risk and potential embodied by different children, and to assign children as early as possible to the intervention that would minimize the risk and realize their potential. This meant that while the institutional matrix of custody remained the same – the rate of institutionalization continued to go up until 1969 – its purpose was being radically reconfigured from within: no longer centered on the exclusion of the socially incapable, it was now an integral part of a surveillance system for early childhood, since the increase in the rate of institutionalization was completely driven by the rise in admissions of very young children. Within this system, medicine, and specifically child psychiatry, was expected to play not only a therapeutic role, but also a predictive, prophylactic public health function, what we called in the introduction the "medical diagnosis of social destiny."

Indeed, the institutionalization wave of the early 1950s must not be understood as the "opposite" of community treatment, as the deinstitutionalization narrative would have it (see Chapter 4), but as one tactical aspect in the new vision of a comprehensive surveillance and placement system. This vision still involved the indictment of mothering and the overriding aim of stabilizing the middle-class family, since it aimed to encompass feeblemindedness within the orbit of child guidance. For precisely these reasons, however, the institutionalization of young children was only an incidental and provisional aspect of this shift. This vision, in short, was much more in continuity with the deinstitutionalization and community treatment movement of later decades than it would at first seem. This very same period also saw a fivefold increase in the number of mentally retarded children enrolled in special education, from 108,500 in 1948 to 540,000 in 1966 (while the total school-age population only increased by 70 percent), the vast majority of whom were served in local public day schools (Mackie 1969, 36–39).

A second wave of child guidance clinics, now focused on evaluation, diagnosis, treatment plans, and lifelong follow-up for retardation, also commenced in the early 1950s. By 1955 there were already 33 such clinics. As envisioned by Kanner, the clinics were multidisciplinary. Their staff included pediatricians, child psychiatrists, nurses, psychologists, social workers, teachers, child development specialists, nutritionists, genetic counselors, as well as occupational, play, speech and physical therapists. The multidisciplinary staff was needed because clinics addressed themselves to the total profile of the child, as well as to the parents and the community. By 1960 the clinics were treating 12,000 children, 75 percent of whom were under 10 years of age. The efforts of the clinics were sanctioned and amplified by the 1963 recommendations of the President's panel on mental retardation to create a "continuum of care," from neonatal screening to identify high-risk children, through comprehensive diagnostic evaluation, to lifelong health supervision (Nehring 2004, 371–80).

As early as 1952, reformers envisioned a locally based system of day care and nursery schools for the retarded, starting at two-and-a-half years of age, to address the problems of early surveillance and placement. Such a system, they said, would be preferable to early institutionalization because it would facilitate much more accurate diagnosis and much better forecasting of the child's prognosis. When the feebleminded are first evaluated, they reasoned, it is difficult to ascertain their status because they come burdened with frustration and with those behavior traits that grow from loss of parental love. They are either "destructive, hostile, and antisocial" or "inhibited, repressed, and withdrawn" and "in due course find their way into the institution for the feeble-minded, the correctional school, or the mental hospital" (Schumacher 1952, 54). But in the child care centers and nursery schools they would get love and security from trained personnel who knew what could be expected of them. The basic method would be a "child guidance approach in the fullest sense of the term," that is, a focus on early prevention, on emotional conflicts, and on family dynamics. It would be possible, then, to sift the absolutely feebleminded from the pseudo- and relatively feebleminded

95

who, with the correct early intervention, could remain in the community. Finally, the program would facilitate research on early diagnosis, prevention, and correct placement, and thus bring "tremendous gain in the health, welfare and wealth of the community and the nation" (Schumacher 1952, 54–56).

We said earlier that the middle-class family was the linchpin permitting feeblemindedness to enter the orbit of child guidance. Indeed, parent organizations, and especially the National Association for Retarded Children, played a central role in the establishment of the new child guidance clinics. At the same time, the clinics' staff encouraged and assisted the formation of parent groups. It was parents' duty to find out what services were available in their community, and if services were lacking, to become activists. Similarly, Schumacher expected the day care centers and nursery schools for the retarded to be organized by parents in cooperation with mental hygiene organizations. Parent activism, at this point in time, was not the enemy of the medical profession but its ally. Doctors, psychologists, members of the American Association on Mental Deficiency, even state officials called upon and mobilized parent activism as a crucial ally in lobbying and securing resources from state legislatures, Congress, and the Federal Children's Bureau. Doctors called upon parents' activism because it was an important outlet for the emotional conflicts of the parents, as analyzed by child guidance, and thus an integral part of the process through which parents would come to accept their children. Schumacher objected to early institutionalization, because it did not address the parents' "intense narcissistic hurt," their denial and resentment. It was necessary, he said, "to accept the parents at the point that they are concerned and to go on from there. Their feelings of frustration, resentment, hostility and guilt must be permitted expression and be adequately dealt with therapeutically" (Schumacher 1952, 55). This could be done in the framework of locally based, parent-organized day care centers, where they would be able to meet with other parents whose predicament was similar, admit and share their secret, and thus come to genuine acceptance of their children. Child guidance clinics, indeed, organized therapy and guidance programs for parents. The idea was to get them emotionally attuned for community activism and cooperation with professionals, rather than wasting their energies in a search for miracle cures. But at the same time it was also hoped activism itself would be "therapeutic," as a psychiatric social worker opined in 1953 (Schumacher 1952, 54–56; Nehring 2004, 374–78; Jones 2004, 329–30; Brockley 2004, 154–56).

This was a fateful moment in the history of mental retardation. Within less than two decades, the drive to institutionalize young children would be reversed, as we shall see in the next chapter, but the receding tide would leave behind it a greatly changed shoreline. The lasting inheritance of the early 1950s would be this unified domain of child psychiatry, stretching from mental retardation to the emotional problems of the middle-class child, and focused on early detection and prevention. In 1970, the report of the White House Conference on Children would recommend early developmental screening and preventative measures to reduce the incidence of mental retardation, along with the now-famous charge to include the mentally retarded in the community. Significantly, it would also recommend the increased use of paraprofessionals, a sign that not only the institution but also established medicine was no longer seen as adequate to the tasks of comprehensive surveillance, prevention, and placement (Nehring 2004, 381–82). This change was intimately related to the other lasting inheritance of the early 1950s, for it would prove impossible to put the genie of parent activism back in the proverbial bottle. Autism would be at the heart of both these inheritances, so that with the benefit of hindsight one could say that the seeds of the spectrum, of the extension of autism to cover an increasing proportion of the domain of child psychiatry, were sown already in the early 1950s. Autism, we saw, was a crucial link between child guidance and mental retardation, since it permitted Kanner to argue that affective disorder and emotional conflict lay hidden behind the complacent mask of feeblemindedness. Yet the active ingredient, so to speak, which caused autism to ferment and spread, like a wine stain on a tablecloth, outward from its middle position between mental retardation and child guidance, was not the agency of the medical profession, not some psychiatric imperialism or quest for increased terrain for the profession, but the parent activism which first – as we saw in the origins of NARC – invited the intrusion of child psychiatry into the middle-class family, but later, as we shall see in Chapter 8 about NSAC, came to resent and resist it as parents of autistic children demanded recognition of their expertise and access to newly emerging behavioral therapies.

— 4 —

DEINSTITUTIONALIZATION

The story of deinstitutionalization of the retarded is different from deinstitutionalization in other fields. It was accomplished by preventing institutionalization (of mostly young children), rather than increases in discharges of (mostly adult) inmates. The deinstitutionalization of the retarded can thus be understood as a tactical reversal within the surveillance of childhood that started years earlier. One aspect of this tactical reversal was the new belief that the middle-class family, in partnership with the state, is a better site for early detection and early intervention in childhood ailments than the institution. This belief was connected also to the "valorization of retarded existence," the emerging moral goal of parent activism that set the stage for autism parenting as we perceive it today.

A new look at the deinstitutionalization of the retarded

Two images come readily to mind when one hears about "deinstitutionalization," as vivid as in a movie scene:

Take One: Willowbrook. NYCLU lawyer Bruce Ennis forces open the doors of hell waving a court order. The inmates are freed; the institution is phased out. The era of a humanitarian, enlightened, "community treatment" begins.

Take Two: Dumping. Ex-inmates turning the traffic divider into their day room, strolling around the neighborhood in their pajamas. The era of "the nursing homes racket," of unscrupulous entrepreneurs cutting deals with a desperate state, has begun.

These two images each come equipped with a story about the causes of deinstitutionalization. The first is a story about the triumph of enlightened and compassionate reformers. The sources of their zeal lay in the sociological critique of total institutions, in the Scandinavian idea of "normalization," and in the example of the civil-rights movement, which taught that psychiatric inmates were citizens deprived of their basic right to be treated in the "least restrictive environment." Their zeal was evoked by the shock and scandal generated by exposés of the plight of the institutionalized, such as Robert Kennedy's surprise visit to Willowbrook in 1965, or the photo essay *Christmas in Purgatory* (Blatt and Kaplan 1966), or Geraldo Rivera's televised raid on Willowbrook in 1972 (Trent 1994; Rothman and Rothman 2005; Wolfensberger 1972, 1–3, 13–24, 46–47).

The second is a story about the fiscal crisis of the state. Exposés of the plight of the institutionalized, shock and public rage, critique of the perverse environment of the institution, trust in the curative powers of a romanticized "community": none of this was new, and yet never in the past were these factors able to overcome the combined resistances of superintendents defending their jobs and neighborhood boards opposed to housing ex-inmates in their midst. What changed during the second half of the twentieth century was the economic calculus facing the state. The development of the welfare state after WWII served as a "pull" factor, making it possible for inmates to subsist (barely) outside the institution, and thus increasing the opportunity costs of keeping them inside. Spiraling state expenditures served as a "push" factor. In the American context, this conjunction of forces was particularly potent because through discharges from state institutions, fiscally strapped states could roll over the expenses to the federal government, which paid the Welfare and Social Security checks of ex-inmates. Similar developments, however, took place also in the U.K. (Scull 1983, 82–89, 96–114, 140–51).

If we want to understand the deinstitutionalization of the mentally retarded, we have to free our minds of the two iconic images presented above. Despite their differences, they share two false claims. First, they both depict deinstitutionalization as a "single, unitary phenomenon" (Scull 1983, 141), a single process that took place concurrently or successively across the whole domain of "social control," in different "human management systems" concerned with various forms of "deviance" (Wolfensberger 1972, 1–3). It is enough to mention the completely different trajectory taken by corrections, and the huge rises in imprisonment (see Scull's 1983 Afterword, 171–81), to cast doubt on this claim, and we will soon see below how mental retardation too does not comport with it. The second claim is implicit in these images' focus on the spectacular moment of emptying the institution. They privilege the dismantling of institutions as the crowning achievement and the overriding motive (whether driven by pecuniary or humanitarian concerns) for an abrupt and radical transformation. The image of patients discharged, *en masse*, is common to both.

But this is not at all what happened during the deinstitutionalization of the mentally retarded. First, it was a gradual and protracted process (Braddock 1981). The rate of institutionalization peaked in 1967 and then began to decline, but in 1977, 83 percent of residents in state and non-state facilities for the mentally retarded still resided in units holding 16 or more individuals. Deinstitutionalization unfolded in fits and starts all through the 1970s, 1980s, and 1990s. It is still going on now (Prouty, Smith and Lakin 2007, 85–88).

Second, despite the prominence of the "Willowbrook wars" (Rothman and Rothman 2005), dismantling the institution was not necessarily central to the process of deinstitutionalization. During fiscal years 1978–1980, for example, states invested almost a billion dollars in renovating existing large institutions. This fits neither the image of liberating the inmates, nor of dumping them for fiscal reasons. Yet it was part of deinstitutionalization. States got about 1.2 billion dollars in federal matching funds for institutions if they met federal standards, which meant that the money was not used to build new institutions, nor to add more beds (in fact bed capacity shrank), but the quality of care had to be improved. At the same time, the five states that accounted for 52 percent of these expenditures – New York, New Jersey, California, Ohio, and Michigan – were also at the forefront of creating smaller community facilities where they relocated the inmates of larger institutions. Contrary to the prevailing images, investment in institutions and the development of community alternatives went hand-in-hand at least until 1981 (Prouty, Smith and Lakin 2001, Chapter 8; Braddock 1981).

Third, despite these modest beginnings, deinstitutionalization in the field of mental retardation went incomparably further and deeper than in the fields of mental health or corrections. The state's commitment to the mentally retarded, as measured by the overall number of mentally retarded individuals in residential settings, was not scaled down, but in fact more than doubled from 1965 to 2005, from around 190,000 to 424,000, but the vast majority of these individuals (84.7 percent) are now housed in smaller community residences, holding 15 or fewer individuals. In fact, 70 percent reside in units holding 6 or fewer persons. The average number of residents per facility in 2006 was 2.7 (Braddock 2001; Prouty, Smith and Lakin 2007, 71–74, 85; Lakin, Anderson and Prouty 1998; Prouty et al. 2005).

Fourth, not only was the deinstitutionalization of the mentally retarded more complete than in other fields, but it was a qualitatively different process. While mental patients were mostly dumped, discharged *en masse* before a system of community clinics and residential facilities was in place to absorb them, the deinstitutionalization of mental retardation was accompanied by rapid increases in the number of community residential facilities. The reduction in the population of institutionalized mentally ill patients was achieved primarily through discharges – in fact, because mental hospitals instituted mandatory discharges at given intervals, for example, 90 days, and because no real community alternatives existed, the rates of admissions, discharges and readmissions all went up together – but the gradual deinstitutionalization of the mentally retarded was accomplished mostly by reductions in new admissions to state institutions, rather than increases in discharges. Rather than by dismantling institutions, it was accomplished by *preventing* institutionalization (Scull 1983; Rothman and Rothman 2005, 1–2, 9, 216; Braddock 1981; Prouty, Smith and Lakin 2007, 14–15, 71–74, 86–87).

The final and most important difference dovetails on this last point – reduction in admissions rather than discharges, prevention rather than dismantling. We need a completely different image to make sense of it. Our suggestion is to think of the deinstitutionalization of the retarded as at least partly driven by a tactical reversal within the surveillance of childhood. This sets it apart from deinstitutionalization in all other fields. It was a two-pronged transformation, one for adults, the other for children, of which the latter was the more important driving factor, manifesting itself over the long term through the reduction in admissions to state institutions.

The proportion of children and youth (younger than 21) in state institutions peaked in 1965 at about 48.9 percent and then began to decline slowly until it reached about 35.8 percent in 1977. Table 4 in Chapter 3 showed the importance of reductions in admissions even for this early change. Between 1968 and 1977, the mean age of first admissions to residential care went up from 13.3 to 18, and the proportion of first admissions between zero to 19 years of age went down from 84.1 percent to 65.4 percent. This seems to indicate that the bulk of young first admissions were adolescents. In 1965, let us recall, children 14 years or younger were the largest category of first admissions! So the modest numbers hide a fairly radical and abrupt change for very young children. During the second decade of

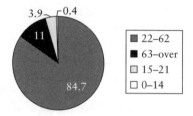

Figure 4: Age distribution of residents at large state facilities in 2006

(Source: R.W. Prouty, Gary Smith and K.C. Lakin (Eds.), 2007, *Residential services for persons with developmental disabilities: Status and trends through 2006.* Minneapolis: University of Minnesota, Research and Training Center on Community Living.)

deinstitutionalization, between 1977 and 1987, the proportion of children and youth at state institutions dove to 12.7 percent, which makes sense if earlier changes were accomplished mostly through the prevention of institutionalization at an early age. In 2006, as seen in Figure 4, the proportion of children and youth at state institutions stood at 4 percent, only 0.4 percent of which were children 14 or younger. There was a "concerted effort by most states to restrict the admission of children to large state institutions" (Prouty, Smith and Lakin 2007, 41). In fact, in 21 states there were no residents younger than 15 in large state institutions in 2006 (14–15).

Were they simply shifted from large (more than 16 residents) state institutions to small private community residences and group homes? This is unlikely. In 2005, as can be seen in Table 6, it was estimated that only 6.2 percent of all persons in all out-of-home placements, private or public, small or large, were less than 21 years old, and only 1.8 percent were 14 or younger. It also shows that the trend in all out-of-home placements of children and youth was similar to what happened at state institutions. From almost half in 1965, the proportion of children younger than 21 years old in all out-of-home placements declined to 36.7 percent in 1977 and 18.2 percent in 1987. Finally, we can see that the sharpest decline took place between 1977 and 1987 in the proportion of children younger than 15, from 15.4 percent to 5.9 percent. Whereas the deinstitutionalization of adults was a gradual and protracted process, it was continuously driven by a more rapid transformation in the status of mentally retarded children, an increased reluctance to place them out of home (Prouty, Smith and Lakin 2007, 36, 40–41; Prouty et al. 2005; Braddock 2001).

Where are they then? Most likely at the home of a family member.[1] Nationally, 57.3 percent of intellectually disabled individuals receiving

Table 6:   Proportion of different age groups in MR residential settings

Age	1965[a]	1977	1987	1997	2005
0–14	N/A	38,161 (15.4%)	15,085 (5.9%)	10,243 (3.0%)	7,926 (1.8%)
15–21	N/A	52,781 (21.3%)	31,448 (12.3%)	15,785 (4.6%)	18,469 (4.4%)
0–21	91,592 (48.9%)	90,942 (36.7%)	46,533 (18.2%)	26,028 (7.6%)	26,395 (6.2%)
Total	190,024	247,796	255,673	342,224	420,216

(Source: Robert Prouty, K. Charlie Lakin, Kathryn Coucouvanis, and Linda Anderson, "Progress Toward a National Objective of Healthy People 2010: Reduce to Zero the Number of Children 17 Years and Younger Living in Congregate Care," *Mental Retardation*, 43, 6 (November 2005), 56–60.)
[a] The numbers for 1965 report the residents of state institutions, because at the time there were few other residential options. The numbers for all later years report residents of all residential facilities, state or private, large or small.

services in 2006 resided in their own homes or the home of a family member. Since, as seen in Table 6, the proportion of 1.8 percent in residential settings represents a huge decline both proportionally and in absolute numbers from earlier years, it is a safe bet that the vast majority of intellectually disabled children 14 years or younger now receive services as they reside with their parents or other family members. Similarly, it was estimated that the proportion of children 15 years old or younger in out-of-home placement in Great Britain declined from 30 percent in 1970 to 3 percent in the mid-1980s. For Australia in 1999, the corresponding proportion was 1.1 percent and it too represented a sharp decline from earlier decades. The progress of deinstitutionalization in Norway similarly confirms the arguments we made based on the American case. Norwegian deinstitutionalization began in the 1960s not with discharges of the adult retarded in institutions, but with a commitment to close all special schools for retarded children, prevent their institutionalization, and educate them in the public school system. By the late 1970s there was nobody younger than 16 in Norwegian public institutions for the mentally retarded (Meyer 2003, 306; Prouty, Smith and Lakin 2007, 81–83; Braddock 2001).

The prevalent images of deinstitutionalization, then, can do with revision. Figure 5 provides an illustration of this rethinking. Deinstitutionalization is usually represented as a sharp break from the ninety-year trend of constant increase in institutionalized populations,

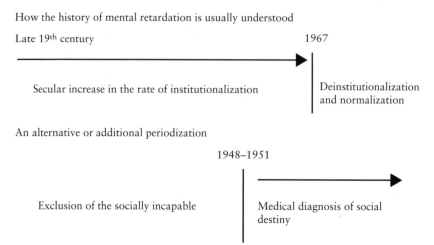

Figure 5: How to tell the history of mental retardation

but if we divide these populations into young children and the rest, there is clearly another story to be told. For the adults, the process of change was much more gradual and protracted than the image of a radical break with the institution conveys. *Pace* Willowbrook, there was no massive *Exodus from Pandemonium* (Blatt 1970), but an improvement of residential facilities and a gradual whittling away of populations through the prevention of institutionalization. For children 14 years old or younger, as we have seen, the change was far more radical and profound, a sudden determination to keep them at home, but the break, of course, was not with a ninety-year trend, but with something that began only twenty years earlier. Previously, we called the institutionalization of young children in the 1950s a merely "tactical" and incidental aspect of a more fundamental change, and we think that its complete reversal within two or three decades justifies this assessment. The essential ingredient in both the sudden institutionalization of young children in the 1950s, as well as their no less sudden deinstitutionalization in the 1970s (or more fittingly, the prevention of institutionalization), was the attempt to put in place a system for the surveillance of childhood, a system that would detect abnormalities very early on, and then seek to minimize the risk they involve and maximize the hidden potential they may mask, through treatment and assignment to an appropriate milieu.

Now we are in a position to provide an alternative explanation for the deinstitutionalization of the mentally retarded. The image

104

we propose is of a tactical rearrangement within the project of the surveillance of childhood. This tactical rearrangement consisted of two outstanding features: first, obviously, the institutional matrix of custody was scrapped as inadequate for the purposes of a comprehensive surveillance and placement system. It was completely eclipsed by the middle-class family, in partnership with the state, as the site for early detection and early intervention in childhood ailments. Second, within this partnership the role of medical expertise was radically reconfigured. In the remainder of this chapter, we will deal with the first feature, that of the institution's replacement by the family. The following chapter, discussing the program of normalization, will describe how it reconfigured medical expertise.

The middle-class family and the "valorization of retarded existence"

Many have noted the crucial role that parent activism played in the deinstitutionalization of the mentally retarded (Trent 1994, 253–66), but it does not suffice to consider parent activism on behalf of the mentally retarded as a tributary of the civil rights movement, as suggested, for example, by Rothman and Rothman (2005), and this despite the fact that the main player, the National Association for Retarded Children (NARC) did change its name in 1973 to the National Association for Retarded *Citizens*. To begin with, as we saw earlier, many parent groups were not opposed to institutionalization in the 1950s, and we must add, many *were* opposed to deinstitutionalization in the 1970s, especially if they themselves were service providers, as in Illinois. The animosity between the New York State ARC and the litigators and activists who brought Willowbrook down was legendary. Personalities played a role, but crucially, ARC and other parent groups were more interested in improving Willowbrook than in closing it down, and they were mortally afraid that massive deinstitutionalization (the sort of massive discharges they already witnessed in the field of mental illness) would siphon off the resources dedicated to community services and special education for their own children, who were typically at home with their parents and less severely disabled than Willowbrook residents (Rothman and Rothman 2005, 60–63, 127–30, 140–41, 171–72).

To understand both the sources of parent activism, as well as the role it played in deinstitutionalization, we must return to its origins in the late 1940s and early 1950s. As we saw earlier, originally parent activism was neither anti-institutional nor directed against the medical profession. In fact, doctors tried to encourage parent activism as a way of channeling parents' emotional energies and conflicts to a useful purpose. NARC literature echoed this strategy when it spoke of activism as the third phase in the parents' process of coping with the realization that their children were retarded: "Your children guide you to a definite form of development" (Egg 1964, 151). Parents typically begin this process by being preoccupied by their own grief. Most parents, however, quickly move into a second, healthier phase in which they become preoccupied with the welfare of their child. Yet they should not stop there. Their concern for their own child should grow, in a third phase, into a concern for all handicapped children (152–53).

Why should parents become activists? As we saw earlier, doctors had their own reasons. One would be entirely justified to add that the ideology of parent activism suited the organizational interests of NARC in increasing its membership base and intensifying the resources – energy, time, dedication to collective interests – it could extract. But we should pay attention also to the specific idiom through which parent activism was justified. Parent activism, as we said, was not originally anti-medical or anti-institutional. It is better to describe its mainspring as "pro-family." The middle-class parents who formed the core of advocacy organizations were demanding the chance to be "normal Americans" like everybody else, which meant being able to lead a normal family life, a life centered on cultivating and maximizing the health and potential of their children. They explicitly turned to the state to help them realize this ideal of domesticity. Only with government help could the family become less exceptional and closer to the ideal of domestic perfection and societal contribution it was supposed to embody. Even their activism was in direct continuity with the practices of civic activity – Rotary clubs and the like – that were an intrinsic part of the postwar image of American middle-class normalcy. It was in the name of this ideal, of normal family life, that children were institutionalized – to protect the family from breaking up, to provide siblings with the normalcy to which they were entitled – but it also fed all the energies channeled into setting up day-care centers, summer camps, and parents' night out programs – that is, everything that could make the exceptional child and the exceptional family more normal. Finally, and this is the crucial point, it was also in the name of this very ideal that civic activism turned into resistance to the institution. It was against a newly formulated ideal of parenting that the institution was judged and found wanting. Measured against the ideal of cultivating children and maximizing their health and potential, the institution was criticized as "warehousing" and waste (Jones 2004, 324, 329–30, 345–46, n.20; Castles 2004, 254–56).

What would appear as an irony of history – how a form of radical resistance, championing the ideal of "normalization," would evolve directly from the most conventional and straitlaced bastion of middle-class normalcy – would become more understandable if we notice that middle-class parents' activism was mobilized not only in search of conformity and fitting in, but also in pursuit of a more *virtuoso* ethical goal of giving their lives a beautiful and inspiring form. The main point was that through the activism of the parents, their child's existence would be valorized and transformed into a social contribution. Explaining her decision, against doctors' advice, not to institutionalize her mentally retarded daughter, Pearl Buck wrote that she "resolved that . . . my child . . . was not to be wasted . . . her existence as it was and as it is today, must be of use to human beings" (quoted in Trent 1994, 231). The distance between this secular, humanist idiom of valorization, and that of Christian writers, was small indeed. Both were attempting to give meaning to what seemed a meaningless and cruel fate, to transform it into secular or religious salvation. Maria Egg instructed parents, in a text sanctioned by NARC, that "we could not possibly say which life is valuable and meaningful and which life is worthless and meaningless. It is not for us to judge; we are not equipped to do so" (Egg 1964, 38). Parents should stop worrying about what caused their child's condition. Knowing the etiology "would not change anything about you and your child. You will still ask: 'why do I have to bear this cross?'" There isn't really a good answer for this question, except the one that parents can give themselves through their activism. A great deal of good can be done through the child. A family grows and matures spiritually by caring for him. Most importantly, through activism "the cross we bear can become a blessing for others."[2] Dale Evans Rogers told readers of her book, *Angel Unaware*, that her mentally retarded daughter, who died at age two, was sent by God on a mission to heal and spiritually strengthen her family. The book was written from the perspective of the dead child, an angel looking from above on the family and describing how it was transformed by her brief visit (Trent 1994, 230–35; Brockley 2004, 154–56; Egg 1964, 38–40, 153).

Incidentally, this idiom of valorization may explain a fact that in retrospect seems shocking and incomprehensible to us (contemporaries also found it disturbing). During this period some parents permitted the testing of the polio vaccine on their mentally retarded children

(Brockley 2004, 154–56). Later decades would see this as prime evidence for the abuse rife in institutions. The litigators-reformers would use it in their drive to dismantle the institution, pointing to the denial of civil rights, since patients' consent was not obtained. Indeed, in many other cases medical experiments were performed even without parents' knowledge or consent, and this power to dispose over the bodies and lives of inmates certainly constituted one of the worst tyrannies of the institution. But the fact remains that some parents approved of the experiment and were proud of it. They saw it as evidence that their children had value and could contribute to society, just like any other children.

Thus, alongside the "infantalization of the feeble mind" (Trent 1994, 241) – the message of NARC's de-stigmatization campaign that mentally retarded people were innocent children in need of protection – there was also a "valorization of retarded existence." This valorization was the impetus and moral goal of parent activism no less than the search for middle-class normality. The phrase "least restrictive environment" had its origins in civil rights struggles on behalf of prisoners and minorities, while the reference to "maximizing the child's potential" – included in case law now as a negative reference point to what the state is *not* obliged to do, precisely because it has become self-evident that this is what *parents* must do – had its origins in this valorization of retarded existence. And so did the radical turn of parent activism against the institution. Measured against the imperative to valorize the child's existence, the institution was secretive, a place where children were hidden from view instead of being a "blessing to others."

This can shed light on the oft-heard phrase that "the most appropriate placement" for a child with mental retardation or autism is at home. One side of this phrase is, no doubt, imbued with concern about the child's welfare, with suspicion of the institution, and with trust in the normalizing influence of family life. But another side of it is much less about the child herself than about the moral mission of parenthood. After all, writers never forget to add (and they would be sorely remiss if they did) that in some situations residential placement *is* a more appropriate and desirable solution than the home (Egg 1964, 148; Lettick and Schopler 1982; Lettick 1979, 106; Schopler and Reichler 1971, 100; Siegel 1996, 160). Yet when justifying keeping the child at home they speak about it as a moral test through which the individual parent or the family as a whole can emerge stronger, more harmonious, possessed of inner peace, having given the child's existence a more beautiful and authentic shape: "You yourselves

must do everything that can help improve your child's condition . . .
A fine and beautiful mission awaits you. You alone can accomplish it
. . . For this, you need no specialized training, no degree or diploma;
your patience, your understanding, your love, your burning desire
to help your child – these are far more important" (Egg 1964, 42).
The outline of this beautiful existence is sketched through contrast
with its opposite. Even when the writer acknowledges that residential
placement may be a more appropriate solution, the parent is admon-
ished that "you cannot put away a child and forget about him." The
implications are well known by now, dramatized by books like *The
Memory Keeper's Daughter*. The institutionalized child becomes a
secret that eats away at family bliss; parents live an unfulfilled life
and an inauthentic existence, most likely ending in divorce (Egg 1964,
42–49, 148).

A direct line of inheritance leads from this valorization of retarded
existence to today's autism world. The contemporary vocation of
autism parenting was built on the strong foundations laid by NARC
parents. Guidebooks for parents of autistic children continuously
repeat that parenting an autistic child is hard and frustrating, but can
also be a rewarding experience, and they depict the process in terms
taken from the earlier discourse. It is the parents' mission to try to
help their child maximize his or her potential, by becoming deeply
involved in the child's treatment program. Why? Because "you see
potential when nobody else sees potential and you see problems when
nobody else sees problems" (Powers 2000, 278). Many parents of
autistic children have written inspirational accounts – often modeled
on the earlier "confessional" books written by parents of retarded
children (Trent 1994, 235–40) – in which the parent is described as
the child's "savior" (see for example, Kephart 1998; Seroussi 2000;
Adams 2005; McCarthy 2007).

By the same token, the moral mission of the parents is reciprocated
by the moral contribution made by the child, who is depicted as their
mentor. Fleischmann (2005) analyzed postings in 33 websites organized by and for parents of children with autism. Postings in 12 of the
websites described the child as a "teacher" from whom one can learn.
Postings in 22 of the web sites described autism as an experience that
enriched their lives, made them stronger individuals and fortified their
families: "Autism is seen by some as a 'holy challenge' that under-
scores for parents the true flavor of life, preparing them to face challenges and empowering them with newfound abilities and strengths.
Thus, autism is viewed in a new light, as having its own 'blessings'
that give meaning to one's trials and tribulations" (Fleischmann

2005, 307). As one mother wrote in her web site, in terms reminiscent of Dale Evans Rogers' *Angel Unaware*:

> More than anything else, I think our family has re-evaluated the meaning of life: God sees every life with a purpose, and although there are challenges and sometimes pain to life itself – we can view it as a time for growth, acceptance, and faith. (Fleischmann 2005; see also Mathews 2002, who describes her son as an "escalator to heaven.")

We heard the same message from parents we interviewed in the course of writing this book. It was common for a parent to say that he or she became a "better person" through caring for his or her autistic child, that their family became "stronger," that everybody in the family, siblings and parents, were taught an important moral lesson by the autistic child. An extreme expression of this message can be found in Mary Sharp's 2003 book: *An Unexpected Joy: The Gift of Parenting a Challenging Child*.[3] There is also a corresponding discourse about autistic individuals making a societal contribution, for example through fostering tolerance for neurodiversity.

None of this is new. Historically speaking, autism parenting as a vocation would have been inconceivable if, first, NARC parents did not manage to invert the sign attached to the presence of the mentally retarded child in the family – from a destructive and disintegrative influence he or she became a factor of family strength and cohesion. Without this inversion, as we shall see in Chapter 8, parental testimony would have remained tainted, too entangled with the child's malaise to be accepted as objective report, let alone a form of radical translation of the child's inner life and contribution to this world. Also important were the quasi-experimental regimes that some parents of autistic children set up at home; the tireless training; the modeling of parenting upon therapy; the sharing of information directly between parents: all this would have been inconceivable if NARC parents did not manage to replace the stain of being a burden on society with the "beautiful mission" of caring for a mentally retarded child. It was their version of small steps becoming giant leaps. The little, step-by-step improvements in quality of life at home, or in the child's ability to communicate and conduct himself outside the home, were magnified a thousandfold on the societal level, where the beautiful mission of the parents assumed a new form – normalization.

— 5 —

"AN EXISTENCE AS CLOSE TO THE NORMAL AS POSSIBLE": NORMALIZATION

When parent activism turned against the medical and psychiatric establishment in the mid-1960s, it found ready allies in the more marginal professions and subordinate forms of expertise – psychology (especially behavior modification), sociology, social work, special education, occupational therapy, speech therapy – whose practitioners were chafing to upgrade their status vis-à-vis institutionalized medicine and psychiatry. Deinstitutionalization must be understood, at least in part, as spurred by jurisdictional struggle among professions to control work, service provision, and clientele in a field in which they claimed relevant expertise (Abbott 1988).

One prominent reformer – Wolf Wolfensberger – was a psychologist strongly influenced by the sociologist Erving Goffman. From 1968 to 1971, he led Nebraska's complete overhaul of its mental retardation facilities in accordance with the "normalization" principle. Another, Burton Blatt, was a professor of special education at Boston College, who became famous in the mid-1960s for the photo essay *Christmas in Purgatory*, which exposed the horrific conditions in the large residential schools for the mentally retarded in Massachusetts. The reformers who forced New York State to empty Willowbrook were civil rights litigators and, crucially, psychologists from Syracuse University's Center on Human Policy, where Wolfensberger had been teaching after he completed his term at Nebraska. Nebraskan psychologists and social workers, involved in the normalization overhaul in their own state, testified as expert witnesses at the Willowbrook trial and assisted in implementing New York State's own program for deinstitutionalization and community treatment.

The common target of all these diverse struggles was not only the institution, but also the monopoly that psychiatry enjoyed in the

111

field of mental retardation. A crucial part of Blatt's crusade against the institution was a demand to break the monopoly of psychiatrists on the directorship of institutions, and to extract mental retardation from the jurisdiction of the Massachusetts Department of Mental Health, whose director was typically a psychiatrist. This was also the demand of reformers in New York. Blatt was, in fact, more successful than he had bargained for, and got himself appointed as the first non-psychiatrist director of the newly created Massachusetts department of mental retardation. He resigned after two years. In New York, a similar administrative rearrangement took place in response to the Willowbrook scandal, and a parent activist – Thomas Coughlin – was appointed to the new position. Wolfensberger, as well, though by no means an "anti-psychiatrist," was scathing in his critique of psychiatry and the limitations of the "medical model." He was far more approving of behavior modification as the therapy most attuned to the spirit of normalization (Rothman and Rothman 2004, 57, 107–10, 127–37; Blatt 1970, 7–9; Wolfensberger 1972, 95–115, 138–47).

The slogan that united parent activism with the peripheral professions and coordinated their attack on psychiatry was "normalization." What did it mean? Was it merely a cover for the pursuit of professional interests? Or were reformers, as a certain retroactive view would have it, mindless zealots and ideologues who advocated returning everybody to the community trusting in its curative powers, and disregarded the real biological disabilities of people with mental retardation and autism? "People who should know better subscribe to the idea that if you pretend that the handicapped are not really handicapped, the handicaps will disappear," Rimland wrote (1993, 3). In this view, compatible with the cynical unmasking of professional interests, the reformers either duped parents or marginalized them in order to pursue the reformers' own ideological agenda against the parents' better interests. There is certainly some truth in this view, especially if it is limited to the tensions between parents and civil libertarian litigators (Rothman and Rothman 2005), but on the whole it says more about contemporary opposition to the tactics and demands of the disability rights movement of the 1990s than about the meaning of normalization (Shapiro 1993).

The second accusation is easier to refute: despite what Rimland says above, normalization was most certainly *not* championed as a panacea that would solve all the problems of the handicapped, making the handicaps "disappear." We are not arguing here whether the reformers were realistic or not. The point is more fundamental. Normalization did not share with medical practice a common agreed goal of treatment, such as "cure" or even "rehabilitation." It was far more radical than that. Normalization *itself* was the goal, or more precisely, it involved a complete recasting of the very goal of treatment. In this respect, normalization responded to a deep discontent within psychiatry itself. Studies accumulated during the 1950s and 1960s demonstrating the lack of efficacy of dynamic therapy (untreated patients improved just as much as treated ones); more important, however, they questioned what the goal of treatment should be. Should it be cure, in analogy with medicine? Or the reduction of inner distress, as the psychoanalysts defensively argued? Or should these lofty and unverifiable goals be rejected in favor of a tangible measure that can be easily operationalized, for example, improvement in social competence and acquisition of adaptive skills, as the new community psychiatrists argued, or simply the removal of symptoms, in which the behavior therapists specialized (Hersch 1968, 499–500)? Normalization opted for the latter formulations, but generalized and systematized them beyond the province of any specific profession into a comprehensive, simple, and parsimonious principle of "human management": "letting the mentally retarded obtain an existence as close to the normal as possible." From a management-oriented point of view, this was a clearly defined goal, from which one could derive realistic, attainable, practical, intermediate-term objectives, open-ended for revision upward or downward after periodic assessment, since it was easy to determine what worked and what did not. By comparison, the goals of psychiatry were ill-defined and idealistic. Cure was much too ambitious a goal, and it led to a fruitless search for etiology, in the absence of which psychiatric custody over the mentally retarded degenerated into "treatment nihilism" (Wolfensberger 1972, 27, 96).

So to reply to the first accusation – that normalization was merely a cover for professional interests – we would emphasize that normalization, in fact, was continuous with developments within psychiatry itself, where discontent had been brewing for two decades before it exploded during the late 1960s. The internal discontent met with external challenges, no doubt, but these came not only from subordinate or competing professions but also from laymen, specifically the patients themselves or their parents. These participants were resisting not just abuse and neglect, but the roles assigned to them by the reigning model of treatment. At issue was not merely psychiatric control of this or that jurisdiction, but the very model of treatment which specified who the patients were, who the therapists were, what it meant to treat somebody, what the goal of treatment was, and how it was to be achieved (Hersch 1968). Consequently, as Coughlin's appointment and Blatt's hurried resignation indicate, it was patently *not* the case that the professional challengers acquired control over the jurisdiction previously held by psychiatry. Instead, they had to share it with both psychiatrists and laymen in a complex and inherently unstable jurisdictional arrangement. In the rest of this chapter we will provide a detailed analysis of normalization as therapeutic practice – its object, subject, goal, and technique of treatment. This leads to a discussion of behavior modification and ABA – the main contemporary therapy for treating autism – showing that contrary to what is commonly assumed it has much in common with the therapeutic and progressive principles of normalization.

Normalization as therapeutic practice

Let us begin with the first question: Who was to be treated? What was the *object*, the human material upon which treatment worked, or more precisely, which was grist to the mill of "human management"? Hersch (1968, 497) says that in the past the patient was whoever came to the clinic and could benefit from what it offered. One recognizes here the "triage" recommended by the mental hygiene movement (Rothman and Rothman 2005, 25–26): deal with the acute cases first, with those who are younger and have better prospects for cure or improvement, and do not waste resources going after chronic, incurable, older cases. In short, acute cases were preferred over the chronic; the emotional problems of the middle-class child took prevalence over the mental retardation of the poor adolescent; urban, educated, and well-off families predominated over the rural poor, the uneducated, and minorities. In short, the best served were those who needed help the least.

We can appreciate, therefore, the contradictions and paradoxes created when, in the early 1950s, mental retardation was brought within the orbit of mental hygiene and child guidance to form a unified domain of the surveillance of childhood. We already saw how the number of children institutionalized increased dramatically. The same was true for mentally retarded children in special education. Their numbers went up from 108,500 in 1948 to 540,000 in 1966 (school age population only increased by 70 percent), but it was estimated that this number only represented half of those who needed services (Mackie 1969, 36–39). Faced with this increased caseload, child psychiatry had little to offer but another triage. The really chronic cases, the "absolutely feebleminded" were to be "institutional material," while, as we saw in Chapter 3, there were repeated attempts to identify a basis upon which to classify a sizeable chunk of the caseload as "clinical material," merely "apparently feebleminded" and curable. Yet the very site of child psychiatry was shifting, and it was slow to adapt. The new urban mental health centers created in the 1960s did not welcome the white middle-class professionals. They were about empowerment, not more mother blaming, and with the health budget tightening there was less tolerance anyway for lengthy psychodynamic treatment (Lakoff 2000, 157–58). When it came to the original middle-class population of child psychiatry, by the mid-1960s it was clear that the triage backfired spectacularly. To the extent that one side of it required removing children from the home, while the other mandated monitoring the parents – criticizing maternal devotion to the child, enrolling the parents in therapy – it provoked the ire of parent organizations and turned them against the nexus of psychiatric control of institutions (where it also increased the waiting lists) (Hersch 1968, 503). Kanner, ever attuned to the changing winds, was already hedging his bets. He warned that autism was over-diagnosed, removed it from competition with childhood schizophrenia, and began to qualify the theory of parental emotional coldness (Kanner 1965, 413). Indeed, within four years he would theatrically declare, speaking before a room full of parents, members of the National Society for Autistic Children, "herewith I officially acquit you people as parents."

This is why deinstitutionalization and normalization are such complex and retroactively misunderstood phenomena. On the one hand, it meant pushing back against psychiatry, which was seeking a mandate to detect, diagnose, and treat even those who did not come asking for its services and were not referred by public authorities. On the other hand, however, it meant expanding the surveillance of childhood, no longer controlled by the psychiatrists, to a population defined by the chronicity, severity, and early onset of their needs. In 1970, the National Association for Retarded Children (NARC) persuaded Congress to introduce a new grouping of handicapped individuals, the "developmentally disabled," who were characterized as needing neither "cure" (because their condition was chronic) nor "rehabilitation" (since they never experienced normal development), but simply "habilitation." The institutional locus of habilitation was a new type of facility, the "Intermediate Care Facility-Mental Retardation" (ICF-MR) defined by federal legislation in 1971. The term "intermediate" meant that these facilities provided "active treatment" specifically focused on the needs of persons with mental retardation, which was more than room and board, but less than medical treatment as in a nursing facility (Shapiro 1993 20–23; Akerley 1979, 222; Prouty, Smith and Lakin 2001, Chap. 8; Centers for Medicare and Medicaid Services 2008).[1] If they were not identical with Wolfensberger's "an existence as close to the normal as possible," habilitation and intermediate care were certainly goals of the same type, differentiated on the one hand from medical cure, and on the other from mere custody.

Normalization thus meant a complete recasting not only of the *goal of treatment*, from cure to habilitation and prevention, but also of its object: who were to be treated, from the individual patient who came to the clinic, seeking relief for an acute crisis, to a *population* originally left out of the mental hygiene triage and defined by the chronicity of its needs. This was no longer the object of clinical practice but of an active surveillance system reaching out into the population. So normalization also provided a new answer to the second question, who is the therapist? Who is the *subject* with the authority to administer treatment? Hersch (1968, 498) says that in the past it was the psychiatrist, though she would delegate some therapeutic responsibility to psychologists and social workers. Yet there was a growing sense that in this respect psychiatry dug itself into a hole, and needed the help of others to get out. Mental hygiene encouraged psychiatrists to identify the antecedents of mental illness and to see the need for their services everywhere, yet it also fettered the expansion of services by mandating an individual-focused, clinical approach and by the long duration of dynamic therapy. This is one of the reasons that psychiatrists encouraged parent activism and why Kanner envisioned a model of multidisciplinary cooperation in the child guidance clinics. As the President of the American Psychiatric Association put it in 1966: "Mental health is everyone's business, and no profession or family of professions has sufficient competence to deal with it whole" (quoted in Hersch 1968, 498). Indeed, by the mid-1960s, many other professionals and paraprofessionals were offering "change-inducing relationships" and a "series of new therapy names [were] coming forth": by far the most formidable colleagues/competitors were the psychologists with their behavior modification techniques. With increased funding from the National Institute of Mental Health, most publications in the field of mental retardation were by behaviorist university-based psychologists (in the past, institution-based psychiatrists dominated). By the early 1970s psychologists constituted 63 percent of board members of the *American Journal of Mental*

Deficiency. But there were also nurses who became clinical interviewers and co-therapists; there were community caretakers such as teachers, police officers, and settlement workers who became front-line mental health change agents (with the psychiatrist as consultant). Crucially, all these groups recruited laymen (mostly laywomen), as their assistants – housewives trained as mental health counselors and parents trained as therapists of their own children (Hersch 1968, 504; Trent 1994, 244–47; Wolfensberger 1972, 100–101, 103).

Maybe the best response to the interpretation of normalization as merely a cover for professional interests is this: the peripheral professions championing normalization were not attacking psychiatry from without, but from within, after psychiatry itself invited them in. They were not seeking to replace psychiatry, but to subsume and subordinate it to the goals of a more comprehensive system of human management, within which it would be purified and improved. Normalization was offered as a solution to the crisis of psychiatry manifested in the lack of consensus over treatment goals, in the mismatch between supply and demand, and in the proliferation of alternative diagnoses. The answer it provided for the question of who is the therapist, who provides treatment, was, therefore, not on the level at which the question was couched. The therapist was not a new actor – psychologist, occupational therapist, nurse. Instead, the answer entailed a double shift of levels, one upwards and the other downwards, so to speak.

The upward shift was to the level of system management. The predominance of psychiatry, a branch of medicine, made sense as long as treatment was understood to address an acute illness and to strive for a cure. The habilitation and normalization of chronic disabilities, on the other hand, required the cooperation of multiple experts and involved not the treatment of illness, but the continuous provision of a form of care that would minimize the risks and maximize the potential inherent in a heterogeneous population of individuals with disabilities. *Pace* Rimland, normalization was not a simple-minded call to return everybody to the community. Note that Wolfensberger carefully formulated the goal as "an existence as close to the normal as possible." For some this could mean independent living, for others it would be a group home. For some only a facility with medical staff would do. What he and the other reformers envisioned was a comprehensive system composed of sequentially ordered residential, educational, and work arrangements, each perfectly adjusted to the potential of the individuals involved, providing just as much integration as they could tolerate. For the adult with mental retardation, he thought at least twelve different types of residences in a continuous chain were needed, and a different set for children.[2] Normalization, he said, was a superior principle of *management*, not a substitute for medical knowledge. Unlike "cure," it was clearly formulated, so that management decisions could be made rationally and defended in ways easy for the public to understand (Wolfensberger 1972, 50–53, 84–85).

Clearly, he envisioned a system that apportioned roles to many different professions, experts, and paraprofessionals. It also empowered a form of expertise that was managerial. This form of expertise would exercise control over all other experts by measuring their decisions and interventions as system components. Others have noted how such a reorganization of the hierarchy of expertise did indeed take place in the fields of corrections and managed healthcare, where managerial-actuarial expertise was superimposed over medicine and other "helping" professions (Feeley and Simon 1992; Castel 1991).

Yet the upward shift was balanced by a downward shift to the level of the disabled individual herself. Treatment was to be, to a significant extent, self-treatment. In Wolfensberger's analysis, the main problem with the medical model and with the focus on cure was that they cast individuals in the sick role, thereby communicating to them that they should let others take care of them until a cure is found. It also meant that they were isolated in a hospital, communicating to outside society that they were different, possibly dangerous. The goal of "cure" implied, therefore, both dependency and stigma. It was a cruel joke at the expense of the mentally retarded person as their condition was "incurable" (Wolfensberger 1972, 41–47; Shapiro 1993, 20–23).

A similar critique was directed at architects. Wolfensberger paid close attention to the "language of buildings" and derided the tendency of architects to design monuments to their own creative and curative powers rather than buildings where they themselves might like to live. In 1976, when the award-winning Bronx developmental center opened, the Willowbrook review panel would not agree to transfer any former Willowbrook residents to it. The young architect designed a self-sufficient, ultra-modern building that shut out the outside world. The reformers were unimpressed. The building was a "monastery," a "gigantic submarine," totally "the wrong concept." A NARC architect pronounced it psychologically harmful to those who would use it. As the Rothmans note, this was an attack not on institutions but on "moral architecture," on the idea that a successfully engineered environment would generate therapy of its own. In this sense, it was analogous to the attack on psychiatry, on the dangerous hubris of the claim to "cure." What came under attack was a particular prototype of the expert, the claim of psychiatrists and architects to possess teleological knowledge – knowledge of values and of the future, of how to engineer human souls, organize their living spaces and daily schedules for their own benefit – and the claim, in the name of this knowledge, to have authority over the lives of individuals, whether in the form of protective custody or in the design of buildings. The shape and direction of this attack cannot be explained merely by referring to professional interests. Many sociologists or psychologists during the 1960s, as evident in the claims of structural functionalism, for example, would have been content to leave this prototype of the expert intact, merely to replace or join psychiatry in laying a claim to represent it best. These sociologists would not have said, as Wolfensberger did, that designing institutions was an immoral mission an architect should not accept, just as one should not accept to design a concentration camp. They would have merely suggested that they knew better how to design them. They would certainly have shuddered to hear Wolfensberger pontificating that architects should direct their energies towards the much smaller and less glamorous task of modifying existing community housing to suit the needs of mentally retarded and otherwise disabled people, and to see, indeed, how instead of sending former Willowbrook inmates to the glorious Bronx Developmental Center, New York City's Metropolitan Placement Unit hired architects to renovate existing apartments for them. Certainly, left to their own devices, many psychologists would not have recognized their mission, the fulfillment of their claim to expertise, in devising methods to toilet train mentally retarded children, as Lovaas did (Wolfensberger 1972, 57–77; Rothman and Rothman 2005, 143–45, 177; Eyal 2006; Bauman 1989; Wagner 1994).

Why would an ordinary grimy apartment be more therapeutic than a newly designed institution? Precisely because it was commonplace. Because it was not visibly different or set apart from its environment, it would promote integration. Crucially, because it was not a one-stop-shop for each and every service, medical or everyday, that the mentally retarded needed, it would be normalizing, it would encourage them to take care of themselves. The willingness of the more marginal professions to completely demolish the pre-existing prototype of the expert, and to accept a much more modest role for themselves, cannot therefore be explained simply by reference to their interests in acquiring professional jurisdiction. A complete explanation must take account of the necessity to strike an alliance with the patients' and parents' organizations, without whom the marginal professions would never have stood a chance. Normalization could never have meant the replacement of one professional dominion with another, since at its core, one of its main engines, were multiple resistances by laypersons – the inmates, the patients, the residents, the parents – to their subjection to expert knowledge, however humane or enlightened. These resistances took the categories of expert knowledge and turned them into identities, rallying points of a campaign for "self-determination." They identified the promise of expert humane and enlightened management of life as iatrogenic, fostering a pathological form of dependency, and therefore championed instead the opposite values and practices of "care of self" (Wagner 1994; Foucault 1982; Roszak 1968, 1–41; Nirje 1972).

To the extent that enlightened custody was seen to be iatrogenic, self-determination, choice, independence, even "the dignity of risk," were therapeutic (Perske 1972). Correspondingly, the expert, whether psychiatrist or psychologist, no longer possessed the bird's-eye view that empowered him to prescribe treatment from without, so to speak. At the most, as with the administrator of "human management systems," they could seek to design arrangements that maximized choice and self-determination, arrangements that maximized self-treatment, the patient's own therapeutic contribution. To the totalizing shift to the level of management, there corresponded an individualizing shift to the level of the choosing agent. All and one – *Omnes et singulatim* (Foucault 1981). It is the clearest in Wolfensberger's declaration that in the future "all education will become special education," by which he meant that all education, not only the education of the mentally retarded, will be structured by the principle of the IEP (individualized educational program), and by extension the whole of the life course with possibly an IRP (individualized residential program), IOP (individualized occupational program), or what have you. In school, grade grouping will disappear, as each student (or more precisely, the parents) will design their own educational course in consultation with the experts, and consequently the problem of integrating mentally retarded students will be much easier. For the moment, Wolfensberger still had to use broad categories and imprecise prescriptions: the mildly retarded would be fully integrated in mainstreamed classrooms with minimal assistance; more severely retarded would be accommodated in special classes integrated into regular schools; some would stay at home, while others would be at boarding schools, foster and adoptive homes, group residences; those for whom vocational training would

120

be suitable would be integrated in industrial work stations located within factories, and so on. But the future he envisioned would be one in which all these categorical distinctions would be eliminated in favor of a fully individualized approach, a spectrum of risk and potential in which – as psychologists have always said about intelligence testing – there would be no clear line dividing the able from the disabled, the normal from the mentally retarded, but merely a gradient, or as it came to be called (and criticized as such) a "continuum of care" (Wolfensberger 1972, 50–51).

In this system, the role of experts is not to cure, nor to design and dictate the whole treatment program and treatment environment. Their role is to assist in what is essentially a course of self-treatment. They act as consultants, provide guidance, "'educe' (lead forth) the learner stepwise into the context in which he is to function" (Wolfensberger 1972, 45). Yet this system also creates the need for what was called in the Introduction "medical diagnosis of social destiny." Somebody would have to be in possession of a sort of medico-pedagogic expertise capable of justifying the assignment of "atypical children" into distinct tracks – Siegel (1996, 274–300) calls it "forks in the road" – going different ways at markedly different speeds; capable of justifying why the goals of the IEP were set the way they were; and capable of resolving the thorny attribution problems of deciding where the fault lay for unmet goals, with the child or with the therapy, and so on. Yet who could possess such awesome authority to decide destinies? Wolfensberger was completely silent on this matter. Child psychiatrists would have been the obvious candidates. We have seen in Chapters 2 and 3 how they sought to introduce prognostic distinctions between qualitatively different forms of feeblemindedness, and how they sought to demarcate an in-between domain of the "apparently feebleminded" where psychiatric expertise could diagnose hidden underlying illnesses, prescribe treatment, and forecast a course of development. We also saw how all of these ambitions were limited by the institutional matrix of custody.

Deinstitutionalization removed this obstacle, and normalization called for an even more ambitious program of early detection, prevention, and differential assignment than originally envisioned. The slot was prepared, but child psychiatry arrived at this juncture too bruised to step into it. Having come under fire for their role as custodians of mental retardation, for their persistent mother-blaming, for their elitism, child psychiatrists severely lacked the symbolic capital necessary to take upon themselves this auspicious role. Nor did anyone else possess it. Hence the legacy of normalization was this empty slot, this eye of the hurricane around which revolves and rages the whole system of early intervention, testing, IEPs and therapies, without ever being able to find its equilibrium. In the following chapters, we will pick up the complementary genealogical thread, the story of the making of a network of expertise that was able to exploit the strategic possibilities offered by this empty slot.

Normalization entailed a major shift not only in the goals, objects, and subjects of treatment, but also in the very "stuff" of treatment, its *techniques*, what it meant to "treat" somebody. This may have been the most important change. In the past, says Hersch, after conducting diagnostic interviews and psychological testing with parents and children, child guidance workers almost invariably prescribed some form of dynamic therapy for both (1968, 499–501). This uniformity, however, was rapidly giving way to more diversity, with different kinds of professionals and paraprofessionals involved, with the points of intervention multiplying beyond the clinic to the "social and educational levels," with a shift to concern with large populations, and a stress on prevention, even social action. Finally, psychoanalysis was eclipsed by the rise of other approaches, of which the most prominent was behavior modification. The following discussion of the role that behaviorist therapies played in the normalization movement is particularly significant for the argument of this book since behavior modification, and specifically Applied Behavioral Analysis (ABA), is today the most widely utilized approach in treating autism. In Chapter 7, we will analyze ABA's transformation from a fairly marginal approach to mental illness into the autism treatment juggernaut it is today. The connection between behavior modification, widely conceived, and normalization concludes this chapter. ABA is often attacked today – unjustly, we think – as being overly rigid, disciplinary, "normalizing" in the pejorative sense. We would like to demonstrate, therefore, its intimate and enduring affinities with the radical and progressive side of normalization.

Behavior modification and normalization

Much has been written about the rise of psychopharmacology and the effect it had on psychiatry and the treatment of mental illness (Scull [1983, 82–89] raised fairly convincing doubts about the centrality accorded to drugs in these explanations). When it comes to mental retardation or autism, however, one can be fairly certain that the effect of the psychopharmacological revolution was close to nil, since, and this is how they most decisively differ from ADHD, there are no pharmacological agents recognized by psychiatrists to have anything but a minimal effect on the core symptoms of these conditions (Siegel 1996, 301–20; Lakoff 2000). In her otherwise penetrating history of autism, Nadesan (2005, 103–78) also seems to miss the mark when she spends the bulk of her time on "the rise of the cognitive paradigm" as well as on "biological psychiatry and geneticization," while dedicating a mere page to behavioral approaches.[3] No doubt, when it comes to theory, these are the reigning approaches today in psychiatry and psychology. Despite their application in theories of autism, they have generated comparatively little by way of treatment when contrasted with pedestrian, theoretically impoverished, old-fashioned behaviorism. Behaviorism has had an unjustifiably bad reputation among critically minded social scientists. Training mentally retarded or autistic children to use the toilet, to eat with a spoon, or to look one in the eye when speaking strays very far from what social scientists see as appropriate employment for themselves. It is both too petty to be significant, and suspiciously conformist. Further, it also has been associated, sometimes rightly, with cruel and unusual punishments.

Yet recall Wolfensberger's express approval for behavior modification therapies, to which he dedicated a chapter in his book. The chapter was written by Philip Roos, executive director of NARC, a psychologist and institution superintendent. Roos argued that the goal of behavior modification was of the same order as normalization: to "enhance human qualities (as culturally defined), increase complexity of behavior, and foster the ability to cope with the environment" (in Wolfensberger, 1972, 147). Wherein lay this surprising affinity? One tends to forget that behaviorism always had a radical, populist side, a sort of "left behaviorism" that was evident very early on in William James, continued in however bizarre ways in Skinner's utopianism, and which certainly came to fruition in the 1960s in the work of people like Ivar Lovaas. The main point, as Roos explained, what made behavior modification particularly suitable for normalization, was that behavior modification did not assume any essential difference between the normal and the pathological. Everybody's behavior is governed by the same basic rules of learning. Behavior modification was not targeted at "mental illness." Mental illness did not exist as a meaningful entity for the behaviorist, since it was too speculative. It postulated some underlying deep cause, whether biological or psychological. The behaviorist was content to be limited to measurable relations between observable behaviors and environmental events (Roos, in Wolfensberger 1972, 138–47).

Correspondingly, the goal of behavior modification was much more modest than "cure." Behavior modification was accused of merely removing symptoms, without curing the underlying real syndrome. An autistic child, for example, could be taught to hug adults, but would that really change the core deficit that Kanner identified as "autistic aloneness" and "basic withdrawal"? The behaviorists countered that they did more than removing symptoms. They changed behavior first, and personality followed (140). The goal of behavior modification was, therefore, more akin to habit reform as one finds, for example, in Alcoholics Anonymous. As Mariana Valverde argues, "habit" is a hybrid category (1998, 35–42). It is conservative, but not unchanging. It is neither a reflex (completely determined and unfree), nor a matter of sheer willpower (merely exercising one's free will). Habit is strategically ambivalent about what is voluntary and what is hardwired, what is illness and what is willfulness. It is therefore well calculated to maximize the autonomy of nonmedical therapies and the extension of the normalization principle. Normalization, for its part, generalizes the model of habit reform and layers more utilities over it. One reforms habits as well as the environment that gave rise to pernicious habits. By "normalizing" one obtains a change in how the environment responds to the individual, and the response acts as reinforcement for desired habits, and so on.

Finally, it may seem that while normalization and behavior modification may share the object and goal of treatment, they would be radically discordant at the level of the subject of treatment, the relations between expert and patient. Roos (in Wolfensberger 1972, 141–47) says this is the most serious objection to behavior modification: that it is "controlling." But this is a misunderstanding. Behavior modification is not more controlling than other therapies; it is simply more successful, his example being the elimination of self-destructive behaviors in autistic children. In fact, control is not an inherent part of behavior modification. "The procedures are, as a matter of fact, well-suited to vesting the locus of control in the client rather than in the behavioral manager" (142). By eliminating pernicious habits and creating useful ones, the behaviorist seeks to give the individual choices where none existed before, to break a certain form of internal slavery, which at bottom is no different than the dependency created by the medical model and the sick role, and to maximize the potential for individual free choice and self-treatment. Moreover, since we are dealing with children, it is important to remember that the principles of behavior modification, including the administration of aversives, were continuous with normal child-rearing practices, which also rely on reward and punishment. Thus, behavior modification is normalizing since it does not set the mentally retarded child apart. He is treated just like other children, albeit in a more structured and systematic manner. Moreover, and this would become the great innovation of the behaviorists, who already in the mid-1960s were experimenting with turning parents into co-therapists, behavior modification empowers the parents and puts them on equal footing with the expert. There is nothing in it that they cannot, with a little training and guidance, do themselves.

By 1972, when these words were written, a great, silent revolution was already underway. The field of mental retardation, and with it, by extension, the whole in-between space of what was now properly termed "developmental disabilities," had been extracted from the jurisdiction of psychiatry. Its boundaries were radically blurred and undefended – the barriers to entry in terms of credentials, funds, and licensing, rather low, while the potential profits in terms of "upgrading" the prestige of occupations that were previously fairly marginal, rather high. It was open and attractive to the incursions of entrepreneurs from adjacent fields – academic psychologists, occupational therapists, speech therapists, special education experts, and activists – each peddling an eclectic, typically low-tech, therapy. Yet the condition for securing the profits available in this space was creating a coalition with parents. In 1970, for example, the University of North Carolina at Chapel Hill began experimenting with the first statewide program for the treatment of "psychotic and autistic children" at the preschool age. The program, known as TEACCH,[4] drew on the lesser therapies, declaring that "in the field of mental health, there is a reluctant but increasing acceptance that paraprofessional and relatively untrained workers are conducting important therapeutic interventions" (Schopler and Reichler 1971, 98). It was premised on giving parents the role of "co-therapists," "primary developmental agents for their severely disturbed child." And in what was to become the major trend for future years, so different from the consensus arrived at by Kanner and Rimland just a few years earlier (see Chapter 6), diagnostic criteria were kept intentionally broad to maximize intake and "avoid premature closure." The target of the new program was "the broad range of severe disorders in which autistic characteristics are prominent" (87–91). In this open space, where they could deal freely and on equal terms with therapists, who were often not much different from themselves, parents and parent-activist-researchers began to shift toward greater inclusiveness and agnosticism (whereas earlier they had restricted the disorder for the sake of de-stigmatization).

The outlines of the spectrum were coming into view. We turn now to the story of how the alliance between parents, activists, researchers and therapists was forged, and a new network of expertise came into being.

— 6 —

CHILDHOOD SCHIZOPHRENIA

To understand the setting for the formation of the alliance, or network of expertise, which was able to make use of the opportunities opened up by deinstitutionalization, we need to reconstruct the unstable and ambiguous position occupied by autism in the decades before deinstitutionalization, a position between mental retardation and what was known at the time as childhood schizophrenia. This would also allow us to demonstrate that deinstitutionalization was a necessary condition for the rise of autism. We turn to the story of childhood schizophrenia.

In the short span from the early 1950s to the mid-1960s, the U.S. experienced three epidemics of childhood disorders, one following another in rapid succession. In each case, however, after the initial alarm and a period of rapid expansion, critics unmasked the epidemic as artificially produced by misdiagnosis, as well as by societal demand for these diagnoses, thus making way for the next wave.

First, for reasons that should be clear from Chapter 3, beginning in the mid-1940s, alarm was raised about an increase in the incidence of mental deficiency. Using intelligence tests, researchers raised the estimate from 1 percent to 2 percent to 3 percent of the school-age population. But the American Association on Mental Deficiency outdid everybody when, in 1961, it estimated that 15.9 percent of the U.S. population (all persons below one standard deviation from the mean IQ) were potential candidates for diagnosis as mentally retarded. Clausen, however, explained that the rise in incidence was due to arbitrary factors such as changes in cutoffs and diagnostic criteria, increased awareness and improved diagnostic facilities (1966, 733–35). Mental deficiency was simply not a single condition, not a disease entity, but a collection of heterogeneous conditions assembled together on the basis of conventions. As social life became more complex and more democratic, conventions changed and with them the incidence rate. In centralized systems such as the U.S.S.R., he explained, the problem of the "higher-grade defective" was minimized through early mandatory placement into vocational tracks, but in the U.S., with an individualist, merit-based system of allocation, an increased emphasis on high school and academic credentials as condition for employment, and increasing complexity of industrial jobs, the problem was exacerbated. Kanner made essentially the same point. The rise in estimated incidence was "an artifact of civilization" (1949, 4–5, 9–11).

These same years also saw an epidemic of childhood schizophrenia. The diagnosis was first proposed in the 1930s, in the New York State hospital system, but was codified during the 1940s by Lauretta Bender of Bellevue Hospital. By 1953, she was ready to propose that it was "more common than generally supposed, especially in institutions for mental defectives," thus cutting to the right, so to speak, into the caseload of the first epidemic. Then she also cut to the left into the caseload of child guidance, since she thought that "any severe psychoneurotic disorder in a child before puberty, whether it is obsessive-compulsive, so-called hysterical or simply severe anxiety, is a reactive response to a deeper, inherent threatening disorder, most often schizophrenia" (Bender 1953, 663–64, 674). No wonder, then, that a few years later, Hilde Mosse complained about "an enormous increase in diagnosis of childhood schizophrenia . . . [that] has filled state hospitals and schools for mental defectives." She thought the diagnosis was misused and unscientific (Mosse 1958, 791). Kanner, too, called it a "pseudo-diagnostic waste basket into which an assortment of heterogeneous conditions were thrown indiscriminately. Infantile autism was stuffed into this basket along with everything else." Childhood schizophrenia, he explained in terms that recalled what was said about mental deficiency, "is not a disease entity," but a "temporary group category," a "species" (Kanner 1965, 417–19). Mosse also thought she could discern wherein lay the societal demand for the diagnosis as a form of ideological obfuscation of social problems: "The most pressing unsolved social problem in the United States today as far as children are concerned is that of juvenile delinquency" (1958, 791). No doubt it was worse in New York City, where the diagnosis of childhood schizophrenia was pioneered. The diagnosis provided an easy solution that "put the problem into a wrong focus, namely into the field of mental illness . . . inherent in the child, instead of into the field of social pathology to which the child is reacting" (791).[1]

Finally, autism. The first autism epidemic, by Kanner's lights, took place from 1951 to 1959. "Almost overnight," he complained, "the country seems to be populated by a multitude of autistic children, and somehow this trend became noticeable overseas as well" (Kanner 1965, 414). He thought, again, that this was due to misdiagnosis: "It became a habit to dilute the original concept of infantile autism by diagnosing it in many disparate conditions which show one or another isolated symptoms found as a part feature of the overall syndrome" (414). Especially, "mentally defective children who displayed bizarre behavior were promptly labeled autistic, and both parents were urged to undergo protracted psychotherapy in addition to treatment directed toward the defective child's own supposedly underlying emotional problem." If in 1949 he characterized the families of autistic children as "emotional refrigerators," and postulated that hidden autism underlay a great deal of "apparent feeblemindedness," by 1965, Kanner had reversed himself completely. True mental defect, he argued, underlay most of the new diagnoses of apparent autism, which merely reflected the "preconceived notions" of a "sizable group of workers, temporarily influential especially in this country," by which he meant psychoanalysts and other dynamically oriented therapists working within the paradigm of child guidance and focusing on the emotional quality of early mother–infant relationship (413, 417).

The first observation one may want to draw from this series of epidemics, which came and went, is that the second autism epidemic, the current one, is one more episode in this long series, especially if one considers that between 1965 and the present moment there were also many other such epidemics, some more long-lasting, others truly episodic. Kanner heaved a sigh of relief in 1965, as "fashion" moved away from autism to "the brain-injured child" (Kanner 1965, 414). The long and gathering epidemic of hyperactivity followed (Lakoff 2000); some today foresee an epidemic of bipolar disorder in children (Groopman 2007). Ian Hacking (1998, 1–2) has suggested the idea of "transient mental illness": an illness that appears at a particular historical moment and place "and later goes away." The illness, he explains, can only exist within certain conditions, or "vectors," as in an "ecological niche," yet disappears almost completely when these conditions no longer obtain. The frequent comings and goings of childhood disorders in the last 60 years, however, seem to be more a matter of diagnostic "fashion" than of ecological niche. At the very least, it indicates that the ecological niche underspecifies who and what could occupy it. To extend the ecological metaphor, one could

129

imagine, as Marissa King (2008) suggests, various diagnoses and their champions (clinicians, but also parents and advocacy organizations) competing for the scarce resources that a niche offers. Certainly the metaphor of ecological niche invites this extension. Indeed, this would account for the fierce competition over the label of "developmental disability" that took place a few years later between organizations representing parents of retarded children and parents of autistic children (Akerley 1979).

One would be hard-pressed, however, to square Kanner's position in 1965 with the notion of competition for scarce resources. Certainly he was reacting to the imperialistic move by Bender, who would categorize autism as one type of childhood schizophrenia, the "pseudo-defective or autistic type," along with the other "pseudo-neurotic" and "pseudo-psychopathic" types. In 1959 she declared flat out that "Kanner's syndrome of early infantile autism . . . is not a clinical or etiological entity" (Bender 1959, 85). So Kanner replied in the same vein concerning childhood schizophrenia. But instead of countering her expansionist move with his own, he retreated. He limited and circumscribed the diagnosis of autism in a way that effectively removed it from competition, and incidentally undercut any idea of a spectrum. What happened with childhood schizophrenia, he said, presents "a rather disturbing dilemma. We seem to have reached a point where a clinician . . . can say honestly: he is schizophrenic, because in my scheme I must call him so. Another clinician, equally honest, can say: he is not schizophrenic because according to my scheme I cannot call him so" (Kanner 1965, 418). The way out of this impasse, he thought, was not to hypostasize autism into another "temporary group category" (though in 1949 he came close to doing so, and of course with the spectrum in 1987, autism once again assumed this role), but to emphasize that unlike childhood schizophrenia or mental deficiency, autism was not a "species" but a "definitely distinguishable disease."[2] Other researchers should follow the example of autism, and lift out of the schizophrenic package other specific and definitely distinguishable conditions, Kanner counseled, just as phenylketonuria was identified as a separate disease and broken out of the continuum of mental deficiency (417–19).

It was no surprise, therefore, that the DSM-II published in 1968 had only a category for "schizophrenia, childhood type," under which infantile autism was included though barely mentioned. We are presented with a historical puzzle: if any condition was ripe to become a spectrum in 1965, it was not autism. This disorder's primary describer declared it should be kept as a distinct syndrome. The likely spectrum disorder was childhood schizophrenia, which threatened to cover the whole field of psychiatric intervention from the "pseudo-defective" (mental retardation) to the "pseudo-neurotic" (child guidance) to the "pseudo-psychopathic" (juvenile delinquency), as well as establishing a firm link between childhood ailments and adult schizophrenia, the province of psychiatry proper.

One clue for resolving this puzzle may come from the sociology of the professions. Andrew Abbott (1988) observes that the relation between the degree of abstraction of professional knowledge and the power of the profession approximates an inverted-U shaped curve. Moderate degrees of abstraction permit a profession to control the knowledge and contributions of other workers within a given jurisdiction, but too much abstraction means that the profession spreads itself too thin, its concepts and knowledge are made to do too much and they become meaningless. The workplace is either dominated by frontline workers or becomes an easy target for the encroachments of another profession. Childhood schizophrenia is a good example of a concept stretched so thin as to become meaningless. As Rutter declared, while delivering what became the death knell for the childhood schizophrenia diagnosis, it "has tended to be used as a generic term to include an astonishingly heterogeneous mixture of disorders with little in common other than their severity, chronicity, and occurrence in childhood . . . We must conclude that the term 'childhood schizophrenia' has . . . ceased to have any scientific meaning or communicative value and it is high time that [it] . . . was politely and respectfully, but firmly, put into its proper place in the section on 'the history of psychiatry'"(1972, 315).

But if the childhood schizophrenia diagnosis lost the battle for the ecological niche because it spread itself too thin, while autism survived by limiting itself to a small number of cases in which the overall syndrome was discernible, then we must revise how we think of ecological niches and the illnesses that occupy them. Not only does the ecological niche underspecify who and what could occupy it, but the niche conditions themselves underspecify the very shape and boundaries of the niche, which as we saw above may expand or contract, thus making the metaphor of "ecological niche" less felicitous. One gets the sense not so much of competition over scarce resources in a given territory, but of successive attempts to make use of the possibilities inherent in a certain strategic situation: a chess game rather than an ecosystem. One player – Bender – instinctively "develops" this situation, making many sacrifices in an effort to translate positional momentum into decisive advantage (but ultimately fails). Another

131

– Kanner – hesitates, but eventually opts to carefully nurture and preserve the limited material advantage he gained.

Experts struggled to define this ecological niche that opened up between illness and retardation, between mental deficiency and mental hygiene. How to make coherent and legitimate the power to provide medical diagnosis of social destiny, demanded by the project of comprehensive surveillance and a placement system for early childhood? What could be the specific province of child psychiatry? If childhood schizophrenia underlay a breathtaking sweep of childhood disorders and was liable to develop into the adult form of schizophrenia, then it would be necessary, wise, even economical, to screen all children, as early as possible, for the telltale signs. But if it was simply the same illness as adult schizophrenia, why would it not be the object of psychiatry proper? Bender attempted, then, to delink the expertise needed to diagnose childhood schizophrenia from that needed for adult schizophrenia (1953, 663). The "signs and symptoms of schizophrenia in childhood" are different "from those in adulthood." Thus she still sought to occupy a niche between illness and retardation.[3] Rutter's attack was so deadly because it was targeted directly at this delinking, no longer permitting childhood schizophrenia to be distinguished from illness pure and simple: "when schizophrenia presents as a psychosis in childhood it does so in a way which is basically comparable to that in adults. The disorder seems the same and there is no reason to give the condition a special name" (1972, 321).

Alternatively, if mental deficiency or retardation was widespread and, as some thought, gave rise to psychoses or juvenile delinquency, then again one would be well advised to screen all children even for mild mental defect, and the sooner the better (Wallin 1949, 71–75). But would it be a medical object at all? Autism, as we saw, could serve as a hinge connecting the two domains of feeblemindedness and child guidance. It could be an illness underlying apparent feeblemindedness, thus a medical object. Yet it was "infantile," a condition with onset in early childhood if not simply inborn, thus withdrawing it from the province of psychiatry proper. By limiting the application of the diagnosis of autism with the "full syndrome" requirement, Kanner was not only avoiding the pitfalls of over-abstraction, but also balancing the emerging ecological niche between the two models of "illness" and "retardation," which threatened to swallow it whole.

Why was this important? Why was the diagnosis of autism eventually successful in its explanatory force, while childhood schizophrenia was relegated to the "history of psychiatry"? One clue, missing from the discussion till now and absent also from Hacking's "niche conditions," is what Kanner and Bender have to say about treatment and therapy. After all, it would be completely useless to detect childhood disorders early, if one could do nothing about them, and it would be fairly useless to wield fine diagnostic distinctions if one's arsenal of remedies was highly restricted. In 1949, Kanner thought that classification of childhood disorders should look not "backward to origin or cause . . . [but] rather . . . forward toward practical communal, educational, and clinical possibilities for human engineering" (Kanner 1949, 6–11). But later he changed his mind and accused the psychoanalysts who championed the concept of "atypical child" precisely of "putting the therapeutic cart before the diagnostic horse" (Kanner 1965, 417). The primitiveness of the diagnostic grid corresponded to a one-size-fits-all approach to treatment. Everybody, regardless of their problems, was assigned to long hours of dynamic therapy, which almost by definition tended to exclude the very young and the seriously intellectually disabled.

How about childhood schizophrenia? How was it to be treated? Bender mentions two principal treatments – electroconvulsive therapy (ECT) and Metrazol, which amounted to the same thing, since Metrazol induced convulsions. Since she believed childhood schizophrenia was a hereditary "encephalopathy" that interfered with maturation, shock therapy – whether chemical or electric – was administered to stimulate maturation. She counseled against psychotherapy aiming to break down neuroses. On the contrary, the child's defense mechanisms against the anxiety caused by inborn defect should be strengthened. Since ECT could only be administered in a hospital environment, institutionalization – temporary or long-term – was part of the regimen, and Bender thought that experiences away from the family would be good for the child. Medications to control anxiety would be useful as well, and could be administered in a hospital setting.[4] Finally, she counseled therapy for the parents. Not because they caused their child's problem, mind you, but "to help them understand their problems," deal with the family conflict that was inevitable when caring for a schizophrenic child, and because "the parent–child relationship or the emotional climate of the family, especially in the first two years, will help determine the defense mechanisms, the ability to handle regressive tendencies, impulses, anxiety, etc." (Bender 1953, 678). She thought this course of treatment, coupled with early diagnosis, before puberty, guaranteed about 50 percent success, namely fair-to-good adjustment (666, 673).

We are fairly sure that this course of treatment is what guaranteed the failure of childhood schizophrenia. Stretched too thin? Perhaps, but so is the autism spectrum today. What mattered most of all was the thinness of the therapeutic arsenal.[5] It is fairly clear from the description above that the way Bender described the syndrome and its etiology was calculated to strike a compromise between the biological and dynamic accounts of mental illness. An underlying biological weakness or deficit gave rise to layers upon layers of neurotic adjustments and defense mechanisms. As Kanner noted, Bender attempted to combine constitutional factors and environmental influences into a single "psychobiologic entity" and thereby put an end to the distinction between "organic" and "functional" psychoses (1965, 416–17; 1971, 17–18; see also Rutter 1972, 316–17).[6] But the price paid for this daring theoretical syncretism was that she remained painfully conventional when it came to therapy, attempting to give both sides their due place and changing very little in the existing matrix of treatment. Hospitalization, medication, and ECT were the standard fare of biologically oriented adult psychiatry at the time, dynamic therapy for the parents a standard issue of child guidance clinics.

Merely on economic grounds it would seem that childhood schizophrenia was doomed. But it was also highly unlikely that one could recruit patients *en masse* with this regimen. Over the course of 18 years at the Children's Ward of the Psychiatric Division at Bellevue Hospital, Bender managed to diagnose 626 children (9.5 percent of the ward's intake) with childhood schizophrenia. She attempted to follow up with about 350 of them in order to "confirm" the diagnosis. She reports that the most difficult group to follow up were those children who were diagnosed with childhood schizophrenia but were not treated, typically because their parents refused permission to give electric shock to their children. Uncooperative to begin with, they were, as she put it, "the least cooperative" at follow-up (Bender 1953, 668–69). The reasons for this uncooperativeness are not hard to fathom. Lower-class or African-American families, who were mistrustful of the medical establishment to begin with, were not likely to cooperate with it once childhood schizophrenia became, as Mosse reported, a standard diagnostic response to juvenile delinquency (1958, 791–92). Gang membership, misbehavior in school, truancy, stealing, were diagnosed as evidence of "childhood schizophrenia" and led to institutionalization and a standard course of twenty ECTs. Then, after six months, the children were typically discharged and the diagnosis was changed to "behavior disorder," but the side effects of ECT were often evident.

As for the dynamic therapy prescribed for the parents, it was an unfortunate adjunct, a peace offering to the psychoanalysts, which they transformed into an examination of maternal ambivalence and the quality of maternal care. Hence, despite Bender's best intentions, childhood schizophrenia was caught up in the groundswell of parental resistance that marked the second half of the 1960s, and which gave rise to, among other groups, the National Society for Autistic Children.

Finally, all this fits nicely with the deinstitutionalization argument. When lifelong institutionalization was common practice, the alliance with parents mattered little, or at least less. Of course, many parents resisted the advice to institutionalize and sought second opinions about their child's diagnosis.[7] But institutionalization was a one-size-fits-all prescription. Differences between therapeutic arsenals were negligible from the parents' perspective. As institutionalization became less common and children were more often staying home with their families, however, the coalition with parents became increasingly salient. Parents could "shop" for a diagnosis that best suited their child's needs, and therapy was likely a major factor in that decision.

There is a more general theoretical point behind these fairly commonsensical arguments. Hacking does not say so explicitly, but we think it is implicit in his account that one of the main "niche conditions" of "transient mental illnesses" must be a set of factors that guarantee the cooperation of patients, that guarantee their willingness to recognize the diagnostic labels attached to them and take them as a basis for their action.[8] In the case of transient *childhood* disorders, this stipulation refers to the need to secure the cooperation of parents, to strike an alliance with them. This highlights the importance of therapy among niche conditions. Bender modeled the therapeutic regime after the medical treatment of acute illness: temporary hospitalization; aggressive treatment with the newest, most expensive and most intrusive medical technology; then discharge. This model minimizes parental involvement and sidelines the problem of cooperation. Obviously, a high rate of cures would do the job of securing parental cooperation, but this is hardly ever the case with mental disorders, and childhood schizophrenia was no exception.

We can look at this also from the point of view of the sociology of the professions. A highly abstract terminology, *pace* Abbott, is not always unstable or weak, provided that it is superimposed upon a complex jurisdictional arrangement in which labor is divided between several groups of experts, in which authority and decision-making power are shared in accordance with some stable formula, *and* in which the therapeutic regime induces the *cooperation* of patients/

parents. This is probably the case with the autism spectrum today, as we shall see in later chapters. The therapeutic regime is not oriented to acute illness but to a chronic condition, not to cure but to improvement of functioning, self-determination, and quality of life, the standards of which are judged and set in collaboration with parents. Hence the solution to the puzzle of why autism, restricted to a "definitely distinguishable illness" by Kanner in 1965, could bloom into a full-fledged spectrum within a decade, and why childhood schizophrenia, which covered the whole field of childhood ailments in the 1960s, would go into disrepute and be practically eliminated by 1980.

The other main actor, besides Kanner, who in the mid-1960s was interested in restricting the diagnosis of autism to a definitely distinguishable disease, was the new breed of parent-activist-researcher represented by Bernard Rimland, who will be the focus of Chapter 8. In his classic *Infantile Autism* (1964), he clearly aligned himself with Kanner, who wrote a brief preface to the book. Why was Rimland, father of an autistic boy, willing to discount Kanner's observations on "emotional refrigeration"? Perhaps because the old man was kind to him and supportive of his work? Instead, the arch-villain of the book was Bruno Bettelheim, who was dismissive of Rimland. But there is also a less personal reason. Just like Kanner, Rimland was concerned to limit the diagnosis of autism. Autism is "very rare," he said, probably the product of a "rare recessive trait." Unfortunately, however, it is over-diagnosed. Many children who only have some of the symptoms receive the diagnosis, while a diagnosis of childhood schizophrenia would probably have been more appropriate. He was emphatic that there was no spectrum: "there is an absence of gradations of infantile autism which would create 'blends' from normal to severely afflicted" (Rimland 1964, 18–21, 52). For anybody familiar with today's parent-activist-researchers, who have played a major role in extending the diagnosis of autism into a spectrum, Rimland's diagnostic asceticism seems odd. Yet it becomes perfectly understandable once we realize that Rimland's main target was the psychogenic hypothesis. If the syndrome is rare and extremely specific, he explained, it was highly unlikely to be caused by the diffuse dynamics of mother–infant relations. For the same reason, he denied any similarity between autism and Spitz's "hospitalism" (37–46). An alliance was forged, then, between Kanner, who wanted to protect his diagnosis from the groundswell of parents' resistance, and the parent-activist-researchers themselves who wanted to destigmatize the condition and put an end to mother-blaming. Yet this alliance was forged precisely around autism as a rare and distinct disease. It is difficult to see how this alliance would contain within itself the seeds of the spectrum, unless as a sort of protective incubator.

The story gets even more complicated. Rimland, in fact, was hugely equivocal on the question of whether autism was a form of mental retardation. In one place he said he was certain autism was a rare form of "oligophrenia," which could mean either brain injury or mental retardation (Rimland 1964, 123). His argument was that autism was a "cognitive dysfunction," a term so general it could easily apply also to mental retardation (79). Yet there was no question of assimilating the two. Autism was a rare and specific condition and mental retardation a "vast conglomeration" (139). He laid down very specific rules for differential diagnosis between autism and mental retardation, and his main arguments repeated Kanner's almost word for word. First, the child's appearance, already noted by Kanner: "The child simply does not look retarded." They are handsome, well-formed, do not have the motor and health problems or the vacuous expression of the feebleminded (10–11).[9] This led him to what he considered the most decisive evidence for the difference between autism and mental retardation: the fact that the parents of autistic children, as Kanner observed, were typically high-level professionals, supremely intelligent though rather cold and preoccupied with their work. They were completely unlike the parents of mentally retarded children, and in fact their demographic profile resembled most of all the parents of gifted children, though they outdid them as well. "The parents," he concluded without a hint of irony (after all, he was himself the father of an autistic boy), "represent an unusual and homogenous group, linked by their sharing of a specific genetic background" (160).

It is easy to dismiss Rimland's arguments as a historical curiosity, no longer relevant, or as evidence merely about how he dealt with his personal anguish. This is, after all, one of the most perplexing aspects of his book, which inaugurated the new era of autism research and advocacy: coupled with its attack on the psychogenic hypothesis, it also affirmed over and over again evidence about the parents' intelligence and personalities – evidence held damning in the past. If the main impetus was to destigmatize autism, to remove the implication of the parents' fault, why flirt with danger in this way? To answer this question without trivializing Rimland's move, we have to break with a narrative of autism's rise and spread as merely a destigmatization campaign and a struggle over scarce resources (King 2008).

What would have happened if Rimland merely destroyed the evidence for the psychogenic hypothesis? In the mid-1960s, this would have meant that autism would have lost its moorings in the domain

of childhood mental illness and would have drifted into the wasteland of undifferentiated mental defect or retardation, and since, as
we saw in this chapter, there were many other labels ready to fill the
vacuum, it would be hard to retrace one's steps. Autistic children
would have become, as in Tredgold's imagery, like all those other
paupers who never possessed a checking account to begin with. So
Rimland's insistence on the parents' unusual intelligence and personalities was calculated to pull autism back into the ethical realm of
illness. "Autistic children," he said, "were to have been endowed with
unusually high intelligence" (Rimland 1964, 124). How do we know
that? Because they would have inherited it from their highly gifted
parents. We beg the readers not to snicker. The awkward phrasing
and scarcely concealed motivation are completely beside the point.
The crucial point about this argument is that it redrew the ethical
limits of illness around autistic children. It was eugenics against itself.
It confounded Tredgold's imagery of illness as "temporary financial
embarrassment," by appealing to the notion of genetic endowment
or potential gone awry: "an infant's road to intelligence lies along a
knife-edged path, and the higher the potential intelligence, the steeper
and more precarious the slope" (127). With this argument, autism
was once again poised midway between illness and retardation,
potentially expanding the no-man's-land between them and blurring
their boundaries. It was "one of the few separate diseases which can
be isolated for study in the massive conglomeration of conditions
which contribute to mental retardation." It "may be used as a fine-
edged tool – an opening wedge – in the general scientific attack on the
problems of abnormal mentality" (139). But it had to be "fine-edged"
indeed. The condition for inhabiting this in-between sphere was, as
we saw, the restriction of autism to a rare and distinctive disorder,
that could never be mistaken for mental retardation.

The crucial difference between the mid-1960s and the late 1970s
is that in between there began the deinstitutionalization of mental
retardation, which ushered a new therapeutic regime and opened up a
space between illness and retardation, between psychiatry and special
education, a space that quickly became populated by therapies cater-
ing to parents and enlisting their cooperation. So Kanner did well to
preserve his material advantage and watch his competitors founder
on the rising wave of parental disaffection. Any attempt to generalize
autism into a spectrum in 1965 would likely have backfired in the
absence of therapeutic mechanisms for enlisting parental cooperation.
One merely needs to imagine what would have happened if Kanner
had heeded Schopler's suggestion to train mothers in how to hug

and provide tactile stimulation to their infants (see Chapter 8). And Rimland did well to restrict *his* initial gambit. In this way he was able to form a fairly cohesive network of expertise composed of parents of children diagnosed as autistic organized in the National Society for Autistic Children. Then, when this network began transacting with the new therapies – which happened in a short while, just a few years after he published his book – it gradually began to expand, and with it expanded also the scope of autism.

One last question: if childhood schizophrenia played such an important role in the history of autism, if, in fact, for a while it occupied the same ecological niche that autism eventually came to possess, why have we chosen to focus on the history of mental retardation and not childhood schizophrenia? The immediate and obvious answer is that quantitatively speaking childhood schizophrenia was far less significant than mental retardation. In 1944, children under 15 years of age constituted only 0.5 percent of first admissions to mental hospitals. This proportion no doubt grew in later years, but the bulk of children institutionalized as mentally ill were probably either in correctional institutions for juvenile delinquents or in residential schools for the mentally defective. When it came to very young children it was almost impossible to distinguish psychoses from mental defect, and while various speculations were rife – that 20 percent of "high-grade defectives" were really psychotic – nobody had any reliable evidence. The prejudice, according to which the mentally retarded were immune to mental illness because of their "simplicity," was long gone, and so wardens of institutions for the mentally retarded were content to admit that many under their care also suffered from temporary psychotic episodes.

From the other side of the fence, Bender's critics pointed out that after discharge, many of the children treated for childhood schizophrenia ended up in state schools for the mentally retarded. The vast majority were "grossly organic cases," with conditions such as encephalitis. One notes also that, sociologically speaking, during this period the cases of childhood schizophrenia were distinguished from autism in precisely the same way that autism was differentiated from mental retardation. Influential studies showed that children diagnosed with childhood schizophrenia, typically with onset after 3 years of age, were vastly more likely to come from poorer or minority families than children who were diagnosed with autism due to earlier onset (Wallin 1949, 70–74; Mosse 1958, 792; Rutter 1978, 151).

This explains why the deinstitutionalization of specifically the mentally retarded, and not of the mentally ill, was the most important

139

development transforming autism from a fairly circumscribed illness to an ever-expanding spectrum. It does not mean, however, that we assign childhood schizophrenia a minor role in the history of autism. On the contrary, the story we are trying to tell is of how autism developed in the interstice opened up between illness and retardation, an interstice occupied by childhood schizophrenia for almost two decades. If, quantitatively speaking, the history of mental retardation is the decisive one, with deinstitutionalization providing the bulk of very young children with no clear diagnosis, the history of childhood schizophrenia, for its part, was nonetheless decisive in the weaving of a diagnostic net with wide gaping holes. They were connected to one another as two parts of a machine, of the "moral blender" that produced a steady stream of "atypical children." By 1968, when the first stirrings of deinstitutionalization began, Ornitz and Ritvo could complain about the multiplication of different labels – infantile autism, childhood schizophrenia, the atypical child, symbiotic psychosis, children with unusual sensitivities – to diagnose what they thought was essentially a "single pathologic process common" to all (1968, 76). They proposed to replace it all with a single disease – autism. Three years later, when the first issue of the *Journal of Autism and Childhood Schizophrenia* was published, the director of the National Institute of Mental Health charged it with the task of bringing together the different clusters of knowledge about "psychotic children" of whatever type. Members of the board intentionally included major spokespersons of all the different strands: Bender, William Goldfarb, and Jacob Lutz for childhood schizophrenia, Kanner, Leon Eisenberg, Rimland, Rutter, Schopler, and Ritvo for autism, Margaret Mahler and Manuel Furer for symbiotic psychosis, William C. Rhodes for mental retardation, and so on (Brown 1971, 2–12). Finally, when the task force charged with writing the DSM-III was formed, a group of child psychiatrists appealed to the chairman, Robert Spitzer, to include within it the diagnosis of "atypical child" (Spiegel 2005, 59). He refused. The task was now to produce a coherent account of what this undifferentiated mass of atypical children all shared with one another, and how they could be meaningfully distinguished, not to recreate Borges' *Chinese Encyclopedia* with its final category of "not included in the present classification."

THE RISE OF THE THERAPIES

. . . his environment is arranged with a simplicity which will protect him from the distractions he is not yet able to ignore. He effects the best relationship to his environment when he is in a small group, with explicit and orderly procedures. He relaxes under routine, for with it he can predict the day's events. He is quieter when there are no distracting displays, or pictures to attract his attention. He is more comfortable and functions better if his desk is turned towards the wall so he is not distracted by the sight of the other children. He may even be at his best if off entirely by himself in another room or working behind a screen or large piece of furniture such as the piano. . . . [T]he classroom is a hygienic environment, arranged to permit his optimum functioning despite deviations. It is a life space which is stable, predictable, and comfortable in which he can find himself in relation to the people and things about him. The confusing world and his role in it become understandable because it can be dealt with in miniature, organized and related to produce a reliable, workable model of reality.

These recommendations come not from a contemporary manual for educating autistic children, though they closely resemble current practices, but from a book on the "Psychopathology and Education of the Brain-Injured Child" (Strauss and Kephart 1955, 174). Compare them with the advice that 40 years later child psychologist Bryna Siegel (1996, 209–30) gives parents about choosing a classroom for their autistic child. Make sure the classroom is a highly structured environment, she says, that is, that there are externally imposed limits, rules that force them to do things, people who monitor them, and consequences for not following rules. Structure, mixed with some choice so as not to make it too regimented, suits autistic children because they are resistant to change. The class environment also must be low-stimulation, no decorations or artwork. Sometimes head-phones are useful.

We would like in the future to describe and analyze the most important therapies currently in use for the treatment of autistic children; we argue that what happens in the course of therapy loops back to modify how autism is diagnosed, conceptualized and experienced, and that an important precondition for today's autism epidemic was the rise and spread of the therapies in the early 1970s. For the moment, however, the point of the above comparison is to alert the reader that *autism therapies themselves have no origin* – that they emanate neither from new discoveries or knowledge about autism, nor even from a previous tradition of work with specifically autistic children. The historical trajectories of contemporary autism therapies begin at multiple, diverse, and obscure points. They were not destined at birth to become autism therapies. Research on the history of these therapies, we argue, should privilege not the moment of their birth, but the moment of their hybridization. Not the moment when they became what they are, a distinct therapy directed at a distinct category of patients, monopolized by a distinct group of practitioners, but on the contrary, the moment of deinstitutionalization, when it became possible for them to be what they are *not*, to blend into one another, cross borders, move laterally and gather patients idiosyncratically, become modular components of treatment programs.

In the rest of this chapter, we will show first that the therapies explicitly billed as addressing autism in the 1950s and 1960s differed from current autism therapies in the role they assigned to parents, in the moral narrative guiding therapy, and in their temporal structure or rhythm. Thus they could hardly be seen as providing the point of origin for contemporary therapies. Second, we will trace two trajectories by which contemporary autism therapies *did* develop – one from the aforementioned perceptual-motor therapy for "brain-injured" children, the other from behavioral therapy for "emotionally disturbed" children. The two therapies shared very little substance, yet they converged and complemented each other in the hybridization to which they both contributed. Perceptual-motor therapy originated in the field of mental retardation yet projected itself outside this field because it treated mental retardation as "injury," a semi-illness that could be cured by a therapy that worked directly to modify the brain of the developing child. Behavior modification originated in the field of mental illness yet it too projected itself outward, because it treated illness as a bad habit that could be unlearned, or a lack of skills that could be corrected. Thus their combined movement blurred the boundary between mental illness and retardation and created a large indeterminate zone between them. As the therapies maneuvered into this zone in order to gain freedom of operation outside the jurisdictions of psychiatry and special education, they settled on three tactical innovations – downscaling, outsourcing, and modularization – which blurred the boundary between expert and layman as well, allowing them to strike an alliance with parents. In this way, they turned the space opened up by deinstitutionalization into an interstitial "space between fields," a space of opportunity and entrepreneurship where it was possible to do things one could not do before, to combine things one had to keep separate if one was within the orbit of the fields of psychiatry or special education. Specifically, it became possible to create new objects of discourse and intervention – indeed, a whole new domain of similarly constituted objects of which autism today is the most prominent example. This is why the moral narrative of contemporary autism therapies differs so significantly from that of 1950s and 1960s autism therapies – because, in fact, the object upon which they work is quite differently constituted.

Autism therapies in the 1950s and 1960s

Contemporary autism therapies, especially those that were able to take advantage of the opportunities opened up by deinstitutionalization, did not typically begin as therapies for autistic children. There is very little similarity or connection between contemporary autism therapies and the treatments practiced at the few schools specifically dedicated to autistic children in the 1950s and 1960s. And this is true even if we exclude or control for the influence of that favorite bogeyman of today's autism world – psychoanalysis. There are three major differences between 1950s/60s autism therapies and contemporary ones:[1] 1) contemporary therapies recruit parents as co-therapists while earlier ones assigned the therapists the role of substitute parents; 2) contemporary therapies are guided for the most part by a moral narrative of construction, laying down the building blocks of development, while 1950s–1960s autism therapies were guided by a moral narrative of discovery, drawing the child outside the fortress represented by autism; 3) contemporary therapies are infused with a sense of urgency, and in terms of temporal structure or rhythm they are divided into ever smaller chunks of time ("discrete trials," "rounds," "circles of communication") during which constant pressure is applied on the child, and a certain measure of progress,

143

however imperceptible, must be recorded. By contrast, 1950s–1960s autism therapies, in accordance with the metaphor of discovery, divided time into long periods of patient waiting and a slow rhythm of coaxing out.

Jacques May was a French physician and father of autistic twins who relocated to the United States in the 1950s. In 1959, he and his wife collaborated with other Massachusetts parents to create the Parents School for Atypical Children, a residential school for autistic children. There was no greater enemy of psychoanalysis than May. He wrote a book – *A Physician Looks at Psychiatry* (May 1958) – in which he attacked the very concepts and approach of psychoanalysis as unscientific; derided psychotherapy for autistic children as useless, wasteful, and serving only to enrich the psychoanalysts; and told a bitter personal story of his exasperating and unhelpful interactions with child psychiatrists and child guidance clinics. Yet the school that the May couple built, and the "environmental therapy" practiced there, were much more similar to Bettelheim's Orthogenic School than to today's autism therapies, with the important exception of the Mays' emphasis on a highly structured schedule, "a well-organized ballet where no surprises ever occur," and on strict rules of behavior (May and May 1959, 438).

To begin with, it was a residential establishment. The children were separated from their parents and families for extended periods of time. Despite the fact that this was a school built by parents, it accorded them hardly any role in treatment. In fact, it replaced them. The first stage of treatment, upon admission, was the creation of a "loving environment," by which the Mays meant that the school was modeled upon the family, with teachers, nurses, and aides playing the role of "mothers" and "big sisters," providing loving care, thus replacing the family from which the children were removed (May and May 1959, 440). When the Bettelheim hunting season was at its height, Schopler (1971, 90) called this sort of arrangement "parentectomy," but we see that it was practiced even where a theory of parental causality was explicitly and vehemently rejected.

The second and decisive stage of therapy at the Mays' school was named "creative gratification." The idea was that through play and art therapy, it would be possible "to discover what the child would have been if he had not been sick – an artist interested in colors, a sculptor interested in reproducing figures . . . after this has gone on for a certain time, we find that the basic traits of the child's personality, that had been completely befogged when the child was obscured by his low threshold of sensitivity . . . begin to uncover themselves and we find that areas of normal relationships between the child and elements of reality expand and increase" (May and May 1959, 441). Unlike most autism therapies today (though there is some similarity with Greenspan's "floor time" and Kaufman's "Son-Rise" program), which emphasize building skills or working directly on one's brain, the image of treatment here seems to be one of "discovery": follow the child's lead, arouse his interest, and draw him out from among the defenses he has erected (Bettelheim's "empty fortress" comes to mind).

A similar moral narrative of "discovery" is found in the description of a 1950s Canadian day nursery – again not particularly influenced by psychoanalysis – dedicated to the treatment of autistic children: "The therapist begins with a very permissive program, feeling her way, following the child's lead . . . She uses stimulation to draw him out from his haven of withdrawal, trying to get through to him through the use of whatever objects seem to give him at least some small satisfaction . . . When the therapist has been able to establish some degree of relationship with the child so that he trusts and depends on her, she begins to lead him into a wider environment and among other people" (Lovatt 1962, 105–6).[2] Note not only the image of therapy as drawing out from a "haven," but also the role of the therapist vis-à-vis the parents. The common principle of contemporary autism therapies is, as we shall see, establishing the parent as "co-therapist" (Schopler 1971), or as in Silverman's felicitous metaphor, "experimentalizing" parenting, turning the home into a "laboratory" (2004, 158). The common principle of these earlier autism therapies, however, seems to be precisely the opposite: turning the clinic into a substitute "home," establishing the therapist as a substitute parent, or let us be more blunt, as a substitute mother. Not because the mother is "cold" or inadequate – both Lovatt and May explicitly reject this interpretation – but because the family and mothering are the model upon which therapy and the therapeutic milieu are structured.

Therapy for mental illness, however technically or scientifically justified, is typically infused with certain moral values. This is because of the element of moral fault we noted in the Introduction: the refusal to recognize oneself as sick, the need for therapy to separate a symptom from an expression of rational personhood. The therapeutic movement thus constitutes a moral narrative. A walking therapy would be a story about restoration to nature; a water therapy would encode a story of purging and purification; underlying occupational therapy there would be a story about the ethical values of work (Foucault

[1954] 1987). Even when dealing with children and developmental disorders, therapies typically are organized around a certain moral narrative. These 1950s–1960s autism therapies are clearly no exception. The moral narrative that underlies them is best captured by the parable of "the castle," reported by Stephen Shore (2003, ix–x), a man with Asperger's disorder. He heard it at the James Jackson Autism Children's Center in Boston, which he attended as a child between 1962 and 1967, and the nursery school teachers in turn heard it from Boston psychiatrist Pierre Johannet. It tells of a young prince locked in a huge castle. You see him from the outside and you want to save him. You break down the gate and scale the ramparts in order to get to him, and yet when you reach him, you find him looking out the window, not at you. You must be careful not to touch or speak to him. You cannot get him out by yourself. You have to enter his world, gain his trust, so eventually he will acknowledge your existence and ask you to lead him out.

All the elements of therapy as "discovery" are here in this story: the main culprit (what the therapy seeks to correct) is the fortress or castle encircling the child. The castle is a symptom of autism, and therapy aims to penetrate it, discover the child within, and lead him out. But the castle is also an expression of the child's rational person-hood, a defense erected against the world. One cannot force the child to come out, as in some of the moral narratives of purging or mirror recognition reported by Foucault. The narrative of discovery is also one of self-discovery and self-healing. To be healed, the child must want to be healed, and the first step in the process is for the child to voluntarily acknowledge the presence of others.

A great deal of this moral narrative of therapy is still with us today, especially the emphasis on self-healing. The image of a child hidden behind the disorder can be found in "autistic autobiog-raphies" (Hacking 2008), in parental heroic rescue and recovery memoirs (Stacey 2003; Kephart, 1998; Seroussi, 2000; Adams, 2005; McCarthy, 2007), as well as in therapies such as Facilitated Communication and DIR-Floortime, which speak about the idea of drawing the child outside his world to our world. The most important contemporary autism therapies, however, either eschew the image of "discovery" (ABA, TEACCH), or superimpose upon it (DIR-Floortime, Sensory Integration Therapy) a constructivist image in which therapy lays down building blocks for development, activates and trains dormant faculties, or inculcates necessary skills. Lovaas is emphatic that "a 'little child' does not seem to be hiding on the inside, waiting for the opportunity to come out from his or her autistic shell, as so many theoretical formulations postulated and still do" (1993, 623). At their most constructivist, inverting the parable of the castle, many contemporary therapies aspire to construct a "prosthetic environment" (Holmes 1990). That is, they do not try to lead the child outside the castle but instead widen the perimeter of the ramparts and moat, so to speak.

The difference in moral narratives between autism therapies of the 1950s–1960s and current ones is most evident in their temporal structure or rhythm. As Shore himself says, the parable of the castle reflects a 1960s sensibility, when the children were treated with the utmost delicacy, and the single most distinctive common characteristic of today's autism therapies – the sense of urgency reflected in what Schopler (1971, 94) terms "the adult's non-specific impingement on the child" – is absent from it. Even contemporary therapies that aim to follow the child's lead and discover his or her potential for development (like DIR-Floortime) cease to resemble this 1960s sensibility when we examine their temporal organization. Time is cut up into minute "circles of communication." Each circle defines a short period of intensive engagement, and once it is "closed," another one should be opened right away (Greenspan 2006; Stacey 2003).[3] Parents and therapists alike report that the effort is exhausting. Put differently, if the temporal rhythm of 1950s–1960s autism therapies was modeled on the leisurely pace of artistic self-discovery, the time of play, contemporary autism therapies, by contrast, are fast-paced, intensive, requiring all of one's concentration and attention, hence are broken down into short durations. Their time is the time of work. "Do your work" is the constant injunction we heard at the school for autistic children where we observed.

While it is tempting to interpret the temporal structure of contemporary autism therapies as merely reflecting the pervasive belief in a fast-closing window of opportunities in early childhood, what Bruer (1999) calls "the myth of the first three years," it is probably a false conjecture. The thesis of the critical window dates back at least to the early 1950s and to the formulation of attachment theory, yet it seems to have had no effect on the pace of earlier autism therapies. Moreover, we witnessed the fast pace, the discrete trials, the injunction to "do your work" applied to severely autistic adolescents with fairly severe intellectual disabilities – that is, the imperative of the closing window was no longer in force. One must seek the origins of this temporal structure and the moral narrative it adjoins elsewhere, in therapies that did not originate to address autism.[4]

Working on the child's brain

So if contemporary autism therapies do not derive from earlier autism therapies, where did they originate? We would like to highlight two trajectories of development, one from treatments for "brain injury", the other from treatments for "emotional disturbance", though doubtless there are many more. What they all share is the fact that *they came from elsewhere* and involved giving a new rationale to very old or even mundane techniques. To be more precise, we can say these therapies came not from elsewhere but from *in-between*, or that they actively hybridized, "blurred," the boundary between illness and retardation. We shall see that they blurred other boundaries as well, most specifically the boundary between expert and layman. Therein lay the secret of their latter success, their "elective affinity" with deinstitutionalization: they represented no technical or scientific breakthrough, but they were socially innovative.

Let us begin with the first set of therapies that claimed to work directly on the child's brain, and with the history of the motor-perceptual therapy for brain-injured children with which we started this chapter. Alfred Strauss was a neurologist and student of Kurt Goldstein, who did seminal work on brain injury in adults. Strauss wanted to replicate this work in children. He became convinced that brain injury was quite distinct from genetically inherited mental retardation, and developed a test to diagnose it even in the absence of somatic evidence. The difference was on the level of "mental organization," especially with certain perceptual and motor skills. These children, he said, were not mentally retarded, but "mentally crippled," with the implication that they should be treated similarly to those who were physically crippled; they should be trained or given aids to cope with their disability. So he opened a school, which later became part of the network of the Cove schools for brain-injured children in Wisconsin and Illinois. Strauss served as president and director of the school network.

Thus far his work was strictly within the field of mental retardation, limited to the children who were referred to his schools. The quote opening this chapter, however, is from a book he wrote together with psychologist Newell Kephart, a book that sought to extend the category of "brain injury" to include children of normal intelligence, the whole population of "slow learners" in public schools. Poor achievement in school, they argued, could be traced to a certain syndrome of perceptual-motor difficulties, which constituted evidence of minimal brain injury, most likely prenatal. The injury could not be detected anatomically. It was not a "lesion." Yet it affected the whole organization of the brain and led to a characteristic pattern of hyperactivity, hyper-emotionalism, impulsiveness, distractibility, and perseveration. Their analysis contributed directly to the formation of the contemporary category of "learning disabilities," but it clearly tapped a large spectrum of ailments partially overlapping with today's autism spectrum disorders.[5] We recall Kanner's sigh of relief as diagnostic fashion abandoned autism and moved on to the "brain injured child" (Winzer 1993, 356–59; Strauss and Kephart 1955, ix, 29–42; Kanner 1965, 414). Our main point, however, is that this therapy developed on the margins of the field of mental retardation, focusing particularly on the indeterminate population previously named "borderline," "dullard," or "dull normal," and it sought to cut itself off from the rest of the mental retardation field by conceptualizing its object as an "injury" leading to "handicap" or "disability."

The therapy that Strauss, Kephart, and their co-worker Laura Lehtinen developed was premised on the idea that brain-injured children were particularly deficient in the faculty of perceptual integration. They perceived details but could not integrate them into wholes. Hence they were also highly distractible. They had difficulty in integrating input from several sensory modalities. So Kephart and his colleagues put headphones on them and they arranged the classroom, as we saw above, to minimize distractions. Or they would do precisely the opposite and stimulate several sensory modalities at once, using especially the tactile and kinesthetic senses to bind vision and audition together. The children were also clumsy because their motor and perceptual systems were not well integrated. The key to therapy was to jump-start and activate the closed-loop system, the "servo-mechanism" binding together motility and perception, for example through a program of visual perceptual stimulation which surprisingly improved motor skills, or motor stimulation to enhance perceptual skills (Strauss and Kephart 1955, 171–87).

The reader who is familiar with contemporary autism therapies must recognize in perceptual-motor therapy some of the main tenets, conceits, and devices of "Sensory Integration Therapy" (SIT), widely practiced today in work with autistic children. The similarity between the two therapies is indeed uncanny, yet it would be wrong to say with Silverman (2004, 158) that Strauss and Kephart's therapy "anticipated" SIT.[6] In fact, the two were contemporaneous, with surprisingly few points of contact. The originator of SIT, occupational therapist Jean Ayres ([1963] 1974, 63–64), cited as her main predecessors and inspiration not psychologists Strauss and Kephart but physical therapists working with patients with motor problems. Her first formulation of the theory and reasoning underlying SIT were in a 1958 article on "the visual-motor function" in the *American Journal of Occupational Therapy*. What we have here is not "anticipation," not a "forerunner" giving rise to mature successors, but simultaneous invention and parallel trajectories unfolding in distinct milieus, yet pulled closer together, modularized and eventually hybridized within the force field of deinstitutionalization.

When we talk about "invention," we do not mean to say that the therapies themselves were new, but that they were socially innovative. To begin with, it was a matter of giving a new rationale to old techniques. Ayres's therapeutic arsenal was borrowed and extremely low-tech – rubbing and brushing parts of the patient's body, swinging and spinning in a hammock-net, rolling on a big ball, riding prone on a wooden board scooter (Ayres 1972, 178–79). Some she borrowed from physical therapists; some harked as far back as Edouard Seguin and his methods in treating idiocy; some she improvised on the spot, based on similar principles. Oftentimes, she said, the treatment is one that occupational therapists have been using for many years (bilateral motor activity, for instance) but now "begins to take on new significance" (Ayres [1963] 1974, 60). As with Strauss and Kephart, the new significance to which she referred was the idea that these treatments directly affected the central nervous system through a feedback loop between movement and perception, helping to correct an "ontogenetically prior" motor-perceptual deficit which underlay children's more evident behavioral, emotional, or cognitive problems (Ayres [1963] 1974, 56–62). The HANDLE[7] therapy, developed independently by Judith Bluestone working with preschool children in the 1970s and 1980s in Israel, is premised on a similar principle. It rejects the specific "labels of ADD, Autism, Dyslexia, Hyperactivity, Tourette's Syndrome, and countless other dysfunctions and disorders" as "superficial" and claims to address "the root causes of disordered behaviors." The main idea is that "the body organizes the brain, and not the other way around." By working on motor coordination or sensory training, then, one is working directly on the brain, reversing the traumatic process.[8]

Like perceptual-motor therapy, sensory integration therapy did not originate in the context of treating autism, but on the margins of the field of mental retardation, beginning work in a traditional domain of occupational therapy – people with epilepsy, cerebral palsy, or "multiple handicaps," (both cognitive and physical). Yet it too sought to cut itself off from the rest of the mental retardation field by means of the idea of "sensory-motor dysfunction," traceable to prior injury and correctable with techniques that modified one's brain. Sensory integration therapy's first major field of application (as with perceptual-motor therapy) became "learning disabilities" and hyperactivity.

Inculcating habits and building skills

Working to modify the brain was only one version of the new rationale given to old techniques. These very same years also saw the beginnings of Ivar Lovaas's treatment program, later named "applied behavioral analysis" (ABA), arguably the most successful and wide-spread contemporary autism therapy. Lovaas never claimed to work on the brain. In the best tradition of behaviorism, he remained agnostic about what could not be measured as observable behavior. Yet he himself admitted that his techniques were very old, and traced their pedigree 200 years back to Jean Marc Gaspard Itard's work with the "wild boy of Aveyron" (Lovaas 1993, 621). The novelty lay not in the techniques themselves, but in their application to children who were previously deemed "emotionally disturbed," and the idea that these children could be treated by unlearning bad habits and acquiring good ones, thus building competencies or skills they previously lacked. These competencies did not so much *underlay* emotional, behavioral, and cognitive development, as in the SIT or perceptual-motor therapy model, but formed a visible and objective *substitute* for dysfunctional behaviors, whose origin in some underlying deficit remained "hypothetical" (Lovaas 1981, x).

This approach to emotional disturbance was pioneered, before Lovaas, by "Project Re-Ed," the brainchild of psychologist Nicholas Hobbs. In the 1950s, Hobbs, who went on to become president of the American Psychological Association in 1966, became disenchanted with "insight psychotherapy." He thought it was ineffective, having nothing to do with "life as it is lived." More damning still was the fact that it was an extremely costly and inefficient way to deliver mental health services, since too few therapists were trained, and typically they did not want to work with the neediest populations. He was much more impressed with an invention originating in Vichy France that went on to become institutionalized in postwar France and Canada. To deal with the problem of war-uprooted children, the French created the new professional role of *éducateur spécialisé* with relatively fast three-year training in *psycho-pédagogie*. Children with various emotional problems were not hospitalized, but re-educated in short-term residential schools by paraprofessionals and special education teachers with the psychiatrists serving as consultants.[9] It is significant that Hobbs cited this French invention, and not the American discipline of special education, as his inspiration, probably because he was seeking to break the boundary between special education and psychotherapy (Hobbs 1979, 3–5).

He obtained funding from the National Institute of Mental Health to begin a demonstration project at Cumberland House in Peabody College, Tennessee. The point was precisely to show that emotionally disturbed children were better served in an educational setting than in a psychiatric hospital. The project started with children between 6 and 12 years old, but later was extended to include children younger than 5 years old. "Emotional disturbance" was a special-education category, a term inherited from child guidance. While it still reflected a certain reluctance to ascribe mental illness to children, within the classification system of special education "emotional disturbance" contrasted with learning disabilities as mental illness did with retardation in the classification system of psychiatry. The differentiating criterion for emotional disturbance was typically the presence of behavior problems, being "incorrigible," evidence for the origins of this category in child guidance's concern with detecting and preventing pre-delinquency. Often the faultline lay, and still does, along racial and class lines (Kugelmass 1987). So with Project Re-Ed, Hobbs was trying to take a category that belonged on the margins of the realm of illness and medicine[10] – and this was especially true for the category of "severe emotional disturbance" (SED), which included autism and childhood schizophrenia – and treat it instead with the tools proper to the field of special education of the mentally retarded. It was education rather than medicine; training rather than cure. Like Lovaas, Hobbs was profoundly agnostic about the ultimate source of the children's behavior problems – though his general approach was "ecological," attributing a great deal of causative power to the environment – and aimed to do away with diagnostic categories. The group treated at Project Re-Ed included children who were violent, therefore, as well as others referred because of developmental delay and learning disabilities. Nonetheless, lest the reader doubt the relevance of Project Re-Ed for the history of autism therapies, we quote Hobbs himself to the effect that "early experimental work at Cumberland house preceded routine programming for autistic children in a number of Re-Ed schools today" (Winzer 1993, 339–50; Hobbs 1979, 4, 17; Kugelmass 1987, 95, 110–12).

The therapy practiced at Project Re-Ed reflected a "preference . . . for a vocabulary of everyday life over a vocabulary of pathology, [and] for the idiom of education" (Hobbs 1979, 6). This meant that instead of diagnosing the child as "ill" and striving for the "extravagant" goal of cure, therapy adhered to a "competence model," defining its goal as the achievement of competence in matters large and small. Compare this approach with Lovaas's rejection of the "disease model" of autism. Lovaas, in fact, doubted whether there "exist[s] a disease called autism," and explained that the therapy he developed was rather "an expertise in dealing with different kinds of behaviors" common to all "children with developmental disorders." "The programs developed to teach autistic children to dress, eat, toilet themselves, talk, or better manage their tantrums, etc., were immediately useful for retarded children, and vice versa" (Lovaas 1979, 321). While Project Re-Ed did not originally utilize behavior modification techniques, the affinities between the two were strong and clear, and in 1965 behavior modification was introduced and credited with "enriching" the process of re-education, making it more precise (Hobbs 1979, 6–16, 19–21; Lovaas 1979, 317, 321–22).

Blurring the boundary between expert and layman

Contemporary autism therapies, therefore, did not begin specifically as therapies for autism. They began on the margins of either mental illness or retardation and moved outward to blur the boundaries between the two, and to create an interstitial and hybrid space where they could operate more freely, outside the jurisdictions of psychiatry and special education. This strategy of expansion relied on three tactical innovations: downscaling, outsourcing, and modularization.

Downscaling, or hands-on

The anthropologist Roy Richard Grinker (2007) noted wryly that all autism therapies are one or another version of the same basic principle – "being in your child's face." This is the same as Schopler's recommendation of "non-specific impingement on the child." Grinker probably meant this as a putdown, but we do not think it should be. This simple principle of "being in [the] child's face" contained within it several far-reaching innovations. First, it marked a direct negation of the more "permissive" and accepting attitude of earlier autism therapies, as captured by the parable of the Castle. Instead of the

153

leisurely pace required to discover the child underneath the disease, the new therapies identify as their object the child's inability to communicate and set out to rectify it by intensifying all forms of interaction (bodily and verbally) (Rutter and Sussenwein 1971, 380).

Second, the simplicity that invited Grinker's derision was in fact a downscaling move that permitted the new therapies to maneuver, so to speak, "under" psychiatry's jurisdiction. Take behavior modification: we do not study or treat "autism," says Lovaas (1977, 320), and the quotation marks are his, since for him autism as a disease, that is, the object of psychiatry, was purely "hypothetical," speculative. Instead, he says, we study and treat the concrete behaviors of autistic children. We take them "apart into smaller units (self-destruction, imitation, vocalizations, units of grammar, labeling, etc.)" so we can learn how to modify each one separately. Similarly, in sensory integration therapy or in perceptual motor therapy the claim is that one is dealing not with autism, but with dysfunction of very basic postural or vestibular or perceptual mechanisms that serve as building blocks for cognitive and psychic growth. Thus, like Lovaas, the occupational therapist is burrowing under psychiatry, so to speak, undermining its object and making it dispensable. Through a set of very simple interactions (Ayres speaks of the child "interacting with gravity") – brushing, rubbing, spinning in a hammock, riding prone on a wooden board – one is seeking to stimulate an "inner-directed adaptive response" and "increasing neural organization" which would eventually manifest themselves at the psychic level. Ayres (1972, 177–81) reported that an autistic girl thus treated for five months showed less bizarre fantasies, more appropriate pretend play, and better engagement with people. Simple physical interventions had results at the cognitive and emotional level at which psychotherapy was couched. So to practice therapy and to treat autism one did not need sophisticated technology, nor license to prescribe medicines, nor deep psychodynamic insight. Needed were only a few simple toys, patience, dogged determination, and the bodily skills necessary to engage a recalcitrant person in one-on-one interaction with a mixture of warmth and firmness.

Indeed, "being in [the] child's face" is quite literally hands-on. It is highly embodied work, about the body and done with the body, and it involves a great deal of touching. ABA, as developed by Lovaas, requires the therapist to physically "prompt" each new learning sequence by holding her hand over the child's hand, or in some versions by physically moving his lips with her hands. The prompts are supposed to be "faded out" gradually, but very often they cannot be.

ABA becomes then a form of "joint embodiment" in which the therapist, most often the parent, becomes a prosthetic device, an extension of the child's body, facilitating the child's communication and interaction with the social world.

Lovaas (1993, 621), in fact, describes the discovery of the utility of spanking (or as he calls it, "contingent aversives") as a major breakthrough in the development of ABA, and gives quite detailed instructions about how to correctly administer it, or how to use just the right amount of physical force to make a child complete his task (Lovaas 1981, 16–18). The TEACCH program, as well, instructed therapists in "how to give him a swat on the behind to clarify communication" (Schopler and Reichler 1971, 94).

This hands-on approach was not limited to the behavioral modification therapies. In the 1960s, Jean Ayres led a revolution in occupational therapy, upgrading it from the supervised teaching of handicrafts to a neuro-physiological approach for treatment of sensory-motor and cognitive problems. But she did so also through a certain downscaling, by removing the taboo on touching the patient's body, about which many occupational therapists felt strongly because it distinguished their expertise from that of physical therapists (Ayres 1974, viii, 50, 66–67, 77–81). Instead of attempting to emulate brainy psychiatry with its increasing resistance to physical propinquity to its patients, the new therapies emulated physical therapists and became expert on spanking. Instead of seeking to establish social distance, on the professional model, the new therapies sought to draw closer to their patients and clients.

Outsourcing

Perhaps the most important innovation of the new therapies, their most distinctive characteristic, was their willingness to forgo any claims to jurisdictional monopoly, and their active attempt to pluralize the relations of expertise and to blur the boundary between expert and layman. They outsourced therapy to paraprofessionals, parents, sometimes even patients themselves. Partly this was, as we noted earlier, a response to the crisis of psychiatry. Certainly this was Hobbs's motivation. But with most of the other therapies this tendency derived from more local constraints: first, their marginal status that prompted them to search for allies; and second, the downscaling maneuver they performed in order to burrow under psychiatry, which committed them to a highly intensive economy of effort. Their techniques were simple but demanded a massive commitment of time, which meant that they could only develop through an alliance between therapists and parents, who became semi-professionals. Correspondingly, the new therapies came packaged together with meticulous systems of recordkeeping and testing, which turned the home into a laboratory. These were some of the reasons why deinstitutionalization was not simply a *coup d'état*, not simply the unseating of psychiatry by some other profession that took its place. It was a wholesale rearrangement of the relations of expertise, involving a downward shift of levels – this outsourcing of therapeutic work to paraprofessionals and parents – as well as an upward shift – connected with the new systems of recordkeeping and testing that turned therapies into modular components of multifaceted treatment programs. From the point of view of administrators, once therapies were all recorded and counted in the same way, very heterogeneous approaches oriented to very different objects could all be combined on the same register as "items of autistic behavior."

The history of perceptual-motor therapy is instructive in this respect. For a short while, it was limited to the few schools opened by Strauss. The crucial innovation came in the late 1950s, when Strauss's co-worker Newell Kephart began a summer school for brain-injured children and their parents at Purdue University. Parents, he said, will be "primary coordinators of and contributors to the child's development and learning" (Silverman 2004, 158; Winzer 1993, 356–59). With this move, Kephart stepped outside the bounds of the institutional matrix of mental retardation; he also outsourced the practice of therapy to parents, content himself with the role of consultant. Many contemporary autism therapeutic programs – TEACCH, RDI[11] – have adopted the same format. Contrary to what we were taught to expect by the sociology of professions – that experts would seek to create a monopoly over their jurisdiction (Abbot 1988; Friedson 1986) – Kephart opted for a strategy of "generosity" (Rose 1992), maximizing not *expert* control but the extent and reach of a particular form of *expertise*. Not only did it mean that parents were empowered as therapists, but it also turned the therapy into something modular, something that parents could practice at home, or institutions pick up as one component of comprehensive treatment programs, something that could be transmitted relatively intact along semiformal networks of information among parents, activists, and educators. It thus permitted the therapy to spread to autism as well.

Rosalind Oppenheim, mother of an autistic child, attended the summer school in the late 1950s, trained herself to use Kephart's methods, and then wrote an article crediting him with "saving" her child. Later, she opened her own school. Amy Lettick, another mother of an autistic child, read the article, corresponded with Oppenheim, and went to the summer school herself. She then opened a school in Connecticut – Benhaven – for autistic children using some of what she learned from Kephart. Perceptual-motor therapy was not the principal means of treatment at Benhaven. By Lettick's testimony, they used anything that worked: direct teaching, behavior modification, sign language, music and auditory therapy, speech therapy, physical therapy, force, even tying two children together with a rope to enhance "relatedness." Having been outsourced to parents, perceptual-motor therapy could become one modular component in a comprehensive treatment program. Lettick kept corresponding with Oppenheim and Kephart, soliciting their advice, and the latter was invited to serve on Benhaven's board (Silverman 2004; Lettick 1979, 11–18, 43–47).

This modularity, even eclecticism, has become a hallmark of contemporary autism treatment. In our interviews and our trolling of the web, we met many parents of autistic children who are "therapy omnivores." They said they were using a "very eclectic" approach; some said they use and combine "whatever works," finances and time being the only limits. Recent surveys found parents of autistic children use about 111 different treatments (Green 2006). In fact, we *never* met an autistic child – in the U.S., in South Africa, Turkey or in Israel – who was receiving just one kind of therapy. It would be easy to paint a picture of the parents as desperate, wacky, or simply exploited by therapists, but this would be to miss the big picture: that modularity and eclecticism are qualities of the social space carved out by autism therapies, not the personal qualities of agents who find themselves within it.

Project Re-Ed also pioneered the extensive outsourcing of therapy to paraprofessionals, and even parents. The staff was composed of teacher-counselors with training in remedial education and behavior management, while psychologists, social workers, and special educators played the role of consultants: "We think it extravagant to use them in direct work with children when their talents can be multiplied many times over by re-conceptualizing their role as knowledge-sharers, as advisers, as enablers of other highly talented people" (Hobbs 1979, 9). When Project Re-Ed was extended into a "regional intervention program," it incorporated training for a group of mothers in how "to deal effectively with behavioral and developmental disorders of their children." Then it recruited these same mothers to train other mothers. Over time, the project developed the role of "liaison-teacher counselor" who works with the family and significant others, getting them to take some responsibility for the child's training (Hobbs 1979, 7–16, 27).

The TEACCH program at the University of North Carolina similarly involved parents as "co-therapists," while the professionals played the role of consultants. Parents came twice a week with the child for a 45-minute session in which they consulted with the therapist or watched a therapist's demonstration, but the bulk of therapeutic work was done at home by the parents. In fact, the program aimed explicitly to blur the boundary between expert and layman, to remove the "mystique and unfounded authority" of the therapist. Observing the therapist at work, the parents could see him or her fail. They could thus become less self-critical and more capable. They were encouraged to compete with the therapist, see who could do better, to become "experts on their own autistic child" (Schopler and Reichler 1971, 93). Schopler reported that "many parents, especially mothers, have developed a degree of objectivity, investment and skill found only in top-notch teachers . . . they are . . . frequently the most effective developmental agents for their children." Many in fact became teachers, volunteers, and advocates. Paraprofessionals, as well, were "conducting important therapeutic interventions" (Schopler and Reichler 1971, 92–94, 98–100).

In his retrospective account of the development of ABA, Lovaas (1993, 622–28; see also Silverman 2004, 171–90) calls parents his "colleagues" and declares that "there are no 'experts' in this field." There were several reasons Lovaas turned to parents and began to involve them massively in the conduct of therapy. One reason was that he was using aversives – spanking, shouting, time-outs – and thought it wise to forestall opposition by keeping the clinic open to everybody and involving the parents. Another reason was the problem of generalization: whatever the children learned at the clinic did not transfer elsewhere. So he decided that they should be trained in their natural surroundings, at their parents' houses. He thereby discovered that parents can be skilled teachers of their children and the best allies one could have to maintain the intensive regime of treatment he thought necessary. By the same means he also transformed behavior modification from a limited remedial technique to a whole way of life, an around-the-clock regime that reorders relations among family members at home.[12]

But probably the most important reason for Lovaas's recruitment of parents was the hostility and lack of cooperation he encountered in dealing with his colleagues, other psychologists and psychiatrists.

Bettelheim said that ABA was harmful to children, like lobotomy. Stanley Greenspan, the developer of Floortime therapy, said that ABA ignores the child's needs and in fact makes behavior even more stereotyped. At one point, Lovaas was even accused by his colleagues at UCLA of fabricating his results. Parents, on the other hand, were his mainstay. Bernard Rimland came to visit Lovaas's lab in 1964 to see if Lovaas could help his son. He liked what he saw, and he and several other parents of autistic children took Lovaas out to dinner where they talked strategy: "It was clear to both Rimland and me that should the parents break the stranglehold exercised by psychodynamic therapists over treatment, it could be achieved only through joint action" (Lovaas 1993, 627).

Both sides had much to gain from the alliance. Lovaas offered parents boundless intensity and pragmatism. Most other therapies, as we saw, waited for the child to "come out of his shell." This was true whether justified in psychodynamic terms, or in terms of finding a creative outlet gratifying for the child (May and May 1959, 441), or in developmentalist terms, as in sensory integration and perceptual-motor therapy, which expected language and communication to follow after the more basic postural and perceptual skills were acquired. Lovaas, on the other hand, was not willing to wait. The hypothesis with which he began his interest in autism was that a child's own verbal response could serve as discriminative stimuli to control his nonverbal behavior. Put in plain language, if you can speak, you gain more control over your behavior. That is why he wanted to work with autistic children. Autistic children who never spoke before he began working with them would not have an "unknown reinforcement history." Hence, he concentrated on teaching them to speak or communicate by whatever means, even in sequences that were counterintuitive from a developmentalist point of view, such as teaching children who never spoke how to read and write. The first thing he did was to get the children to respond to a verbal prompt, from which he built some simple linguistic skills. Not growth, but communication, dictated the sequence of therapy. This pragmatism obviously made his work very appealing to parents. Special education teachers, as well, were eager to receive training in ABA, probably for similar reasons. Though there were always tensions about the use of aversives, NSAC picked up ABA and promoted it aggressively (Lovaas 1993, 627; Silverman 2004, 178–81). We will further analyze the parents' reasons for this alliance in the next chapter.

Lovaas obviously needed parents to disseminate word about his work, since his colleagues were hostile, and as he put it, "you do not get tenure" doing this type of intensive, uninspiring, theoretically dull work. More important, he developed the principles of ABA working with only one subject, an autistic girl. As he came to appreciate the amount of work and persistence involved, it became clear that it would be impossible to replicate what he managed to achieve in his laboratory without a whole army of paraprofessionals. To transform ABA from a laboratory technique to a viable intervention required finding this army and training it, something that Lovaas did not yet know how to do. What he did know was that the very idea of treatment had to change. Treatment should no longer be addressed to some key deficit, which once fixed will generate change across a large number of behaviors, because in autism no such generalization takes place. One needs to intervene on all behaviors, in all environments, with the help of all significant persons, all waking hours, for a good part of one's life. There are not enough professionals to deliver this. "This means that we will have to give away our professional skills to lay people, and the sooner the better" (Lovaas 1993, 628; Silverman 2004, 190).[13] Thus, ABA was ready to be modularized, to become one set of skills at the command of parents and paraprofessionals taking an experimental and syncretic approach, ready to adopt, as in Benhaven, "whatever works."

Modularization

By modularization we mean two complementary movements. First, therapies needed to be unmoored from their local contexts in the laboratory or the residential school. This was achieved through downscaling, outsourcing and repositioning the expert as consultant. Second, a device had to be found that could integrate and link the therapeutic work now undertaken in the family, the day school or the day nursery, the community clinic – in scattered, sporadic, local, and only weakly bounded contexts characteristic of the new institutional matrix. This was typically achieved by adopting a system of observation, recording, planning, reporting, monitoring, and testing that bound the various therapies together as components of a comprehensive treatment program, and measured their input on a common scale of explicitly defined and precise goals.[14]

This system was variously called "precision teaching" or "precision programming," after the methods developed by Ogden Lindsley, a student of B. F. Skinner. Essentially, it was a device for recording and charting behaviors in a way that permitted measurement of the effectiveness of any teaching technique. At Project Re-Ed, "what they do might best be called precision programming": identify the problem; decide on means to effect change; specify the outcomes sought "preferably in behaviors that can be counted, measured or consensually validated"; assign responsibility for carrying out the plan by a target date; periodically evaluate progress and keep everybody informed of goals, means and outcome (Hobbs 1979, 15–16).

At Benhaven, Lettick adopted a version of precision teaching after consulting Lindsey. The teachers would do about 1,800 chartings of behavior a week. It was completely modular, since teachers had freedom to choose whatever technique they deemed suitable, as long as the results could be charted and measured. It anticipated the system of IEPs made mandatory in U.S. special education in the mid-1970s. Lettick reports that Benhaven did not need to adapt when the legislation was passed, because they were already practicing a superior form of goal setting, charting, and reporting. If outsourcing transformed treatment into endless training and therapy into a whole way of life, as happened with ABA, modularization by precision teaching transformed training into a system of testing. With everything measured and counted, every round of training was also a test for both student and teacher, so that, as Lettick observed, "there is some form of testing going on almost at all times" (Lettick 1979, 145–49). No child was left behind. As Silverman (2004, 158) says, what happened from the late 1950s to the early 1970s was the "experimentalization of [special] education," or more precisely downscaling, outsourcing, and modularization permitted to replicate the laboratory experiment on a larger scale.

North Carolina's TEACCH program was similarly modularized. It combined methods of special education together with operant conditioning,[15] perceptual-motor therapy, physical and occupational therapy – in other words, whatever worked. Any problem or skill was broken into manageable parts and then taught piecemeal, with daily logs tracking change and progress. Goals were predefined, in fact, for both parents and children – increasing parents' involvement was a goal of the program, one way it could measure its success or failure – and measurement was continuous (Schopler and Reichler 1971, 95–100). In the U.K., Rutter's treatment program was similarly outsourced and modularized (Rutter and Sussenwein 1971).

The space between fields

Summing up the state of the therapeutic art in 1983, Rutter (1983, 210–11) admitted that the search for medical treatments for autism had led nowhere. The main advance was the rise of educational and behavioral methods of treatment that have replaced insight psychotherapy. The new therapies changed the site of treatment from the hospital and the laboratory to the school and the home, and involved parents as co-therapists. They have broadened therapeutic goals and were extended to ever younger children, no doubt due to deinstitutionalization (see also Rutter 1971, 376), yet none of them could significantly undo severe initial handicaps of intelligence and language (Oppenheim, as well, told Lettick that perceptual-motor therapy "has nothing to do with the basic problem," that is, autism [Silverman 2004]) and in general the claims of therapy enthusiasts far exceeded what could in fact be accomplished. Fifteen years later, this was still the conclusion of a comprehensive assessment of the efficacy of autism therapies (Howlin 1997).

The success and spread of the new therapies, therefore, cannot be attributed simply to their technical superiority. They did not "cure" autism, nor did they claim to do so – in fact, the appeal of ABA and similar techniques in many respects lay precisely in *not* claiming to cure autism. One could say that they were "better" than earlier therapies, precisely in the sense that by not claiming to cure autism they freed themselves to offer parents pragmatic help with simple mundane goals of everyday functioning. This is no doubt true, but requires one to take into account deinstitutionalization and the change in the institutional matrix. Earlier autism therapies did not need to offer such pragmatic help because they existed within a custodial institutional matrix meant to relieve parents of such needs altogether. Long into deinstitutionalization, parents of autistic children continued to complain about the lack of residential custodial institutions and to lobby for their creation and funding (Sullivan 1981). They were not bad or unfeeling parents. No doubt, ABA is the most effective way to teach some of the basics without which life with a disabled child could be hell. But even with it life is still hard, incredibly so, and ABA outsourced much of its management to the parents. On purely pragmatic grounds, it is not clear whether the bargain was worth it, and certainly one cannot explain the success of ABA or other therapies simply in these terms. The success and spread of the new therapies had just as much to do with their social innovation and their affinity with the new institutional matrix of early intervention and community treatment.

Deinstitutionalization opened up a vast space between the fields of medicine/psychiatry and special education. It was a space of opportunity and entrepreneurship where it was possible to do things one could not do before, to combine things one had to keep separate if one was within the orbit of psychiatry or special education. First, it became possible to create new objects of discourse and intervention – indeed, a whole new domain of similarly constituted objects. Normalization blurred the distinction between mental illness and mental retardation and reconfigured the space between them as an open-ended terrain of "developmental disabilities." For a short while, the advocates for the mentally retarded sought to occupy the whole of this space and act as gatekeepers, positioning mental retardation as the prototypical developmental disability. Autism advocates and parents resisted their exclusion from the domain of developmental disabilities, and eventually prevailed. All the while, however, below the radar of the lobbyists and legislative politics, therapies such as ABA or perceptual-motor therapy, and comprehensive treatment programs such as TEACCH, were undermining the viability of a distinction between mental retardation and autism-qua-illness, inscribing them on the same register, so to speak, and thus preparing the ground for autism to become a spectrum and to begin to edge out mental retardation.

Second, the barriers to entry into this space in terms of credentials, licensing, and types of expertise were radically lowered, and it became possible to create new assemblages of expertise. The 1973 "Bill of Rights for the Mentally Retarded" sponsored by Sen. Jennings Randolph and Sen. Edward Kennedy made no mention of psychiatry among the services that should be available to the residents of institutions for the mentally retarded, nor did it require that the chief executive officer of the facility be a psychiatrist. By comparison, the legislation explicitly required that the staff of such facilities would include persons capable of providing special education, music, art or dance therapy, occupational therapy, physical therapy, speech pathology, psychological testing, and behavioral therapy. Yet, the Senate Committee was not too picky about the credentials of the therapists. When it came to occupational therapy, for example, the legislation permitted that specific credentials were not required of the provider. A physical therapist, a psychologist, or a special education teacher could do the work of an occupational therapist just as well.[16]

Outside the institution, in the community centers or in special education, as one could imagine, the regulation over the specific credentials of providers and therapists was even less stringent, and the competition much fiercer. To use the example of occupational therapy once more, leaders of the profession were warning that with the move to the community, a major area of their professional jurisdiction, their work with the mentally ill or mentally retarded, would "cease to exist because other professions are rapidly absorbing our body of knowledge, they appear to the public to be offering the same services that we offer and they are selling their programs to other professionals and the public more effectively than we are" (Woodside 1971). The threat felt by occupational therapists was due to the lower barriers to entry as well as the modularity and pragmatism of therapies that permitted unorthodox combinations and borrowings between types of expertise: "Whatever works" was operative here too. A program such as TEACCH recruited its staff from education, psychiatry, psychology, and social work, but the main criterion for selection was not "professional identity . . . but skill in teaching autistic children and advising their parents." They were supposed to be well-versed in methods of direct teaching, behavior modification, and perceptual-motor therapy, as well as more traditional psychological counseling (Schopler and Reichler 1971, 92). Speech therapists would work together with physical therapists to devise programs designed to improve relatedness and language skills through gross motor training or gym games. A speech therapist introduced sign language with great success, a music therapist sought to elicit speech from mute children, and so on (Lettick 1979, 33–37, 78–80).

Deinstitutionalization opened up a potential space between fields, but the distinctive character of this space and the fact that it has remained open for as long as it has are due to the influx of the new therapies into it and the principle of hybridization they constantly activate. On one side, this space is bounded by the system of special education, yet it permits the position of the educator to be occupied by altogether different agents – parents, speech therapists, psychologists, even psychiatrists. On the other side, it is bounded by established medicine and psychiatry, yet the therapeutic function, the discourse of "cure," is taken up by occupational therapists, or even by parents who establish themselves as quasi-medical experts (such as Rimland). Hence the power and attraction of the category of autism; hence the reason the new therapies began to define themselves more and more as therapies for autism, since among all developmental disabilities it offered the most extensive scope for the art of therapeutic combination. ABA improved certain behaviors of autistic children – so principles of behavior modification were incorporated in Rutter's treatment program, in TEACCH, or in Benhaven; SIT seemed to have a calming, "organizing" effect – so most schools and centers for autistic children incorporated "sensory gyms" into their programming; visual schedules, social stories and picture exchange systems improved communication and made the environment more predictable for autistic children – *everybody* has them now (Green 2006).

Downscaling, outsourcing, and modularization made sure that such combinations were relatively easy, and autism's balancing act between illness and retardation significantly reduced the rigidities specific to either the medical treatment of illness or the special education of the mentally retarded. By the same token, the influx of new therapies and the assembly of new forms of expertise loosened autism further from its moorings in either mental illness or retardation, turned it more and more protean, more and more a "free-floating signifier" sanctioning therapeutic creativity, improvisation, and hybridization.

Perhaps the mythical Proteus, the shape-shifter subdued by Menelaus, is not the right metaphor with which to represent the autistic spectrum. Mickey Mouse might be a better candidate. The Soviet filmmaker Sergei Eisenstein, watching early Disney cartoons, was fascinated by the way Mickey Mouse's hands might mimic a musical score: they would stretch well beyond the limits of their normal representation in unison with a high note. He observed how the neck of a surprised horse might extend to implausible lengths. He called this dynamic quality of Disney images "plasmaticness." Plasmaticness is not Protean shape-shifting, since the transformation is always a matter of stretching (or contracting) lines and shapes already traced. The power and attractiveness of plasmatic images resides precisely in the combination of continuity and utter heterogeneity. Eisenstein's neologism seems to us to capture what autism has become in the space between fields. The therapies trace a line of continuity – the so-called "spectrum" – which nonetheless attains substantial freedom from any stable form. It brings together children who are overly sensitive to certain stimuli and those who are undersensitive, the mute together with the verbose, the withdrawn together with the clingy. The secret of this plasmatic quality, we argue, lies in the relative openness of the space between fields, as autism morphed like Mickey's hands in harmony with whatever particular therapeutic tune it encountered.

This openness, however, would have remained inert if, apart from the lowering of barriers to entry by deinstitutionalization, there were not also high potential profits to be realized by treating developmental disabilities and autism more specifically. Such profits were monetary, but also symbolic, in that marginal occupations got upgraded in prestige. Lettick (1979, 30–37) observed that deinstitutionalization was propelling "towns to develop classes for lesser handicapped children within their own school system," leading to increased demand for special education teachers; speech, occupational and other therapists;

and educational psychologists. By the same token this meant that more schools like Benhaven were needed in order to absorb the more severely handicapped or more disruptive children.

Securing these potential profits depended on striking a coalition with parents. Deinstitutionalization created enormous new challenges for parents, who were now expected to care for their young disabled children at home. Anything less than that was understood as abdicating one's moral responsibility. Books and movies like *The Memory Keeper's Daughter* have driven this point home all too well. Yet deinstitutionalization also empowered parents, vindicated their struggle against the medical establishment. They were now invited to become co-therapists and celebrated as "experts on their own children." Their presence in IEP meetings was now mandatory, and at least some could parlay it into real voice and influence on the process of categorization, assignment and treatment. When the psychiatrist left the field, his mantle did not descend on anybody else. Nobody stepped forth to claim jurisdiction over the diagnosis of social destiny. Instead, the coalition between therapists and parents depended on postponing the pronouncement into an indefinite future, and internalizing the prognostic function – now euphemized as "assessment" – into therapeutic practice. In return, parents became the main – and formidable – champions of therapies that without their support would have disappeared since they were completely marginal, minor and unprofitable within the academic or scientific or special-education spheres. NSAC's campaign in favor of ABA is only the most outstanding and successful example of these coalitions. We turn now, in the next chapter, to the story of these parents' rise from obscurity and stigma to the position of experts.

— 8 —

BERNARD RIMLAND AND THE FORMATION OF NSAC

Within a week of publishing his landmark book, *Infantile Autism*, Bernard Rimland began receiving letters from parents. The letters contained pleas for help with severely afflicted autistic and psychotic children as well as completed E-1 checklists (Rimland 1964, 1971). The checklist was published as an insert in Rimland's book and was to be completed by parents and then sent to him. Rimland was excited about the enthusiastic response, but bewildered about what to do next. He had very little to offer parents in return but his sympathy, since the thrust of his analysis in the book was to refute the psychogenic hypothesis and establish autism as a neurological disorder, for which, however, there were no known medical interventions. At this critical moment, he heard talk about O. Ivar Lovaas, a behavioral psychologist at UCLA, who was developing a method for the treatment of autistic children. Within weeks he made the trip from San Diego to meet Lovaas. He was invited to observe Lovaas at work with patients or in training sessions with therapists and students. He spoke with some of the patients. Utterly impressed with what he saw, Rimland underwent something like a conversion experience. Returning home, he tried the method on his own autistic son, Mark – and his domestic experimenting bore instant, if modest, success. Further, Rimland brought Lovaas along with him to a dinner with local parents with whom he had corresponded, thereby forging a connection between the researcher and the parents and paving the way for Lovaas, a few years later, to incorporate parents into the therapeutic process (Rimland 1972; Lovaas 1971).

While not a lone pioneer, Rimland is nevertheless especially significant because of his central position in a nascent parent movement. Through the notoriety of his book, he became the central node through which parents from across the country, dissatisfied with available services (or lack thereof), could be connected and organized. Lovaas was being inundated with letters from parents, as was Rosalind Oppenheim, a mother who in the summer of 1961 published an article in the *Saturday Evening Post* titled "They Said Our Son Was Hopeless," describing her success in treating her autistic son (Silverman 2004; Lane 2008). Both passed the letters along to Rimland, who added the names to his by now very long list. In 1965, a number of television and news outlets ran features on autism and autism treatment, including a famous *Life* magazine feature introducing Lovaas's work to a popular audience (Moser and Grant 1965). During this time, Ruth Christ Sullivan saw a television special on autism and, recognizing characteristics of her son Joe, contacted the father featured on the show, New York playwright Robert Crean, who put her in touch with Rimland (Warren 1984, 102). She and Rimland then decided to organize a meeting of parents and began contacting names on Rimland's list. To the emerging alliance between Rimland and Lovaas, Sullivan brought another set of skills that proved indispensable. She cut her teeth lobbying for the League of Women Voters and knew a thing or two about creating an effective lobbying and advocacy outfit (Park 1971a). The two men, in fact, were soon joined by a formidable cadre of women activists who had already accumulated experience in the women's rights movement.[1] The founding meeting of the National Society for Autistic Children (NSAC) took place in Teaneck, New Jersey, on November 16, 1965 (Warren 1984 101–3; Lane 2008). Both the name and later the puzzle-piece logo were borrowed from the British Society, founded three years prior by Lorna Wing – with whom Rimland corresponded – and other parents (Warren 1984, 102).

Not much else, however, was borrowed from the British Society. At its founding, the U.K. organization made a strategic choice to model itself after the earlier Spastics' Society, and not to follow in the footsteps of the National Society for Mentally Handicapped Children (NSMHC). The choice was between acting primarily as a lobbying and pressure group, like the NSMHC, or to become a service provider, like the Spastics' Society. At its founding, the British NSAC put as the first aim on their agenda "to provide and promote a day and residential centre for the treatment and education of autistic or psychotic children" (Allison 1997). The American NSAC, on the other hand, made a point of not becoming a service provider. From the beginning, it organized itself as "a national self-help group, not an organization of people who support a service delivery system"

(Warren 1984, 105).[2] The lobbying experience of Sullivan and her colleagues probably played a role in this decision, but it must also have been inspired by the example of NARC, which shunned service provision and attempted to instruct state ARCs to do the same. By 1965, the example of NARC, which was fast becoming one of the most effective national lobbying organizations, must have been decisive. This was a crucial decision, and it explains why we chose in this book to tell the history of the American NSAC and not the earlier British organization. Choosing to avoid service provision and concentrate on advocacy meant that NSAC was poised to go along with deinstitutionalization and utilize the opportunities it opened up. As we saw earlier, when parents' organizations provided services and managed residential institutions, they typically opposed deinstitutionalization. Knowing how intense and acrimonious debates about deinstitutionalization were within NSAC in the 1970s, we know that NSAC's willingness to go along with it was by no means a foregone conclusion (Sullivan 1981). Hence the importance of its difference from the British society.

At the founding meeting in 1965, Rimland acted as chairperson.[3] He passed out a list of things parents could do with their children (Warren 1984, 102). He also gave a speech based on his observations of Lovaas and his own reading of the behavioral literature, titled "Operant Conditioning: Breakthroughs in the Treatment of Mentally Ill Children." "It was intended to be, and succeeded in being, a summons to parents to come forward and insist upon the abandonment of Freudian theory and the adoption of a totally new and different concept in the treatment of autistic-type children" (Rimland 1972, 573). Most important in this context, Rimland noted that operant conditioning was a "technique that parents could learn with demonstrable success" (Rimland 1972, 573).[4]

We have dwelled at some length on the story of NSAC's founding and the role Rimland played in it because it contains all the necessary ingredients for the argument of this chapter. What was NSAC? How do we understand the role it played in the history of autism? Sociologists typically approach a question like this from a "political" perspective, which is compatible, in the language we used in Chapter 1, with a demand-side account for the autism epidemic. NSAC is analyzed as a lobby, an advocacy group concerned with de-stigmatization and resource mobilization (King 2008). There is a great deal of cogency to this approach. It certainly makes sense of the role played by Sullivan and her comrades. Yet it is also partial. What do E-1 checklists or behavioral therapies have to do with the politics of lobbying and resource mobilization? The approach we will take in this chapter is, therefore, complementary to the political one. We will analyze NSAC not as a lobbying outfit, but as a *network of expertise* connecting parents, activists, researchers, clinicians, and therapists. This analysis will be compatible with a supply-side account of the autism epidemic, because it will demonstrate the ways in which the concept of autism was broadened within this network.

So is NSAC's story another example of the construction of "lay expertise," like the case of AIDS activism analyzed by Epstein (1995)? There are some superficial similarities. ACT-UP activists fought to remove the stigma of AIDS; parents of autistic children fought to remove their own stigma as "bad parents." ACT-UP activists targeted the medical establishment; NSAC parents the psychiatric powers. ACT-UP activists developed working knowledge of the relevant science, and ultimately were accepted as credible experts in policy forums; parents of autistic children read voraciously and translated their knowledge into effective lobbying. But here the similarities end. Epstein's analysis remains wedded to a "political" approach. The expertise of ACT-UP activists is mobilized as a resource in their struggle against the medical establishment. It is agonistic. The oxymoron of "lay expertise" merely signifies that at the end of the day, when the dust settles, the two are left quite distinct: experts are on one side, and laymen on the other. It is not hard, therefore, for Collins and Evans to classify it as "interactional" expertise, ultimately subordinate to the truly "contributory" expertise of practicing scientists (2007). They would be hard pressed to do so in the case of NSAC. ACT-UP activists plugged into existing networks. NSAC took the existing network of expertise apart and wove a wholly new and alternative network of knowledge production and dissemination. It was not a mere teaming-up of adjacent groups, parents on one hand and practitioners on the other. Rather, it involved the hybridization of identities, blurring of boundaries between expert and layman, and crucially "co-production" of common objects of inquiry and treatment. NSAC is similar not to ACT-UP, but to the French Muscular Dystrophy Association (AFM) analyzed by Vololona Rabeharisoa and Michel Callon (2004). And for good reason: in both cases, parents and researchers were dealing with chronic incurable conditions. In both cases, the struggle was to define a level of intervention between cure and neglect, and to develop a network of expertise adequate to this level.

This chapter, therefore, also aims to contribute to the "third wave in science studies" represented by an emerging sociology of expertise and experience (Collins and Evans 2002). The main question is, what makes one an expert? One possibility is that expertise is a real and substantive skill possessed by an individual by virtue of being socialized into a group of similar experts. This is what Collins and Evans argue, with a strong normative tinge (2007), and arguably this is also Bourdieu's position (1975). The alternative is that expertise is not something possessed by an individual, but a property of a network – which is what we argue. Collins and Evans dismiss "relational" or "network" approaches as merely "attributional": treating expertise as merely the assignment of a label (2007, 2). While the analysis of attributional struggles is certainly an important part of the network or relational approach, and we will have occasion in this chapter to analyze one such crucial struggle, we think that it is about much more than the mere assignment of a label. If expertise is a property of a network, then struggle within it is about rearranging relations and rechanneling flows within it. Obviously this is harder to do in heavily capitalized sciences, where the price tag for entry and transformation is set incredibly high (Bourdieu 1975), and therefore a relational approach would seem to be merely about "attribution." These are the sciences or forms of expertise – for example, gravitational wave physics – about which Collins and Evans write. In these sciences, the distinction between interactional and contributory expertise is productive, because the fuzzy zone between the two is minimal (70–76). The only way to possess contributory expertise is to practice science. The only way to practice science is to work in a state-of-the-art laboratory. The boundary between interactional and contributory expertise is, therefore, fairly clear. In less heavily capitalized sciences or forms of expertise, however, the fuzzy zone between interactional and contributory expertise is bigger, and the distinction, we argue, is unproductive. Parents, who seemingly possessed only interactional expertise, were able to emerge out of the "attributional" struggles with upgraded "contributory" expertise, while the expertise of dynamic clinicians and therapists was downgraded. This is good evidence that it is useful to treat expertise as a network property, since the parents' coup involved taking apart a set of relations within which they were subordinate and their expertise merely "interactional," and "rewiring" it by redefining almost everything about the expertise (its goals, techniques, subjects and objects) that was relevant in the field of autism.

Our argument in this chapter will proceed in the following steps:

1. A new type of actor emerges with NSAC: the parent-activist-therapist-researcher. This actor is not represented by only a few

charismatic individuals – Rimland, Lorna Wing – but constitutes a new modality of expertise anchored in networks of knowledge exchange among parents, researchers, and therapists.

2. The key problem to solve in order to craft this form of agency, in order to jumpstart the circuit of exchange among parents, was how to reconstitute parents as credible witnesses and their testimony as worthy currency.

3. To resolve the problem of credibility NSAC evolved a two-step strategy. It devised a counter-narrative about the etiology of autism and the genesis of parental attitudes that took apart the existing network of expertise and rearranged it around the position of the parent-researcher-therapist-activist. It then invented and disseminated a new style of being a parent – "autism parenting" as a vocation, as the "expert on your own child" – so as to guarantee that this position will be filled by agents with the correct attitudes.[5]

4. Once autism parenting became a vocation and a credible source of knowledge, it rendered superfluous Rimland's initial restriction of the syndrome. As autism parenting contracted with therapies that blurred the distinction between expert and laymen, as well as between mental illness and mental retardation, the scope of the syndrome became open-ended, capable of becoming a spectrum of disorders that had in common their responsiveness to these therapies.

The parent-activist-therapist-researcher as a new type of expert

Roy Richard Grinker (2007) has argued that autism awareness increased in part "because some of the most influential parents, such as Bernard Rimland and Lorna Wing, happened to be mental health experts able to communicate to large audiences through scientific publications" (2007, 156). Admittedly, this is not a central component of Grinker's argument, but we still think he is being too cavalier. A great deal of work, personal transformation and social innovation is hidden behind this misleading word – "happened."

To begin with, NSAC did not "happen" to have a parent leader who was a mental health expert. Rimland, as we saw, founded NSAC after he wrote his book. The list of potential members to contact was compiled in part on the basis of responses to his E-1 checklists and letters of inquiry from parents. NSAC is unique among similar organizations – and this justifies our choice to analyze it as a network of expertise – to have been founded as a follow-up to a book, and a scholarly book at that! Was it activism that needed expertise to support it, or expertise that needed activism to supplement it?

As it happened, none of these parent-experts – and there were many more than Rimland and Wing – were able simply to use their previous expertise. All would first need to stretch outside their prior professional domain into other areas. All were trained professionals. Rosalind Oppenheim was an educator. Amy Lettick, a mother who communicated with Oppenheim and initiated an intense in-home behavioral education program with her son Benjie, was a special-education teacher.[6] Clara Claiborne Park, whose 1967 book *The Siege* chronicled her daughter Jessy's[7] first eight years in microscopically insightful detail, had a master's degree in English (Park 1967). Sullivan was a registered nurse. Rimland earned his doctorate in psychology, specializing in psychometrics. Wing was a psychiatrist. They all faced the peculiar demands of raising a disabled child in the absence of credible, accessible, and helpful expert advice and institutional support. They dismissed institutionalization as an option, and so their predicament led them outside their original professional domain into new areas such as behavioral techniques, orthomolecular medicine, legislative processes, or neurological debates. They did not *possess* credibility and expertise; they had to *cultivate* it. To be sure, Rimland's PhD and Wing's MD gave them a certain authority and allowed them to make critical connections. But they both commented on issues far afield from their original areas of expertise. Rimland's book, for example, grew out of voracious ransacking of library collections in his spare time and an ever-increasing stack of notes. His neural theory was in no obvious way connected to his psychometric work for the Navy. Being steeped in research methodology and scientific terminology no doubt advanced his cause, but he did not "happen" to be an expert on mental health who had an autistic child. Neither did any of the other parents described here. They *made* themselves into experts.

In fact, as the example of NARC proves, to become an effective lobbying outfit NSAC hardly needed Rimland's expertise. It was the other way around. Rimland needed to found NSAC in order to advance his (and other parents') claim to expertise. Here he was, a Navy psychologist attempting to compete with psychiatrists and MDs. His knowledge of his subject matter, however extensive, was – despite occasional references to his son, and even to himself – bookish. *Infantile Autism* was the book of an outsider, marked by the

173

stigmata of looking from the outside in. It was admittedly speculative. It was a book based on "interactional expertise," but not a "contributory" one (Collins and Evans 2007). He summed up the results of others' research, but had very little of his own. Without a clinic, like the psychiatrists, or a laboratory, like Lovaas, how could he make them stop and listen to him? What tools did he possess to support his claim for expertise? He turned to what he knew best – psychometrics, the E-1 checklists – and this brought him in touch with other parents. Activism and the formation of a parents' association were an extension of this quest to forge a new type of expertise, or to rearrange relations in the existing network of expertise, not vice versa.

One should note that Lovaas's situation was not all that different from Rimland's, which explains why he was keen on cooperating with him. As we explained in Chapter 7, he developed the principles of Applied Behavioral Analysis (ABA) working with only one subject and needed the parents' support in order to generalize and replicate his results. Rimland, with his E-1 checklists, and then with his privileged position in NSAC, provided a solution (Lovaas 1993, 628; Silverman 2004, 190).

It is similarly misleading to say that Rimland and his colleagues were able "to communicate to large audiences through scientific publications" (Grinker 2007). The most distinctive feature of the expertise network represented by NSAC was the knowledge exchange and dissemination that took place *within* it, among parent-activist-researchers, and not *outside* it, in the scientific literatures. That is why we emphasize the innovative nature of Rimland's E-1 checklists. They involved a model of knowledge exchange around which the whole network was organized, and which served to bypass the reigning authorities in the field of autism research. In Collins and Evans's (2007) terms, it transmuted Rimland's (or Lovaas's) interactional expertise into contributory expertise, and by the same token downgraded the expertise of the psychiatrists into an interactional one; or, in our language, this model of knowledge production took apart the existing network of expertise in which parents reported to clinicians, and rewired it to go through the parent-activist-researcher. Rimland's gambit was to treat parents as credible witnesses of their child's development and symptoms. The checklists he received allowed him to generate an independent database with which to challenge the psychiatric establishment. Wedded to the clinical case method, the latter lacked a similar resource and was an easy target (Lakoff 2000). Rimland fulfilled his own side of the bargain by publicizing his findings first in parents' forums, and especially by creating the link with

Lovaas and disseminating information about "operant conditioning" directly to parents. As in the case of the French Muscular Dystrophy Association analyzed by Callon and Rabeharisoa (2004), this meant placing at the center of the exchange not the unreachable and ever-receding goal of "cure," but the workable problem of managing a chronic condition.

Rimland's exchange became the model for the communication and expertise network built by NSAC. Clara Claiborne Park put her graduate training to work editing NSAC's newsletter, informing parents directly of advances in research and treatment. NSAC also supplied parents with information and referrals (a service run by Ruth Sullivan); it sold books and articles about autism; it compiled and provided bibliographies and lists of relevant films. Most important, parent-activist-researchers like Lettick, Oppenheim, and Rimland set up quasi-experimental programs at their homes, and later in the schools they founded, and exchanged information directly with each other about what worked in treatment of their own children, and what did not.

This meant that NSAC's parent-activist-researchers were poised to collaborate with the established experts from a position of strength, on their own terms. They did not come knocking on their doors begging for advice and help. They did not, as did ACT-UP, bang on experts' doors demanding attention, in order to plug into the existing network (Epstein 1996). Rather, they invited the established experts *in*, to plug into their *own* network, into the protected space they created in NSAC, wherein parents were credible witnesses and a different type of expertise was recognized. In 1969, NSAC began hosting a national meeting and conference for autism research and treatment. Researchers, clinicians, and therapists were invited into this forum, where they had to speak directly to parents. They were thus compelled to come face-to-face with parents and their needs for concrete solutions, and had to reckon with the parental point of view about autism and its history. The new terms of discussion were set in the inaugural meeting, when Kanner famously "exonerated" parents of any blame or guilt for their children's disorder. In return, one could say, he was rewarded with the stewardship of the new *Journal of Autism and Childhood Schizophrenia*, inaugurated two years later by two members of NSAC, both parents of autistic children, one of whom owned a publishing house.

Thus the new type of autism expert, the parent-researcher-therapist-activist exemplified by Rimland and Wing, was not parlaying his or her scientific credentials to translate what parents knew into scientific language in order to plug into existing scientific networks. These parents rewired the relations of expertise and in the process invented a completely different type of network. Crucial to their development as experts were alternative modes of public circulation and extra-scientific forums, provided by the national societies. The ties between the American and British societies were exceptionally strong, but from the very beginning the network of expertise was extended to other places around the globe, either through the dissemination of Rimland's articles and his reception of E-1 checklists from parents abroad, or through personal visits, by Park and other parents who met with parents of autistic children in France and other countries.

The problem of credibility

For the network of expertise to be rewired, the problem of the credibility of parent testimony had to be resolved. Witnessing is the ideal of empirical science, but it can never really be achieved. Even in public experiments, there is the background of failed attempts in the private laboratory. Thus, testimony has to replace witnessing, which raises problems of credibility. Steven Shapin (1988) has demonstrated how, in seventeenth-century experimental science, the problem of credibility was resolved by moving from the juridical model of examination to one of gentlemanly "virtue," by restricting access to gentlemen witnesses and relying on their status and code of honor to legitimate their testimony. From then onwards, spatial arrangements – from the gentlemen's house to today's laboratories – have served to legitimate empirical science by controlling access, constructing visibility, and creating a smooth flow of "virtual witnessing" (Ophir, Shapin, and Schaffer 1991).

How could parents, each in a private home, each with an obvious interest, be taken as credible witnesses whose testimony could be trusted? To make matters even more difficult, by the mid-1960s parents of autistic children were among the least credible, the most discredited, of all witnesses. They were caught in an economy of blaming that made their very attempts at accurate, credible testimony serve as the basis to downgrade their credibility. As Ruth Christ Sullivan, the first elected president of NSAC, noted, parental testimonies were the ground on which Kanner built the syndrome in the first place – while using them to discredit the parents who gave them. The detailed diaries, reports, and remembered developmental minutiae, Kanner wrote, "furnish a telling illustration of parental obsessiveness" (Kanner 1943, 250, cited in Sullivan 1984, 239). "Yet," Sullivan points out, "when *he* is struck by the same phenomena and writes thirty-three pages of detailed description of these children's unusual behavior *based on those mothers' notes and good recall*, he is called the 'father of autism' and hailed as a gifted observer, which, of course, he was" (Sullivan 1984, 239). She may have been too kind to the old man. After all, he was not the only gifted observer of the children. His keen observation of the *parents'* "obsessiveness" served to erase *them* as gifted observers, and especially as credible witnesses. Over the next two decades after Kanner's article, parents became an erased or inert node in the expertise network that gave rise to clinical acumen. Through the discrediting of parental testimony, the clinician was positioned at an obligatory point of passage in this network, from which he could appropriate parental reports, erase the work that went into them, and accumulate them in his hands as scientific capital. Put differently, the "contributory" status of the clinician's expertise depended on downgrading the contributory element in parental reports. The "obsessiveness" of the parents was taken as testimony to their overly intellectual approach to their children, proof of their pathogenic coldness. In this economy of blaming, every argument or observation that a father like Rimland might come up with could be turned against him and used to establish his culpability and justify his exclusion, just as it served simultaneously to buttress the objectivity of the syndrome and the authority of the clinician.

No doubt this was precisely why Rimland was able to create NSAC so quickly. His book was published in 1964, and the society formed a year later. A number of engaged and educated parents had been chafing against this state of affairs for a while. After bruising encounters with the psychiatric establishment, they opted out. People like Jacques May, Oppenheim, and Lettick were educating their children at home, devouring available literature, and liaising with interested experts at the fringes of special education, psychology, and psychiatry. They were ripe to be organized. They had a common enemy in dynamic psychiatry, and a concrete goal: to reinstate parents as credible witnesses so as to project their observations, opinions, and interests into public and professional discourses about autism. Rimland (1971, 163) spoke for them all when he argued: "Since diagnosis depends at least in part on retrospective information (age of onset, behavior in infancy, etc.), there is no way of circumventing parents' reports in any case." Parental testimony was already being used, already treated as a credible source of information. It was simply high time this fact was recognized.

177

Yet the initial strategy upon which Rimland settled in his struggle against the psychogenic hypothesis was ill-suited to serve parents' purposes. He accepted that parents of autistic children were different from other parents. To avoid, as we saw earlier, the stigma of mental retardation, he was willing to concur with Kanner's observations about the parents, if it was granted that their intellectualism and coldness were the cause of their children's condition only in the genetic sense, as a "rare recessive trait." Beyond the possible impression that he was merely splitting hairs, his strategy had the added disadvantage of radically restricting the diagnosis of autism, thus restricting the potential pool of parents to be organized, or alternatively and much more destructively involving the fledgling society in a bruising and potentially fatal conflict over who is "really" autistic and who is not.

Schopler and the new economy of blame and worth

Help came from an unexpected corner. Or maybe it was not so unexpected after all. It came from the other side of the emerging parent-practitioner network, from another actor interested in rewiring relations in the network of expertise, another psychologist who turned to parents as allies in the struggle against the domination of the field by psychiatrists and clinicians. Eric Schopler, who earned his doctorate in child developmental psychology at Chicago during the height of Bettelheim's popularity there, initially accepted the psychogenic hypothesis but sought to moderate it, to achieve some compromise in the impending struggle over the allocation of blame. Over time, however, as he drew closer to the nascent parents' movement and drew on parents as his allies, he devised a more radical narrative that inverted the economy of blame and worth, and with it also the relations of expertise.

In 1965, Schopler's analysis still placed him halfway between the parents and the psychiatric establishment. Like Rimland, he accepted as proven the claim that the parents of autistic children were different from other parents, that they were colder and overly intellectual. We already saw that Rimland interpreted this as proof, not of the psychogenic hypothesis, but that autism was a genetic disorder. Schopler sought to split the difference. He made essentially the same point as Rimland: the parents of autistic children had other normally developing children. The quality of parenting could not, therefore, be the sole cause of their disturbance. There must be also a "constitutional dysfunction." Both cold parenting and constitutional deficit were necessary conditions (Schopler 1965).

178

This analysis explains why in 1966, along with Robert Reichler, Schopler began a five-year pilot study in North Carolina, treating autistic children in collaboration with their parents. Collaboration with mothers, specifically, was necessary because the therapy involved providing adequate tactile stimulation, as well as swinging and patting games. Reichler and Schopler were not the first to collaborate with parents. As we saw in the previous chapter, several therapies on the margins of the fields of mental retardation and emotional disturbance were experimenting, already in the late 1950s and early 1960s, with various forms of "outsourcing" therapeutic work to parents. Nonetheless, Schopler was the first to introduce this innovation into the treatment of specifically autistic children. The initial impetus for this collaboration, however, was not quite parent-friendly. It was still guided by a theory of maternal deficit.

This collaboration with parents, however ambiguous to begin with, proved decisive in shaping Schopler's trajectory. After a few years had passed, he sought to turn this pilot study into a statewide treatment program known as Treatment and Education of Autistic and related Communication-handicapped CHildren (TEACCH). Schopler needed parents as allies, not only in the conduct of therapy, but in order to establish the credibility of his treatment program, lobby on its behalf, and provide it with extra support against possible attacks from the better-endowed psychiatric establishment. While not parents themselves, in 1970 Schopler and Reichler helped parents establish a North Carolina chapter of NSAC, which would play an instrumental role in lobbying the state legislature to fund TEACCH as a statewide autism treatment program. Reporting the tremendous political success of Frank Warren and other parents and specifying a model of parent–professional collaboration, Schopler put it simply to the NSAC audience, "parents have more political clout than professionals" (Park 1971b, 4). And he wrote his seminal article, drawing on the pilot study experience, to suggest that parents serve as "co-therapists" in autism treatment programs (Schopler and Reichler 1971). The article was first circulated as an NSAC publication, and later published in the new outlet of the combined parent–practitioner expertise network, the *Journal of Autism and Childhood Schizophrenia* (*JACS*). Schopler would later describe the relationship between the parents and professionals as necessarily involving a "common front" when it came to community advocacy (Schopler et al. 1984, 79).

The new narrative that Schopler devised in the early 1970s seems part of this "common front." Through his collaboration with parents, he too, like Rimland, was now keenly interested in reinstating parents as credible witnesses, but unlike Rimland, he was not as concerned to restrict the scope of the disorder. He came up with an effective strategy that involved inverting the whole economy of blame and worth, which, as we saw, allocated clinical acumen to clinicians and pathogenic blame to the parents.

First, Schopler now argued that the "obsessive" or "cold" parental behavior described by Kanner was not even a partial cause of autism, but its consequence. He no longer split the difference, but bent back the arrow of harm – which meant he did not need to restrict the scope of the disorder as Rimland did. In the "refrigerator mother" hypothesis, it was the unloving mother (and perhaps father) who harmed or disturbed the otherwise normal child. Schopler argued the inverse. The parents of autistic children differed from other parents precisely because they lived with an autistic child, a child who did not reinforce the mother's initial emotional overtures and presented unique behavioral problems. The mother's difference was not a cause of the child's difference, but rather an effect of it. In his words, "it was increasingly clear that parents of psychotic children are disorganized in *reaction* to their disorganized child" (Schopler and Reichler 1976, 355). The child went from being disturbed to disturb*ing*. The arrow of harm bent back – now from child to mother and beyond, to the entire family. There was no longer any reason to be suspicious of the trustworthiness of parents' testimony. It was the best data to be had, as Schopler and Reichler's research seemed to indicate (1972).

Second, Schopler introduced the notion of "scapegoat." Why were clinicians unable to see that the arrow of harm went from child to parent and not vice versa? Because, he argued, they were baffled by autism, secretly frustrated, and needed to find a scapegoat. Schopler thus provided a dynamic interpretation of dynamic therapy, downgraded the clinicians to the status of patients, and discredited their testimony. Autism was such a recalcitrant, untreatable disorder, and autistic children were so hard to reach, that even the most optimistic and indefatigable play therapist became frustrated. The behavior of autistic children was confusing. It resisted dynamic explanation and interpretation by even the most inventive psychoanalytic minds. Backed into a corner, unconsciously compensating for their failure and frustration, psychoanalysts blamed parents and promised unrealistic outcomes. The economy of blame and worth was thus completely inverted, with parent testimony becoming credible and clinical insight discredited.[8]

In the third and final move, Schopler's analysis displaced culpability not simply from mother to child, nor to his or her biology, but also to an unhelpful psychiatric profession and an unsupportive insti-tutional arrangement (Schopler and Reichler 1976, 348–49, 366–68). Without the proper infrastructure, the bent arrow of harm could turn into a vortex. Confused by contradictory advice and lacking adequate support, parents and children would mutually negatively reinforce one another, endlessly exacerbating the situation.

Schopler's analyses of parents as affected by the child rather than vice versa, parents as both "scapegoats" and "co-therapists," were immediately picked up and echoed in the parent literature and at parent meetings. This was indeed his intention. No longer the scape-goats of psychoanalysts, parents would now be co-therapists in the establishment of a new regime of treatment and care focused on the individual child's needs. NSAC, he argued, would provide the umbrella under which they could all come together to develop the critical mass needed to resist psychiatric accusation and develop this new regime of treatment (Schopler 1971). The articles in which this new narrative was articulated were made available to NSAC members. Professionals also embraced this inversion of the economy of blame and worth; Schopler's etiological argument and idiom of parents as co-therapists became a sort of mantra for many professionals at the early NSAC conferences. Even Kanner would write, in a 1971 speech read in absentia by Victor Winston, "parents are beginning to be dealt with from the point of view of mutuality, rather than as people standing at one end of the parent–child bipolarity; they have of late been included in therapeutic efforts, not as etiological culprits, nor merely as recipients of drug prescriptions and of thou-shalt and thou-shalt-not rules, but as actively contributing co-therapists" (Kanner, cited in Park 1971a, 7–8). Presenters at NSAC meetings continually reiterated the party line – parents are no longer part of the problem; they are part of the solution.

In 1974, now the new editor of *JACS*, Schopler published, some-what tongue-in-cheek, a letter from a member of the *JACS* board of directors. "Your expectation that the contributors would include parents suggested to me that the scientific level might well be lowered as a result," wrote E. James Anthony. Schopler's response pointed to the vision of parent–professional relations he foresaw. "I believe that an attempt at reasonable dialogue over scientific and clinical material will enhance the scientific level rather than diminish it" (Schopler 1974, 93–94). Further, he had noticed early on how important was the contribution of parent-researchers. Witness a note he sent Ruth Sullivan after the second NSAC conference in 1970, cited by Sullivan in the introduction to the published proceedings:

I have attended both of the first two annual conferences and continue to be impressed with the interest, vitality and quality of the parents' participation. They seem to talk to each other more and make better use of available information than do most participants of professional meetings. Maybe it's the groups' combined energy and talent, and living in more of a pressure cooker than their professional counterparts that makes for that vitality. Let me take this emotional climate one step further and consider the intellectual output of this group. If you rack up the contribution of parents like Rimland, Wing, Park, Kysar, May, Eberhardy, Junker against the professional contributions to the literature on autism, these parents may easily have made a more lasting contribution than the professional group. (Sullivan 1971, 2)

Finally, Schopler saw scientific specialization as detrimental to the care of disabled children. He was a generalist through and through and he preferred that the therapists at TEACCH be without specialized training. He felt theoretical allegiances and a tendency toward specialization in psychiatry were a detriment to families of autistic and otherwise "communication-handicapped" children. Thus the team he first assembled in 1966 was purposefully interdisciplinary: Schopler himself along with a child psychiatrist, an arts and crafts teacher, an academic teacher, a social worker, and a music therapist.[9] Everyone had to know every aspect of the system and of the child. However, he noted, only one person could truly have such a holistic view – the parent. Thus, he told the audience at the 1970 NSAC meeting, "I advocate that parents must become experts on their own autistic child. They have the most complete and relevant information available, from their daily life with the child. They have the highest motivation for helping their child and maintaining their family equilibrium" (Schopler 1971). Here Schopler articulated a vision of the parent not simply as a credible witness, but perhaps the *most* credible witness.

Nothing captures better the new economy of blame and worth and the rewiring of the network of expertise introduced by Schopler, than his pioneering use of a one-way screen to teach parents how to work with their children. Parents would first observe the therapist working with their children through the one-way screen; then they would try to replicate at home what they saw. The one-way screen takes away "the mystique and unfounded authority" of the therapist, Schopler told the audience of the 1971 NSAC conference (Park 1971b). Over time, parents would learn to discriminate between superior and inferior therapeutic performances, would become able to criticize the therapist for failures or mistakes they saw, and would acquire confidence in their own powers as therapists. Schopler testified, indeed, that some parents have come to surpass the therapists who originally trained them. The one-way screen complemented Schopler's critical narrative. It established a relation of transparency between expert and parent, a new regime of visibility wherein no room for scapegoating remained. Only techniques that therapists had themselves proven to be successful – through meticulous record-taking and one-way screens – would be passed along to parents. The therapists could not entertain unrealistic expectations and therefore would not blame parents for lack of improvement. Put differently, accusation and the assignment of blame was still possible, but it was disciplined in two ways. First, it was now a two-way street. Just as therapists could criticize parental practices, parents could criticize therapists' performance. This was enough to tone down accusations. Second, and more important, accusation had to be conducted through a transparent medium, either the one-way screen, or the videotapes that are now the common currency of instruction, supervision, and training among DIR therapists, or the detailed reporting systems we discussed in the previous chapter.

The one-way screen also demonstrates that thinking of expertise relationally, as a network, is not the same as thinking of it as merely an "attribution," the assignment of a label that, by implication, is empty and arbitrary. Here was a concrete device, a physical apparatus that rewired the flow of information within the network of expertise, and was analogous with Rimland's E-1 checklists and complemented them. Neither clinician nor therapist was positioned in the obligatory point of passage in the newly rewired network. By being able to observe the therapists, parents became – as Lovaas (1981) was suggesting they should be – "managers of treatment teams," the supreme "experts on their own autistic children" whose proximity and entanglement with the child was no longer culpable, but on the contrary, the only position into which flowed all the relevant information, and the only one wherein synthesis was possible. These parent-manager-therapists, these small nodes or obligatory points of passage, now turned around and communicated directly with larger nodes or obligatory points of passage represented by parent-activist-researchers like Rimland.

Autism parenting as a vocation

The critique of scapegoating represents the negative moment of transformation, the moment when the barriers to the development of the new network of expertise were removed. By the same token, the positive moment was represented by the example set by the early founders of NSAC. To transform parental testimony into "virtual witnessing" it was necessary, first, to disentangle it from a too-near relation to that on which it was reporting, where the accusation of "obsessiveness" had placed it. In the second place, however, it had to be re-entangled in it again, but this time armed with a shield of unassailable *virtue*. Just as gentlemanly virtue resolved the credibility problems of early experimental science, a new style of parenting – autism parenting – assured the credibility of parental testimony. This is fairly counterintuitive. How could parental love, presumably everything that love is – emotional, subjective, one-sided, and "blind" – serve to lend credibility to a claim for objective observation and reporting?[10] Counterintuitive, but not unprecedented. We saw in Chapter 4 that the origins for this generalization of parental love into an objective social virtue lay in the "valorization of retarded existence" attempted by NARC parents, some years earlier.

This new style of parenting was modeled for NSAC members by its early board members, people such as Rimland, Oppenheim, Lettick, and Park. NSAC provided venues for parents to learn from one another, to experiment with and report back on different therapeutic modalities, creating circuits of knowledge accumulation outside of the professional journals. Rimland openly used his home-baked experiments as evidence, as did Oppenheim, Lettick, and Park. In fact, in speeches to audiences at NSAC meetings or in newsletter articles, these parents would often describe their personal experiences with methods of treating their children. They modeled a fearless experimental spirit, not unlike the heroism of the pioneers of experimental science. For instance, in a newsletter summary of a conference presentation, Park writes, "the editor [Park herself] tried it on 13-year-old Elly, whose passive, iron negativism, as readers of *The Siege* know, has always been the most frustrating accompaniment of her condition" (Park 1971b, 6). She reported incremental but "unprecedented" improvement.

Their experimentalism was not mindless, not "everything goes," but it was certainly pragmatically oriented, outcome-driven, and hence at least in principle open to anything that "worked" even if it was marginal to contemporary research programs. This pragmatism was conditional on the fact that, as we argued in Chapter 7, together with blurring the boundaries between expert and layperson, there was also blurring of the boundaries between mental retardation and mental illness and hence a more flexible, open-ended definition of the goal of therapy: of what it would mean for a therapy to "work." As Chloe Silverman points out, parental acceptance of, experimentation with, and advocacy for behavioral methods was a necessary ingredient to their dissemination and eventual ascendancy to "gold standard" status in autism treatment (2004, 172). In the mid-1960s, Lovaas's research program was marginal, bordering on the nonexistent – limited to one subject, detached from the advances in cognitive psychology that were to become the dominant paradigm a decade later (Nadesan 2005). Autism itself was limited in scope and derivative. As we saw in Chapter 6, Lauretta Bender's construct of childhood schizophrenia had a lot more purchase than autism but, as we argued, it lacked precisely this seedbed in which the autism spectrum and ABA germinated – an alliance between parents and therapists, a network of expertise that blurred the distinction between the two, brought them closer, and additionally, translated and coordinated their interests by blurring the distinction between mental illness and mental retardation, thus giving them concrete and achievable goals.

A major aim of NSAC early on was to show that autistic children were not uneducable (Silverman 2004). Rimland often cited his "discovery" of operant conditioning and his desire to show parents that they could teach their children as the impetus for founding NSAC in the first place (Rimland 1992, 3). With operant conditioning, he had something to give back to parents in return for their participation in his research program, in return for their completed E-1 checklists, and their willingness to set up quasi-experimental designs in their homes. What he and Lovaas and Oppenheim and Lettick gave back to parents was a concrete and achievable goal, and the set of technical means adequate to it. As one NSAC spokesperson said in 1969, "it is time we once and for all dismiss the untenable idea that these handicapped children are unreachable and un-teachable" (Burns 1969). The technique gave the organization a clear message about the educability of autistic children and a pragmatic tool to disseminate. As Rimland reported in 1970, "I'm sure that the operant conditioning workshops set up in various cities by groups of NSAC parents, with the help of Dr. Lovaas and Dr. Lindsey, have had much to do with the wide acceptance of operant conditioning today" (Rimland 1971b, 56). Through NSAC's promotion of Lovaas's method, individual successes accumulated and Lovaas's therapy would enter the space opened up by deinstitutionalization from a position of strength.

As they reported on their home-based experiments, leading figures such as Park or Rimland modeled a style of parenting for NSAC readers and audiences. And through these reports and testimonies, a prototype of the autism parent began to coalesce – experimenting, observing, keeping detailed records, varying treatment regimes in accordance with the evidence, contracting with schools (or creating their own schools) to extend further the experimental and prosthetic environment they created at home, communicating with other parents, providing them with advice, and lobbying legislators on their behalf. These parental experiments and reports also accumulated through parental testimonies at meetings, or through letters to Rimland and others.[11] Individual reports iteratively demonstrated the importance of parental observations, cumulatively solidified their credibility, and lent weight to particular therapies' credibility.

One might object here that this relatively small group (NSAC's membership was estimated at only 2,000 in 1970 and 4,000 by 1972 [Griffith 1973, 2]) was not in any way representative of the experience of the majority of parents at the time. This, to be sure, is not the claim we are making. Nor are we arguing that parents were met with open arms by helpful professionals who did not pathologize them. And not all parents then, or ever since, fully inhabited the role of the "autism parent." We are tracing the development of a critical nucleus, comprised of a set of moral entrepreneurs – both parental and professional – who anticipated a historical necessity and did most of the (conceptual and pragmatic) heavy lifting early on to prepare the way for the autism spectrum to become the paradigmatic childhood disorder.

The implications of behavioral therapy

As the new network of expertise was rewired around the exchange among parents, not only the subject of expertise changed – from the clinician / dynamic therapist to the parent-activist-researcher-therapist – but also its object. In fact, the change of technique, goal, and object came as a package deal with the adoption of behavioral therapy as valid currency in the exchange between Rimland and the parents.

One of the advantages of behavioral therapy (or "action therapy," as he called it), argued Rimland, was that unlike "insight therapies" (read: psychoanalysis) it did not require the child to be physically or biochemically intact. In fact, Rimland made a point to note, "the method has been shown to work on pigeons, cats, rats, dogs (even with half their brain cut away), mongoloid children, blind deaf-mutes like Helen Keller" (Rimland 1972, 576). His examples, taken from published case studies by other researchers, included Dicky, a "psychotic and retarded boy," and Nelson, "a severely withdrawn 8-year-old who has never developed a meaningful relationship with anyone, despite three years of psychotherapy, and still had not developed speech" (Rimland 1972, 581).

Ultimately, therefore, behavioral therapies did not discriminate between autism, childhood schizophrenia, mental retardation or any of the other overlapping labels of the day. How could Rimland square this with the line he took in his book, according to which autism was a rare and distinctive disorder – only superficially resembling mental retardation; the neurological inverse of childhood schizophrenia? The currency – operant conditioning – with which he was paying parents back for their completed E-1 checklists, threatened the very reasoning upon which these checklists were based. In 1968, he published a successor E-2 form: *The Diagnostic Checklist for Behavior-Disturbed Children* (DCBDC; Rimland 1968), an eighty-item multiple-choice questionnaire to be completed by a parent or caregiver based on the behavior of their three-to-five year old child. It closely followed Kanner's description of the syndrome. Each response was scored as +1 or -1 point based on whether the item was characteristic of autism or not, with the total score being the sum of all eighty item scores. Based on a sample of 2,218 psychotic children, Rimland (1971) determined a cutoff score of +20 to be indicative of autism. He found that roughly 10 percent of his sample had a score of 20 or higher, thus conforming to Kanner's contention that only 10 in every 100 children labeled autistic really exhibited early infantile autism. Against a growing current of opinion, as we shall see, Rimland used the E-2 checklist to stick to the defensive line he and Kanner formulated in the mid-1960s: autism is a rare and distinct illness. It has nothing to do with mental retardation or childhood schizophrenia. It is over-diagnosed. It is not a spectrum. But how could he square this position with his advocacy of behavioral therapy?

The checklists, however, provided Rimland with a way out of this quandary. Behavioral methods seem to help children with different diagnoses, he argued, but how do we know that these diagnoses are reliable? His E-1 and E-2 checklists gave him a unique insight into the nosological mess that was the diagnosis of childhood disorders during the years when the institutional matrix of custody was being dismantled, an insight that nobody else possessed. Remember, there were no Center for Disease Control studies of developmental disability records back then. There was no "developmental disability"! But parents of course knew how truly serpentine was the route to a final diagnosis, and they reported it to Rimland. They reported receiving multiple, conflicting diagnoses. One mother was given ten different labels for her child (Rimland 1971a, 165). A table comparing agreement between diagnosticians, Rimland argued, "shows how arbitrarily these diagnoses have been assigned by presenting an almost random pattern of labeling" (166). Thus the checklist, by rerouting newly credible parental reports directly to him, allowed Rimland to downgrade the expertise of clinicians and to question also what they said about the efficacy of behavioral interventions.

As he digested the evidence about diagnostic unreliability and the wide applicability of behavioral methods, and as he tried to reconcile both sides in the exchange model he established, we find Rimland shifting his position. Thus it was under the pressure of therapy, or more precisely of an emerging coalition between parents and therapists that was to solidify in later years under deinstitutionalization, that autism became a spectrum. On the one hand, Rimland (1971, 162, n.3) proposed to call the residual diagnoses his checklists produced not "childhood schizophrenic" children but instead "autistic-type" children. The checklists no longer identified autism as a distinct and rare disorder against its nosological other, but instead traced a continuum of conditions with autism being the paradigmatic form of childhood developmental disorder. Correspondingly, he also recommended that NSAC's slogan be inclusive; their letterhead and newsletters read "dedicated to the education, welfare and cure of all children with severe disorders of communication and behavior" (Rimland, 1993, 3).Thus, he situated autism on a common plain with other similar disorders (mental retardation, brain damage, psychosis, and so on) on the basis of their common responsiveness to therapy, though he reserved for autism a paradigmatic position. The British National Society followed suit a few years later. In 1972, Lorna Wing reported to the crowd at the annual American NSAC meeting and conference, "like the National Society in the U.S.A. the British Society has broadened its outlook to cover *all* children with severe disorders of communication and behavior. This is appropriate because techniques of teaching and managing classically autistic children are successful with other children with severe language problems. It soon becomes clear in the field of communication problems how pointless it is to draw sharp lines between autistic and 'not really autistic' in educational practice, even if this distinction is of great theoretical interest. The question to ask about each child is – what are his handicaps, what are his skills and what can we do to help him?" (Wing 1973, 118).

On the other hand, Rimland still attempted to "split the difference" or maintain autism as a unique disorder, by arguing that "true cases of infantile autism . . . seem to respond especially well" to behavioral therapy and autism-like cases respond less reliably. Within the continuum, in fact, he introduced an opposition between the ethical economies of illness and retardation that could have easily broken it up. In "true cases," he argued, there was "magnification of effect of small therapeutic change"; meanwhile, for the presumably "untrue" cases, therefore, the "thimbleful" approach, where one fills a bucket one thimble at a time with the economy of effort associated with mental retardation, would be appropriate (Rimland 1972, 581, 583). We can see that under the pressure of the alliance with behavioral therapy, Rimland reluctantly and gingerly began navigating autism towards the space between mental retardation and mental illness, the space between fields that deinstitutionalization would open up, yet he was ready to revise course if the opportunity presented itself. If it never did, it was because deinstitutionalization solidified and tightened the relations within the new network of expertise, so that Rimland remained locked into them, somewhat reluctantly perhaps, and increasingly irrelevant. The future of autism, at least nosologically, belonged to Wing, much less to Rimland. We will return to Rimland, however, in Chapter 11, since his advocacy of biological treatments continues to exert an important influence in the space of autism therapies. Paradoxically, it is his vision of autism as illness, which one would expect to express the interests of the medical profession, which blurs the boundary between established and alternative medicine in the space of autism therapies and contributes to its especially open and dynamic character.

Schopler, as well, saw the implications of behavioral therapy and seemed much more comfortable with the route taken by Wing. He seemed to have a clear vision of the space opening up between mental retardation and mental illness, between the fields of special education and psychiatry. Drawing on a psychiatrist-father's account (Kysar 1968), he described two camps between which parents were often helplessly caught. One told them the problem was purely medical, the other purely educational. But neither had the full story. The medical camp could not treat autism and the educational camp could not properly classify or predict outcomes. Thus, he aimed to take up the mantle of medical diagnosis of social destiny by focusing efforts on quantitative diagnostics that could make distinctions on the basis of potential therapeutic benefits.[12] He felt the behaviorists were throwing the baby out with the bathwater when they said autism was no more than a cluster of measurable behaviors. But he also thought

Rimland's attempt to narrow the scope was an "*etiological* classification," and a premature one at that (Schopler and Reichler 1976, 351). He sought to rescue diagnosis, but in a modified form, one tightly bound to therapeutic intervention. In his words, "Nosology is not to be definitive, but only to provide a changing, developing language for communication. For prescriptive purposes, a diagnosis should also imply a preferential hierarchy of treatments" (Schopler and Reichler 349–50).

Schopler's innovative techniques and pragmatism explain why in later years he (and others) came to eclipse Rimland, while always paying homage to him as the "founding father." During the same time that Schopler and Wing led the charge into the space opened up by deinstitutionalization, Rimland was following leads on megavitamin therapy. He was convinced from the start that the best hope for autism treatment was in dietary and biomedical therapies. He saw phenylketonuria – which involved behavioral disturbances and mental retardation, and which could be treated by a strict diet – as a paradigm case, one he sought to emulate (1972, 574). However, in pressing this view, Rimland became increasingly marginalized. Thus, in 1974 when Kanner passed on the stewardship of *JACS*, Schopler was there to take the helm. And his first order of business was to add two new features to the regular menu – the "Parents Speak" column, to be edited by NSAC, and a "Questions, Answers, and Comments" forum through which parents and practitioners could query authors.

Conclusion

To recap our argument: as the network of expertise was being rewired around the parent-researcher-activist-therapist and around the alliance with behavioral therapy, its object changed. Autism finally became capable of being stretched into a spectrum, though this subterranean shift would be reflected in actual diagnostic change only many years later. To fully grasp the causes for this change we need to return to the analysis of the therapies we presented in the previous chapter, the therapies that blurred the boundaries between mental retardation and mental illness, and thus created the conditions for a spectrum between them. Then in the following chapter, we will look at how, in the wake of deinstitutionalization, a new institutional matrix within which a spectrum of developmental disabilities, with autism as its paradigmatic case, could become a reality. For what remains of this chapter, however, we would like to spell out the profound implications of this change in the object of expertise.

Being stretched into a spectrum meant that the relations between autism and mental retardation began to be reorganized. It became possible for them to coexist as concurrent diagnoses, and while autistic children were now identified with varying degrees of mental retardation, by the same token it also became possible to construe the whole of mental retardation on the model of autism, to foresee the moment when, in Lovaas's (1981) words, "there will be no more mentally retarded people," only developmentally disabled persons needing various levels of help with language and daily living skills. It is significant, moreover, that this possibility was first foreseen by therapists like Lovaas, and then within NSAC, even before it started to take institutional shape in early intervention programs and even though it never received explicit codification in diagnostic manuals.

No doubt Lorna Wing is commonly understood to be the "mother" of the autism spectrum precisely because hers was the most powerful statement of this new way of reconceiving mental retardation. She is famous for extending the spectrum to include higher-functioning people with her landmark paper on Asperger's syndrome (more on this in Chapter 10). But she also extended the spectrum to include those previously considered to be mentally retarded. In a presentation at the 1972 NSAC conference, Wing discussed the relationship between autism and mental retardation. Research clearly showed, she argued, that autism can and does occur in concert with mental retardation.[13] Dismissing the common complaint that autistic children scored low only because IQ tests were poorly administered, she argued, "a more cogent criticism is that autistic children do badly because of their perceptual and language handicaps" (Wing 1973, 112). Further, she saw no reason not to extend this argument to the whole of mental retardation. She argued instead for looking at the specific skills and deficits of each child in order to offer individualized education. "The idea that mental retardation exists as a unitary condition has, on the whole, impeded progress in education," she asserted in no uncertain terms (Wing 1973, 113). Here, in a key move, Wing used the sensory and language problems associated with autism as an idiom through which to level a critique of the concept of mental retardation as global deficit. She saw autism as one identifiable constellation of features. These features could be found in different combinations among children labeled as mentally retarded or those edging closer to the "normal."

This idiom of communication and sensory deficits was to have

191

profound influence in restructuring the whole domain of developmental disabilities. First, it infused treatment with a problematic of *radical translation*, long before it gained notoriety in contemporary debates about facilitated communication (Biklen 1990), neurodiversity, and autistic autobiographies (Hacking 2009b). Citing studies in the late 1960s by Hermelin and O'Connor, Wing (1973, 111) wrote: "they came to the conclusion that autistic, meaning 'socially withdrawn,' is a completely inappropriate label to apply to these children. They believe (as I do) that autistic children have all the normal emotions appropriate for their mental age, but are severely handicapped in *showing* them" (1972, 111). In this view, autistic children, and increasingly developmentally disabled children with various diagnoses, have emotions, intentions, preferences, the capacity for choice (the hallmark of late-modern personhood) like anyone else, but are unable to express these in normative ways, instead emitting a confusing cacophony of autistic behavior and/or idiolect. They cannot represent themselves. They must be represented, or more precisely, translated.

But who could claim to possess enough knowledge and discernment to undertake such a task of radical translation? In the passage quoted above, Wing added that "many parents who have learned the special language of their own autistic child are of the same opinion [that the handicap is in showing emotions, not having them]" (111). The second point, therefore, is that the task of radical translation was construed as continuous with the experiences and practices of parents, especially with autism parenting as a vocation. If the vocation of autism parenting was modeled after the therapist-experimenter, then, it is also true that therapy was infused with the parental relation of representing/translating the child. Think of it as a radio. It is not that children with autism are not transmitting, Wing argued. Each child is just on his own frequency and it takes a committed parent to tune in and receive the message, to decipher the child's own "special language" and translate it for others. Thus parents took over the task of translation, of interpretation. But it was not the deep interpretation of psychoanalysis. Theirs was the everyday interpretation of the give-and-take of daily emotional travails – and it was always tentative and inferential. Parents like Clara Claiborne Park modeled this sort of parenting. Through cleverly calibrated social experiments in her home, she devised schemes through which she could break through her daughter's stoic resistance and involve her in their family life. Contemporary therapists, from Stanley Greenspan to Soma Mukhopadhyay, now use videos and training sessions to model this sort of translation work for parents. A session with the child is taped. Then parents and therapist, or apprentice therapists, watch it together and point out moments when it seems the child was trying to communicate. Gradually, one becomes adept at interpreting the child's idiosyncratic mode of communication.[14]

Finally, the task of radical translation, and with it the image of the autism parent as the ultimate translator and advocate, enjoyed affinity with one of the core principles of the new institutional matrix that would replace custody: "normalization." Thus it was generalized into a principle guiding public policy. Reflecting on a decade of profound change, Frank Warren averred that "NSAC historically has asserted that parents of autistic offspring are the persons with the highest degree of investment in the lives of persons with autism, understand their own children better than anyone, and are, therefore, most able to understand the personal goals of their offspring, and to translate that understanding into policies guiding the operations of the society" (1984, 111). Thus, in order to normalize society, and hence the disabled person's life, parents were called upon to represent and translate their child's interests. Similarly, Wolf Wolfensberger, the main advocate of normalization, together with NARC, suggested pairing up each "retardate" with his or her own personal "citizen advocate" (not the parent) who would represent the person's needs (emotional, physical, economic). Thus, while NSAC privileged the parent's position as a sort of organic advocate, a natural proxy citizen, one who knew best and was most interested in the child's personal goals, NARC privileged the citizen-advocate as a Big Brother or Big Sister, probably to avoid paternalism and because NARC was more attuned to the problem represented by adult populations. Yet, both were different takes on the same task of representing and translating the wishes and communication attempts of those who could not quite represent themselves. Both shared a radical critique and resignification of mental difference, analogous to Wing's displacement from brain or psyche to the senses and linguistic capacities. Autism, however, had pride of place in being the paradigmatic, early, and extreme version of the problem of radical translation. As Lapin and Donnellan-Walsh argued, "parents of an autistic child collided head-on with the responsibility to 'speak for' their child early on" (1977, 191). They saw this as a common problem among the handicapped, but one particularly salient in the case of autism. "Parents of autistic children function as advocates on a daily basis," they argued.

— 9 —

THE ATYPICAL CHILDREN

By the time deinstitutionalization began rolling, as we saw in earlier chapters, the whole system of classifying childhood ailments was in turmoil. The DSM-II, published in 1968, papered over the confusion by recording a single diagnostic category – childhood schizophrenia – and ignoring the set of competing labels championed by different clinicians at different sites: childhood schizophrenia was specifically diagnosed in the New York region by Bender at Bellevue Hospital and Goldfarb at the Ittleson Center in Riverdale. At the Masters Children's Centre in Manhattan, Margaret Mahler distinguished symbiotic from autistic psychosis. From Boston came the category of "atypical child" or "atypical development," proposed by Rank, Putnam, and Pavenstedt, who tended to apply it to children "in whom relatedness was not as disturbed as to make the term autistic appropriate" (Ornitz and Ritvo 1968, 77). Bergman and Escalona at the Menninger clinic specialized in the diagnosis of "children with unusual sensitivities," while at the Langley Porter clinic in San Francisco, Szurek diagnosed a spectrum of childhood psychoses. Autism was the creature of Kanner at Johns Hopkins. As we saw in Chapter 6, Kanner opted to restrict its application. Ornitz and Ritvo at UCLA, on the other hand, proposed the term be used to identify "a unitary disease . . . a single pathologic process common to early infantile autism, certain cases of childhood schizophrenia, the atypical child, symbiotic psychosis, and children with unusual sensitivities" (Ornitz and Ritvo 1968, 76). Other labels were also bandied about that could accomplish this syncretic feat. Some spoke of "pseudo-retarded" children whose intellectual potential belied their appearance, while Reiser suggested the term "infantile psychosis" to replace all other terms and to encompass any pathology up until age 5 (Ornitz and Ritvo 1968; Bruch 1959).

The newly inaugurated *Journal of Autism and Childhood Schizophrenia*, first issued in 1971, reflected this confusion and turmoil. During the first two years of its existence, each issue led with an article by one of the champions of differing diagnoses – Kanner, Bender, Spitz, Louise Despert, Stella Chess, Mahler, Goldfarb. They all agreed, provisionally, to treat the common object of the journal as "childhood psychosis," but these were just two thin words standing over a wide abyss. In the pages of the new journal, Rimland complained that "to see the lack of agreement between diagnosticians who have seen the same child is to be convinced that the state of the diagnostic art is chaotic" (1971, 165–66). He used the reports that parents had been sending him since 1964 to show that out of 445 children who saw two different clinicians only 55 received the same diagnosis! Having been diagnosed as "autistic" by one clinician only gave one a 25 percent chance of being diagnosed so by the second, and one was just as likely (or even more likely) to be diagnosed with childhood schizophrenia, retardation, brain injury, or emotional disturbance.

To some extent, this situation was not unique to childhood disorders, but was the rule throughout the domain of psychiatry. The DSM-I and II had very little effect on what clinicians did. Studies conducted in the 1950s and 1960s found a low (20–42 percent) agreement rate between clinicians, due to the fact that they simply used different diagnostic criteria and different labels. Partly it was due to the "antinosographic" bent of dynamic therapy and the clinical case method, and partly due to the dispersal of child psychiatry in specialized clinics and hospitals where the diagnosis tended to be subordinated to the therapy offered. This is true to some extent even today, despite the enormous prestige of the DSM and the rise of descriptive psychiatry, as noted by Tom Widiger, head of research for DSM-IV: "there are lots of studies that show that clinicians diagnose most of their patients with one particular disorder and really don't systematically assess for other disorders. They have a bias in reference to the disorder that they are especially interested in treating and believe that most of their patients have" (Spiegel 2005, 58, 63; Lakoff 2000, 154–58).

But when it came to childhood disorders, the classificatory chaos had other sources as well. Diagnostic disagreement extended beyond the domain of illness and – as indicated by terms such as "pseudo-retarded" or "apparent feeblemindedness" – into the domain of retardation, where the terms used held even less communicative value. To begin with, the very term used to identify this sphere was indeterminate. Today we grimace at the term "mental retardation" and prefer euphemisms such as "intellectual disability" or "developmental disability." As we note in the introduction, terms like "mental retardation," "mental deficiency" or feeblemindedness were often introduced as euphemisms meant to indicate the mildest cases. Each in turn came to be associated with more severe cases and acquired pejorative connotations. By 1970, "mental retardation" was edging toward the end of this cycle, becoming less useful as it took on stigmatized meanings and encompassed even the most severe cases.

The accepted internal differentiation within this realm, which held for about fifty years, was in disarray. Up until 1952, the usual distinctions were, from most to least severe, "idiots," "imbeciles" and "morons" (or "feebleminded" or "mentally retarded" or "subnormal"), with some accommodation made for higher-functioning individuals considered "borderline" or "dull normal." These were legal distinctions that fit well within the institutional matrix of custody, since they were subdivided as gradations of social incapacity and minority. "Idiots" were equal to infants. They lacked the power of self-preservation, could not guard themselves against common physical dangers. Imbeciles were equal to young children. They could take care of themselves in terms of ordinary personal needs, but could not manage themselves or their affairs, nor be taught to do so. The morons, or feebleminded, resembled older children in that they could manage themselves, but required care and supervision for their own protection and the protection of others. This subdivision clearly worked well for the institution. It distinguished, for example, between wards, or between those who could and could not work, as well as between those who could be released (with or without sterilization), and those who could not. Yet, as the institution was gradually inserted into a system for the surveillance of childhood, as its functioning was more and more measured by goals such as prevention or minimization of future risks, the more this subdivision appeared useless. It merely recorded legal status at a given present moment, but could say very little about prognosis (Wallin 1949, 33–36).

So in 1952, the DSM-I replaced this nomenclature with the categories of mild, moderate, and severe mental defect, and in 1961 the American Association on Mental Deficiency (AAMD) manual added a fourth category: profound mental defect. These were supposed to correspond strictly to IQ scores, but in reality still reflected the exigencies of institutionalization. For example, the AAMD manual defined mild mental retardation as an IQ of 85 or lower (below one standard deviation), but in reality the line was drawn at IQ of 70. Hardly anybody thought that individuals with IQ over 70 should be institutionalized. Hardly anybody, in fact, was willing to ascribe predictive, prognostic value to IQ scores, especially since a child's IQ may change over the life course. IQ was a continuous variable, and any division along the scale was merely conventional and arbitrary. The main advantage of using IQ scores was the consistency and reliability with which annual reexaminations could be done. This meant that IQ testing was recommended primarily as a surveillance device, not as a meaningful system of classification. And to the extent that it was used to classify individuals, it merely recapitulated the threefold distinction of moron-imbecile-idiot, since this is what the institutional matrix of custody needed. Thus the AAMD manual introduced another distinction in 1961 between the "educable" retarded (those whose IQ lay between 50 and 70), the "trainable" retarded (IQ between 25 and 50), and by implication the "nontrainable" or "custodial" retarded (IQ below 25) (Clausen 1966, 735, 742–43).

An etiological or physiological classification also existed, the most important element of which was Down's syndrome, but by and large it covered only a very small portion of the full range of mental defects, leaving the greater part of this range undifferentiated. Kanner's distinction between absolute, relative, and apparent feeblemindedness was a road map to another future for mental retardation, a wish list, not a system of classification. No wonder then that with deinstitutionalization, which as we saw began by ending the practice of institutionalizing very young children, clinicians and practitioners were confronted with a huge undifferentiated mass of what, for want of other terms, could be called "atypical" or "exceptional" children. Recall Tredgold's point that mental deficiency was a legal concept, denoting simply those who were "socially incapable," by which he meant those who, left to their own devices outside the institution, would not be able to work and fend for themselves. Just as autism was meaningless within the institution, so now, within the institutional matrix of community treatment and normalization, this distinction between the socially capable and incapable was rendered meaningless. Nobody was going to be left to their own devices, but everybody had to be "social" in a different sense: interactive and communicative at home, in the classroom setting, and with age peers. Gradually, a different continuum of "social impairment" was taking shape and coming into view.

The struggle over inclusion in the Developmental Disabilities Act

If anything, the moral blender of deinstitutionalization and normalization tended to agglomerate the mass of atypical children even further.

These years saw the invention of the category of "developmental disabilities," first used by Congress in 1970 to "describe a subgroup of handicapped individuals who, because of the severity of their impairment and because they had no normal developmental experience on which to draw, needed habilitation as opposed to *re*habilitation" (Akerley 1979, 222). The group was thus defined by the substantiality, chronicity, and early onset of a "handicap" and the common need for similar services it entailed.[1] The law specified mental retardation, cerebral palsy, and epilepsy as members of this group (no doubt because each had a formidable association and lobbying outfit to represent it), but stipulated also that "other neurological conditions" may be included, if the Health, Education, and Welfare (HEW) secretary would consider them "similar to mental retardation or requiring similar treatment" (Akerley 1979, 223). This wording reflected the political reality of the superior clout of NARC over the less-powerful United Cerebral Palsy (UCP) association and the Epilepsy Foundation of America (EFA). It reflected the historical context in which the term was introduced as part of a bill to reauthorize the Kennedy bill originally targeted solely at mental retardation. Mental retardation advocates considered the bill "theirs" and 90 percent of the members of state developmental disabilities councils were representatives of NARC. Finally, the wording reflected the fiscal reality: the resources appropriated for the bill were well below what was needed, and the competition for scarce resources was fierce (Akerley 1979 222–25; Maryland Developmental Disabilities Council 2008). Regardless, at least at the level of legislation, access to services, and the political campaign mounted by associations and activists, the law placed a premium on representing other conditions, of which autism was the most visible, as akin to mental retardation in being "neurological," that is, possessing some diffuse etiology which mainly served to exclude any implication of psychological or emotional origins.

The legislation forced NSAC to get its act together and become an effective lobbying force in Washington, since HEW, pushed by NARC representatives, did not find autism "similar to mental retardation" and hence it was ineligible to reap the benefits of the act. A neurologist member of the national council on developmental disabilities explained that the causes of autism were "psychological" not "neurological." In response, NSAC members inundated HEW with letters arguing that autism was a physiological disorder. They had the support of Donald Cohen, child psychiatrist at the Yale Child Study Center and the new special assistant to the director of the Office of Child Development at HEW, who wrote a memo to the director of the division of developmental disabilities explaining that autism was "a generalized central nervous system disorder." This is how the destigmatizing campaign, begun by Rimland, was transformed: in order to refute the psychogenic hypothesis he needed to show that autism was a rare and specific illness, only superficially appearing similar to mental retardation. The key to success in a struggle over scarce resources was still to refute the psychogenic hypothesis, but now in order to demonstrate an essential similarity and affinity between autism and mental retardation. In fact, in order to prevail, autism advocates pushed for a "noncategorical" legislation that would not identify any specific disabilities, but merely the functional limitations shared by all developmentally disabled individuals. First, in 1975, autism was simply added to the legislation, but finally in 1978, after all the different organizations banded together to form a lobbying consortium, and after Congress threatened to discontinue funding if they did not resolve their differences, the noncategorical approach won out and became legislation (Akerley 1979, 225–31; Maryland Developmental Disabilities Council 2008). The political need to avoid destructive competition and bickering by the different constituencies thus created a vastly changed landscape in which the various conditions and disorders were much less differentiated from one another.

Autism as concurrent with mental retardation

This, however, is only half of the story. We already saw how the conditions for autism's expansion in later years into a spectrum were prepared in advance by the new therapies that blurred the boundary between mental illness and retardation, and by the network of expertise forged by parents of autistic children. If the story was merely about political mobilization, destigmatization, and struggle over legislation and scarce resources, it is not at all clear that they would have led to the expansion of the diagnosis into a spectrum. All that the legislation required was that autism would be *analogous* to mental retardation as a neurological disorder. This stipulation could have easily coexisted with Rimland's and Kanner's initial restriction of the scope of the diagnosis. The fact is that autism's expansion into a spectrum in later years was achieved not via an analogy with mental retardation, but through removing the obstacle, originally laid down by Rimland and Kanner, to considering the two together as overlapping and concurrent conditions. In his book, Rimland equivocated about how autism was related, if at all, to mental retardation, and ultimately sought to erect a "firewall" between the two. He concurred with Kanner that the parents of autistic children were unusually intelligent, if personally cold, in order to pull autism back into the ethical realm of illness in the same way that the term "apparent feeblemindedness" was meant to do – to protect it from disappearing into the vast wasteland of mental retardation.

What happened between 1964 and 1978, however, was deinstitutionalization. As we saw in Chapter 4, the most immediate change was the rapid abandonment of the 1950s practice of institutionalizing very young children suspected to be mentally retarded. Correspondingly, clinicians now expressed much less certainty about diagnosing mental illness in very early childhood. "Behavioral disorders, deviant affective manifestations – in short, the whole pathology which we equate with psychiatric problems," said Rene Spitz (1971, 240–43), "are not psychiatric at all during" the first and second years of life. Since the psyche is not yet established, "we can speak at best only of an impairment of the innate potentiality to develop a psychic system." He suggested, therefore, thinking of the "adaptive disorders" of these early years "as nosologic entities *sui generis*, defined as developmentally determined age-specific entities." Autism, he thought, was a "transitional form" between these "totally dependent" adaptive disorders and the "increasingly autonomous, volitional . . . psychiatric disease proper" (Spitz 1971, 242–43).

The whole domain of early childhood developmental disorders was becoming relatively autonomous, and psychiatrists no longer had sole jurisdiction. Recall those child psychiatrists who approached Robert Spitzer trying to resurrect Rank's idea of "atypical development" and turn it into a *bona fide* DSM diagnosis, so as to reclaim psychiatric jurisdiction over this zone. Recall also that Spitzer, who himself did research on childhood schizophrenia, threw them out. Within this autonomous zone, no longer split between illness and retardation, new kinds of relations between autism and mental retardation became possible. Within this domain, the new therapies and the network of expertise forged by parents of autistic children fit hand in glove. With normalization proclaiming a universal right to an existence "as close to the normal as possible," Rimland's dogmatic assertions about the rarity of the disorder and the unique intellectuality of the parents, calculated to balance autism between illness and retardation, were no longer necessary and came under critical scrutiny. We saw in the preceding chapter that already in 1972, speaking to a NSAC audience, Wing effectively called for dismantling the distinction between autism and mental retardation. Similarly, at her Indianapolis Clinical

Research Center for Early Childhood Schizophrenia, Marian DeMyer began a research program designed to show that Rimland was wrong, that the parents of autistic children were not uniquely educated or intellectual, and that, in her words, "evidence . . . links autistic children more closely with subnormal than normal children in terms of neurological integrity" (Allen et al. 1971, 325). Though they were aware that many parents of autistic children "believe that the intelligence of their kids is basically normal" (322, n.9), DeMyer (1972), Lockyer and Rutter (1969), Rutter (1978), Ando (1979/1980), Wing and Wing (1971) and countless other researchers during the early 1970s began to argue on the contrary that "autism and mental retardation frequently coexist."[2]

Saying that autism and mental retardation coexist is very different from talking about "apparent feeblemindedness" or "pseudo-defective children." In earlier formulations, autism or childhood schizophrenia underlay, preceded, and completely determined mental retardation. They had the value of an inner state, a "disease entity," while mental retardation had merely the value of a symptom or an observable expression of this inner state. Or, in the debunking move, mental retardation became the real thing, and autism or childhood schizophrenia merely a misdiagnosis, which shows, precisely, that they could not coexist. If, in the early 1970s, it suddenly became possible to strike this new relation between them, to juxtapose autism and mental retardation as states existing side by side, it is precisely because they were now inscribed on the same register, given the same value as observable behaviors by the new modular treatment programs (Lovaas 1979). For them to coexist in this way presupposed the capacity to distinguish between them as observable behaviors (which presupposed the capacity to record and count and chart these behaviors), to mark meaningful thresholds where one ended and the other began.

Indeed, in the early 1970s there suddenly developed an intense interest in the differential diagnostics of autism and mental retardation. The issue was no longer to determine which one was real and which was apparent, but to discern how they differed as objects of therapeutic intervention. The overall finding reported in countless studies in the U.S., Britain, and the Netherlands was that there were many autistics among the mentally retarded, but that they were different and far more problematic, because they did not communicate: they were aloof, avoided eye contact, did not interact with age peers, and many did not speak. They scored lower on scales for social skills, communication, and social competence, all things that would have been under the radar in the institution. Additionally, they were distinguished by

problem behaviors – self-injury, aggression, hyperactivity, stereotypical routines and behaviors, withdrawal, lack of self-control, problems
with toilet training – precisely the sort of things that in the past would
have gotten one in the back ward of the institution and literally out of
sight (Krajier 1997, 30–34, 40–42; DeMyer 1972).

Autism now became differentiated within a new institutional
matrix that served as what Foucault (1972) would call a "grid of
specification." The key to this development, as we have argued, was
the deinstitutionalization of mental retardation, and the therapies
that were deployed by the new institutional matrix of early intervention, special education and community treatment. These therapies –
behavior modification, sensory-motor therapy, occupational therapy,
speech therapy, sensory integration therapy, developmental therapy,
special education techniques – were applied equally to mentally
retarded children, autistic children, schizophrenic or "psychotic"
children, children with learning disabilities or language disorders, and
children with "special sensory sensitivities," thus establishing equivalency between them, arraying them on the same register, so to speak,
and then drawing internal distinctions between them so they became
"nosologic entities *sui generis*." This meant that one no longer faced
Rimland's quandary. Autism no longer needed to be a disease entity,
or to be restricted into a rare syndrome, in order to avoid blending
indistinguishably with mental retardation. Against the background
of therapies that sought to establish communicative rapport with the
child, a certain set of behaviors would become particularly visible and
differentiable as the recalcitrant material requiring, as Schopler and
Reichler (1971, 94) put it, "the adult's non-specific impingement on
the child," requiring an intensification of the efforts of the therapists
and the mobilization of all available agents, especially the parents.

The therapy devised by Michael Rutter (Rutter and Sussenwein
1971, 376–83) in Britain was identical in all essential details to the
TEACCH program established by Schopler in North Carolina. Like
TEACCH, Rutter's program was responding to an increase in the
referral of very young children, caused by deinstitutionalization, and
the need to develop techniques appropriate to this age group. His
was a similarly modular blend of behavior modification techniques,
direct teaching, and a "developmental" approach, all linked and integrated by systems of observation, coding, and reporting. He adopted
TEACCH's innovation of mobilizing the parents as "co-therapists."
Most importantly, Rutter's program was similarly organized around
the cardinal principle of the adult's "non-specific impingement,"
making sure that the child could not accomplish anything without the

mediation of an adult and thus imposing the need to establish some sort of communicative rapport. Within this treatment and research program, he explained, it no longer made sense to ask the traditional question – "What is autism?" – but rather to read it from right to left in a decidedly nominalist fashion: "To what set of phenomena shall we apply the term *autism*?" (Rutter 1978, 141).

Compare this with Lorna Wing's retrospective recounting of her thinking as she devised the study that would provide the basis for the new idea of an autism spectrum:

> What Judy and I wanted to do was not come along with an absolutely set definition you know, these are the points that define autism and anything else outside those points we're not interested in. We had a different angle on this. What we wanted to do was see how much items of autistic behavior, features of autistic behavior, how often they occurred among children in general. We were interested in anything that was anything like the features of an autistic disorder. Even one single thing, like having odd stereotype movements interested us. So therefore we were approaching the thing bottom up, instead of top down.[3]

Taking this "bottom-up" approach, Wing and Gould arrived at a formulation not much different than Rutter's (1978) a year earlier and Schopler's (Schopler et al. 1980) a year later. A large group of children shared a "triad" of impairments in language, social interaction, and repetitive behaviors. All three were formulating new diagnostic criteria and a new understanding of autism as a spectrum from within programs that crucially blended research and diagnosis with comprehensive treatment and experimentation with new therapies. The prevalence of this triad was about four to five times higher than the prevalence of "classical autism," distinguished by the use of idiosyncratic phrases, reversal of pronouns and elaborate repetitive routines, yet Wing and Gould did not see much point in maintaining this distinction. They averred that "the distribution of the variables among the subgroups suggested that they formed a continuum of severity rather than discrete entities" (Wing and Gould 1979, 26). Let us immediately note that the "distribution of variables" did not show, nor could it show, any such thing. Looking at Wing and Gould's results one could reach the conclusion that classical autism is a unique syndrome (since the behaviors of children with known history of classical autism differed significantly on two important measures from the behavior of children without such history), or that Wing and Gould's "aloof" type was simply a better way of diagnosing this unique syndrome, or, most credibly, that what we know and the behavioral symptoms we

can measure simply do not provide enough discriminating information to decide whether there were one or more syndromes here or a
continuum. Seeing a "continuum of severity," as Wing admitted later,
and as Rutter was quite forthright about, was a pragmatic choice.
Rimland and Kanner, believing or choosing to believe that autism was
a rare disorder, objected precisely to this procedure in which the full
syndrome is broken into items, each of which can become a metonym
of "autism," and all of which arrayed according to severity. If you
believe that autism is rare, you will see here illegitimate inference. If
you believe that it is widespread, or – more to the point – that it is
useful to treat it as widespread, you will see a continuum of severity.
Two years later, introducing "Asperger's syndrome" and arguing
that it too should be included within the syndrome, albeit on the least
severe side, Wing (1981, 124) was very clear about why it was useful
and legitimate to take this "bottom up" approach:

> The justification for regarding them as related is that all the conditions
> in which the triad of language and social impairments occurs, whatever
> the level of severity, are accompanied by similar problems affecting
> social and intellectual skills. Furthermore, individuals with the triad
> of symptoms all require the same kind of structured, organized educa-
> tional approach, although the aims and achievements of education will
> vary from minimal self-care up to a university degree.

To translate into our own idiom: what brought together all these
"atypical children," many of whom would be diagnosed with mental
retardation as well, was their recalcitrance, the resistance they
afforded to the sociability demands of the new institutional matrix,
which required them to be interactive and communicative in various
domains. What brought them together was also the promise that this
recalcitrance, in whatever shape it appeared, could be treated by an
identical set of therapies, themselves representing mostly an intensification of existing features of the institutional matrix (e.g., "non-
specific impingement"). Finally, what brought them together was the
capacity of these therapies to break the syndrome down to a list of
"items of autistic behavior," to array these on the same register as the
behaviors exhibited by the mentally retarded, so that one no longer
needed to choose between illness and retardation.

Looping and the transformation of autism

In 1979, the *Journal of Autism and Childhood Schizophrenia* was renamed *Journal of Autism and Developmental Disabilities*. Schopler et al. (1979, 1–4) explained that a majority of the board wanted to change the name already in 1975, when the new Developmental Disabilities Act including autism was passed, but had to wait until the publisher agreed. In the meantime, during the journal's eight years of existence only 6 percent of publications were about childhood schizophrenia. When the journal began, the name reflected thinking that autism might be an earlier form of childhood schizophrenia, but further research showed they were unconnected. Autistic children do not develop into schizophrenics. Autism is an inborn condition and diagnosed between birth and three years of age. Schizophrenia is an illness that strikes much later. So a simple early-onset criterion can distinguish between the two without overlap. Regarding the new name, "administrative and political conclusions coincide with the empirical evidence . . . Our current state of knowledge has demonstrated that autism frequently coexists with other disabilities of development. . . . Mental retardation, cerebral palsy, epilepsy, and autism all refer to overlapping states with different causal mechanisms" (Schopler et al. 1979, 4). This was to be the state of affairs for the next decade. Autism no longer needed to contend with childhood schizophrenia as a competitor. Childhood schizophrenia was banished from the space between illness and retardation. At the end of the decade, when, as Rutter predicted, the childhood schizophrenia diagnosis was already a musty thing belonging strictly to the section on the "history of psychiatry," the late-onset exclusion would be removed by DSM-III-R with little ceremony.

By the same token, Schopler et al. (1979, 4–6) explained that research and treatment would profit if autism was no longer considered "a unitary disease entity" but as overlapping, concurrent, and deeply intertwined with all the other developmental disabilities – mental retardation, cerebral palsy, epilepsy, speech and language delays, learning disabilities – because many symptoms ("items of autistic behavior") were shared between these conditions, and because often the siblings of autistic children would exhibit one or more of these other conditions. The journal's new scope would include developmental disorders that are not well understood, any delays or distortions of development, including sensory sensitivities. Autism was fast becoming something new, altogether different from what Kanner saw and described – despite ritual protestations to the contrary and periodic affirmations of renewed fidelity to the Master's original intentions.

There is no better evidence for this than the sort of things that began to fall out of the triad as incidental and no longer part of the core syndrome. Note that Wing and Gould's "triad" included hardly any mention of self-injurious behaviors such as the head-banging and hand-biting that in the past constituted such an important part of the syndrome. Rimland (1964, 59) quotes Jacques May (surgeon and father of autistic twins) approvingly, when he says that "I do not know any one of these children who did not have the rocking and banging of head." In the DSM-III (1980), self-mutilation was one of the criteria for childhood-onset Pervasive Developmental Disorder (PDD). In the DSM-III-R (1987) criteria, however, self-injury became merely an "associated feature." These criteria were developed by Wing on the basis of her 1979 article, and in her role as member of the advisory committee on PDD for the DSM-III-R (Waterhouse et al. 1992, 528–29, 535–36). They also reflect NSAC's definition of autism, developed by Ritvo and Freeman (1978), where self-injury was not considered part of the core syndrome of autism.

Finally, in the DSM-IV (1994) there is no longer any mention of self-mutilation or head-banging. By that time, Bryna Siegel (1996, 74), another member of the advisory committee, could assert – in a book written for parents – that self-injurious behaviors like head-banging and hand-biting were in fact quite rare in autism. What happened between 1964 and 1994? Siegel goes on to say that "it's my clinical impression that there is a lot less hand biting now than twenty years ago." Why? Whether her impression is accurate or not, we think that the condition permitting to *formulate* this impression was the fact that self-injurious behaviors, and self-stimulatory behaviors more generally, came under the jurisdiction of behavior modification therapies in the 1970s. Lovaas certainly made them one of his prime targets. Self-injurious and self-stimulatory behavior came to be seen as treatable or at least controllable by these therapies, and consequently came to be discounted as outside the core symptoms of autism. Schopler (1978, 169) said as much: behavior modification can eliminate self-destructive behavior in autism, but this is relevant to the treatment of "any severely disturbed child." "Only a few" autistic children "are seriously self-destructive." Hence self-injurious behaviors as well as repetitive movements and stereotypy are "associated features," not part of the core disturbances. It is against the background of these therapies that Wing as well demoted self-mutilation and head-banging from the foreground as behaviors that are merely "associated" – that is, they should not be used to diagnose autism, they are not part of the "core symptoms." Over time, they were almost completely eclipsed by the special sensory sensitivities of autistic children, to which therapies such as perceptual-motor therapy and sensory integration therapy paid particular attention (Siegel 1996, 60–72). In NSAC's 1978 definition of autism, "responses to sensory stimuli" constituted an independent dimension, into which were collapsed some behaviors that counted as stereotypy or "alone-ness" in Kanner-influenced definitions, such as lack of eye contact, spinning, hand-flapping, and so on (Ritvo and Freeman 1978, 162). Today, sensory sensitivities, especially as defined by sensory integra-tion therapy, constitute the unofficial fourth dimension of the triad.

Even more dramatic, because so central, was the fate of Kanner's "cardinal symptom" of autistic aloneness and utter lack of interest in people (Rimland 1964, 8). Under the pressure of the therapies' "non-specific impingement," Wing was able to make distinctions between the very few who were aloof and indifferent in all situations, those who liked merely physical contact with others, those who were indif-ferent only toward other children but not toward adults, those who were passive but amiable when approached, and finally those who made active social approaches but in inappropriate ways (Wing and Gould 1979, 14–15). This could be translated into the more general idea of an "impairment of social interaction," so that what in the DSM-III was a nonnegotiable demand for the presence of "perva-sive lack of responsiveness to other people (autism)," had become in DSM-III-R a variable of "qualitative impairment in reciprocal social interaction" of which the aloofness and flat affect noted by Kanner were possible but no longer necessary components.

Two autism diagnostic scales were published in 1980, between the two versions of the DSM-III. One, Krug et al.'s (1980) Autism Behavior Checklist (ABC), harked back to Kanner's original criteria and Rimland's Form E-2. It assigned almost half of the maximum number of points to the areas of "relating" and "body/object use": the repetitive, stereotyped, and ritualized behaviors that are today referred to as "classic autism" and that had orginally served to constitute the syndrome as strongly distinct from mental retarda-tion. Many of these received the heaviest weights (4 points) on the ABC: whirling around oneself, odd speech intonation, rocking oneself, hand-flapping, stimming,[4] covering ears at sounds, echolalia, ritualistic behaviors such as lining up toys, toe-walking, staring into space for prolonged periods of time, and the like. When compared with today's "gold standard" of diagnostic instruments, the ADOS

(Autism Diagnostic Observation Schedule [Lord et al. 1989]), only two ABC descriptors with a weight of 4 are still considered relevant today: lack of eye contact and the failure to develop friendships. Not surprisingly, the ABC has been losing its validity over time. Volkmar et al. (1988) found that only 57 percent of the children with autism in their study were classified as probably autistic by the ABC. Wadden et al. (1991) reported that only 49 percent of their children with autism had ABC scores that indicated a high probability of autism, while Sevin et al. (1991) found that 50 percent of their subjects were misclassified as not autistic by the ABC. Damningly, the ABC seems unable to differentiate autism from mental retardation in accordance with the DSM-IV, classifying children as mentally retarded whom researchers consider to be autistic by the DSM-IV criteria (Rellini et al. 2004). Currently, the ABC has been pronounced by the American Academy of Pediatrics as not useful for diagnosis and is now used primarily by school psychologists for designing intervention strategies (Baron 2004).

But the nail in the coffin for the ABC seems to have been its under-performance in comparison with Schopler et al.'s Childhood Autism Rating Scale (CARS 1980), published in the same year. If the ABC harked back, the CARS was "ahead of its time," or more precisely it expressed the diagnostic consensus arrived at somewhat independently by Rutter, Schopler, and Wing, without being bound by the forces that still shaped the DSM-III diagnostic criteria. Already in 1980 it was implementing what would later become the DSM-III-R criteria. Unsurprisingly, later studies utilizing the DSM-III-R criteria found the CARS to be far superior to the ABC. Sevin et al. (1991) found the CARS to be accurate 92 percent of the time and Rellini et al. (2004) found an accuracy rate of 100 percent for the CARS.

On a variety of levels, autism, as defined by the CARS, was no longer the same thing as the autism that served as the object of the ABC. The "classic" stereotypical and repetitive behaviors that the ABC tended to weigh so heavily – rocking oneself, hand-flapping, lining up toys – were collapsed into the categories of "body use" and "object use" in the CARS, which meant that exhibiting *all* of these behaviors would only add a maximum of 8 points to the child's CARS score (and so a maximum of 13 percent of the total score), while they would have constituted 24 percent of the ABC total score. Thus, the CARS restricted the importance of this category for a diagnosis of autism. In fact, it is no longer a necessary condition.[5] Similarly, while the ABC included only one item coding for eye contact (with a weight of 4 points), with the CARS there are at least two (and possibly three) scales on which this symptom can be scored. A collateral consequence was a changed relationship to mental retardation: downgrading the significance of stereotypical and repetitive behaviors effectively raises the status and weight of other CARS categories – verbal communication, adaptation to change, emotional response – that overlap with mental retardation. It thus increases the likelihood of diagnostic substitution. Most important, the CARS scales were scored to reflect degree of impairment, thereby stretching autism into a spectrum, whereas the ABC was only concerned with whether a particular behavior was present or absent, thus still treating autism as a distinct disease entity. Additionally, while the ABC was essentially a list of specific behaviors (for instance, "strong reactions to minor changes in routine/environment"), CARS was composed of scales each constituting a *category* of behavior (such as "adaptation to change"). Thus, unlike ABC, the CARS forced practitioners to think of autism as a multidimensional spectrum rather than a small subset of symptoms constituting a syndrome.

Thus the claim of the DSM-III-R advisory committee to have corrected the DSM-III by "return[ing] to the criteria of Kanner's original case study descriptive accounts" (Waterhouse et al. 1992, 526) must be taken with a grain of salt. Waterhouse and Wing did review Kanner's case study accounts and pulled out items that were then added to the DSM-III-R criteria, but this was, after all, precisely the procedure to which Kanner objected in 1965. Autism in the DSM-III-R was no longer the same thing as what Kanner saw and described. We will return to the DSM-III-R and the making of the spectrum in Chapter 11. For the moment, let us underline the significance of this argument: that the spectrum was no longer the same as Kanner's syndrome. This is not a critical argument. We are not saying that either Kanner or Wing was wrong, that one was closer to the reality of autism and the other farther. We do not think anybody is in a position to make this argument. Further, we think that such a critical argument misstates the relation between the diagnostic classification "autism" and the reality of autism. It expects the one to reflect the other as closely as possible, while the transformations we began to chart indicate that the two interact and "loop," as Ian Hacking (1995, 1999) puts it. Classifying and naming autism set in motion processes that act on the phenomena classified and possibly change them in ways that, in turn, react back on the classification, leading to its revision.

For example, Rimland and Kanner restricted autism in the mid-1960s to a rare and distinct disorder. We do not know whether they were wrong or right in doing so, but what we do know is that their act of classification began a dynamic that undid their assertion. Rimland insisted on the rareness and distinctiveness of autism in order to defeat the psychogenic hypothesis and remove the burden of guilt from parents, without at the same time collapsing autism into the vast territory of mental retardation. Kanner did the same for his own reasons: to remove his concept from competition with childhood schizophrenia and to forge an alliance with parents. To the extent that both were successful, however, they destigmatized the condition and gave rise to an active parents movement, both of which meant that the diagnosis was becoming less rare, and in due course, less distinctive. This was the first, 90-degree loop. It did not yet lead to an official change of diagnostic criteria, but it enabled, as we saw, the insertion of autism-qua-developmental disability into the new institutional matrix created by deinstitutionalization.

Within this matrix, a second loop took place, now from the therapies addressing themselves to developmental disabilities back to the new diagnostic criteria devised by the researcher-therapist-advocate-parents, codified in diagnostic scales and eventually also picked up by the DSM. As we saw, the therapies gradually identified certain behaviors like head-banging and self-injury as treatable and therefore incidental to the syndrome, thus trimming away at its edges and blurring its boundaries. The therapies also established an equivalency between the multiple ways – from aloofness to oddness – in which the communicative rapport necessary for therapy could break down, thereby stretching, as it were, what was understood to be the core of the syndrome. So over the long term, what happened between autistics and therapists began to redefine what autism really was and what it was not, both the boundaries and the core of the syndrome. What happened between therapists and autistics began to change what the clinicians knew they should be looking for – if they used the CARS, for example. Then it was reported back to parents in books such as Siegel's, which meant that clinicians would indeed see in their offices more or less what they were looking for, that demand and supply were being adjusted to one another. Then eventually the DSM was twice amended to reflect these new points of dynamic equilibrium. In this way, the movement started by Rimland and Kanner in the mid-1960s completed a full 180-degree loop. It substantially revised how autism looks and feels; how it is understood, classified, and counted. How else could one characterize this change but to say that autism was no longer the same thing? The irony was, of course, that precisely those behaviors that initially differentiated autism from among the atypical children and made it the privileged object of the therapies

– the problem behaviors and the noncommunicativeness – were the ones that mutated. The problem behaviors were the most responsive to the therapies, and therefore became residual. Aloofness became the main target of the therapies and therefore became capable of assuming many different forms. The result was the precise opposite of what Rimland and Kanner hoped for. Autism became protean, a spectrum that could encompass increasing varieties of disorder with differing degrees of severity. As noted earlier, the spectrum could even include stark opposites such as profound intellectual disability together with savant abilities (recall Rimland's "knife-edged path"), hyper-sensitivity and hypo-sensitivity, aloofness and over-attachment (recall Mahler's "symbiotic psychosis"), flat affect and aggressive tantrums.

—10—

ASPERGER AND NEURODIVERSITY

One name has been conspicuously absent from this book up until this point: Asperger. We trust the readers are by now familiar with Leo Kanner, his work, his acerbic humor, his influence, but they have not heard much about Hans Asperger. Yet one could argue that, over the past three decades, he and the syndrome that bears his name have come to eclipse Kanner and his syndrome (to which, as we have shown, the criteria for autistic disorder today bear only superficial resemblance) in terms of shaping the autism spectrum and contemporary autism discourse. Asperger's influence is recognizable, in particular, in the rise of a whole new category of individuals – autistic self-advocates like Temple Grandin, Daniel Tammet, and Donna Williams – who now serve as some of the most recognizable faces and voices of the autism spectrum. What do they have to do with the story we have told up until now, of liberation from the institutions of yesteryear, of the network of expertise, of the rise of the therapies and the carving of a space between mental retardation and mental illness? It is time, therefore, we reckoned with Asperger's influence and with the phenomenon represented by these ambassadors of autism and neurodiversity.

The story of Asperger's syndrome is extraordinary and quite perplexing. First, there is the uncanny fact of the simultaneous yet completely independent discovery of autism by Kanner and Asperger in 1943 and 1944, respectively. Why did their descriptions coincide so well in time and in substance if they were unaware of one another's work? Then there is the fact that, despite their simultaneous discovery and the very similar terms they used to describe and name what they saw, for 45 years the professional consensus was that these were two different syndromes, two different clinical entities. What kept

Kanner's "infantile autism" and Asperger's "autistic psychopathy" separate for so long? Finally, there is the no less extraordinary fact that despite these decades of determined mutual isolation, the two conditions were brought into connection in 1994 in DSM-IV. What made it possible and practical to conceive of Asperger's disorder and Kanner's autism as connected on a continuous spectrum? The story of Asperger's disorder, therefore, is a composition in three movements: twinborn, separated at birth, twins reunited. *Finale*.

The riddle of simultaneous discovery dissolved

The Atlantic Ocean and WWII between them, Leo Kanner and Hans Asperger chose exactly the same term to describe the children they saw – "autistic." The Swiss psychiatrist Eugen Bleuler coined the term decades earlier to describe his schizophrenic patients.[1] Bleuler's patients went into states where they seemed totally detached from the outside world. Disconnecting from the world around oneself and basking in fantasy was something any person did to a certain extent, Bleuler thought. He dubbed this state of disconnection "autism" and spoke of "autistic thinking" as one modality of thought that all humans engaged in (Bleuler 1913).[2] Grinker (2007, 44) reminds us that autism was a *symptom*, not a syndrome, for Bleuler and those who came after him. It only became a syndrome after Kanner and Asperger penned their descriptions. Asperger thought Bleuler's term good enough but not quite right, and Kanner would retrospectively say he felt the same (Asperger [1944] 1991, 39; Kanner 1965, 1973). It was not quite right because autism was *not* a temporary-if-persistent state for the children they described. It was a durable way of being. It was not a retreat from the world, but a different kind of *contact* with it. And this word, "contact," is notably present in both their original writings as well as Bleuler's. It found its way also into the Dutch "contact disorder."

The simultaneous use of these terms – contact, autism – is important since, after all, this was not really so much a case of simultaneous *discovery* as of simultaneous *description*. Kanner was not a Pasteur, bending over his microscope and discovering a new entity, the bacillus, never before seen. Asperger was neither Watson nor Crick, manipulating a model of molecules until he arrived at the elegance of the double helix. Kanner and Asperger saw something that many others had seen before them or around the same time, but they described it differently, using the word "autistic."[3] What is important is that it was not possible to *be* an autistic person, to experience oneself as such and to interact with others on that basis, until Kanner or Asperger, each in his own way, redescribed what he saw in terms of a new syndrome (Hacking 1995, 1999, 2007). With their writings, Kanner and Asperger each conjured into being a new type of person, and as we saw in previous chapters, this set in motion looping processes that caused the original category to morph (Hacking 1995, 1999, 2004, 2007). In this chapter, we will be able to add more depth and credibility to this story of looping, but before we do so we have to answer some initial questions. First, why would these two men, at the same time, dust off and refashion the same term to describe children with attributes that others had seen and described differently?

Ultimately, the convergence is not as uncanny and mysterious as it may seem. After all, the two men came out of a similar tradition. They were formed professionally within similar intellectual and clinical milieus. Both were born in Austria; Asperger was trained in Vienna, Kanner in Berlin. In the U.S., Kanner worked with Adolph Meyer, the leader of the mental hygiene movement, who brought the thinking and concepts developed within the Austro-German milieu to America. Among these were the refinement of the concept of psychosis, and a focus on development, personality, and childhood coming out of the Freudian legacy. These trends explain in part why their writings would come at the same time and share so much (Grinker 2007; Nadesan 2005; Hacking 2007b).

More important, from our point of view, were similarities in the institutional location of the two men, their similarly interstitial position between disciplines. In earlier chapters, we have emphasized that the concept of autism, in Kanner's hands, was geared to stitch together child guidance with the institutional care and treatment of mental retardation. It served as the hinge connecting the two, mental illness and mental retardation, and unifying them into a single field of observation and treatment. Kanner envisioned this field as the proper domain of child psychiatry, organized around an object that consequently could have been identical with neither illness nor retardation. Asperger, in fact, was even more interstitially located in what was called *Heïlpädagogik* (or remedial pedagogy). *Heïlpädagogik* was not exactly "special education." It was more like an attempt to combine medical and pedagogic expertise in the same institutional location, and possibly in the same person. According to Asperger (1979, 46), his was the first institution to combine clinical research and educational treatment of child psychiatric patients. At his clinic, "education and therapy were the same thing" (Frith 1991, 8), much as they are in today's autism world. Further, Kanner himself was certainly aware of *Heïlpädagogik* and held it in high regard (Kanner 1964, 141; Neve and Turner 2002, 388).

Why is it important that both were located interstitially, at some intersection of medicine and education? Recall the choice of the term "autism" by both men. They plundered it from Bleuler's tool box in order to articulate a clinical entity that could be assimilated neither to the realm of mental retardation nor to that of mental illness. Even if Kanner wavered on this, allowing autism to be placed temporarily within the realm of psychogenesis (or at least not resisting that move for a time), his choice of terms for describing what he saw was the same as Asperger's, and he similarly strove to define an object proper to the new domain he was trying to open up. The two key words in Kanner's *"inborn autistic disturbances of affective contact"* (1943, 250) were "inborn" and "contact." Asperger used similar words, with precisely the same meaning. First, speaking of an "inborn" or, as Asperger put it, "constitutional" disturbance, was meant to distinguish the condition from mental illness with acute onset and a precipitating, perhaps psychogenic, trauma (Frith 1991, 9). Asperger was emphatic that of the 200 patients he saw over the years, only one developed something like schizophrenia. There was no biological or genetic relationship to schizophrenia (Asperger [1944] 1991, 87). Second, speaking of a disturbance of "contact" was meant to indicate that it was not an intellectual disorder either. As Asperger (1979, 46) noted, by the 1930s intelligence testing had become fashionable even in Vienna. He could certainly have opted to interpret the results of such tests as indicating an intellectual deficiency in the children he saw and described, but he was convinced that the "disturbance was elsewhere and made one think of personality traits which the then current psychiatric circles did not describe or clarify" (1979, 46). The essential abnormality in autistic psychopathy is "disturbance of the lively relationship with the whole environment." Autistic psychopathy thus was not an intellectual disturbance, not retardation; like Kanner's, it was one of *contact*, whether *affective* (having to do specifically with people) or *lively* (having to do with both people and objects) (Asperger 1991, 58, 86–87; Grinker 2007, 59; Frith 1991).

In short, the riddle of simultaneous discovery is more apparent than real. Asperger and Kanner did not discover the same thing, but used a similar set of terms to describe what they saw. They did not need to talk to one another to arrive at a common set of terms. They functioned within a common universe of discourse and formulated their concepts in dialogue with the concepts and approaches of a small group of discursive interlocutors – Sigmund Freud, Eugen Bleuler, Adolph Meyer, Kurt Schneider. They gave these terms analogous meanings because they were similarly located at the intersection of disciplines and similarly strove to open up the space between these disciplines.

"Personality trait" vs. "psychotic process"

In 1971, Leo Kanner wrote a review of a book on infantile autism. In his acerbic style, he tore it to pieces. In doing so, he made his first and perhaps only reference in print to Asperger's work, distancing it mightily from his own construct. In spite of a reference to "meticulous proofreading" in the book under review, Kanner noted,

> There is repeated mention of "Ansperger" who is cited as having "confirmed Kanner's syndrome" in 1944. The name is Asperger, and the man, at that time, could have no knowledge of Kanner's publication; instead, he independently described what he called "autistic psychopathy" which, if at all related to infantile autism, is at best a forty-second cousin . . . and has received serious attention from investigators not confused by klang [sic] associations. (Kanner 1971, 390)

A forty-second cousin! To be sure, as we have noted, by this time Kanner had chosen to restrict autism to a rare and unique disorder. Connecting it to Asperger's more able children would have further expanded and watered down autism, and Kanner worried that over-diagnosis of autism was already threatening to sap the category of any relevance (Kanner 1965). Nonetheless, it is clear that there is a second historical puzzle here to be solved: considering all the similarities between the two concepts, why were they kept apart for so long? Why were the twins turned into cousins, forty-two times removed?

The usual answer one finds in the psychiatric and autism literature is language. Asperger wrote in German, the story goes, and therefore his work was simply unknown (or little known) to English-reading audiences until Lorna Wing introduced it in 1981 (Wolff and Chick 1980, 88; Wing 1981, 1986, 2005). This explanation, however, is thin at best. Asperger's work was known in the English-speaking world, and not only to Kanner.[4] The Dutch psychiatrist D. Arn Van Krevelen began writing about it in English in 1962 and published a paper on the relationship between Kanner's autism and Asperger's "autistic psychopathy" in the very first issue of the *JACS* in 1971 (edited by Kanner – clearly this was a connection he wanted to dispatch as soon as possible).[5] It was by no means unknown outside of Europe. Bernard Rimland had briefly mentioned Asperger's syndrome in his 1965 book, *Infantile Autism*, though in a letter to a colleague shortly after sending the book off for publication he admitted: "I don't understand Asperger's syndrome very well, except that the children tend to be quite bright (IQ over 130) but are decidedly deficient in warmth" (Rimland 1964b, 2). What he knew of Asperger, he told his correspondent, he learned from Van Krevelen's work. Rutter as well discussed Asperger's syndrome and its relation to autism, repeating Van Krevelen (Rimland 1964, 54; Van Krevelen 1963, 1971; Van Krevelen and Kuipers 1962; Rutter 1978, 145). Kanner, Van Krevelen, Rimland, Rutter, Wing – one could not have assembled a more eminent group of experts to disseminate information about Asperger's work to non-German-reading parents and experts. In fact, as we shall see later, in the mid-1970s there was agitation within the two national parents' organizations – the American and the British – to gain greater recognition for the problems of higher-functioning, or "near-normal," autistics. In short, the latency of Asperger's uptake relative to Kanner's was not caused by a language barrier. We must seek a different, more contextually sensitive explanation.

How did contemporaries justify the separation and disconnection between Kanner's "early infantile autism" and Asperger's "autistic psychopathy"? They said, with Van Krevelen, that the latter was a *static* "personality trait" while the former a "psychotic process" with a *course* (1971, 83, 84; see also Rutter 1978, 145). This was the key difference Van Krevelen used as the basis for his argument that they were "two entirely different nosological syndromes" (1971, 84). He also listed six other points on which the two constructs diverged, but the distinctions he drew were nebulous. For example, Kanner's child "lives in a world of his own," while Asperger's "lives in our world in his own way" (1971, 84) – hardly a sharp nosological hook on which to hang a diagnosis. In fact, he went as far as to suggest a possible common genetic basis for both, though with autism involving a further organic injury. He presented a clinical case of a family who had one child with autistic psychopathy and another with infantile autism (and said he knew of two other similar cases). "It is possible," he noted, "to think that the patient with early infantile autism is an organically damaged child who, if it were not for the organicity, might have developed into an autistic psychopath of the kind described by Asperger" (1971, 85).[6] This is good evidence that the distinction between personality trait and psychotic process was the decisive element separating the two syndromes within a discursive

217

economy quite different from our own. Change the terms a little bit in Van Krevelen's formulation, and you can turn it into a sentence that looks to our twenty-first-century eyes like an unproblematic spectrum statement: "low and high functioning autistic spectrum disorder share a common genetic basis, as shown by their co-occurrence within families. The children with low functioning ASD may suffer from additional injury." Yet in Van Krevelen's work the same statement sits comfortably within a text geared to explain that the two are *not* merely "quantitative variants" of the same thing, but rather qualitatively different.

What's in a name? Why is it important that one condition is described as a personality trait and the other as psychotic process? The most obvious point is that the two terms indicate different levels of severity. Already in 1964, as shown by the quote from Rimland above, Asperger's disorder was understood to be milder and the children affected highly intelligent. Crucially, Van Krevelen argued that autistic psychopathy and infantile autism should be differentiated on the basis of prognosis (1962). This was, in fact, the meaning of the opposition between a static personality trait and a psychotic process with a course. What was this course? In the case of infantile autism, Van Krevelen argued, the personality disintegrates and in time "pathology predominates more and more, even to such an extent that the parents are often obliged to have their child placed in an *institution*" (Van Krevelen 1963, 304). In effect, Van Krevelen was suggesting that Kanner's autism be used to designate those autistics who would be simply "institutional material," because in severe cases it "can hardly be distinguished from idiocy" (1963, 320). "Psychotic process" was thus meant, however paradoxically, to assimilate autism to the realm of mental retardation. By contrast, children with autistic psychopathy were less impaired; their condition involved a "peripheral" anomaly of the personality. Differentiating it from Kanner's autism, he cites Asperger noting that his patients are "amenable to influence and education" (Van Krevelen and Kuipers 1962, 20), while Kanner's autistics are not. Finally, Asperger's syndrome, on his view, was not a disorder of contact in the same way as Kanner's autism. Children with infantile autism are totally disconnected, no contact. Meanwhile Asperger's children merely lack intuition, which leads to a different kind of contact with the world. Readers should recall that within the new institutional matrix of autism therapies that intensified interaction, this distinction between the totally disconnected and the differently connected could give way to a set of much finer distinctions concerning the quality of contact that could set the two

218

up as quantitative variants rather than qualitatively different entities. Within the matrix of autism therapies, total disconnection is simply not an option.

While, as we saw, the context for the two men's initial simultaneous description of autism was similar, there were also subtle differences that became more significant as the new language invented by the two men had to be disseminated and assimilated by colleagues. It was the context of reception that configured the two descriptions differently and set them on different paths of development.

First, as Nadesan (2005, 77) shows, the concept of "personality" had a decidedly different value in the American and Austro-German contexts. In American psychiatry, to speak of "personality" placed one on the psychodynamic, even psychoanalytic, side of the opposition between psyche and soma. In the Austro-German world, on the other hand, "personality" belonged to a unique synthesis of Gestalt psychology, phenomenology, and psychoanalysis, developed by people such as Kurt Schneider, as an alternative to either medicalized or purely psychodynamic ways of thinking about personality. This alternative lineage helps explain why Asperger could classify what he saw as a "psychopathy," while Kanner chose to describe "disturbances of affective contact."

Second, while both men, as we argued earlier, wrote from an interstitial position, their faces were turned in opposite directions, addressing different audiences. Kanner occupied the first chair of child psychiatry in the U.S. and wrote the discipline's first textbook. He was at the helm of the emergent domain of child psychiatry, carving a new space for it with his synthesis of child guidance and the care of mentally retarded children. His audience was first and foremost American psychiatrists and clinicians. He was involved in competition where the prize was diagnostic autonomy. This explains why he joined with Leon Eisenberg to systematize his initial clinical and exploratory observations, distilling them into the discrete "cardinal symptoms" of autistic aloneness and an insistence on sameness (Eisenberg and Kanner 1956; see also Kanner 1958). It was a systematization facing towards medicine and clinical psychiatry.

Asperger's face, on the other hand, was turned toward education. He was an educationalist at heart and he worked at the remedial department of the university pediatric clinic in Vienna (not the psychiatric clinic [Frith 1991, 9]). This clinic pioneered a combination of special education and pediatrics. Unlike Kanner, Asperger's referral funnel originated in the schools (which may explain the higher functioning abilities of the children he saw). Indeed, Asperger said that the family could typically absorb the peculiarities of the children in the early years, but in school they became no longer tolerable (1944). They were then referred to child guidance centers and from there to him. All the conduct problems that are part of fitting children in class (hyperactivity, hypersensitivity, bullying) thus played an important role in the analysis. The children were referred to Asperger not for diagnosis, as with Kanner, but for remedial treatment. They came from the school and they were to be returned to the school. The "surfaces of emergence" (Foucault 1972, 41) of infantile autism and autistic psychopathy were thus subtly different, setting them on different courses in the context of the custodial institution.

We can see here why the two men's clinical styles and approaches to classification were rather different. Both wrote highly memorable and evocative case studies, but as Schopler (1998, 387–89) notes, Kanner wrote "clinically lucid" and "behaviorally observable" descriptions meant to be reproduced. And they were. Shortly after the publication of his original paper, the U.S. and U.K. were abuzz with discussions of autism. By 1952, Van Krevelen had made the first diagnosis of the disorder in continental Europe (Van Krevelen 1971, 82). Asperger never distilled his syndrome into "cardinal symptoms" like Kanner (Eisenberg and Kanner 1958), and Van Krevelen's attempts to do so were never sharp enough to make distinctions in the clinic. Schopler charged that Asperger described his patients individually and unsystematically, without concern for generalization.

But perhaps it is more correct to say that Asperger was not seeking to formulate a list of diagnostic criteria designating a clearly bounded diagnostic entity. Why? Perhaps because of his concern for "implications of remedial education" – to which he dedicates a much longer portion of his monograph than Kanner ever did. His background in phenomenology and Gestalt psychology gave him a different vision of classification altogether. He aimed to delineate a series of prototypes among which there was "family resemblance," but whose distinctive features were no less important because they could guide therapy. Douwe Draaisma, a Dutch historian of psychology, helpfully explains Asperger's approach (2009, 1475–76). [7] In the first seven pages of his 1944 monograph, which Frith omitted from her English translation, Asperger outlined three approaches to classification in psychopathology. The first two – using *polarities* like introversion/extroversion or *essences* like depression or neurasthenia – he considered unsatisfactory because they were too one-dimensional. As Draaisma explains, Asperger opted for an approach in which "each human being . . .

must be understood as an alloy of traits, as a unique blend of capacities and inclinations. To be a good diagnostician, one will have to develop a sensitivity for what he called the '*Zusammenklang*' or Gestalt of the child – his voice, face, body language, intonation, gestures, gaze, expression and diction . . . This Gestalt-like orientation precluded the description of syndromes, in terms of lists or assemblies of atomistic traits." Hence, autistic psychopathy was not a "personality trait," as Van Krevelen misleadingly translated it for Anglo-Saxon psychiatry, but a personality Gestalt, a unique human type admitting of infinite variation and nuance. The structure of Asperger's monograph reflected this orientation, Draaisma notes. The case studies were constitutive of the paper, not supplementary. Beginning with a long and detailed description of Fritz K., Asperger sought to evoke an image in the mind of clinician-therapists of the "Gestalt of the child."[8] The next two children were described more and more briefly, and the fourth was a negative case, showing that similar symptoms could be caused also by brain damage.

To be fair, the case studies in Kanner's initial paper are not mere appendices either; they make up its core.[9] Donald, Kanner's first case, is described in meticulous and fascinating detail. The paper is stripped of any deep interpretation or theoretical posturing and it could be rightly said to operate by a similar Gestalt principle, as Donald is described much more extensively than the cases that follow. As father and anthropologist Roy Richard Grinker (2007, 49) notes: "Today, as I read Kanner's vivid descriptions . . . I see my own daughter on almost every page" (2007, 49). The important point, however, is that Kanner felt compelled to systematize and distill his descriptions because of his orientation to a field of competing diagnostic labels, while Asperger was concerned to specify and further particularize them, to provide a solid guide for remedial education. In words that presage normalization and the IEP system, he wrote, "we can demonstrate the truth of the claim that exceptional human beings must be given exceptional educational treatment, treatment which takes account of their special difficulties . . . We can show that despite abnormality human beings can fulfill their social role within the community, especially if they find understanding, love and guidance" (Asperger [1944] 1991, 37).[10]

Kanner's quip about a forty-second cousin, and the separate histories of autistic psychopathy and infantile autism, are intelligible consequences of the opposing orientations of Kanner and Asperger in the context of a custodial institutional matrix that did not permit the two to be brought together. Kanner operated on the margins of the institution, in a fuzzy zone where it became possible to challenge the distinction between the socially capable and incapable (recall the "apparent feeblemindedness" of autistic children). Yet he was decidedly oriented toward the center of this matrix. The children, like Virginia, were brought to him *from* institutions, or because their parents challenged the recommendation to institutionalize them. Not a few ended up in institutions, as shown by his 1971 follow-up study (Kanner 1971). Asperger's referral pattern, from and to the school; the type of milieu therapy he practiced (children were separated from their parents and placed at his clinic for a period that ranged between a few months and few years); the higher functioning of the children he saw: all this meant that he was facing toward the outside of the custodial institutional matrix. The children he saw were not likely to have been deemed "socially incapable," and he provided them with short-term milieu therapy meant to return them to school and family. Consequently, he focused on exceptional qualities pertinent to remedial treatment. Van Krevelen's distinction between personality trait and psychotic process, therefore, merely replicated and then reflected the line traced around the institution, a line that only deinstitutionalization was able to erase.

The following story provides final evidence that Asperger's latency was not due to a language barrier but reflected the custodial institutional matrix's inability to synthesize his and Kanner's descriptions. In 1958, two American clinicians presented a paper at the American Psychological Association annual meeting on what they were calling, for lack of a better term, "children with circumscribed interests." In many ways, their cases resembled Asperger's. The children "developed special interests and sometimes special skills" and there was "a restriction of social interests and a limited establishment of interpersonal relationships" (Robinson and Vitale 1958, 755). The authors suggested a similarity to Kanner's autism, but noted many differences in degree of severity – less withdrawal, less obsessiveness, greater emotional responsiveness in infancy, and so on. Here was a diagnosis that from a contemporary point of view, one influenced by the idea of the spectrum, neatly captured what autism and Asperger's disorder have in common (Wing's "impairment in social interaction"). Kanner commented favorably on the paper. He thought it was an important addition to the field, and used the opportunity to make the case for an empirically based descriptive psychiatry. He agreed, however, with the authors' judicious choice to emphasize the differences between their own label and his autism. The two were not the same.

Twins reunited

As we have said, Lorna Wing's 1981 paper, "Asperger's Syndrome: A Clinical Account," is seen as the turning point in the career of Asperger's category. By Wing's count, based on the National Autistic Society's database, there were two articles published on Asperger's syndrome before 1981 and a total of 900 by 2004, with 126 in 2003 alone (Wing 2005, 197).[11] But if others knew about Asperger's work before her and if her innovation was not simply to make it available to English speakers, then why was she so effective in putting Asperger on the map – and why hadn't he been there before?

Part of the answer was given already in the preceding analysis. By 1981, deinstitutionalization was in full force. A domain of developmental disabilities was constituted and within it the therapies operated to break autism down to a list of "items of autistic behavior," to array these on the same register as the behaviors exhibited by those diagnosed as mentally retarded, so that one no longer needed to choose between illness and retardation. By the same token, the register could be extended to include the behaviors described in Asperger's case histories and the cases Wing saw in her clinical practice. Finally, there was no longer any meaning to the distinction between personality trait and psychotic process (autism was no longer psychosis, and personality became an axis of the DSM, combinable with diagnoses made using a different axis). If Asperger would have been translated into English in the 1950s, perhaps his cases would have been assimilated to the category of "children with circumscribed interests," but in 1981 there was a place for him on the spectrum, and Wing could use the idea of a spectrum to dissolve any difficulties posed in the past by the differences between Kanner's and Asperger's descriptions. She used her own epidemiological findings to support the concept of an autistic continuum (Wing and Gould 1979). Among their many subjects, she and her collaborator, Judith Gould, found only a small percentage of children fitting either Kanner's or Asperger's descriptions. Children's symptoms did not sort perfectly into the two rows suggested by Van Krevelen, she argued; they mixed and matched. Autism, as Kanner described it, was only one possible permutation in the combinatory matrix offered by the spectrum. Other permutations were possible. The idea that the types of children Asperger and Kanner described differed quantitatively, not qualitatively (by "severity" if you will), was not new (Bosch 1962). It had been around for years. But it could have no practical meaning before deinstitutionalization. Recall that Wing's final argument was that whatever the level of severity, autism and Asperger's were accompanied by similar problems affecting social and intellectual skills, and required the same kind of structured, organized educational approach (1981, 124). For practical purposes, then, on the register established by the therapies, it made sense to regard them as related.

But this is not all. Or rather, this account still lacks a crucial actor – parents. The story we told above remains either at the "micro" level of the actions of one charismatic individual, or the "macro" level of wholesale institutional changes. The mediating "meso" level of mechanisms is absent. But the relatively favorable (though by no means unanimous) reception for Wing's proposal was not due to her charisma alone, nor to the charisma of truth. The niche in which the diagnosis could thrive was prepared in part prior to her proposal, which in many respects catered to already existing and effective demand.

Wing did not effect the U-turn in Asperger's fortunes all on her own. There was a constituency waiting to champion the diagnosis by the time of her writing. A need, a demand, was articulated within parent organizations for the very thing Wing offered, and she herself was well-placed to be aware of it. The U.S. and U.K. parent associations collaborated in the early 1970s on a project about "the near-normal autistic adolescent." Margaret Dewey from the U.S. and Margaret Everard from the U.K. coordinated the transatlantic project, which involved airmail correspondence over the course of a year between parents and professionals in the two countries working with fifty individuals in this "subgroup." Dewey was the mother of Dicky, a poster child of sorts for the American national society who found a niche as a piano tuner. Dicky's life was often reported in the NSAC newsletter, and he was even interviewed on stage at the 1970 annual NSAC conference (Park 1971b). Everard, also a mother, edited the British National Autistic Society's journal, *Communication*, and herself would later do some research on high-functioning autism (Frith 1991).

In 1974, the two women published an article in the *Journal of Autism and Childhood Schizophrenia* titled, "The Near-Normal Autistic Adolescent," in which they described the unique deficits and talents of these young adults. This group, they concluded, "would benefit . . . from the recognition of their condition as a separate category of autism" (1974, 355). They thought that getting their own label would stimulate broad interest as well as further research, open up possibilities for sheltered employment and assisted living, and facilitate the dissemination of information and managerial strategies for assisting these individuals. In 1979, Everard published a translation of a speech Asperger gave in Switzerland in 1977 on the relationship of his syndrome to Kanner's. The work Everard and others did within the national associations prepared the ground for Wing's linking of the two. Recall that Wing was a founding member of the British society and she has remained active in it throughout her life. No doubt she was aware of these developments. Thus, we must see her essay as more than a collection of astute clinical observations by a veteran psychiatrist in the field. She was not exploring virgin territory, but was accompanied by other parents with whom she communicated. She was one, albeit important, node in a network of expertise. Her real ingenuity lay in the invention of the autism spectrum as a device for translating and aligning the multiple interests of members of this network: autism researchers, clinicians, therapists, parents of severely afflicted autistic children, and parents of near-normal autistic adolescents, and ultimately also these adolescents and children themselves.

At the same time, the choice to retain the separate label "Asperger's syndrome" revealed an astute awareness of the forces of demand put into motion by deinstitutionalization. It also reveals that diagnostic labeling is a form of representation, "making up people," that requires political acumen. Five years after her initial paper, Wing responded to what had become a minor controversy over whether Asperger's was a distinct entity or not and whether the distinction was useful. She gave as reason for offering the label that "parents and professional workers tend to be more receptive if told that the person has an interesting condition called Asperger's syndrome" (1986, 513). "Though no curative treatment is available," she continued, "parents are relieved and comforted to have a name for the condition and an explanation for the odd behavior. The connection to autism can be introduced later so that help can be obtained from other parents through the relevant voluntary society for autistic people" (514). In other words, it was a back door into the world of autism therapy and advocacy, one unhampered by the popular image of the autistic child as mute and utterly unsociable. It scrapped the old prototype and offered a new one next door. These considerations also explain why Wing jettisoned the term "autistic psychopathy" in favor of "Asperger syndrome" (although the term had been in circulation before her writings).[12] Psychopathy resonated in translation in unintended ways, conjuring an image of malign criminality and sociopathic behavior. There was a clear need to dissociate from this image in order to gain wide acceptance, especially among parents.[13]

For the same reasons, she also vehemently rejected all speculations about a possible connection to schizophrenia. Asperger's syndrome was definitively not a "schizoid personality disorder," as Sula Wolff had argued a year earlier (Wolff and Chick 1980). Wolff's category was "vague and ill-defined," and "there is no firm evidence of a special link between this [Asperger's] syndrome and schizophrenia" (Wing 1981, 123). Hence she was completely silent about Asperger's well-known observations about malice, masturbation, and sexual deviation associated with the condition. She called it "impairment of social development" (123), "handicap," "developmental disorder," all terms calculated to maintain a peaceful coalition with parents.

Loops of self-advocacy

The account above leaves out, perhaps, the most important fact. All of this is not enough to explain Wing's "success" – because she was not successful, at least not immediately so. Asperger's disorder was not added to the revised edition of DSM-III-R in 1987. The official decision to add it would have to wait until the 1994 DSM-IV,[14] 13 years after Wing's article. While Wing got her wish to remove the early-onset restriction – something she speculated would promote the autism diagnosis for children who fit Asperger's description (Wing 1986, 514) – the committee was very clear that it saw no need to explicitly include Asperger's disorder in the spectrum (Waterhouse et al. 1992, 538). Eric Schopler was from the beginning, and remained after 1994, opposed to the concept of Asperger's disorder. There were no differences, he argued, in course, cause, or treatment between a person meeting the criteria for Asperger's disorder and one with "high-functioning autism." The label is redundant. Schopler was not alone in this view and criticism only intensified after Asperger's disorder went on the books in 1994. A 2001 article reported research showing that a clinical diagnosis of the disorder using the DSM-IV was "unlikely or impossible" (Mayes, Calhoun, and Crites 2001, 263).

How to explain, therefore, the adoption of Asperger's disorder in DSM-IV (or ICD-10) and its current centrality in the autism world if clinical opinion was split, and in the face of such trenchant critique? The missing link is looping. By herself, Wing would not have been able to attach Asperger's disorder so decisively to autism.[15] But she, or rather the whole network of expertise in which she and parent activists played a crucial role, brought a new type of person into being. More precisely, they made it possible to embody and claim affinity with this type of person, and this claim rapidly spread, in channels over which the parents and the clinicians no longer had any control, making Asperger's disorder a cultural and public identity before it was recognized by an official diagnostic gesture.

The rapid rise to prominence of Asperger's disorder is sometimes chalked up to the movie *Rain Man*. The story of *Rain Man*'s impact and of its crafting, however, is more complex than it would seem from these arguments, and fits rather neatly with the argument about looping. How did *Rain Man* come about? How did Dustin Hoffman learn to play such a convincing "autistic savant"? And where did the idea of autistic savants come from in the first place anyway? Where else? From parents of autistic children themselves. Bernard Rimland reports being contacted in 1986 to have a look at the film's script, which he did. It had promise, he thought. But he had many suggestions, most crucially that Dustin Hoffman's Raymond be an "autistic savant," rather than an "idiot savant" or a "retarded savant."[16] Indeed, Rimland himself was the first to use the neologism "autistic savant" in print in 1978. He gave Hoffman books, articles, and educational films to help him study for the part. Rimland also put the actor in touch with several families, including Ruth Christ Sullivan's. Her son, along with a savant Rimland had earlier studied, became Hoffman's main source of inspiration. The film was a huge success, both in the box office and in the popular press. Sullivan went on Oprah and remarked that the film had "advanced the field of autism by twenty-five years!" It put autism on the map in a whole new way, sparking a fascination with real-life savants that we think is continuous with the current public interest in Aspies like Daniel Tammet and Temple Grandin. In fact, Grandin, who at the time had recently published her first book, *Emergence: Labeled Autistic* (1986), was asked to comment about the film in a *Boston Globe* article alongside established autism giants like Rimland. Many books and countless radio and newsprint interviews later, we can see that this was, one could argue, one crucial step in the process of Grandin becoming a widely recognized international spokesperson for autistics, the first "self-advocate." Thus, *Rain Man* was not simply a fortuitous event. It was engineered, at least in part, by parents. As such it can be viewed as a concentrated publicity campaign of sorts. Having firmly established himself as an expert, Rimland was able to contribute to the film's crafting, using it as an opportunity to disseminate a sympathetic and intriguing image of autism.

The other development, of course, was Grandin's book *Emergence*, the first book-length autobiographical account written (or at least co-written) by an autistic person. In his Foreword, Rimland vetted Grandin as one of the few *truly* recovered autistics, among the many pretenders (Rimland in Grandin 1986, 5–7). It must have been among the materials Rimland shared with Hoffman as well, as the actor quotes her, chapter and verse, in an interview shortly after the film was released (Guthmann 1988). First considered brain-damaged as a child, Grandin showed characteristics of classic autism and was eventually diagnosed as such. In her book Grandin tells of her halting development, the crucial mentors who worked with her autism, and especially of her mother who created a structured but supportive environment in which she could "emerge" from her autistic shell.[17] She also gives fascinating descriptions of her sensory experience of the world and attempts to translate them into a neurological idiom. When her aunt hugs her, "It was like being suffocated by a mountain of marshmallows. I withdrew because her abundant affection overwhelmed my nervous system" (24).

From the perspective of looping, Grandin is a bridging figure (Hacking 2007). As a child, she approximated the prototype of Kanner's infantile autism enough to become associated with the label, but she grew into something that was previously unthinkable to many people, an independent living, self-reflexive, highly articulate if idiosyncratic autistic adult.[18] In becoming a public figure, she stretched the autism prototype, making room on the spectrum for others who may not have shown such classic autistic traits as children but identified with her circumscribed interests, visual thinking, or particular sensory experience of the world.

Thus the response to the popularization of Asperger's disorder and the interest in autistic savants soon took on a life of its own. It led to a wholesale change in the image of autism in the public imagination, and to the emergence of a new type of autism expert – the self-advocate. It played a role, therefore, in creating the epidemic even before the DSM was changed. Psychiatrist Fred Volkmar, a major advocate of the Asperger's label and main author of the Asperger's entry in DSM-IV, tells that in 1993 he received an inquiry from the Learning Disabilities Association of America, asking if he could send them some information on Asperger's syndrome. Shortly after that information was published, 600 parents from around the country wrote him and his colleagues to say that they thought their child had Asperger's.[19] This was one year before the diagnosis was added to DSM-IV. As we put it before, drawing on Hacking's notions of "making up people" and "looping" (1986, 1995, 1999, 2007),

228

individuals and their families were seeking to attach themselves to this new type of person. Adults and adolescents once considered learning-disabled or schizophrenic were now seeking to reclassify themselves as having Asperger's or autism. Previously undiagnosed people living independent lives could now be given an Asperger's label. Sometimes it was a self-diagnosis. Other times a physician made the call. Either way, Asperger's and high-functioning autism became powerful ways of reordering and reorganizing symptoms. Physical aggression no longer had to be seen as rooted in anger, but might rather stem from social anxiety and sensory overstimulation. Years of heavy drugging and institutionalization gave way to social skills therapies and modified environments (Macdonald 1998). People were, indeed, coming out of the woodwork to receive a diagnosis of Asperger's syndrome. As Draaisma argues, public representations and media portrayals of autism and autistic experience further shape the prototypes that are shared by clinicians and the wider public. Changes in the DSM are secondary and derivative. While they play a role in the moment of making an official diagnosis of autism, the prototype perhaps plays a greater role in shaping the population of actual diagnoses. The prototype intervenes at multiple levels: the way parents understand their child's delayed speech development, the way a teacher deals with a misbehaving student, the way a socially isolated adult understands himself and his own reactions to other people. Articles, websites, biographies, magazine and newspaper articles all play a role in directing these individuals, oftentimes before they ever make their way into a psychiatric clinic for evaluation. Draaisma, drawing on Hacking's work, points us to the ways in which these media representations interlock with scientific representations to shape the prototype of an autistic child or a person "on the spectrum."

But this is only one side of the looping process. When new types of people come into being, new types of agency – new ways of acting, speaking, and representing – follow. Such new kinds of action can affect the prototypes and official classifications in unexpected ways. Some of the individuals who most successfully came to embody the prototype of Asperger's disorder – the most well-known being Temple Grandin, Donna Williams, Jim Sinclair, Stephen Shore, Ari Ne'eman, Daniel Tammet – became self-advocates, spokespersons on behalf of the whole spectrum or a portion thereof. They developed a type of expertise superior, at least in some respects, to that of both professionals and parents. When it comes to reporting on the experience of being autistic, what it feels like, and therefore what it might mean when an autistic child says or does something peculiar, their word is considered the best currency around.[20] This constituted a second wave of restructuring autism expertise. Now, alongside parents, and often in direct and open conflict with them, people diagnosed on the spectrum inserted themselves into networks of information and knowledge production. Boards and committees, like the Autism Coordinating Committee, now stipulate that there be a person with autism among the group. Following the disability rights movement of the 1980s and 1990s, these self-advocates come bearing the slogan "nothing about us without us," and they demand respect for "neurodiversity" ("diversity of human wiring") as one axis of human difference among others, like race, class, or gender.

Self-advocacy is connected in complex ways to the parents' movement. On the one hand, we must emphasize that the second restructuring of the network of autism expertise did not originate as a backlash against the first restructuring undertaken by Rimland and NSAC. Nor was it independent of it. It was continuous with it, grew out of it. Indeed, as we showed above, parent societies and parent-activist-researchers were the main constituents championing the extension of autism to encompass more "high-functioning" people. And they played critical roles in making Asperger's disorder an official diagnosis and *Rain Man* a Hollywood success. Further, Jim Sinclair, a major figure in the autism rights movement, notes that self-advocates first took the stage (literally) as a result of requests from parents who invited them to speak at conferences and to act as interpreters on behalf of their children, and it was at parent conferences or through parent lists that they began to meet and form a community (Sinclair 2005). Recall also that Dicky Dewey spoke on stage to parents and researchers at a NSAC conference as early as 1970. On the other hand, however, over time there have developed some serious rifts between parents of so-called "low-functioning" children and "high-functioning" self-advocates. The former frequently mobilize around ABA, the search for a cure, and genetic research, drawing on a disease model of autism (see Broderick and Ne'eman 2008). The latter are oftentimes critical of behavior modification (as was Asperger himself) and refer to parents, researchers, and anyone else not on the spectrum in derogatory ways, as "cure-bies" or "neurotypicals."

These tensions are serious, sometimes agonizing. Online discussions can quickly become acrimonious. At their worst, they lead to balkanization. A group of individuals with Asperger's disorder has, in fact, staged a vocal revolt within the British NSAC, and eventually split from it (Wing 2005, 201). In the U.S. and elsewhere, there formed many independent organizations of "Aspies" who no longer want to be associated with the main autism organizations. Their message is, with Sinclair, "do not mourn for us."[21] They do not need to be cured, and there is nothing sad about their lives or who they are. Autism is a form of difference, they say, not a disability. Some parents of severely afflicted autistic children find it hard to sympathize. They tend to depict the self-advocates as fellow travelers, incidental tourists whose claims for association with autism are self-made, dubious and injurious to the more serious campaign.

At the same time, these struggles – which we do not wish to belittle – show no signs of dissolving the reality or the unity of the spectrum in any way, perhaps because both sides have in fact a vested interest in its existence. Moreover, as Hacking (2009b) insightfully and productively argues, the lines are not drawn as clearly as they sometimes seem when we read the programmatic statements of prominent activists. The "autistic autobiographies" of self-advocates, though they may sometimes offend parents, serve a function symmetrical to that of social skills therapies. Just as social skills therapies allow autistics to recognize and interpret the actions of non-autistics, these autistic autobiographies give non-autistics pictures and a language with which to describe and interpret autistic behavior. The point is not whether these are really accurate images or descriptions of what it is like to be autistic; the point is that this sort of language begins to constitute the experience of what it is to be autistic by telling stories that connect words from ordinary language (recall Grandin's aunt's marshmallow hug), used to describe emotions and mental states, with the behavior of autistic children, thus making this behavior intelligible to parents, experts and conceivably also to autistics themselves. In this way, the spectrum is cemented in place. These accounts tie the "high-functioning" person to the "low-functioning" one, not only discursively, but within common forms of life. Thus, as high-functioning individuals begin to represent themselves publicly, they create enduring links that tie the spectrum together, rendering the question of whether autism and Asperger's are really quantitatively or qualitatively different null and void.

Our interviews and experience with families of so-called "low-functioning" children support Hacking's thesis, albeit with some caveats. The writings of self-advocates such as Temple Grandin can provide these parents with a language with which to understand and frame their child's behaviors. What seemed enigmatic can be interpreted as a way to relieve stress, to dissipate pent-up anxiety. Further, it gives them a powerful language with which to critique what they see as harmful and discriminatory devaluations of their

231

child's experience. Not disconnected from the social world, but differently connected to it; not brain-damaged, but differently wired; not senselessly rocking, but self-soothing: as Hacking has pointed out, these transformations allow a "thicker" or richer image of the autistic child's emotional life to emerge. The self-advocates embody the idea that one's child, no matter how disconnected he may seem, could be an emotionally thick – if radically different – person with a complex inner world. They encourage parents to interact with the child on that basis and to invite others to do so as well. Eventually, this image lends support to therapies like Facilitated Communication and Rapid Prompting Method (see the next chapter) that attempt to allow individuals, like Tito Mukhopadhyay – who present the classical image of the mute, rocking, impenetrable autistic – to represent themselves. We have two points to add. First, contrary to what one might think, this image of neurodiversity and the technologies of behavior management are not mutually exclusive. Rather, they coexist and hybridize. Within the same home, one finds a room for structured discrete trial ABA and a bookshelf housing biographies by Grandin and other self-advocates. Parents move seamlessly between talk of their child's "perseveration" and her "sensory sensitivities." ABA-based schools allow students to work to earn "sensory breaks," or they teach them to request a "sensory toy" instead of lashing out when they feel uncomfortable or become stressed. Second, parents did not need to wait for the self-advocates to provide them with this "thick" image of their child. Recall Wing's 1972 comment that autistics do not lack emotional experiences but simply express them differently, and that parents come to learn the "special language" of their own child. Or consider Clara Claiborne Park's thick portrait of her daughter in *The Siege* or Rimland's son who became a successful artist. The point is that some parents could reach the conclusion that their child had a rich emotional and intellectual life before the autobiographies that described them in that way. Nonetheless, the accounts of the self-advocates provide parents with a language with which to imagine and interpret their children's actions and they expand the prototype of autism in the public imagination so that these interpretations can appear plausible or defensible to others.

By the same token, parents, from Rimland's *Rain Man* connection to today's bloggers like Autism Diva and neurodiversity.com's Kathleen Seidel, have supported self-advocacy in numerous ways. They run websites, speak publicly, are featured in magazine and newspaper articles and lobby for neurodiversity causes and autistic rights. Academics such as Roy Richard Grinker, Majia Nadesan, and

Kristin Bumiller, who are parents of autistic children, have made a powerful case in their writings for a more progressive perception of autism and the potential value of autistic lives and possibilities for personhood articulated through new social movements. It seems that when proper boundaries and rules of engagement are negotiated between the two constituencies, as the self-advocacy group Autism Network International (ANI) seems to have done, good relations between parents and self-advocates are possible, and they are able to collude with minimal conflict. Ultimately, both sides need each other. Without the spectrum, who would pay attention to the Aspies? At the same time, deinstitutionalization has saddled parents with the task of representing, advocating for, and translating their children for neighbors, teachers, and many others on a daily basis. The self-advocates provide them with the language, confidence, and support to make these translations.

THE SPACE OF AUTISM THERAPIES AND THE MAKING AND REMAKING OF THE SPECTRUM

Work on revising the diagnostic criteria for autism in preparation for DSM-III-R began in 1984. An advisory committee chaired by Robert Spitzer met and debated an initial draft of diagnostic criteria written by Lorna Wing and Lynn Waterhouse, based on the triad of symptoms introduced by Wing five years earlier. Committee members were unanimous that earlier DSM-III criteria for autism were lacking detail and precision, and that Wing's triad not only fit better with the developmental data, but also conformed better with Kanner's "original case study descriptive accounts." They adopted the triad with only marginal changes (Waterhouse et al. 1992, 526).[1]

It is common wisdom that the autism epidemic followed hard on the heels of these changes. It is customary to date its beginning to around 1991 (Croen et al. 2002a), and supply-side explanations for the autism epidemic have no difficulty making the connection with the new DSM-III-R criteria (Grinker 2007). As we saw in the introduction, the early-onset (before thirty months) requirement stipulated in DSM-III was dropped. The diagnostic criterion of complete lack of social responsiveness was changed to simply abnormal social responsiveness, and so on. These were changes that were likely to increase the number of children diagnosed with autism, and the committee seems to have been well aware of this prospect: "taken together, three of the five changes in DSM-III-R – eliminating COPDD [Childhood Onset Pervasive Developmental Disorder], eliminating age at onset for AD [Autistic Disorder], and revision of the AD criteria – will increase the number of children receiving the diagnosis of AD as compared with the number of children who received a diagnosis of IA [Infantile Autism] in DSM-III" (Waterhouse et al. 1992, 545).

Yet the committee also seems to have been utterly unprepared for

234

the size and rapidity of the increase, evidenced by the fact that one of its key members could say, in retrospect, she "never thought that there would be an increase in the number of children diagnosed via DSM-III-R criteria."[2] Why? Because by 1987 they had evidence that clinicians were not, in fact, adhering to the DSM-III criteria, but were giving the diagnosis of autism – as DSM-III-R would require it – to children who fit DSM-III criteria for "Atypical PDD" and "Childhood Onset PDD" (Waterhouse et al. 1987). In essence, the committee was saying that since clinicians were already working with a different understanding of autism – not as "a single valid underlying core disorder" but as a *spectrum*, a category free "from arbitrary boundaries," with "greater descriptive coverage" adjusted for the purposes of *surveillance* – this justified the introduction of new and relaxed criteria and was unlikely to create a major upheaval (Waterhouse et al. 1992, 546). As we saw in Chapter 9, diagnosticians using the CARS in the 1980s were in fact diagnosing children on the basis of criteria similar to what DSM-III-R would require, years before the latter was written and published. It is important to note, however, that the second edition of the CARS, published in 1988, was even more likely to raise the number of diagnoses not because it broadened diagnostic criteria – these were essentially the same as in 1980 – but because it was easier to use: it could be used not only by trained diagnosticians in psychological test sessions, but by other professionals such as medical students, special educators, and speech pathologists. After reading the manual and viewing a 30-minute training tape, these other professionals produced ratings not significantly different from autism specialists. Direct observation of the child was not necessary for administration of the second edition of the CARS, as the scales may be rated from medical records, parent reports, and classroom observations (Schopler et al. 1988).

Ten years later, when attempting to account for the epidemic, Croen et al. (2002a) noted a similar phenomenon, namely, that DSM criteria follow practice rather than vice versa. DSM-III-R may have drawn a distinction between autism and Pervasive Developmental Disorder, Not Otherwise Specified (PDD-NOS) and excluded Asperger's disorder altogether, they say, but clinicians probably did not adhere to the letter of this so-called psychiatric bible. Faced with increasing demand for services – especially as the prestige of Lovaas's treatment program was growing and states were passing early-intervention legislation in compliance with IDEA – they "give children with Asperger's disorder and PDD-NOS a diagnosis of full syndrome autism so that they could qualify for regional center services" (213–14). DSM-IV, of course, added Asperger's to the spectrum of autistic disorders in 1994. Grinker (2007) also quotes Judith Rapoport, chief of child psychiatry at the National Institutes of Mental Health, who told him: "I'll call a kid a zebra if it will get him the educational services he needs" (131). Recall also the study by Bearman and his collaborators mentioned in Chapter 1. They show that in California during the 1990s and the early 2000s living in very close proximity to a child previously diagnosed with autism significantly increased the risk of being diagnosed with autism, and significantly lowered the risk of being diagnosed with mental retardation. Effective demand for diagnostic change and diagnostic substitution, therefore, was supported by networks of social influence and information diffusion among parents living in distinct geographical clusters (Bearman and King unpublished).

So supply-side accounts swing full circle to rely on demand-side and social influence explanations. Changing diagnostic criteria create the epidemic, but the new criteria either reflect pre-existing practice and presumably pre-existing demand, or are ignored and stretched by besieged clinicians. Did the dog wag its tail, or did the tail wag the dog? We tend to root for the tail, or more precisely we think that the key for changes in both supply and demand is to be found in the open-ended and dynamic nature of the space between fields, the space of autism therapies. It is the ground upon which demand and supply are able to find one another. Every twist and turn of the spectrum, from its initial formulation by Wing in the late 1970s to its consecration in DSM-IV, every stretch it underwent, downwards because the DSM-III-R committee eschewed any IQ cut-off, upwards to include the Aspies – every expansion had its underlying precondition in the constant blurring of boundaries at the edges of this interstitial space. From this point of view, it is immaterial whether the authors of diagnostic criteria strove for greater precision or left things fuzzy, or whether they intended and foresaw the rise in the number of diagnoses or were surprised by it. Their battles and debates seem like a tempest in a teacup in comparison with the silent shifting of tectonic plates that opened up the space between fields, and with the determined troops of therapists, parents, and advocates who set out to explore its terrain and push its boundaries.

The return of Rimland

In this chapter, we would like to describe in detail one example of this blurring of boundaries that shaped the spectrum "from beneath," so to speak. We do not have space in this book to describe the full range of processes taking place at the boundaries of the spectrum, but perhaps it is better to tell one story well, rather than spread the account too thin. Let us return to Bernard Rimland and pick up his story where we left off in Chapter 8. In the mid-1970s, Rimland, who was universally recognized as *the* global expert on autism, was becoming increasingly marginal to the movement he founded, and to mainstream autism research. Schopler, as the readers may recall, and not Rimland, was chosen to replace Kanner as editor of *JACS*. Lovaas's treatment program had become independent and no longer needed Rimland's mediation. The last word on diagnosis belonged to Lorna Wing's triad. By comparison, Rimland's campaign for megavitamin therapy seemed idiosyncratic and likely to doom his chances of ever regaining his stature. He was fast becoming alienated from the central thrust of autism research and from the network of expertise that used to be centered around him.

Rimland, however, did not go quietly into the night. No doubt his quest for biological therapeutics initially marginalized him and severed at least some of the ties that made his node a central one, yet in characteristic fashion he worked diligently to rewire the network of expertise in another direction, just as he did in the mid-1960s. The research institute he opened in 1967 – originally called the Child Behavior Research Institute (CBRI), then later changed to Autism Research Institute (ARI) – allowed him to maintain close connections to parents and pursue his own agenda, crafting a viable career as an autism research scientist outside academic or government medical institutions.

For the next two and a half decades, Rimland used the ARI as a platform from which to promote alternative biomedical interventions in autism, especially megavitamin therapy, supplements, and diets. His first lead on the potential therapeutic use of megadoses of vitamins came from parents. A nurse who had seen success treating her granddaughter wrote to him. Canadian researchers at the hospital where she worked were experimenting on schizophrenic patients with this treatment, and they were seeing results (Rimland 2006, 17). Rimland was skeptical at first. "But," he told the audience at the 1970 NSAC conference, "as the letters accumulated I began to get more interested in the reports . . . As the number of parent-experimenters grew, it began to include more parents whom I knew personally to be highly intelligent and reliable people" (1971b, 57). As with Lovaas's therapy, Rimland tried it on his son Mark and saw success (Rimland 2006, 22). So he included relevant items on his E-2 checklist (1971b, 58–59). The idea, however, was never able to get traction in mainstream circles.

In 1987, Rimland began to publish his own newsletter, the *Autism Research Review International* (*ARRI*). In its pages, he weighed in on contemporary debates, published "letters to the editor" from parents, professionals, and scientific researchers alike, and penned reports on the latest research, complete with citations and the authors' contact information, presumably for parents to pursue leads. Then, in 1994, he convened a "think tank" with a physician (Sydney Baker) and a chemist (Jon Pangborn, a fellow parent-researcher) in order to survey the state of the art of biomedical treatments for autism. This led to the formation of Defeat Autism Now! (DAN!), a coalition of parents, health practitioners and researchers interested in "biomedical treatments" for autism.[3] They held their first meeting the next year and switched to meeting twice annually in 2001. These DAN! meetings are nucleating sites for what Chloe Silverman calls an "experimental community," "a practical movement based on unlikely alliances and built on experiential knowledge and pragmatic interventions firmly situated within daily life" (2004, 4).

The final chapter in the story of the Rimland network – Rimland himself passed away in 2006 – is the controversy over the link between autism and vaccination. While Rimland played a marginal role in the recent controversies over thimerosal preservative in vaccines and the MMR vaccine (Kirby 2006; Rimland 2003), he began tracking parents' reports of the ill effects of vaccination already in 1968 and argued early on that autism can be caused by vaccinations. DAN! is certainly one of the major proponents of the theory as well as of detoxification therapies (Edelson and Rimland 2003, 13–18, 20–24, 58–61). In the vaccination controversy one discerns what is probably Rimland's most significant legacy: an alternative network and model of research that is the direct challenger, competitor, enemy, and detractor of experimental science's ethic of "virtual witnessing" – an alternative network that attempts to subordinate virtual witnessing to the ethical vocation of autism parenting.

To follow the story of Rimland, ARI, and DAN!, therefore, is to follow a genealogical thread that does not lead one from the roots to the tree, from heterogeneous origins to a settled identity, but like a rhizome splits apart, wraps around, then spreads out and disappears into the earth. It is to follow not a process of consolidation, but a constant movement of fuzzing, weaving in and out of science; back and forth between medicine, alternative medicine, and the market; blending therapy, parenting, and advocacy; and collecting new and heterogeneous symptoms and gluing them to the spectrum until it forms a tuberous agglomeration.

The agonistic network

If the story we told earlier was similar to what Rabeharisoa and Callon (2004) call "co-production" – where parents and experts (and parent-experts) collaborate to create a new and joint object of discourse, research, and intervention – Rimland's later trajectory, after he split from the mainstream of the parents' movement, is a story of *dissidence*, of the agonistic production of counter-objects aimed at unseating official dogma. Rimland certainly interpreted his whole career in this light. "Our children are victims of both autism and dogma," he said and brought as an example the 1960s dogma that behavior modification was futile in autism. The skepticism about his megavitamin therapy he interpreted similarly: "false – just as their view was false that autism was caused by bad mothering" (Edelson and Rimland 2003, 13–18). He styled himself as a renegade parent expert and his arch-nemesis was established psychiatry. He had long ago seen, with the psychogenic hypothesis, its "lack of intellectual integrity," and he sought, once again, to create circuits of information exchange that could circumvent it. "Founding the ASA [aka NSAC], as well as the ARI [aka CBRI], were expressions then, as now, of a lack of confidence in the community of professionals who dealt with autism" (Rimland 2006, 17). Not only are they married to dogma and too fond of drugging their patients, but they are simply too slow, too slow to recognize the truth – about the epidemic and about vaccinations – even as it hit them in the face. In 1995 he published an editorial in *ARRI* replying to explanations of the epidemic emphasizing awareness or diagnostic change (Rimland 1995, 3); years later he would remark, "they were wrong – the increase is very real" (Rimland and Edelson 2003, 13–18, 58–61; Rimland 2006, 7, 17–19).

Whom should you trust, if you cannot trust the experts? Parents (and especially mothers), he argued, were always ahead of the curve, aware of aspects of autism treatment long before medical doctors: "As the years went on, I continued to find, repeatedly, that parents, especially the mothers, were remarkably effective at identifying treatments that were helpful to their autistic children. They were also very observant in detecting factors that caused their children to become worse" (Rimland 2006, 18). These factors, for Rimland, were vaccinations as well as wheat and milk (the basis for gluten-free, casein-free [GFCF] diets).

This mistrust of the experts and valorization of parents' observations was given concrete form in how Rimland rewired his network. He used the E-1 and E-2 checklists to rewire the relations of expertise around the exchange between parents and himself and away from the psychiatric profession. While the use of Form E-2 appears to have dwindled significantly after 1980, probably because of competition from Krug's ABC and Schopler's CARS, and because of its poor performance as a diagnostic tool (Morgan 1988), this had very little effect on Rimland's network, since he already acted to insulate it from such competition. He probably never intended Form E-2 to be primarily a diagnostic tool. He certainly did not design it to be plugged into the network of established psychological and psychiatric expertise. It was written in order to create his own *alternative* network. Unlike what is customary for other diagnostic scales, scoring rules for the items on Form E-2 were never published. So unlike the CARS, which as we saw became a flexible tool, used by multiple actors, nobody, including trained diagnosticians, could use Form E-2 without surrendering control to Rimland. Clinicians were unlikely to agree to such a bargain. The form was intended to be used primarily by parents, who had to send it to ARI once it was completed. The institute, essentially Rimland and an assistant or two, then sent a score and a brief report back to the parents with an explanation about what the answers said about their child. The circuit of exchange excluded clinicians and established a direct link between the little parent-experts and the big Parent-Expert, Rimland.

What was Form E-2 designed to do, if it was not primarily a diagnostic tool? It was a research tool, meant to build a database that would allow Rimland to investigate biological variables and biomedical treatments through a direct exchange with the parents. The newsletter, *ARRI*, was meant to serve a similar function. Rimland routinely advertised in its pages, searching for parents who had experimented with specific therapies.[4] "ARI's basic premise," he noted, "is that parents are the best source of information on what helps – and what doesn't help – autistic children" (Rimland and Edelson 2003, 6). Here was a mechanism, pioneered by NSAC, that provided an alternative to established experimental science with its double-blind controlled experiments. In Rimland's hands it was turned into a weapon against established experimental science, challenging its ideal of virtual witnessing and seeking to subordinate it to the ethical vocation of autism parenting.

In Barron Lerner's (2006) phrase, NSAC's model of exchange among parents multiplied the "*n* of 1" cases so they can stand up to scientific scrutiny. Each parent reported on results of work with one child, and by aggregating all reports, Rimland had enough numbers in his database to make his arguments strong. Recall Lovaas's difficulty getting attention for his results because they were obtained with only one subject. More than twenty years passed before he felt he had accumulated enough observations to report on the success of his method in a fairly marginal psychology journal (Lovaas 1987), and even then the number of subjects was very small, the results not statistically significant, the assignment into groups not really random, and potential biases from time period and parental work unknown. No wonder he was roundly criticized, even accused of fudging his results, and no wonder he retreated to henceforth publishing in the *Journal of Applied Behavior Analysis* – another alternative network. "Stand up to scientific scrutiny"? Perhaps not, but the device of multiplying the "*n* of 1" cases produced an *alternative* mode of research that potentially could bypass and undermine the circuit of exchange upon which depends the legitimacy and viability of experimental science.

"Normal" experimental medical science typically strives to delink the subjects of experiments from the consumers of results. Between them stand three figures: first, the experimenter, protected from public scrutiny by spatial arrangements as well as by the ethos of "virtual witnessing." At the laboratory the experimenter aggregates the individual complaints in order to produce black-boxed facts about populations. The second interpolation is the regulator, typically a whole network of expertise composed of bureaucrats and expert advisory committees. They assess the credibility of the results produced at laboratories and develop policy recommendations, again with respect to populations, "acceptable risk" levels, and so on (Jasanoff 1991). Third, the doctor intervenes, the pediatrician or psychiatrist who is the direct audience for facts and policy recommendations, and who disaggregates them in the form of diagnosis, medical advice, and treatment of individual clients. The whole circuit of exchange relies on the production of what Lakoff calls "diagnostic liquidity," the ability to extrapolate from research subjects to similarly diagnosed populations by means of general, context-independent, currencies of exchange (the black-boxed fact, the diagnostic scale [2005]). When experimental subjects and consumers are unified in the body of the same person – as ACT-UP strove to do with AIDS research (Epstein 1995) – the lonely, secure, and fortified existence of the laboratory scientist is breached, the monopoly of medical advice is challenged, and diagnostic liquidity is compromised. The subject/consumer is capable of exercising influence on the construction of experiments, the selection and assignment of subjects, and the interpretation of results. Rimland's alternative network strove to "eliminate the middleman" (and his liquid currency). It first made parents themselves the experimenters; next it reported the aggregate results of experiments directly back to parents in a mode useful to them, thereby eliminating the need for regulatory science, peer-review, NIH or CDC endorsement, and consultation with a doctor; third, it created an experimental community that allowed parents to share their results, to query one another about specific problems, and to utilize the specific expertise of DAN! scientists, physicians, and parents.

Edelson and Rimland's (2003, 7, 84–85) *Treating Autism: Parent Stories of Hope and Success*, published by ARI, is a good example. The book is organized in two parts. In the first, Rimland and other researchers lay out their approach. The second part of the book is composed of 31 parent-written accounts. This part is preceded by a table, "Autism Symptom Profile." The horizontal axis lists the 31 children, each in his or her row, and the vertical axis lists their symptoms. The table is meant to be used by parents reading the book. Instead of reading black-boxed facts about populations, the product of experimental research, they can directly compare their child's symptoms with those of the children described, find one that is similar, and then leaf forward to the parent-written account to find out what worked and what did not work in treating this child. They can then attempt to replicate the successful treatment given to this type of child, devising their own experimental design at home, and in due course report back their experiences to other parents. Each of the 31 children is treated as a "prototype," if you will, a best example representing a certain category (Rosch 1978). The "*n* of 1" is multiplied, but only to be disaggregated in a mode calculated to be consumed directly by parents. No diagnostic liquidity, more like diagnostic and therapeutic potluck.

"Every child is biochemically unique," is a central tenet of DAN!, along with "autism is treatable." The insistence on each child's uniqueness is clearly the polar opposite of diagnostic liquidity.[5] And it is fast becoming a commonplace in autism discourse. Respectable clinicians subscribe to the oft-repeated mantra that "no two children on the spectrum are alike," "there is no one-size-fits-all autism treatment," "if you know one autistic child, you know one autistic child," and so on (Siegel 1996, 14). One must experiment with what might work, determine what does and does not work, and eventually over time tailor a regimen to the child's particular "biochemical profile." DAN! suggests a whole regimen of tests and supplementation, and a cottage industry has grown up around providing these services, including for-profit manufacturers such as Kirkman Laboratories, with whom Rimland had longstanding relations. Rimland gives suggestions for making one's experimentation more scientific. For instance, he advises against alerting the child's therapists of changes in the child's medical treatment. This way, the professionals will take accurate and unbiased records of the child's progress; "each child thus becomes, in effect, a subject in a double-blind 'mini-study'" (2006, 25; see also p. 10).

Not only is this diagnostic and therapeutic potluck a viable alternative to the circuit of generalized exchange of experimental science, it attempts to subordinate the latter to its own purposes by submitting the results of experimental science directly to parental scrutiny. Recall how Rimland published the contact information of researchers in *ARRI*, so parents could find and contact professionals researching children like their own. In short, he was attempting to produce something similar to the "autism symptom profile" table, only with experimenters and their peer-reviewed articles playing the role of the parent-written accounts of individual profiles and treatment regimes. Instead of experimenters reporting black-boxed facts, they have parents peering over their shoulders, looking at half-baked controversies before they are black-boxed and hardened into facts (Latour 1987). Instead of experimenters producing knowledge about populations, to be disaggregated by the doctor middleman, their reports are taken as particular accounts about particular types of children, and judged with respect to the particular needs and experiences of parents. Similarly, experimental science's "gold standard" of the randomized, double-blind, placebo-controlled trial is subordinated to what McCandless calls the "silver standard" of clinical efficacy. The circuit of exchange among parents short-circuits the lengthy procedures of experimental science. Most therapies first come to meet the "silver standard" of clinical efficacy long before they are ready to be submitted to the "gold standard" test of double-blind placebo trials. By that time, however, says McCandless, it is unethical to withhold treatment, so the "gold standard" is a bit like King Midas's golden touch – never to be used (McCandless et al. 2003, 117). Ultimately this leads to suspicions concerning the integrity and credibility of the laboratory scientist, especially the government-funded one, who no longer enjoys a secure and lonely existence, and no longer can claim the presumption of virtual and virtuous witnessing.

The idea that parents should try whatever is available, and try it fast, further accentuates the agonistic network's resistance to the randomized controlled trial method. McCandless articulates a heavily morally laden image for autism parents, showing how the ethical vocation of autism parenting claims to subordinate the one of "virtual witnessing":

> Imagine you are standing on a pier. Your child is drowning (he or she has developed autism or one of the other autism spectrum disorders) and you can't swim. You desperately look for help or a life preserver (a physician or treatments that might work). You find a rope tied to the pier (special diets, nutritional supplements, anti-fungal/anti-viral treatments, Secretin, chelation for heavy metal toxicity – all of which you have learned are safe and help many of these children). However, authorities warn you not to use it because it has not been proven that the rope is strong enough (the treatment option has not received final approval by "authorities" who are waiting for reports of completed scientific studies appearing in peer-reviewed journals). Meanwhile your child is drowning (exhibiting autistic/ASD symptoms). (McCandless et al. 2003, 137)

If you were a parent, you would not wait, she tells her readers. You would grab that life preserver and give it a hurl. The worst that could happen is that it breaks after your child is pulled a bit closer to shore. In the context of this "try everything" philosophy, where can one find a treatment-naïve child? Parents of autistic children are therapy omnivores. Green et al. (2006) have found that parents of autistic children in the U.S., Canada, and Australia use 111 different types of treatments. The mean number of current treatments to which a child is subjected is 7, with children between the ages of 6 and 10 undergoing the most treatments, and the more severe their disorder, the more types of different treatments they undergo or experiment with. In this context, it is plainly impossible to create uncontaminated control groups for research, unless of very young infants, or perhaps children in countries with less developed medical systems. Thus, the agonistic network and the ethical vocation of autism parenting render randomized controlled trials problematic.

Blurring the boundary between medicine and alternative medicine

Underlying Rimland's search for biochemical treatments was his earlier understanding of autism as a distinct and rare *illness*. He claimed, among other things, that children with high E-2 scores responded better to a multivitamin treatment regimen than did those with lower scores (recall that he argued this about ABA therapy as well), and that children with high scores also had high levels of serotonin outflow. This meant that for Rimland, while Form E-2 and other diagnostic tools constructed autism as a spectrum, there was a distinct biological disorder camouflaged by the spectrum, which corresponded to classical Kanner-type autism and which Form E-2 gradually allowed him to identify (Rimland 1971a).

A curious reversal of roles ensued. In the 1960s, established medicine and psychiatry conceived of autism along an illness model and strove to cure it. NSAC, on the other hand, of which Rimland was a co-founder, linked autism to the model of lifelong, incurable "developmental disabilities," which like mental retardation were to be treated with behavioral and educational approaches seeking not to cure but to "habilitate." Over time, the network of expertise represented by NSAC extended itself into the medical establishment, and now collaborates with it to co-produce autism as a lifelong disability for which the treatment "gold standard" is a combination of nonmedical therapies, and the goal is not cure but equipping children with habits, skills, and prostheses that would allow them to better manage their disability. Conversely, the radical faction of the parent movement led by Rimland has gravitated toward something that looks like an illness model of autism, and their "fringe" treatment protocol is composed precisely of medical and semi-medical treatments aiming at cure or "recovery" (we shall see below the significance of this term). The opposition between these two treatment approaches is more radical on paper than in practice. In reality, many parents use the medical and semi-medical therapies (vitamins, diets, anti-fungals, chelation) with an eye to amelioration of specific symptoms rather than cure. Parents combine medical, behavioral, and educational therapies indiscriminately. Whatever works. Indeed, Edelson and Rimland (2003, 9) themselves observe that the biomedical treatments they recommend "are most effective when combined with intensive educational approaches . . . they 'open the children up' to the experience of learning. We strongly encourage parents to pursue educational and biomedical treatments concurrently to maximize their children's progress." Yet the opposition is significant for two related reasons: first, the agonistic network stakes a position counter to established medicine precisely by deploying the medical model of illness and cure, and the consequent role reversal blurs the lines between "mainstream" and "alternative" medicine, between science and pseudo-science, between medicine and home-baked cures. This then serves to maintain the "pull" that suspends autism between illness and retardation, stretching the spectrum between them and permitting it to collect new categories of children in its fold.

Why is the boundary blurred between mainstream and alternative medicine? First, because the individuals involved in the agonistic network often come from within the medical establishment, yet they are also parents (or grandparents) of autistic children. Rimland formed DAN! in collaboration with John Pangborn, an academic chemist, and Sidney Baker, a Yale pediatrician. They were soon joined by Jaquelyn McCandless, a psychiatrist with an autistic grand-daughter named Chelsea. DAN! maintains a list of doctors who are affiliated with it, and whom parents are encouraged to consult. To be affiliated with DAN! means that one is willing to consult the DAN! protocol, titled *Biomedical Assessment Options for Children with Autism and Related Problems*. To be clear, it means that one is recommending diets, vitamin treatments, chelation, and a variety of other treatments that the medical establishment considers "fringe," "unproven," "alternative," or even positively dangerous. It may mean that one agrees with parents that vaccines have caused their child's autism, which is precisely where the battle lines are drawn between established medicine and its enemies. Yet many physicians with autistic children join DAN! – so many, in fact, that there was even a special panel for them in the 2002 DAN! conference. Among the parent-contributors to Rimland's volume there were also a pediatrician and a neurologist (Edelson and Rimland 2003, 19, 24, 123–26).

Second, the boundary is blurred because Rimland and DAN! actively deconstruct the distinction between mainstream and alternative medicine. I do not promote alternative medicine, says Rimland, but "intelligent medicine" (Rimland 2003, 3), and he traces the lineage of his method to Linus Pauling and "orthomolecular medicine." Jacquelyn McCandless, writing in a more sociological mood, provides a social constructionist analysis of the distinction between mainstream and alternative (2003, 116–17). The "popular press makes a big deal about the dichotomy," but a historical view reveals fluid movement in both directions. What was mainstream can become alternative and vice versa.[6] Why is the use of vitamins "alternative," they ask, and the prescription of drugs by psychiatrists "mainstream"? Rimland deconstructs the history of DMG's (dimethylglycine) introduction to the American market to show that pure historical contingency and regulatory fiat led to its being classified as a food supplement and not a drug (Edelson and Rimland 2003, 40–42). This is good, he says, since it does not require prescription, it is cheap, and parents can use it freely. But it does not mean therefore that its use is "alternative" and not "medical." He and McCandless target the complex of relations between big pharmaceuticals and established medicine and accuse the latter of "simply drugging . . . autistic children [instead of] . . . effectively treating them" (ibid.). Appendix C in Edelson and Rimland's book contains the results of a "Treatment Effectiveness Survey" of parents (364–65). It compares diets and supplements with drugs to show that the former are safer and more effective. Very early on Rimland developed a close working relationship with Kirkman Laboratories through which he helped foster an alternative supply channel that could respond to increasing demand for multivitamins, DMG, digestive enzymes and other supplements. A small but thriving market emerged, alongside and intermeshed with the market for pharmaceuticals.

It is the therapy itself, however, and the ethical model of intervention embedded in it, rather than what is said about it or who practices it, which serves to open up a whole fuzzy zone between established and alternative medicine. The moderate success he experienced experimenting with vitamin therapy led Rimland to introduce a small but crucial modification in his understanding of autism. There was a "remarkably wide range of benefits . . . better eye contact, less self-stimulatory behavior, more interest in the world . . . fewer tantrums, more speech, and in general the children became more normal, although they were not completely cured." He concluded, therefore, that "autism . . . is in many cases a vitamin B6 dependency syndrome" (Edelson and Rimland 2003, 26–28). Conceiving of autism as "dependency" is, of course, not inconsistent with also thinking that it is a genetic illness, but it allows Rimland to activate a principle of fuzzification within the medical model of illness and cure. Dependency, as Mariana Valverde (1998) notes, is a morally laden metaphor, one that links a moral image with a somatic condition, it conjures a whole world of hybrid entities, from "diseases of the will" (Ribot 1910) to speaking bodies – if they get hyperactive, says Rimland (Edelson and Rimland 2003, 49–50), it is "their way of telling you they need more folic acid." It is a highly flexible term. On the one hand, it can mean something like "deficit," which is the closest to the illness model – find the correct dose of the missing substance and the child is cured. On the other hand, it may mean a permanent condition and identity, closest to the model of disability and retardation – "once an alcoholic, always an alcoholic." In between the two, there is the image of a body out of homeostasis, either poisoned from the outside as in the vaccine theory or GFCF diets, or depleted on the inside as in the image of *Children with Starving Brains* (McCandless 2003), or the two images are neatly combined in the notion of "autoimmune disorder," a body that poisons itself.

To dependency and its brethren disruptions of homeostasis corresponds not cure per se, but "recovery." Rimland explains that vitamin therapy is "not a cure," but it makes a "big . . . difference" (Edelson and Rimland 2003, 36). The title of the aforementioned 2003 book was changed for the 2006 second printing from *Treating Autistic Children* to *Recovering Autistic Children*, to reflect what Rimland claimed was a major breakthrough, an explosion of "recovered" children; an impossibility had become "commonplace" (Rimland 2006, 6). The use of the term "recovery" is significant for several reasons: first, in the hierarchy of treatment outcomes it strays just below the level of "cure." It connotes a longer and less certain, potentially reversible process, but unlike "improvement" (below it in the hierarchy) it is still within, or on the fringes, of the *restorative*. Second, it resonates with the image of a child, hidden behind the disorder (recall the fable of *The Castle* in Chapter 7), who is snatched back, "recovered," by his parents from the "empty fortress" of autism. It interpellates, therefore, a particular moral mode of parental agency. Indeed, among the parents writing short reports in Edelson and Rimland's book is Karyn Seroussi, who in no uncertain terms explains how "we rescued our child from autism" (ibid., 299–305; see also Seroussi 2000).

Recovery in this view is an individual and unique process. A disease may be cured, but only a unique individual can recover. As Rimland (Edelson and Rimland 2003, 20–24) explains, there is no way of knowing if vitamins or diets will help, because "every child is very different from every other child." Recovery, therefore, is something that only parents, experimenting on their child, day in and day out, can achieve. Recall the "Autism Symptom Profile." Nobody can tell you what is the right amount (of vitamins, supplements, detoxification), says Rimland, not only because every child is different, but because "dependency" and its brethren disruptions of homeostasis (deficit, poisoning, auto-immune disorder, and so on) imply recovery as a delicate fine-tuning of chemical balance that can only be achieved in individual cases and only through trial and error. What is involved is not a science of illness but an art of healing (Edelson and Rimland 2003, 48–49; Gadamer 1996). The result is a fuzzy zone where established and alternative medicines are indistinguishable, and the expertise of doctors is not superior, but additive (advisory, in Abbott's [1988] phrase) to the expertise of parents. It would seem, perhaps, that it is still possible to distinguish between the two, since one prescribes drugs and the other administers vitamins/nutrients/food supplements:[7] "a drug acts by blocking or interfering with a natural body process, while a nutrient permits or enhances these processes" (Edelson and Rimland 2003, 48). The very nebulousness of this distinction, however, demonstrates the principle of fuzzification activated by the model of dependency/recovery. To begin with, the distinction between "blocking" and "permitting" is altogether fuzzy. Is slowing down the reuptake of a neurotransmitter, for example, blocking or permitting a natural process? Isn't dependency itself a natural process? Moreover, since the target of treatment – recovery – is imagined as enhancing a natural process tending toward homeostasis, then any adverse result can be interpreted as simply failing to achieve the correct balance (and therefore to require a bit more or a bit less of the same).

As a term signaling an art of healing, "recovery" is not only individualizing but holistic. The whole individual is treated through a sort of therapeutic bricolage, not just his or her autism. Or more precisely, as Chloe Silverman (forthcoming) argues, a variety of symptoms, previously understood as "co-morbidities" and not essential to the diagnostic prototype of autism (gut dysfunction, but also yeast infection, allergies, sleep disorder, eating disorder, aggression, "self-stimming," seizures, hyperactivity) are now translated differently, as relevant symptoms of autism-qua-disruption of homeostasis, as legitimate objects of treatment the reduction of which signals recovery. They can be treated by "correcting body chemistry" (Edelson and Rimland 2003, 52), thereby indicating that one is acting on the underlying imbalance responsible for the total condition of the child. Thus, we agree with Silverman when she argues that this "leads to a blurring or reframing of the diagnostic category of autism itself" (Silverman, forthcoming). In particular, the fuzzy zone between established and alternative medicines serves as a channel through which a variety of late-onset or "regressive" types of autism were attached to the spectrum and came to modify its prototype. This process began long before the late-onset exclusion was dropped, and it is still continuing.

Take, for example, the case of anti-fungals. A small number of children exhibiting autistic symptoms were reported recovered following treatment with Nystatin, an anti-fungal. Rimland argues that this shows something he had claimed in 1966, that between 5 to 10 percent of children diagnosed with autism, especially the late-onset or regressive type, are actually suffering from a yeast infection, with the *Candida albicans* fungus (Edelson and Rimland 2003, 55–57). They were given antibiotics for ear infections at an early age. The antibiotics disrupted the delicate balance in which the fungus is kept in check by the body and by other competing microorganisms. The fungus began to release toxins which cause pain, disrupt the immune system, and also affect the brain. The children regressed. Treatment with anti-fungals assists the body to restore balance and therefore the children recover. He says that physicians are skeptical of this theory, but mothers have flocked to the therapy. Very few physicians will prescribe anti-fungals, but the result is uncertain because there are many different strains of the fungus, hence one needs to experiment also with diets (that will reduce nutrients favored by the fungus) or even move to a drier climate, he counsels. One can see how in this case the blurred boundaries between established and alternative medicines allowed a whole set of new symptoms (especially allergies, repeated infections, and so on), and with them whole new populations, to infiltrate the spectrum and swell the ranks of the epidemic.

The space of autism therapies

Fuzzy zones, like the one between established and alternative medicine, surround the space of autism therapies on all sides, each in its own way blurring the edges of the diagnostic category of autism and extending the spectrum to new populations of children. Figure 6 is a schematic representation of the space of autism therapies. It is a space between the fields of medicine and special education, between academia and the market, a space relatively open to incursions from all these other fields. It is characterized by low barriers to entry in terms of credentials, funds, and licensing, by high potential profits, both monetary and symbolic (in terms of upgrading the status of marginal occupations); yet it is also typically the case that realizing these profits is conditional on striking a coalition with parents. Finally, this space is characterized by fuzzy boundaries with medicine, special education, academic psychology, the market and advocacy, and by the principles of blurring or hybridization activated by actors within it. In the previous section, as we followed the story of Rimland, we found ourselves weaving in and out of advocacy, medicine, alternative medicine, and the market, tracing a characteristic movement that imparts to the space of autism therapies a significant measure of its dynamism. We saw how the therapeutic function, the medical

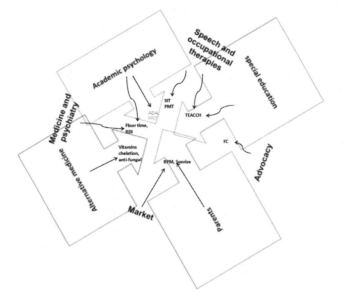

Figure 6: The space of autism therapies

discourse of "cure," is taken up by parents and advocates who estab-lish themselves as quasi-medical experts, who then form alliances with various medical professionals who straddle the fuzzy boundary between established and alternative medicine, or with entrepreneurs like Kirkman Laboratories. Medical cure is then transformed into a set of hybrid goals modeled after recovery from dependency and imbalance, which authorize this constant weaving and blurring of boundaries.

On the other side of the space of autism therapies, an analogous movement unfolds. We do not have the time or space here to chart its course; however, since it is characteristic of the mainstream of the parents' movement, the reader may recognize its outline from earlier chapters. A full-fledged analysis will have to wait for another book. On the right-hand side of the space of autism therapies, autism is not an illness or a quasi-illness (dependency, deficit, imbalance) but a developmental disability (or delay, or even pure difference), and the position of the special educator is occupied by multiple agents – parents, speech and occupational therapists (many operating as entre-preneurs of this or that therapy, many as advocates), psychologists, even psychiatrists. In their transactions across disciplines and fields,

Table 7: Leading autism therapies

Therapy	Founder or central figure	Date	Organizational format	Main techniques
Perceptual-Motor Therapy (PMT)	Newel Kephart, psychologist	Late 1950s	Summer camp, strictly advisory	Visual and tactile stimulation, "structure"
Applied Behavioral Analysis (ABA)	Ivar Lovaas, UCLA psychologist	Late 1960s	Association, certification	Operant conditioning
Sensory Integration Therapy (SIT)	Jean Ayres, USC occupational therapy	Late 1960s	Non-profit, certification	"sensory gym," forming "adaptive responses"
TEACCH ("developmental therapy")	Eric Schopler, UNC psychologist	Early 1970s	State program	Eclectic
"son-rise"	Barry Neil Kaufman and Samahria Lyte Kaufman parents	1974	Training center, certification	Imitate the actions of the child
Facilitated Communication (FC)	Rosemary Crossley, speech therapy	1970s	Institute, training but not certification	Hand over hand typing
Floor Time (also known as DIR)	Stanley Greenspan, GWU psychiatrist	1980s	Foundation, certification	Circles of communication
Pivotal Response Training (PRT)	The Koegels, UCSB psychologists	Early 1990s	Research center, certification	ABA in "natural" interaction
Relationship Development Intervention (RDI)	Steven Gutstein, UT psychologist	1990s	Consultation and training center, certification	Experience sharing interaction
Rapid Prompting Method (RPM)	Soma Mukhopadhyay mother	2001	Non-profit, certification	Teaching academics using paper cards

they blur the boundaries between special education and academic psychology on one side, and between special education and advocacy (or even for-profit entrepreneurship) on the other. The approaches they deploy are known by various outlandish acronyms. Some of the information about them is summarized in Table 7.

The object of these therapies, as they freely admit, is no longer autism-qua-illness. They pragmatically sidestep, ignore, neutralize, the antinomies of medical discourse. They move easily in the space opened up between illness and retardation, thereby giving rise to a new ethical economy of intervention. The ethical substance of this economy, the object upon which it works, is not an illness, though it is invariably understood as an inborn and lifelong condition. Lovaas expresses the inner truth of the principle of hybridization these therapies activate when he says that the idea of autism is "superfluous" or "hypothetical," and that what ABA does is interchangeable among diagnostic categories (1981). Patients are neither "ill" with autism, nor are they "retarded," he says. They are developmentally disabled persons who score low on IQ tests and need help with language. ABA, SIT, Floortime, have all gathered into the fold of the spectrum children with diagnoses of ADHD or learning disabilities, or those simply defined as "challenging" children with "special needs." If a newer and less established therapy, like RPM, developed by the mother of an autistic child, presents itself as specifically and solely for "classical autism," this merely reflects its status as newcomer to the space of autism therapies. Before it can expand to other parts of the spectrum, it needs to gain recognition by scoring successes at the core.

As we noted earlier, the techniques deployed by these therapies in working on their objects are low-tech, typically developed a long time ago, all versions of what Grinker (2007) calls "being in your child's face" or Schopler and Reichler (1971) describe as "the adult's non-specific impingement on the child." All involve a great deal of immediate physical co-presence and involvement with the child, including touching. They brush the children's bodies, swing them in a hammock (SIT), play with them (DIR), use flash cards (RPM), instruct them to type (FC), prompt them for correct response by guiding their hands, drill language into them, even spank (up until the mid-1980s) and shout (ABA). To what end? "Being in your child's face" means that therapies identify as their object the failure to communicate, and they react to it by intensifying interaction – bodily, verbally, any which way. Consider Asperger's phrase: "One has to seek contact with the contact-impaired!" (1979, 51). What desired effect is to be gained from intensive interaction? We already know from previous chapters:

it can be meant to build skills and inculcate habits (ABA), that is, be a thoroughly bottom-up, constructivist approach, where one starts with elementary behaviors and forms of communication and works one's way up slowly to more complex behaviors. It can also be meant to work directly on the brain, to jump-start a certain faculty, some natural potential that has been lying dormant, encircled in defenses (PMT, SIT). To these two interpretations we may add a third, this one thoroughly top-down, where intensive interaction is understood as primarily *representing* a child who cannot communicate but whose thought is intact and on a high level (FC, RPM).

These three interpretations contain the residues of a medical model of cure (as in the awakening of "dormant faculty"). Their origins in the field of special education and retardation (as in the inculcation of habits) are also clear, and the relatively later intervention of advocacy organizations and the neurodiversity movement can be traced as well (as in representation). These differences in interpretation are also a matter of relational positioning and niche-building in a highly uncertain market. They represent differences in the timing and mode of entry, whereby early leaders, like ABA, with its superior organization, can afford to impose the longest waiting periods, while newcomers must opt for a top-down interpretation and promise quick results in order to attract clients. At the level of therapeutic practice itself, however, the differences are much less stark. Coaching habits, awakening a dormant faculty, representing; in some sense all three are present in any of the therapies. Top-down approaches, like FC and RPM, also do a great deal of habit training, while bottom-up approaches like ABA also seek to engage a certain dormant faculty. Lovaas's discussion of tantrums is extremely revealing in this regard: tantrums are rational, he says, they are effective means of communication (1981). The child is seeking to intimidate you and gain control. The tantrums, in fact, are something that the therapist should seek, because through them communication is established and one arrives at the child's "basic humanity." Precisely over this issue there was a split within ABA, and two of Lovaas's disciples splintered off to create Pivotal Response Training (PRT). Certain behaviors are pivotal because "it is believed that by changing them, other associated behaviors will change without being specifically targeted." And ABA, which relies heavily on prompting, can also become a form of representation, almost *joint* embodiment, as parents or therapists prompt the child verbally and physically, serving thus as their interpreters and advocates in everyday encounters. In the actual practice of any of these therapies, then, the boundaries between behaviorist psychology, special education, occupational and speech therapy, advocacy, even parenting, are blurred.

This blurring between, for example, advocacy and psychology is particularly evident when it comes to the way the goal of therapy is defined. Unlike in medicine, the goal of intervention is not envisioned as "curing" an illness. There is no illness, and there is no end point. Therapy will be lifelong. The first step in treatment, says Karen Siff Exkorn, is acceptance that one (or one's child) is going to live with autism for the rest of one's life (2005). Like "once an alcoholic, always an alcoholic," this assumption of an autistic identity is a paradoxical precondition for beginning the process of self-healing, or "improvement." Autistics and parents are led away from expecting a quick cure (though this is obviously less true for newer and less established therapies), and asked to adjust their expectations. We hear echoes of Alcoholics Anonymous' slogan "one day at a time" in Lovaas' advice to "set small goals so both you and your child will be rewarded. Find pleasure in small steps. Don't struggle for an absolute and unattainable ideal of normalcy" (1981). Unlike the treatment of retardation, however, the goal of intervention is not passive adjustment to society, but an active relationship to oneself and to one's environment. First of all, "improvement" means that the goal of the therapies can be characterized as a continuum: it could mean fairly complete recovery, or very modest gains in terms of quality of life. Second, it means that the art of therapy consists in guiding students and parents toward independence. The trick is to provide just the right amount of "structure" – a key term in all these therapies – so as to foster the self-organizing powers of parents and students, to create a "prosthetic environment" wherein the autistic person can function relatively independently (Holmes 1990). Third, it means that even when this is achieved to the fullest, autism is not cured, but simply better managed, or in the language of the TEACCH program, it is "sufficiently camouflaged . . . to be unnoticeable" (Schopler and Reichler 1971). The habits of communication coached by the therapies – to which one should add social skills classes, "empathy" teaching, face recognition workshops – are technologies of the autistic self. They equip it with tools for living, for relating to itself and to others. They manage or channel its excesses. But they do not do away with the underlying condition. They only camouflage it.

To what end? Lovaas states it plainly: "there will be no more retarded persons" (1981). He means two things: first, normalization in the sense of integration and adjustment of the individual, who is taught to become a functioning member of whatever "track" and prosthetic environment he or she inhabits. Siegel says it means "making the 'mainstream' more diverse, with roles for people with limited cognitive ability, but who can be helped to feel useful doing a small, well-defined vocational job" (1996, 274–300). The second meaning of this slogan, however, is the more radical meaning of "normalization," inherited from the struggles against the institution. Autism, retardation, developmental disability, will be normalized in the sense of destigmatization, in the sense that society too will be changed and adapted to the needs of individuals who are different, and are not going to stop being different. Rather than merely enveloping the person within a prosthetic environment, advocacy comes to infuse the very goal of treatment – to extend the walls of the prosthetic environment further out until they come to overlap with a much fuller range of social environments and experiences. As stated plainly in the mission statement of TEACCH: "the environment should be modified to meet the needs of children with ASDs, not vice versa" (quoted in Siff Exkorn 2005, 111).

CONCLUSION

The argument we presented in this book was not a simple story of cause and effect – if A, then B – but a complex tale of necessary though not sufficient historical conditions, of active ingredients that set in motion looping processes, and of the interaction between all these pieces in the form of a puzzle. While the preceding pages have examined the pieces in detail, it is helpful in conclusion to step back and reflect on the scene that appears when they are fitted together.

Our main point was that the recent rise in autism diagnoses represents not an epidemic, but a change in the institutional conditions under which we perceive and treat childhood disorders. How we understand what used to be called "mental retardation" has been crucial to the change. The very category of autism, we have shown, emerged in the interstice between mental retardation and mental illness, as part of an attempt to stitch them together into a comprehensive program for the surveillance of childhood. To perform this role, however, autism did not need to be any more than a rare disorder, one more form of "apparent feeblemindedness."

In putting together the puzzle of contemporary autism, therefore, we argued that the best place to start is with the question of why autism was rare in the past, and with the existence of a population of individuals housed in custodial institutions for the mentally retarded who *could* have been diagnosed with autism. The institutional matrix of custody defined this population, as we saw, not by intelligence but by social incapability, and within this matrix there was little motivation or even meaning to differential diagnosis. Add to this arrangement the social distance between the diagnoses – between the potentially dangerous and mostly lower-class and racial-minority "morons" and the white, middle-class, potentially intelligent autistic

– and the mutually exclusive moral images associated with autism-qua-mental illness as against mental retardation, and you get the reason why autism remained a rare disorder, unable to make its appearance among the institutionalized populations.

Several other factors, however, intervened to create a spiral of looping processes that extended autism into a much larger spectrum now covering an ever-widening expanse of the domain of developmental disabilities. The parents' movement blurred the boundaries between expert and layperson, and began extending the category to include less typical manifestations of the disorder. This movement developed in tandem, as we saw, with the elaboration of a system for the surveillance of childhood. Parent activism in NARC, for example, was originally not anti-medical but pro-family, and it collaborated with psychiatry's intrusion into the middle-class family. When it turned against the custodial matrix in the late 1960s, with both NARC and NSAC, it did not reject the effort to establish medical surveillance of childhood, but rather offered the middle-class family as a central subcontractor of such a system, superior to the custodial institution. With NSAC, in particular, this has meant that parents' expertise was valorized and a new network of expertise began to be forged.

Crucially, however, the middle-class family was not abandoned to its own devices. The blurring of boundaries between lay and expert in NSAC was complemented by the emergence of new therapies that blurred the boundary between mental illness and mental retardation. The historical moment of these therapies came, as we saw, with deinstitutionalization. As normalization redefined the goal of treatment from cure to habilitation and its object from retardation to developmental disability, the therapies flooded into the space opened up between medicine and special education and began contracting with parents to decenter the subject of treatment from the sovereign psychiatrist to a network of expertise, increasingly including parents. These therapies were unique in that they blurred the boundary not only between expert and layman, but also between mental illness and mental retardation. This blurring was a precondition for the expansion of autism into a spectrum, because the aim of these therapies was tailored less to a diagnosis than to the specific deficits of the individual. A condition was addressed from the bottom up, not from the top down, thus ushering in an alternative, more finely tuned means of classification: if, as Lorna Wing suggested, if we focus not on global diagnoses but instead on specific handicaps, then there is little reason to differentiate so sharply between mental retardation and autism.

Rather, it was more useful to see them as overlapping conditions, different combinations of symptoms pulled from the same pool of deficits. To understand autism as a spectrum meant to define it not as a specific constellation of symptoms, but increasingly as the very pool of deficits itself. Therefore, *multiple* combinations of symptoms could be represented as regions on the spectrum, which by this new definition would include milder cases of Asperger's as well as the more severe cases previously categorized as mental retardation.

We have shown how, with the change of institutional matrix and extension of the therapies, especially behavioral ones, the autism prototype began to change, in particular by becoming concurrent and overlapping with mental retardation. Other dynamics were modifying the prototype and extending the spectrum as well, especially the addition of Asperger's syndrome and the emergence of self-advocates. But from the point of view developed in this book, the crucial dynamic, the real revolution of lasting significance was this rearrangement of the relations with mental retardation. Co-morbidity or concurrence of the two paradoxically meant that they became interchangeable, preparing the ground for diagnostic substitution driven mostly by demand factors, by social influence and the interests of parents. As Siegel (1996, 128) says, parents try to "bargain away" the retardation component in the diagnosis, presumably because it is perceived as more of a "life sentence" than autism. As Bearman and King (unpublished) show, net of other factors, living in very close proximity to a child previously diagnosed with autism significantly increases another child's risk of being diagnosed with autism, *and significantly lowers their risk of being diagnosed with mental retardation.* Hence the final chapter in the looping process was massive diagnostic substitution during the 1990s, which has given rise to the perception of an autism "epidemic."

Diagnostic substitution is no doubt driven by proximate demand forces, such as the interests of parents, but the precondition for this dynamic was this much longer process that established the peculiar boundary between autism and mental retardation. The boundary was blurred, making substitution possible, but it was consequential for the ethical economy of treatment – otherwise substitution would not be attractive. Treatment of mental retardation is still perceived and institutionally defined as *dis*economical, especially after a certain age, whereas the "critical window" implicated in autism, and the new ethical mode of intervention it triggers, renders its treatment economical. Unlike mental retardation, a diagnosis of autism postpones the medical diagnosis of social destiny. Yet historically, this peculiar

line at once differentiating and linking autism and mental retardation
was a product of the institutional matrices and networks of expertise
surrounding the diagnoses. It is much too uncertain and provisional
to serve such an auspicious social function.

This sociological and historical analysis, we must emphasize,
finds support in the findings of genetic research we cited in the
Introduction. Geneticists are currently showing that the autism spectrum overlaps with mental retardation not only on the phenotypic
level as co-morbidity, but also at the genomic level of QTLs and rare
mutations, as well as on the level of endophenotypes (Laummonier
et al. 2004; Marshall et al. 2008; Abrahams and Geschwind 2008).
Scientists were quick to recognize that a fruitful research strategy
would "require more rigorous definitions of *specific* components of
the social, language, and repetitive behavior dimensions of autism,
using clinical, neuropsychologic and neurobiological markers" (Rapin
and Tuchmann 2008; emphasis added). In other words, like the clinical understanding of autism, genetic research needed to be "spectru-
mized." Consequently, the search for a single autism gene has largely
been abandoned. In its place came the search for CNVs, QTLs, and
the specification of endophenotypes. But many of the endophenotypes
in autism – lack of language, age at first word, gender, IQ, repetitive
behaviors – are also typical of mental retardation, and this calls seriously into question the logical leap from symptom to disorder, for
we would be hard pressed to explain why certain loci associated
with language delay in autism would necessarily differ from those
associated with the same characteristic in mental retardation. In fact,
some researchers suggest that genetic analyses of syndromes that are
co-morbid with autism could be valuable for indicating genes important to the etiology of ASDs, and that "many of the CNVs identified
[for autism] overlap with previously identified mental retardation
(MR) loci or chromosomal syndromes" (Bill and Geschwind 2009,
273).[1] The same authors note that "the majority of ASCG [Autism
Susceptibility Candidate Genes] are not ASD specific and have been
implicated in other neurodevelopmental disorders such as intellectual
disability, epilepsy, or psychiatric conditions" (276). These findings,
we believe, support the argument we developed in this book, since
they indicate a substantial overlap between autism and mental retardation. Common CNVs between schizophrenia and bipolar disorder
have forced some to challenge the notion that the two are distinct
conditions (O'Donovan, Craddock, and Owen 2009). We think the
same logic may apply for childhood developmental disorders. Taken
together, the findings suggest that autism and mental retardation are

less distinct disorders than originally conceived. While inconclusive with respect to permitting statements of the type "autism is caused by X, mental retardation by Y," recent results indicate that what *can* be said with confidence is that any such simple statements are patently false. Even estimates of heritability have varied widely over the years, with some in the 1970s as high as 90 percent and others in 2009 as low as 19 percent for boys. Why such a large discrepancy? While it made sense both clinically and educationally to redefine autism as a spectrum, this "phenotypic renaissance" resulted in an increase in genetic heterogeneity, which greatly complicated the task of geneticists (Bill and Geschwind 2009, 272). With the spectrum continuing to increase in scope, we can speculate that heritability estimates will continue to decrease.

As the overlap and links between mental retardation and autism become more substantial, it is the former category that begins to be understood differently, and on the model of autism-cum-developmental-delay: impairment being specific rather than global; diagnosable early rather than late; temporary, amenable to intensive intervention at the right moment, or at the very least not fixed and without progress (see also Siegel 1996, 97; Greenspan and Wieder 1998, 8–9); Down's syndrome being the exception rather than the prototype.

This is, after all, what the advocates of autism originally wished for. Recall Lovaas's wish that "there will be no more retarded persons," recall also Wing's dismantling of the idea that mental retardation exists as a unitary condition. Yet, paradoxically, the rise of autism has also meant a certain marginalization of mental retardation; otherwise parents would not have had to try to "bargain it away." With a great deal of resources and effort now dedicated to early diagnosis and early intervention in autism,[2] those with other diagnoses (specifically mental retardation), those who are deemed too impaired, and also those who are too old, are marginalized. The image of the fast-closing "window of opportunity" legitimizes intensive investment specifically in early diagnosis and intervention for autism, with the promise that this is how we will secure the most dividends in the form of more spontaneous recovery or marked improvement. By the same token, it shunts to the side sustained investment in those individuals who either are evaluated as unlikely to make progress sufficient to justify this allocation of resources or those who have aged and for whom the window has presumably closed – remember Siegel's "forks in the road."[3] And since nobody is in the position to assume the mantle of medical diagnosis of social destiny, the fateful

261

decision as to this allocation of categories, resources, and destinies is preempted by arbitrary forces such as the differential clout of parents, place of residence, social proximity to other affected families, differential access to services, and more. Moreover, even if we had in place an objective and rational system of assignment and allocation, what would happen to these very same children when they grow up into adolescents and adults with autism, in all likelihood not "cured" or sufficiently improved to lead fully independent lives? Prevention, early intervention and improvement of diagnosis would no longer be relevant for them. As many parents can testify, there is a stark discontinuity in the lives of their children as they grow up. Sometime around early adolescence, the intensive therapeutic regime they underwent as toddlers and youngsters is gradually whittled down, replaced by very little that is targeted, and they and their parents are left to their own devices.[4]

When the significance of autism, by contrast, is grasped as a new ethical mode of intervention; when, by the same token, mental retardation is construed no longer as a unitary category but an aggregate of specific disorders, overlapping and analogous to autism; the implication is that the proper response to the rising number of diagnoses is not prevention and eradication of an epidemic, but guaranteeing equity and continuity in access to services and therapies. Intervention still can (and should) start early, but with a wider perspective on autism as a lifelong condition and the autistic *person* – not just the child – as a member of society. This was precisely the political and ethical question raised by normalization: what adaptations is society willing to make, and how many resources is it rational to invest, in order to convert the formal rights of even its most disabled citizens, at whatever age, into substantive and meaningful experiences of membership in society? This framing does not ignore or marginalize the needs of autistic adults or persons with disabilities in general. We reject as invidious the distinction between those who are more and less likely to make progress, not because we are starry-eyed and believe in everyone's limitless potential, but because we know that it is but one more iteration in a historical series of distinctions between the "deserving poor" and "nondeserving poor" of the economy of childhood disorders and their treatment. As with the welfare state, with which this distinction is intimately connected, we opt for a universal model. It is the case today that the autism diagnosis provides access to far more services – hours of therapy, aides in the classroom, autism-only classrooms, IEPs geared toward maximizing the child's potential even where the law explicitly does not require it – than do diagnoses for children with other developmental disabilities, most notably mental retardation in its various forms and euphemisms. If one follows the argument of this book, as well as the findings of genetic research, then one must acknowledge that this distinction is arbitrary, and the sooner we get rid of it, the better. This was, indeed, the promise of autism as a new ethical mode of intervention. Recall what Wing had to say already in 1972 about these distinctions: it is "pointless . . . to draw sharp lines between autistic and 'not really autistic' in educational practice. . . . The question to ask about each child is – what are his handicaps, what are his skills and what can we do to help him?"

We should note that this point of view comports, as we tried to show, with the nature of the intervention itself, that is, with the therapies and the moral narrative that guides them. When parents start their journey in the autism world, they find themselves in a confusing and uncharted territory. It takes them some time to realize how very open and unbounded this world is. Yet the temporal structure of their experience of the journey hardly permits them to lift their heads and look around. From all sides they are being urged to take action fast, often with rhetoric not unlike McCandless's parable of the drowning child, and often with a particular therapy being peddled as the salvation they desperately crave, as the only "scientifically proven" panacea. At the same time, they may hear talk about autism therapies, especially behavioral ones, as being authoritarian and conformist, something to avoid. This view is typically voiced by some self-advocates and scholars sympathetic to their perspective. Ian Hacking (2007, 311) says that "the point of behavioral therapies for autism" is "to make unfavorable deviants as close to normal as possible," and Bumiller (2008, 976) opines that "the pressures for social integration that accompany these practices result in professionals devaluing deviant groups or accepting them only when they appear like members of the mainstream." We think neither view does justice to the complexity and flexibility of autism therapies *taken as a whole*. The moral narrative common to autism therapies, we argued, is the idea of "prosthetic environment." This narrative is inclusive. Regardless how impaired one may be, or how old, it is always possible to structure an environment in which one is enabled, and then gradually seek to extend it. From this point of view, it is misleading to paint the significance of autism therapies, especially behavior modification therapies, as authoritarian and constraining. To be sure, therapies may work toward the adaptive goal of normalization, training individuals to pass as normal or, as in Schopler's phrase, to

263

"camouflage" the disorder, but at the same time they also reconfigure what counts as normal and *how* someone can pass as such. They make the mainstream, as Siegel says, more diverse, or put differently, they extend the perimeter of the prosthetic environment further into the mainstream (1996, 274–300). Is communicating one's desire to go for a walk by passing a PECS picture to another person normal? In the context of autism therapies – yes, it is. Is squeezing, rubbing, and spinning a "sensory toy" in order to diffuse anxiety or tension "normal"? Sure – *now* it is. For the same reason, it is misleading to represent the matter of therapy as a choice between "rescuing" children or letting them drown. Autism therapies are technologies of the autistic self, and they reconfigure the goal of treatment. They come equipped with a whole host of prosthetic devices – PECS books, personal communication computers, wristbands, and more. They are meant to be tunable to the child's individual strengths and weaknesses, and calculated to extend outward and blend into the environment. "Work with autism, not against it" – this slogan invented by some self-advocates could also be the slogan greeting people at the entrance to the prosthetic environment (yes, even of the environment where ABA is practiced!) as this is the principle that governs action within it. As we said in Chapter 10, touching on this issue, within the same home one can find a room dedicated to structured discrete trial ABA and a bookshelf housing memoirs by self-advocates; ABA-based schools know how to "work with autism" by allowing students to earn "sensory breaks."

The idea of the "prosthetic environment" is, in some sense, paradoxical. It aims at achieving maximum independence, autonomy, agency, and sociability – all the trappings of the modern subject – yet these are often achieved – better, approximated – through hybrid arrangements involving therapists and parents who prompt the child or translate his utterances and behaviors, computers that project typed or touched words, or environments geared to the child's sensory sensitivities or distractive proclivities. Because these therapies expand the range of environments in which the individual can function, they practice a sort of (micro) politics of recognition, seeking recognition for approximations of "normal" sociality – a prompted hello, a computer-articulated request, a loose interpretation of the sign-language gesture for thank you, eye contact in the general direction of another person. If these are impositions at all, they do not impose a constraining norm but force the individual to engage socially, or to exercise the faculty of choice even when he could not care less about it (Schelly 2008).

We are well aware that the relations between parents and therapists can often be quite tense, and that our reading of the significance of the therapies may seem overly idealistic to parents who have to monitor, dismiss, bargain with or implore, cajole, evaluate, even instruct the whole rag-tag army of therapists in their role as treatment managers and advocates for their children. We hope to make amends in a second volume that will describe and analyze the moral career of the autistic child, where the analysis would draw closer to the experience of contemporary parents of autistic children. In this volume, however, we attempted to draw out the global historical significance of the therapies *taken as a whole*, of this whole interstitial space between fields, and to point out the commonalities between some of the practices and legitimating narratives employed by therapists.

At the heart of these narratives, as we tried to show, was the idea of a prosthetic environment governed by *sui generis* communicative norms wherein the autistic person can acquire thickness, almost always, however, assisted by aides, advocates, most often by parents. We would like to end this book with this moral narrative of therapy – idealistic, we admit, maybe even saccharine – as captured in a contemporary movie, *Lars and the Real Girl* (2007). Without mentioning autism by name, this movie captures a dimension of the contemporary experience of autism and the ethical mode of intervention it represents, which is absent from *Rain Man*.

It is a movie about mental disorder, perhaps somehow related to autism or Asperger's, we are not told what it is. The opening scene has the actor, Ryan Gosling, looking out the window, transfixed, at some play of sunlight on the snow – an unmistakable reference to some such disorder. It is instructive to compare the representation of mental disorder in *Lars* with movies from twenty or thirty years ago that dealt with mental illness. In earlier films, mental illness was typically represented as something not immediately obvious, not on the surface. At first scarcely recognizable under a layer of normality, yet in moments of crisis what lurked beneath became evident (for instance, Peter Falk in *Woman Under the Influence*). Or, mental illness was related to a secret in the past, a deeply buried traumatic experience; one needed to dig deep to recover it to begin the healing process. Again, a violent confrontation, a crisis, was sometimes needed to do so. None of this is true about mental disorder in *Lars*. It is obvious from the very first moment that something is not quite right about Lars. Illness is not buried; it is wholly on the surface. If something is lurking below, it is Lars's normality – or more precisely, his desire to communicate with others, understand them and be understood.

One cannot shake the feeling that the old idea of illness as an evil agent still permeated the depictions of mental illness in earlier movies. Notions such as a secret buried deep in the past, a trauma still lurking just underneath the surface, which could only be made manifest through crisis and confrontation, gave this agent of evil a body and a voice, and depicted healing almost as exorcism. Nothing could be further from this than *Lars*. Here illness is not an agent, it is a state of being. It is who Lars *is*. Illness pervades Lars's existence, not underneath the surface, but in his every habit and behavior, and it consists of a fundamental incapacity to communicate or to understand what others are communicating to him. Most important, the psychiatrist or psychoanalyst, as the locus of authority and as the hero doing battle with madness, is gone. Instead, we get a small-town doctor who is also a psychologist of sorts, but most of what she does is to go along with Lars's device or story and encourage others to construct the prosthetic environment within which he can practice his first halting steps. For one brief session we see her practicing with him a behaviorist trick – desensitization – but even this is done casually, almost like prescribing aspirin: "Here is something that can help." The movie makes it clear that Lars is treating himself, and his way of doing this is of course to procure Bianca, the Real Girl, and to begin practicing with her all the things that one would do if one were normal: to communicate to her and through her what he wishes and feels; to listen to her in a touching attempt to understand what others might want and feel.

Now it is true that if we go back to the early alienists, one finds them practicing something very similar to what the doctor and the whole town do: going along with the patient's "delusion" in order to heal him. But there is a crucial difference between this technique, as Foucault analyzed it, and what happens to Lars. The old alienists used the technique of going along with the patient's delusion because at bottom they were convinced that delusion or insanity was error, and therefore they trusted that by going along with its "argument," they would be able to follow it to its illogical conclusion, to its *reductio ad absurdum*, where the patient too would have to confront the error in his thinking. There is very little of this sense of delusion in *Lars*. The only one who holds onto it, however briefly, is Lars's brother. He attempts to argue with him, show him the absurdity of his ways. He is the one who, in a pathetic gesture inadequate to the enormity of what is taking place and to Lars's humanity, types into an internet search "mental illness" and introduces the term "delusion" in talking to his friends. But the men really have very little control or understanding of what the town does in response to Lars. The women are in charge. They are the ones who construct the prosthetic environment where Bianca is accepted as a real girl. But most important, Lars is in charge. Fundamentally this is a story about self-healing through the most absurd means. The town, especially the town's women, go along with Lars's device (let us no longer insult it with the term "delusion"; nothing in the movie makes you feel that Lars is deluded any more than children are deluded who play "doctor and nurse" or "Mommy and Daddy"), not in order to demonstrate to Lars the error of his thinking, but in order to let Lars, who never truly communicated before, communicate with others, mingle with them, practice how to be part of "normal" town society. At the same time, we are reminded that the townfolk themselves are not really altogether normal, that the line between sanity and insanity is blurry and arbitrary, that people crisscross these lines continually in their daily lives. At the crucial church meeting, where the whole town is recruited to accept Lars, the decisive argument that wins the day is that everybody present in fact has a relative who was quirky or downright crazy. Moreover, Lars belongs in his work environment – in front of the computer – and among his co-workers even before he strives to communicate. The girl who takes a fancy to him is immaturely attached to a teddy bear, and the movie makes it clear that this (fairly common) attachment is at bottom no different, no less or more rational, than Lars's use of Bianca. The guy who shares his cubicle is attached to action figures, though he clumsily tries to disguise it by claiming that "they are worth a lot of money." This is the very same person who first introduces Bianca to Lars. He introduces Bianca ostensibly as a sex toy – but who knows, maybe his interest in pornography is at bottom also a clumsy rationalization, like the financial value of the action figures, for the desire for human contact, a desire that Lars expresses and performs far more authentically. We can easily recognize this stereotypical depiction of Lars's work environment and co-workers as "geekdom": a virtual domain removed from reality, populated by characters who cannot properly communicate, who mask their vulnerabilities in the bravado of gory fantasy games. Lars shines through this dim mirror because he does not opt for any of these masks. With Bianca he is authentically himself – and as the movie at bottom seeks to teach: whatever is authentic cannot be mad.

Fundamental incapacity to communicate; radical otherness as a way of being; self-healing; the construction of a prosthetic environment rather than the imposition of normality; integrating otherness without demanding that it forego itself: these are elements of a new experience of mental disorder, a new ethical mode of intervention that is most evident today in autism, though not peculiar to it. Autism is construed as the inability to understand how others may feel, what they intend and how they may react to one's words or deeds. Consequently, it is also the systematic incapacity to express one's self through typical means. Autism is now constructed as radical otherness, as a different way of being that is neither illness nor retardation but one's identity, how one thinks and sees the world. In autism, therapists assist with a host of behavioral "tools for living," but ultimately the responsibility is on autistic persons themselves and their parents to heal themselves, or more precisely to acquire means of communication – however absurd – with others, upon whom it is incumbent to tolerate and accept this otherness as it is, to converse using its own means (special interests, PECS), because ultimately what autistic people may want and feel, despite the grotesque means used to communicate, is at some level no different than what everybody else wants and feels. Autism has been assimilated to geekdom in fictional (D'Amato 2004; Moon 2003) and even serious scientific representations (Baron-Cohen 2006); autism as a different way of being, and normality, too, as "neurotypical" with its own absurdity, at least from the point of view of the autistic.

In a memorable scene, Lars explains to the doctor that he is concerned about his brother's wife. She has a problem, he says, she wants to hug everybody. She does not understand that people do not want to be hugged or touched (it hurts, he says, invoking another of contemporary autism's unmistakable signs – sensory hypersensitivity), she does not understand that people like to be left alone. Bianca is Lars's "assistive communication device." She is not a delusion or a sexual perversion. The doctor reminds Lars's brother of the obvious facts: Lars is functional. He holds a job and takes care of himself. He is not violent. He does not constitute a danger, neither to himself, nor to others. The unspoken point is that Lars should not be institutionalized. In fact, he cannot be institutionalized. In today's age of patients' rights, if you know where you are, who you are, where you live, and you are not a danger to yourself or others, there are no grounds to hold you in a mental hospital. Recall that *Rain Man* ended with the autistic person played by Hoffman returning to the sheltered but stifling environment of the institution, an ending which raised many eyebrows (and some ire) among parents of autistic children and advocates like Grandin. Bianca no longer constitutes legal evidence of Lars's insanity and/or social incapacity anymore than – as the movie presses – it constitutes psychological evidence of one's abnormality.

But the most important affinity with autism lies in the movie's moral narrative of therapy. As in the parable of *The Castle*, told in Chapter 7, the whole town enters Lars's world, participates in his peculiar way of seeing, constructs the prosthetic environment wherein he can practice normality (as one form of impression management among others, how Goffmanian!), and lets Lars eventually lead the way out (he announces that Bianca is dying, then buries her, making room for the really real girlfriend). We warned you it is saccharine sweet.

NOTES

1 http://www.cdc.gov/ncbddd/autism/faq_prevalence.htm (last accessed: December 8, 2008).

2 http://www.autism-society.org/site/PageServer?pagename=community_world_incidence (last accessed: December 8, 2008); http://www.cdc.gov/ncbddd/autism/documents/Autism_PrevalenceSummaryTable_updated_06–2007.pdf (last accessed: November 11, 2009).

3 What else could one call this peculiar relationship by which the psychiatrist built a case history primarily using parents' reports, and then turned around and used it against them, detecting the myriad ways in which their own faults and neuroses rebounded and amplified in their children? What else could one call it but the precise Marxian categories of "expropriation of the direct producers [of knowledge]" and the "alienation" of their labor in psychiatric accusation? We will develop this analysis further in Chapter 8.

4 Although "mental retardation" (or MR) has been superseded by "intellectual disability" (or ID) as the term of choice of several professional and advocacy organizations as well as parents, it is still used in many settings, notably the Individuals with Disabilities Education Act (IDEA) and by states' Departments of Developmental Services.

5 President of the Autistic Self Advocacy Network, Ari Ne'eman, writes, "there has been a general perception in the autistic community that 'person-first' language does not adequately represent the perspective of autistics" (http://www.autisticadvocacy.org/uploads/smartsection/19_neurodiversity_and_the_autistic_community.doc).

6 And what counts as mental retardation depends on the "Flynn effect" and on the "re-norming," every decade or so, of the IQ test. Before the re-norming of the Wechsler Intelligence Scale for Children in 1991 the numbers of children scoring below seventy (within the retarded range) were falling steadily, and then jumped up when the new test was introduced (Gladwell 2007).

7 Though Waterhouse (2008), for these and other reasons, concludes that the autism research program at the moment is not progressive, with researchers

proposing ad hoc replacement theories rather than linking their findings and theories with others.

8 See also Waterhouse et al. (2007, 309): "the behavioral syndrome of autism may represent an aggregate of many sub-disorders, most of which arise from genetically significant distinct endo-phenotypes."

9 QTLs are stretches of DNA that are closely linked to several genes, the interaction between which is associated with a phenotypic trait that varies in degree. Identifying QTLs can be an early step in identifying and sequencing these genes. http://en.wikipedia.org/wiki/Quantitative-trait-locus (last accessed: August 2009).

10 New research, and especially large scale studies (Szatmari et al. 2007), are using the Autism Genetic Resource Exchange (AGRE). AGRE is a DNA repository and family registry housing a database of genotypic and phenotypic information that is available to autism researchers worldwide. It was created by Autism Speaks in collaboration with geneticists in response to early recognition of substantial genetic heterogeneity in the autism spectrum disorders, and the need for large patient cohorts. Being primarily a parents' organization, Autism Speaks was able to persuade parents and patients of the importance of contributing DNA samples. Consequently, AGRE is by far the largest such database and it aggregates samples from all over the globe (Abrahams and Geschwind 2008, 349; http://www.agre.org/ [last accessed: August 24, 2009]).

11 *De novo* mutations are new mutations that occur in a germ cell and are then passed on to an offspring. They are not, therefore, inherited from the parents, neither of whom possesses the mutation themselves. A copy number variation (CNV) is a segment of DNA in which copy-number differences – due to deletion or duplication – have been found by comparison with two or more genomes. CNVs may be inherited or *de novo* and have been associated with susceptibility to various diseases. http://en.wikipedia.org/wiki/Copy_number_variation (last accessed: August 24, 2009).

12 http://ghr.nlm.nih.gov/condition=fragilexsyndrome; http://www.ninds.nih.gov/disorders/rett/detail_rett.htm (last accessed: August 9, 2009).

13 See, for example, http://autismnaturalvariation.blogspot.com/2006/03/is-genetic-mini-epidemic-possible.html; http://osdir.com/ml/culture.autism/2005-03/msg00079.html (last accessed: August 25, 2009).

14 http://www.allkindsofminds.org/about_approach.aspx (last accessed: December 11, 2008).

15 A prototype is a "best example" that stands for a whole category, the way a robin, for example is a prototypical bird, but the ostrich is not. Cognitive psychologists argue that human concepts are not constructed as a strict logical definition of necessary and sufficient conditions, but by chains of diminishing family resemblance to a central prototype (Rosch 1978).

16 We are not suggesting that these traits occur at the same time in the same individual, but rather that they are all associated with the autism spectrum.

17 We are ignoring here, of course, psychoanalysis and similar dynamic therapies, which as Luhrmann (2000, 136–140) convincingly demonstrates, now handle this "complicated question" by erasing from the very beginning the veracity of all mental states, including those of the normals, especially the therapist's own. Mental states are complex, layered, full of unconscious intentions, ultimately unknowable. Psychoanalysis can thus suspend

judgment about the ultimate worth of patients' intentions precisely where the biomedical approach experiences its most stark dilemma: do they reflect the disease or do they reflect rational personhood?

18 The case of psychosomatic illness demonstrates that this distinction is really a continuum composed of characteristic movements rather than static positions. Psychosomatic illness is a process that begins with subjective complaint yet fails to achieve localization. The more attempts at localization fail, the more the recourse to the "mental" in order to manage the patient, the more the idea of "resistances" that need to be overcome becomes appealing to doctors. The characteristic movement in the other direction is "brain disease." It begins with objective complaint, proceeds to persuade the patient of its validity and as it secures recognition by the patient, becomes a physical "brain disease." The more voluntary and complete the recognition granted by the patient, the more she is treated for all practical purposes as suffering from a physical disease.

19 This explains why medical and psychiatric researchers typically eschew these sorts of questions as unanswerable in principle: "Neither disease nor health has ever been strictly and unambiguously defined in terms of finite sets of observable referential phenomena. Medical textbooks rarely devote even passing reference to the subject, and it seems perfectly possible for a medical professional to practice medicine and treat illnesses without using an overarching concept of disease" (Jablensky 2007, 157–58). Jablensky further quotes Carl Jaspers to the same effect: "the medical person is least concerned with what healthy and sick mean in general . . . we do not need the concept of 'illness in general' at all and we now know that no such general and uniform concept exists."

20 See Landsman for an ethnographic account of the ways parents negotiate in interactions with doctors over the use of "developmental delay" instead of "disability" in order to assert their child's personhood or potential (Landsman 2002).

21 See the acrimonious debate on the subject of "cure" between the leading autism parent organization – "Autism Speaks" – which funds and encourages research for the purpose of curing autism, and a small organization of individuals with Asperger's disorder – Global Regional Asperger Syndrome Partnership (GRASP) – which opposes the language of "cure" as offensive to its members, for whom Asperger's is not an illness, but simply who they are. As the representative of GRASP notes: "The word 'cure,' like the word 'disease,' has historically reflected conditions, syndromes, and diagnoses that are *acquired*, meaning that you got it from somewhere after you were born. Now granted, genetic alteration – as proven by a Welsh lamb a few years ago – is not the impossibility we once thought it to be. And depending on what dictionary you're consulting, the descriptions of these words may not match the populist manner in which they are used. But in general, most people who believe that autism and AS are genetic do not use the words 'cure' or 'disease' because they feel primarily that what you were born with, i.e. your genes, you will die with. However, if you *do* believe that autism is acquired, then the word would seem to be medically appropriate." Michael John Carley, "GRASP and the word 'Cure'" in http://www.autismspeaks.org/whatisit/cure_intro.php (last accessed: January 23, 2008). For a science fiction novel that articulates forcefully the dilemma of genetic alteration, making it possible to "cure what you were born with," see Moon (2003). We will return to this debate in Chapter 10.

22 Hearings decisions from July 1, 2005, to the present are available at: http://www.oah.dgs.ca.gov/Special+Education/SE+Decisions+and+Orders.htm.

23 Of course there are other non-economic social concerns at play in these cases, as debates over cochlear implants in deaf communities have made clear (Dolnick 1993).

24 Medicine, originally uninterested in these "incurable" diseases, had to be dragged kicking and screaming by patient-rights and parents groups to assume jurisdiction over the quality of life of chronic patients (Shapiro 1993; Rabeharisoa and Callon 2004).

25 State of New Jersey, OFFICE OF ADMINISTRATIVE LAW, OAL DKT. NO. EDS 1547-05 AGENCY DKT. NO. 2005 9682.

26 Juliette de Wolfe, personal communication. (8/5/2009).

CHAPTER 1 THE PUZZLE OF VARIATION IN AUTISM RATES

1 The highest autism rate, in fact, is likely to be in the fifty-first state of the United States, namely the military. Some independent estimates suggest that the rate of autism among children of active duty and retired military personnel is 1 in 88 children. We find the calculation to be suspect. The base number of 22,356 diagnoses is drawn from a Department of Defense document, but the calculation of the actual rate is not, and the military says that it cannot be calculated based on the figures it has. Nonetheless, it is a safe bet that the rate of diagnoses is likely to be at least as high as in Maine, if not higher. From the point of view developed in this chapter, this is hardly surprising, since the military boasts, by comparison with U.S. states, a superior and more generous welfare state and a better developed program for the surveillance of childhood disorders. For the estimate of 1 in 88, see http://www.ageofautism.com/2008/07/autism-in-the-m.html (last accessed: January 27, 2009). It contains a link to the Department of Defense figures obtained through the Freedom of Information Act.

2 These are not the actual numbers reported by these studies, but figures recalculated by Eric Fombonne, who attempted to render comparable a set of very diverse studies using a range of very different criteria. For this reason, we preferred not to report later studies not reviewed by Fombonne.

3 In fact, there is some anecdotal evidence that supply-side increases attract families who move across state borders to enjoy the benefits of better autism services. Indiana, with the third largest prevalence in 2001, had a special Medicaid program for reimbursing services for individuals with autism spectrum disorders. The same was true for Maryland, which was also above the national mean. Oregon and Minnesota, however, the national leaders in 2001, did not have such a program (Mandell and Palmer 2005).

4 If anything, the 2008 elections produced an even neater correlation. Now *all* seventeen states above the mean voted for Obama, but there were twelve states below it that also voted with the Democrats. Yet by 2008, autism was an issue for both parties. During his campaign, the Republican nominee, Sen. John McCain, made numerous references to autism, including one during a debate with then Sen. Obama, when he mentioned the fact that his running mate, Governor Sarah Palin, was mother of a child with special needs, in order to talk about autism, even though her son suffers not from autism but from Down 's syndrome.

5 The well-established finding that maternal education correlates with risk of autism has been interpreted by some researchers as indicating that these parents are better informed and better equipped to secure the diagnosis of autism for their children (Croen et al. 2002; Bhasin and Schendel 2007). The superior clout of highly educated parents in dealing with the special-education bureaucracy has been documented by Ong-Dean (2004). The involvement of highly educated parents in forming autism advocacy organizations is reported in Silverman and Brosco (2007), as well as in later chapters of this book.

6 http://cms.education.gov.il/EducationCMS/Units/Special/HaagafBepeula/ NetuneyKitot/ (last accessed: January 4, 2009).

7 Classification Française de Troubles Mentaux de l'Enfant et de l'Adolescent.

8 http://www.fondation-autisme.org/content/view/64/110 (accessed December 30, 2008).

9 Noa Herling. Personal Interview. July 9, 2008; Daphna Erlich. Personal Interview. July 9, 2008.

10 According to the criteria of the Israeli National Insurance Institute, "a disabled child is any one of the following: a) a child (from age 3) dependent on the help of others for the performance of everyday functions to a degree significantly greater than is normal for his age group; b) a child (from age 91 days) in need of constant supervision; c) a child with a special impairment, that is: – (from birth) Down's syndrome or a deterioration in hearing; – (from age 91 days) a vision impairment, *autism (including PDD and Asperger)*, psychosis or a severe developmental retardation (the last until age 3); d) a child (from age 91 days) in need of special medical treatment as defined in the regulations, due to a severe chronic disease." National Insurance Institute of Israel, annual reports:http://www.btl.gov.il/פרסומים/pub/Skira_shnatit/skira2007/Documents/ chap-2007-4.pdf); http://www.btl.gov.il/פרסומים/pub/Skira_shnatit/skira2007/ Documents/chap-2007-6.pdf. (last accessed: March 26, 2009).

11 *Otizm Platformu Bildirgesi, 2008*, www.otizmplatformu.org.

12 Tohum Otizm Vakfi, http://www.tohumotizm.org.tr/IcSayfa.asp?PageID= 64andSubPageID=63 (last accessed: December 30, 2008).

13 http://cms.education.gov.il/EducationCMS/Units/Special/HaagafBepeula/ NetuneyKitot/ (last accessed: March 26, 2009).

14 The rate of deinstitutionalization was calculated as follows. For each year between 1977 to 2000, and for each state, we calculated the percentage of persons younger than 21 years old among the residents of state institutions for the mentally retarded. Then we performed a regression analysis to calculate the rate of deinstitutionalization, that is, the rate of change over time in these ratios, or put differently, how fast this age group declined as a proportion of state institutionalized population. The starting point of 1977 is completely arbitrary, and may bias these results. In 1970, the federal government stopped collecting figures on the population of people with mental retardation at state institutions (Lakin et al. 1982). Only thanks to the valiant efforts of researchers at the University of Minnesota's Institute on Community Integration, who beginning in 1977 annually publish a report on "Residential Services for Persons with Developmental Disabilities," do we possess the current figures. It might be possible to extrapolate trends using figures from before 1970, but we have not done this yet.

15 http://seocura.org/Family_Update_Final_07.pdf (last accessed: December 1, 2008).
16 Mental Health Statistics, Volume I, Institutional admissions and separations. Dominion Bureau of Statistics [Statistics Canada], Health and Welfare Division, Public Health Section. 1964–1979.
17 http://www12.statcan.gc.ca/english/census06 (last accessed: February 4, 2009).
18 http://www.leapoursamy.com/ (last accessed: December 30, 2008).
19 "Integrated National Disability Strategy," White Paper, Office of the President. The Republic of South Africa. (Ndabeni, Western Cape: Rustica Press, 1997.) http://www.independentliving.org/docs3/sa1997wp.pdf.
20 See at http://www.molsa.gov.il/MisradHarevacha/Disabilities/Mental Retardation/Dormitories/ (last accessed: March 26, 2009).
21 Dahava Eyal. Personal communication. January 22, 2009.
22 See also data in http://www.health.gov.il/download/mental/annual/43.pdf for years 1975–1999 and http://www.health.gov.il/download/mental/annual2006/children.pdf for years 2000–2005.
23 On the Higashi school, see http://www.musashino-higashi.org/english.htm (last accessed: October 10, 2008).
24 Dahava Eyal. Personal communication. January 22, 2009.
25 On the greater acumen of Japanese clinicians, see http://www.emedicine.com/ped/TOPIC180.HTM (last accessed: October 29, 2008).
26 In fact, Rimland reported that his visit to Higashi had a profound effect, causing him to rethink his view of one-to-one education, seeing it now as a "Helen Keller model" to which Americans have clung too tightly (ibid.).
27 http://www.handle.org/index2.html (last accessed: January 21, 2009).
28 In the acrimonious debates over whether autism is caused by the MMR vaccine or by a mercury-based preservative in vaccines, the interpretation of evidence from Denmark and Japan, respectively, played a crucial role (Madsen et al. 2003; Honda et al. 2005).
29 http://www.autismspeaks.org/about_us.php?WT.svl=Top_Nav (last accessed: January 21, 2009).
30 In the provinces of Prince Edward Island, Nova Scotia, and New Brunswick, inclusion in regular classrooms is the *only* option for students with disabilities. Even in places offering a "continuum of services," first priority is usually given to the regular education classroom (this is even mandated in Ontario legislation) (Dworet and Bennett 2002).
31 See, for example, "Agencies decry Ontario's funding of child autism treatment" (Babbage, Maria, July 20, 2008, *The Globe and Mail*).
32 See www.tohumotizm.org.tr, accessed September 5, 2009.
33 Interview with Aylin Sezgin (co-founder of Tohum Autism Foundation), July 9, 2009.
34 *Aut-Talk*, newsletter of Autism South Africa, July 2005, no. 6, p. 1; May–July 2008, no. 13, p. 2.
35 See, for example, *Aut-Talk*, April/May 2007, no. 11, pp. 10–14.
36 http://www.autismwesterncape.org.za/about%20us.htm?sm[p1][category]=100, (last accessed: September 3, 2009).

Chapter 2 The Feebleminded

1 In a *New York Times* article about a case of retroactive diagnosis, Fred Volkmar, a major figure in autism research, noted, "There is unfortunately a sort of cottage industry of finding that everyone has Asperger's" (Goode, Erica, Oct. 9, 2001, "CASES; A Disorder Far Beyond Eccentricity," *New York Times*). For more examples, see http://www.child-autism-parent-cafe. com/famous-people-with-autism.html. For a truly canonic example of this genre, see "Diagnosing Bill Gates," *Time Magazine*, January 24, 1994. This sort of retroactive diagnosis is so widespread that one can find on Wikipedia a rather long list of "people speculated to have been autistic," http:// en.wikipedia.org/wiki/People_speculated_to_have_been_autistic. See also a recent letter to the editor of an autism journal titled, "Did Hans Asperger have Asperger's syndrome?" (Lyons and Fitzgerald 2007).

2 According to the influential Vineland classification devised by Henry H. Goddard, based in part on IQ testing, idiots had a "mental age" of 2 years or less, imbeciles, 3 to 7, and morons 7 to 12. The term "moron" expressed Goddard's belief that this was a condition of "moral idiocy," that morality was acquired and learned in adolescence, but that morons could not learn to abide by moral rules because they were stuck in an earlier developmental phase (Trent 1994, 162; Kline 2001, 41).

3 The celebrated 1975 Supreme Court decision, which changed the rules for involuntary commitment of the mentally ill, dealt with the case of a Florida patient, who in 1956 at the age of 48 was committed by his parents. A panel composed of two ordinary physicians (neither psychiatrists nor psychologists) and a deputy sheriff took but a few hours to determine that he was mentally ill (suffering from a "persecution complex") and within a day a judge had committed him to a state institution (from which he was released only in 1971) (Rothman and Rothman 2005, 55).

4 Writers at the time were quick to notice the "selection bias" in Kanner's sample, particularly since Kanner deduced from it that autism was a condition specific to the highly educated. Bender (1959, 22) commented derisively that "it is not clear what he means by saying that there is evidence that autistic children have greater intellectual potentialities, unless he is referring to the family background of his colleagues, professors and intellectual sophisticates who have selected his services." Rimland (1964, 23–30) mounted a vigorous defense of this finding: "Very few parents, regardless of intellectuality, are acquainted with the differential expertise of child psychiatry. It is the family physician or other professional worker who must make the referral. Such a process could hardly begin to account for Kanner's findings" (29). This is hardly convincing. If the family physician diagnosed mental retardation, the educational status of the parents becomes a good explanation of their willingness and ability to resist this diagnosis and to seek out Kanner. One need assume neither psychogenic nor genetic causation here.

5 Hilde Bruch (1959, 15), who worked from 1941 as a psychiatrist in Kanner's clinic, thought that the correlation he observed between autism and upper- or middle-class origins was due to a "sociological fact: namely, that it takes a high degree of intelligence in the parents to make such detailed observations on a child's behavior." With time, it was bound to disappear: "The picture

by now has become well known and the syndrome is recognized more commonly in clinic patients."

6 Though for a while in the South, racial segregation "protected" black children from institutionalization. For a long time the institutions in the South did not house African-American inmates. Only in 1939, when the first all-black Petersburg state colony was opened in Virginia, did black people enter such institutions in the South. This is, of course, an exception that proves the rule. Noll (1995, 133, 143) indicates that "with control enforced by legalized segregation, there appeared little need for institutions for the feeble-minded to further control black deviants."

7 There is some contemporary evidence for this conjecture, since while autism is no longer understood to be correlated with class (though maternal education is often found to be a significant risk factor), co-morbidity of autism with mental retardation still differs significantly by class and race. In a recent study in Atlanta, Georgia (Bhasin and Shendel 2007), white children were over-represented in the category of those who received the diagnosis of autism only, with no mental retardation (white-to-black ratio of 2.9:1). The same was true for children of higher social class. The racial ratio was inverted, however, the lower one went down the IQ ladder, to 0.8:1 in children with mild mental retardation, and 0.5:1 in children with profound mental retardation. Similar results were found in California (King 2008). It is highly likely that these differences reflect the effect of differential access to the healthcare system, since African-American and/or poor kids were significantly more likely to be diagnosed only once they began school. Moreover, other studies have shown that pediatricians and clinical psychologists, as late as 1987, still believed (against the claims of epidemiologists and the instructions of the DSM) that autism was overrepresented in higher socioeconomic classes (Stone 1987), no doubt reflecting clinical experience and referral streams. Even much later, Cuccaro et al. (1996) found that clinicians were more likely to ascribe autism in hypothetical cases to high-socioeconomic-class children. This is reflected by the fact, reported by the *Los Angeles Times*, that while it took white children an average of four visits to specialists over four months to be diagnosed with autism, African-American children required thirteen such visits over ten months (Brink 2007).

8 Mental health statistics. Volume I, Institutional admissions and separation. Dominion Bureau of Statistics, Health and Welfare Division, Public Health Section.

CHAPTER 3 THE SURVEILLANCE OF CHILDHOOD

1 And as we shall see in Chapter 8, Kanner escaped blame, and not simply because he reversed himself publicly and apologized to the parents of autistic children, absolving them from blame in a 1969 meeting of the National Society for Autistic Children (NSAC). Another reversal was more important – it got him invited to the meeting in the first place! In the mid-1960s, he decided to restrict the scope of the autism diagnosis and to disavow any connection to mental retardation. It was music to the ears of Bernard Rimland and other founders of NSAC, who were interested in establishing autism as

277

a rare disorder, removed from the stigma of mental retardation. The two exchanged letters and Rimland got Kanner's blessing for his 1964 landmark book, *Infantile Autism*, which not only disproved the "psychogenic" theory of autism, but launched the parents' movement with Kanner as its ally.

CHAPTER 4 DEINSTITUTIONALIZATION

1 Foster homes are another possibility, and in some states they play an important role, but overall their numerical significance (total of 35,000 individuals in the whole of the U.S. in 2006) pales in comparison with the number residing in family homes (total of 569,020) (Prouty et al. 2007, 79–83).
2 For a discussion of how some contemporary parents articulate the significance of parenting a child with disabilities, see Landsman 1999.
3 This attitude is by no means universal. Many are the parents who do not speak, or explicitly reject, the idiom of valorization of autistic existence. These parents tend to, but do not always, present a "thin" image of the inner life of the autistic child (see the Introduction). Blastland (2006) writes that his son considers everyone, including his dad, as a "universal vending machine," which he pokes repeatedly to get what he needs. These parents present themselves as realistic and might even at times refer to raising an autistic child as "hell." Overall, our impression from our interviews is that ordinary parents – as distinct from memoir-writers – do not need to choose between these two idioms and are not wholly converted to either view, but rather switch back and forth between them as two complementary narrative frames.

CHAPTER 5 "AN EXISTENCE AS CLOSE TO THE NORMAL AS POSSIBLE": NORMALIZATION

1 Centers for Medicare and Medicaid Services, "Background and Milestones Intermediate Care Facilities for People with Mental Retardation (ICFs/MR)" http://www.cms.hhs.gov/CertificationandComplianc/Downloads/ICFMR_Background.pdf (last accessed: March 26, 2009).
2 Indeed, this is also the principle governing the provision of services for some organizations that offer educational and residential placements to individuals with autism (See Holmes 1990; Siegel 1996, 274–300).
3 See also Bumiller 2009 for another geneticization account of the history of autism.
4 Treatment and Education of Autistic and Related Communication-handicapped CHildren

CHAPTER 6 CHILDHOOD SCHIZOPHRENIA

1 For a perceptive historical account of the social model of mental illness see Michael Staub's *Madness Is Civilization* (forthcoming).
2 Ornitz and Ritvo (1968, 76) went the opposite direction from Kanner. They proposed that "a single pathologic process [is] common to early infantile autism, certain cases of childhood schizophrenia, the atypical child,

symbiotic psychosis, and children with unusual sensitivities. It will be shown that these descriptive categories are variants of a unitary disease," which they thought was best characterized as autism.

3 Additionally, the idea that the main pathology in childhood schizophrenia was "plasticity" transformed it from an illness pure and simple to a constitutional condition underlying an infinite variety of clinical manifestations (Bender 1953, 673). See Foucault (2003, 306–13) about this peculiar notion of "condition," which is not an illness, but a permanent causal background on the basis of which illness may develop. He calls it "a radical discriminant of abnormality with a total etiological value," since it could lead to any number of diseases, and even without their full development marks the individual as abnormal. It is a notion capable of integrating a whole field of abnormalities, and of retranscribing it upon a physiological, medical register, typically one of heredity.

4 She also was part of a small cottage industry in the 1960s that experimented with the use of LSD and amphetamines in the treatment of disturbed children and enthusiastically reported her positive findings (Bender 1963). For a selection of articles about LSD studies on autism and childhood schizophrenia, see http://www.neurodiversity.com/lsd.html.

5 To do justice to Abbott's nuanced account, he also emphasizes the importance of effective treatment: "The final tests of such [jurisdictional] claims are their practical results" (38).

6 Schopler (1965, 334) too was aiming in a different way to reconcile the psychogenic and biogenic hypotheses, as well as to settle the boundaries between autism and childhood schizophrenia. He thought it should be possible to develop an early screen to predict and distinguish autism and childhood schizophrenia. Tactile hyposensitivity at four to five weeks after birth would indicate autism. Hypersensitivity would indicate a tendency towards childhood schizophrenia. To develop norms for such a test, however, he thought it would be necessary to norm also the "optimum range and amount of stimulation" in mother–infant interaction. Then one could counsel mothers about holding, hugging, and caressing their infants in the right amount to prevent autism from taking over. One can see how the origins of autism as a sensory sensitivity disorder – a matter almost completely absent from Kanner's initial descriptions, but which is so prominent today – were perhaps in this attempt to domesticate the psychogenic hypothesis and the mother-blaming incited by Kanner's "emotional refrigerator" phrase. Mothers of autistic children merely had to learn to provide more touch, more cuddling, than was the case with normal infants.

7 Key examples are the founding members of the National Society of Autistic Children (Bernard Rimland, Clara Claiborne Park, Ruth Christ Sullivan), and the Washington state families chronicled in *Becoming Citizens* (Schwartzenberg 2005).

8 Hacking's point is more specific. One of the "vectors" of the ecological niche is that "the illness, despite the pain it produces, should also provide some release that is not available elsewhere in the culture in which it thrives" (Hacking 1998, 2). This vector is meant to account, we think, for the agency of patients, their willingness to produce the requisite symptoms, their collusion with the therapists. But the way Hacking formulates it seems to us too restrictive.

9 This image is reinforced in many contemporary accounts. For example, Uta Frith begins her book, *Autism: Explaining the Enigma*, with one of the "many puzzles of the disorder called autism." "The typical image of the child with autism is surprising. Those familiar with images of children who suffer from other serious developmental disorders know that these children usually *look* handicapped. In contrast, more often than not, the young child with autism strikes the observer with a haunting and somehow otherworldly beauty. It is hard to imagine that behind the doll-like image lies a subtle yet devastating neurobiological abnormality" (1989, 1).

CHAPTER 7 THE RISE OF THE THERAPIES

1 The characterization of contemporary therapies in this paragraph, and in the rest of this section, relies on observations of therapy sessions by the authors, to be reported in a follow-up book.

2 The program described, the West End Creche, was not some obscure day nursery, but the very first clinic in Ontario, and probably in Canada as well, dedicated to treating children with autism. In later years, it became a major center of autism treatment in Canada. A Czech immigrant, Dr. Milada Havelkova, worked there for 30 years, and was the first child psychiatrist in Canada to initiate studies into the etiology and natural history of autism. She wrote a guide for parents of autistic children that was published in 1966. Today, the autism program is incorporated as part of the Child Development Institute (CDI). http://www.childdevelop.ca/secondpage/history/index.html (accessed January 28, 2009).

3 Stanley I. Greenspan and Serena Wieder, "The Developmental, Individual-Difference, Relationship-Based (Dir^tm) Model." Http://Www.Icacd.Org/Articles/2.Pdf (last accessed: March 26, 2009).

4 Nonetheless, the link to the notion of a fast-closing window of opportunity obviously served as a strong "elective affinity" between these therapies and the newly emerging field of early intervention. A key figure in forging this affinity was Greenspan, the originator of "Floortime" therapy for autism, who in the mid-1970s also founded *Zero to Three: National Center for Infants, Toddlers, and Families* and served as its president during the years 1975–84. This organization seeks to educate parents and professional caregivers about the crucial role played by the earliest emotional experiences in fostering healthy cognitive development (Greenspan and Greenspan 1985; Greenspan and Greenspan 1990; Greenspan and Salmon 1993; Greenspan and Salmon 1995; Greenspan 2003).

5 One can recognize in their account many of the hallmarks of the autism diagnosis, past and present, such as "insistence on sameness," rote memory, difficulty with abstract linguistic concepts, etc. They write of brain-injured children who, especially when young, attempt "to order their world to maximum stability, sometimes to such a degree that to normal persons it appears invariant. The child may insist upon his own dishes at every meal, or refuse to drink chocolate milk which is ready mixed since he is accustomed to seeing it mixed . . . and in many other ways arrange as unchanging world as possible." This is due to a "central disturbance in the individual's ability to organize relationships," which leads to the development of "splinter

skills," to rote verbal learning without application, or even inability to grasp linguistic concepts altogether (Strauss and Kephart 1955, 176–77, 182–84).

6 Silverman's groundbreaking research, nonetheless, was the first to call attention to the importance of perceptual-motor therapy in the origins of autism treatments and to the early links between Kephart and parents of autistic children. We owe a great deal to her generosity in sharing her research findings.

7 Holistic Approach to NeuroDevelopment and Learning Efficiency.

8 http://www.handle.org/abouthdl/handouts/Introduction_to_HANDLE-9-15-04.pdf. (last accessed: October 17, 2008).

9 Even before the French, the Germans and Austrians invented the discipline of "remedial pedagogy" and created similar short-term residential institutions, practicing milieu or environmental therapy. Hans Asperger's discovery of an "autistic psychopathy in childhood," the subject of Chapter 10, took place in such a context ([1944] 1991, 58). He worked at the remedial department of the university pediatric clinic in Vienna, a place that pioneered a combination of special education and pediatrics. Children came who were referred by schools, and they stayed for extended periods, separated from their parents. Therapy consisted of a highly structured schedule and set of rules presented as impersonal and universal. At the end of their treatment period, the children were released back to their families and schools. The Dutch, too, had a similar arrangement at the Eekwal "observation home" (Kraijer 1997).

10 It was under the jurisdiction of child psychiatry, at least its "remedial" wing. The American Orthopsychiatric Association was created in 1924 to "disseminate information on therapeutic and educational measures for emotionally disturbed children" (Winzer 1993).

11 RDI stands for Relationship Development Intervention.

12 For a description of such in-home regimes in the case of children with ADHD see http://www.nytimes.com/2006/12/22/health/22KIDS.html?_r=2andsq = behavior%20children%20mental%20healthandst = nytandoref = s loginandscp=4andpagewanted=allandoref=slogin.

13 Despite Greenspan's scathing attack on ABA (see above), the DIR model outsources therapy in exactly the same way as ABA. Greenspan even uses exactly the same phrase as Schopler: "Parents and therapists are partners in helping the child. Therapists are experts in their individual fields of specialization; parents are the experts about their child." In the DIR model, parents are expected to work directly with their child, as well as train other service providers and take upon themselves the role of a "team leader" coordinating the work of all the therapists who work with the child. This is good evidence, and we will return to this point in the conclusions, that the commonalities between autism therapies are more important than their differences. www.floortime.org/ft.php?page=The%20Parent's%20Role (last accessed: February 5, 2007).

14 In interviews we often found that parents, especially early in the child's life, themselves end up taking on the role of bridging or coordinating between various service-providers – speech therapists, occupational therapists, behavioral therapists, etc. – who work with the child independently.

15 Operant conditioning is a term introduced by B. F. Skinner to describe all methods that aim to shape voluntary behavior by assigning its occurrence

with differential consequences such as reward and punishment. It is roughly synonymous with "behavior modification" in this context.

16 Subcommittee on the Handicapped of the Committee on Labor and Public Welfare, U.S. Senate. "Developmental Disabilities Act Extension and Rights of Mentally Retarded, February 8, 1973" (Washington, D.C., U.S. Government Printing Office: 1973).

CHAPTER 8 BERNARD RIMLAND AND THE FORMATION OF NSAC

1 S. Clarence Griffith, the second elected NSAC president, noted that his wife used what she had learned working with the League of Women Voters in order to lobby Georgia lawmakers to include autism in their 1968 "Exceptional Child Act." He told the NSAC crowd in 1970 that they should join forces with the League, the Federation of Womens' Clubs, and the Jaycees in order to lobby effectively for services (Griffith 1971).

2 On July 1, 1977, an NSAC bylaw amendment officially prohibited chapters from providing services (Warren 1984, 106–107).

3 There were no elections yet, although Mooza Grant was appointed president at the meeting (Warren 1984, 103).

4 In the seven years that passed until it was finally published in a professional journal, copies of Rimland's talk were already circulated via informal channels to nearly all English-speaking countries and it had been translated into six different languages (Rimland 1972, 573). It was a testimony to the emergence of a new network of expertise, shared between parents and researchers, which gradually supplanted the usual channels of professional communication.

5 This argument is very much indebted to Chloe Silverman's work and her analysis of the formation of the identity of "autism parent" in these years around the use of an unproven therapy, applied behavioral analysis (2004, 184).

6 As noted earlier, Lettick went on to open the Benhaven School for children with severe handicaps in 1967 and Oppenheim opened The Rimland School for Autistic Children in 1971 (Silverman 2004, 158, 193).

7 The name is changed to Elly in the book.

8 In D'Amato's (2004) murder mystery, Schopler's scapegoat argument underwrites the plot: in it, a therapist – a scarcely concealed Bettelheim – is murdered. He turns out to have abused the autistic children entrusted to him for treatment, because of his frustration with being unable to understand or help them.

9 http://ericschopler.blogspot.com/2006/07/remembering-eric.html (accessed January 29, 2009).

10 See Silverman 2004 for a more extended account of the role of love in the history of autism in the U.S.

11 This is precisely how Rimland claims to have become convinced of the efficacy of megavitamin therapy, which he would champion for decades. "But as the letters accumulated I began to get more interested in the reports . . . As the number of parent-experimenters grew, it began to include more parents whom I knew personally to be highly intelligent and reliable people" (1971b, 56–57).

12 Rimland tried to do something similar with the checklist. But his efforts

always sought to validate his initial insistence that autism was unique and relatively rare, constituting 10 percent of the "psychotic children."

13 In 1968, John Kysar, a psychiatrist and father of an autistic and mentally retarded son, published an article in the *American Journal of Psychiatry* where he described two camps – one neurological, the other psychological-emotional. "Members of this [latter] camp seem unable to say (even when it seems most accurate and appropriate): 'This child is autistic *and* retarded.' The effects of this limited viewpoint on the child, his family, and the schools and agencies who work with them can be very destructive." Schopler also wrote in 1974: "As experience with autistic children grew, we recognized that a child can be autistic, can have clear signs of brain damage, and can also be retarded" (Schopler 1974, 194).

14 Interview with Barbara Harmon. March 22, 2007.

CHAPTER 9 THE ATYPICAL CHILDREN

1 Recall Rutter's (1972, 315) complaint that "childhood schizophrenia has tended to be used as a generic term to include an astonishingly heterogeneous mixture of disorders with little in common other than their severity, chronicity, and occurrence in childhood." These were precisely the same three broad criteria that were used to create the overall domain of "developmental disabilities."

2 There were, in fact, Dutch specialists who, as early as 1960, asserted that autism occurred frequently among mentally retarded children, and even coexisted with Down's syndrome (Kraijer 1997, 5, 21–30, 37–40, 348–49). Unlike in the U.S. or U.K., this argument about concurrence was made from within Dutch institutions for the mentally retarded, and not as a result of deinstitutionalization – which seems to have been minimal in the Netherlands (Hatton et al. 1995). Nonetheless, we do not think the Dutch case undermines our argument that autism was "below the radar" of the custodial institutional matrix. The Eekwal Observation Home, where this research was done, took in a small number of children, no more than twenty, all with a diagnosis of mental retardation. Over a period of six months to a year, a team of psychiatrists, psychologists, pediatricians, and various therapists worked out a thorough diagnosis of the children's problems and developed a treatment program to be carried out at home and school upon release (Kraijer 1997, 46–48). The only places in the U.S. where similar conditions prevailed were small, private residential schools run by parents, who had no interest in adding another label to their children (May and May 1959).

3 Interview with Lorna Wing, http://www.autismconnect.org/core_files/interviews/transcripts/lorna_wing.htm (accessed April 25, 2008).

4 A "repetitive body movement that self-stimulates one or more senses in a regulated manner" http://autism.wikia.com/wiki/Stimming (accessed March 26, 2009). See Siff Exkorn (2005, 47–50) for a discussion of "stimming," or self-stimulating behaviors.

5 While including items that code for stereotyped and repetitive behaviors, the Autism Diagnostic Observation Schedule, today considered the "gold standard" of diagnostic instruments, does not include these items in the diagnostic algorithm (Lord, Rutter, DiLavore and Risi 2002).

283

CHAPTER 10 ASPERGER AND NEURODIVERSITY

1 Indeed, Bleuler also coined the term "schizophrenia," and spoke more precisely of a "group of schizophrenias," as a replacement for Kraeplin's "dementia praecox" (Kuhn and Cahn 2004; Hacking 2007).

2 Interestingly, Daniel Tammet, a world-famous autistic savant, discusses autistic thinking in a similar fashion in his recently published second book (Tammet 2009).

3 Today, the literature abounds with the retroactive discovery of autism before Kanner and Asperger (Frith 1989; Houston and Frith 2000; Wing 2005). We have no intention to add to it, yet it is indisputable that during the two decades preceding the naming of autism, there were many cases in which clinicians reported similar symptoms in young children, but chose to name them differently – typically referring to "psychosis" and "childhood schizophrenia" (for reviews of the previous clinical literature, see Wing 1981, 2005; Wolf and Chick 1980; Bosch 1970; Kanner 1965). Kanner and Asperger were in a direct line of continuity with these other accounts. After all, they too chose to raid the black box of "schizophrenia," open it up and plunder from it this single expression: "autism."

4 Wing reviewed many of the relevant discussions of Asperger's autistic psychopathy in the English-language literature in her 1981 article. Nonetheless, we find the argument that language was the main or sole barrier to the popularization of autistic psychopathy in the U.S. and U.K. before Wing's article to be insufficient.

5 There were also Russian research programs that picked up on Asperger's work and published articles in major English-language academic journals (e.g., Isaev and Kagan 1974; Mnukin and Isaev 1975).

6 In more direct terms, Van Krevelen asserted in a 1963 article: "One could say that the patient suffering from 'Early Infantile Autism' is a brain-damaged autistic psychopath" (321).

7 To hear Draaisma present a slightly expanded version of this paper, go to http://royalsociety.org/podcast/audio/DM2008_08/Draaisma.mp3 (last accessed February 20, 2009).

8 And apparently some clinicians felt they got the hang of it. "A good observer," Van Krevelen and Kuipers wrote, "recognizes the autistic psychopath at first glance" (1962, 23).

9 Draaisma also notes this (2009, 1495).

10 There is good reason to think also that Asperger's emphasis on the higher intelligence and abilities of the children, and crucially his choice to describe them as a personality type rather than mental illness or retardation, were connected to his desire to defend them from Nazi eugenic policies (Frith 1991, 7). This is not altogether different from Rimland's "children who were to have been endowed with unusually high intelligence."

11 While there were many more than two publications on Asperger before 1981, we think the dramatic change is faithfully reflected in Wing's statistics.

12 In his 1979 paper, or at least in the translation, Asperger uses this eponymous name as does Rimland in his book (1964).

13 From Everard's trenchant critique of Asperger's description of autistic malice one can see that parents were uneasy with this aspect of his writings (Everard 1991).

14 Though it was added to the World Health Organization's *International Classification of Diseases, Tenth Edition* (ICD-10) already in 1990.

15 Of course, Asperger's syndrome also sparked the interest of many autism researchers and cognitive scientists, which helped Wing's cause as well (see Nadesan 2005).

16 "It was largely on my recommendation," Rimland wrote, "that Dustin Hoffman played an *autistic* rather than a retarded savant" (Rimland 1995, 3).

17 See Broderick and Ne'eman (2008) for a critique of autism metaphors such as Grandin's "emergence."

18 For an account prior to Grandin's, although not a first-person one, of a recovered autistic who was diagnosed at age 4 by Kanner himself, see Bemporad 1979. Grandin cites this article as well.

19 Fred Volkmar, interview by Terri Gross, *Fresh Air*, May 5, 2004, *National Public Radio*. http://www.npr.org/templates/story/story.php?storyId=1872 620 (last accessed August 27, 2009).

20 See Hacking 2009b.

21 However, we should note that Sinclair's organization, Autism Network International, decided to include parents and has developed strong relationships with them after a rocky beginning (Sinclair 2005).

CHAPTER 11 THE SPACE OF AUTISM THERAPIES AND THE MAKING AND REMAKING OF THE SPECTRUM

1 The consensus was hardly surprising since committee members included Schopler and Rutter, whom we already saw were running research and treatment programs analogous to Wing's, and who penned their own similar "triads." Other members included Donald Cohen – the Yale psychiatrist who was an ally of NSAC – and Lynn Waterhouse and Deborah Fein who collaborated with Wing and who were preparing a study criticizing the DSM-III criteria (Waterhouse et al. 1987; Waterhouse et al. 1992, 528). Rutter, however, was the one significant voice of dissent. He was opposed to removing the early-onset requirement. He thought it should be kept, since late onset might indicate a different, typically regressive and disintegrative, disorder and was likely to have a different etiology. He and Wing had a short exchange about whether keeping or removing the late-onset exclusion would better encourage research into etiology. The compromise was to remove the exclusion, but keep the distinction in the form of further qualification of the same diagnosis as either infantile onset or childhood onset.

2 Lynn Waterhouse, private communication, October 20, 2008.

3 We refer the reader to Chloe Silverman's excellent ethnographic and historical work on Rimland and the DAN! movement (Silverman 2004, esp. pp. 350–451; Silverman forthcoming).

4 For an example, see Rimland 1988.

5 However, a famous DAN! doctor, Jacquelyn McCandless, herself the grandparent of an autistic child, is sure to note as a disclaimer that these treatments will help most but "*not all*" autistic children (McCandless et al. 2003, 68; her emphasis). See Silverman 2004 (Chapter 5) for a discussion of DAN!'s "autism is treatable" campaign.

6 For instance, dietary interventions, previously considered "alternative," are

increasingly being recommended by "mainstream" practitioners as a treatment for autistic children, especially children suffering from gastro-intestinal issues.

7 However, in cases where parents research pharmaceuticals and seek prescriptions for their children, the boundary is blurred further still.

CONCLUSION

1 The authors give the example of Phelan-McDermid Syndrome. Deletions of 22q13 – which is what constitutes the definition of the syndrome – have been found to overlap with deletions on an Autism Susceptibility Candidate Gene (ASCG) (Durand et al. 2007). They note, "This is not a surprise, as 94% of the original Phelan-McDermid Syndrome patients met ASD criteria via the CARS phenotyping tool" (Bill and Geschwind 2009, 273).

2 "President Obama himself has made autism a priority, promising to put $1 billion in funds towards research. The NIMH grants support research on topics like early intervention and diagnostic testing" (http://blogs.wsj.com/health/2009/03/24/autism-research-gets-stimulus-money-for-a-short-term-boost/
?mod=rss_WSJBlog, accessed March 27, 2009). In a recently released "Strategic Plan for Action," Autism Speaks noted two trends in funding: first, the funding portfolio for treatment shows that efforts have focused on preschool and school-aged children to the neglect of adult populations (2009, 33); and second, treatment has been underfunded in favor of risk factors, neurobiological research, and investigations into diagnosis (2009, 35). In their defense Autism Speaks made these self-criticisms in a public document; one hopes they will attempt to correct these lapses. Additionally, treatment comprises a larger portion of their total funding portfolio than it does in non-Autism Speaks funding.

3 If these more severe and recalcitrant individuals are represented in these arguments at all, it is often in terms of the specter of lifelong disability and the drag that disabled adults put on the economy. A recent *New York Times* opinion piece by two parent-advocates provides an example: "If we do not help these children [by giving them forty hours a week of intensive early intervention], we are essentially condemning them to a lifetime of disability, unemployment and, for many, institutionalization. On human grounds, this is tragic. But it's also bad economics. The few hundred thousand dollars needed to do intensive early intervention for four or five years – while a lot – is only one-tenth the expected cost of supporting someone for a lifetime on the dole" ("Studying Autism Isn't Enough," Garland, Cathryn and O'Hanlon, Michael, November 21, 2006). The final phrase sums it up – "a lifetime on the dole." In this way, the economic arguments made to justify early intervention effectively obscure the ethical questions we have tried throughout this book to reinsert into the debate.

4 An Easter Seals online survey among 1,652 parents of children (aged thirty and under) with autism reveals that nearly 80 percent of the parents are extremely or very concerned about their child's independence as an adult. Only 14 percent feel that their child will be able to make life decisions. Only 17 percent think their child will make friends. And most parents report that they're "financially drowning," with concerns for their child's financial future (http://www.easterseals.com/site/PageServer?pagename=ntlc8_living_with_autism_study_homeands_src=autism_studyands_subsrc=a4ahomepage).

REFERENCES

Abbott, Andrew Delano. 1988. *The system of professions: An essay on the division of expert labor*. Chicago: University of Chicago Press.

Abrahams, B. S. and D. H. Geschwind. 2008. Advances in autism genetics: On the threshold of a new neurobiology. *Nature Reviews: Genetics* 9 (May): 341–56.

Abramson, Larry. September 26, 2007. Family wins suit for autistic son. *National Public Radio Morning Edition*.

Adams, Christina. 2005. *A real boy: A true story of autism, early intervention, and recovery*. New York: Berkeley Books.

Akerley, Mary S. 1979. The politics of definitions. *Journal of Autism and Developmental Disorders* 9(2): 222–31.

Akkök, Füsun. 2000. Special education research: A Turkish perspective. *Exceptionality* 8(4): 273–79.

Alarcon, M., R. M. Cantor, J. Liu, T. C. Gilliam, and D. H. Geschwind. 2002. Evidence for a language quantitative trait locus on chromosome 7q in multiplex autism families. *American Journal of Human Genetics* 70: 60–71.

Allen, John, Marian K. DeMyer, James A. Norton, William Pontius, and Ellen Yang. 1971. Intellectuality in parents of psychotic, subnormal and normal children. *Journal of Autism and Childhood Schizophrenia* 1(3): 311–26.

Allison, Helen G. 1997. Perspectives on a puzzle piece. In *Webpage of National Autistic Society*: http://www.nas.org.uk/nas/jsp/polopoly.jsp?d=364anda=2183 (accessed October 18, 2008).

American Psychiatric Association. 1980. *Diagnostic and statistical manual of mental disorders: DSM-III*. Washington, D.C.: American Psychiatric Association.

– – – . 1987. *Diagnostic and statistical manual of mental disorders: DSM-III-R*. Washington, D.C.: American Psychiatric Association.

– – – . 2000. *Diagnostic and statistical manual of mental disorders: DSM-IV-TR*. Washington, D.C.: American Psychiatric Association.

Ando, Haruhiko, and Ikuko Yoshimura. 1979. Effects of age on communication skill levels and prevalence of maladaptive behaviors in autistic and mentally retarded children. *Journal of Autism and Developmental Disorders* 9(1).

Ando, Haruhiko, Ikuko Yoshimura, and Shinichiro Wakabayashi. 1980. Effects of age on communication skill levels and prevalence of maladaptive behaviors in autistic and mentally retarded children. *Journal of Autism and Developmental Disorders* 10(2).

Asperger, Hans. 1979. Problems of infantile autism. *Communication* 13(3): 45–52.

– – –. [1944] 1991. "Autistic psychopathy" in childhood. In *Autism and Asperger Syndrome*, ed. U. Frith. Cambridge: Cambridge University Press.

Aviram, Uri. 1981. Facilitating deinstitutionalization: A comparative analysis. *International Journal of Social Psychiatry* 27(1): 23–32.

Ayres, Jean. 1974. *Development of sensory integrative theory and practice.* Dubuque, IA: Kendall/Hunt Publishing Company.

Ayres, Jean, and William Heskett. 1972. Sensory integrative dysfunction in a young schizophrenic girl. *Journal of Autism and Childhood Schizophrenia* 2(2): 174–81.

Bailey, A., A. Le Couteur, I. Gottesman, P. Bolton, E. Simonoff, E. Yuzda, M. Rutter. 1995. Autism as a strongly genetic disorder: Evidence from a British twin study. *Psychological Medicine* 25: 63–77.

Baron, Ida Sue. 2004. *Neuropsychological evaluation of the child.* New York: Oxford University Press.

Baron-Cohen, Simon. 1997. *Mindblindness: An essay on autism and theory of mind.* Cambridge, Mass.: MIT Press.

– – –. 2006. The hyper-systemizing, assortative mating theory of autism. *Progress in Neuropsychopharmacology and Biological Psychiatry* 30(5): 865–72.

Baruch, Yehuda Moshe, Yaakov Kotler, Joy Lerner Benatov, and Rael Strous. 2005. Psychiatric admissions and hospitalization in Israel: An epidemiologic study of where we stand today and where we are going. *IMAJ* 7(12): 803–7.

Bauman, Zygmunt. 1989. *Modernity and the Holocaust.* Ithaca, N.Y.: Cornell University Press.

Bearman, Peter, and Marissa King. 2009. Diagnostic change and the increased prevalence of autism. Forthcoming in *International Journal of Epidemiology.*

Bearman, Peter, and Marissa King. Unpublished. Social influence and the autism epidemic.

Bemporad, Jules R. 1979. Adult recollections of a formerly autistic child. *Journal of Autism and Childhood Schizophrenia*, 9(2): 179–97.

Bender, Lauretta. 1953. Childhood schizophrenia. *Psychological Quarterly* 27(4): 663–81.

– – –. 1959. Autism in children with mental deficiency. *American Journal of Mental Deficiency* 64(1): 81–86.

Bender, Lauretta, Gloria Faretra, and Leonard Cobrinik. 1963. LSD and UML treatment of hospitalized disturbed children. *Recent Advances in Biological Psychology* 5: 84–92.

Bernard, Sallie. 2004. Association between thimerosal-containing vaccine and autism. *Journal of the American Medical Association* 291(2): 180.

Bettelheim, Bruno. 1967. *The empty fortress: Infantile autism and the birth of the self.* New York: The Free Press.

Bhasin, Tanya Karapurkar, and Diana Schendel. 2007. Sociodemographic risk factors for autism in a U.S. metropolitan area. *Journal of Autism and Developmental Disorders* 37: 667–77.

Biklen, D. 1990. Communication unbound: Autism and praxis. *Harvard Educational Review* 60(3): 291–314.

Bill, Brent R., and Daniel H. Geschwind. 2009. Genetic advances in autism: Heterogeneity and convergence on shared pathways. *Current Opinion in Genetics and Development* 19: 271–78.

Bishop, Dorothy V.M., Andrew J. O. Whitehouse, Helen J. Watt, and Elizabeth A. Line. 2008. Autism and diagnostic substitution: Evidence from a study of adults with a history of developmental language disorder. *Developmental Medicine and Child Neurology* 50(1–5).

Blatsland, Michael. 2006. *Joe: The only boy in the world*. London: Profile Books.

Blatt, B., and F. Kaplan. 1966. *Christmas in Purgatory: A photographic essay on mental retardation*. Boston: Allyn and Bacon.

Blatt, Burton. 1970. *Exodus from Pandemonium: Human abuse and a reformation of public policy*. Boston: Allyn and Bacon.

Bleular, E. 1913. Autistic thinking. *Journal of Insanity* 69: 83–86.

Bockman, Johanna, and Gil Eyal. 2002. Eastern Europe as a laboratory for economic knowledge: The transnational roots of neoliberalism. *American Journal of Sociology* 108(2): 310–52.

Bolton, P., et al. A case–control family history study of autism. *Journal of Child Psychology and Psychiatry* 35, 877–900 (1994).

Bosch, Gerhard. 1970. *Infantile autism: A clinical and phenomenological-anthropological investigation taking language as the guide*. Trans. D. Jordan and I. Jordan. New York: Springer-Verlag.

Bottomer, Phyllis Ferguson. 2009. *So odd a mixture: Along the autistic spectrum in* Pride and Prejudice. Vancouver: University of British Columbia Press.

Bourdieu, Pierre. 1975. The specificity of the scientific field and the social conditions of the progress of reason. *Social Science Information* 14(6): 19–47.

Braddock, David. 1981. Deinstitutionalization of the retarded: Trends in public policy. *Hospital and Community Psychiatry* 32: 607–15.

Braddock, David, Eric Emerson, David Felce, and Roger J. Stancliffe. 2001. Living circumstances of children and adults with mental retardation or developmental disabilities in the United States, Canada, England and Wales, and Australia. *Mental Retardation and Developmental Disabilities Research Reviews* 7(2): 115–21.

Brink, Susan. 2007. It takes a miracle worker. *Los Angeles Times*, May 19.

Brockley, Janice. 2004. Rearing the child who never grew: Ideologies of parenting and intellectual disability in American history. In *Mental retardation in America: A historical reader*, ed. S. Noll and J. W. Trent. New York: New York University Press.

Broderick, Alicia A. and Ari Ne'eman. 2008. Autism as metaphor: Narrative and counter-narrative. *International Journal of Inclusive Education* 12(5, 6): 459–76.

Brown, Bertram S. 1971. A task force with a goal. *Journal of Autism and Childhood Schizophrenia* 1(1): 1–13.

Bruch, Hilde. 1959. The various developments in the approach to childhood schizophrenia. *Acta* Psychiatrica et Neurologica Scandinavica 34 (Supplement 130): 5–27.

Bruer, John T. 1999. *The myth of the first three years: A new understanding of early brain development and lifelong learning*. New York: The Free Press.

289

Bumiller, Kristin. 2008. Quirky citizens: Autism, gender, and reimagining disability. *Signs: Journal of Women in Culture and Society* 33(4).

Bumiller, Kristin. 2009. The geneticization of autism: From new reproductive technologies to the conception of genetic normalcy. *Signs: Journal of Women in Culture and Society*, 34(4): 885–99.

Burns, Kathy. November 9, 1969. Parents of handicapped urge more educational opportunities. *Chicago Tribune*, SCL6.

Burstejn, C., and P. Jeammet. 2002. Autisme et psychoses de l'enfant dans la CFTMEA R-2000. *Annales medico-psychologiques* 160(3).

Buxbaum, J. D. et al. 2001. Evidence for a susceptibility gene for autism on chromosome 2 and for genetic heterogeneity. *American Journal of Human Genetics* 68: 1514–20.

Buxbaum, J. D. et al. 2004. Linkage analysis for autism in a subset families with obsessive-compulsive behaviors: evidence for an autism susceptibility gene on chromosome 1 and further support for susceptibility genes on chromosome 6 and 19. *Molecular Psychiatry* 9, 144–50.

Campbell et al. A genetic variant that disrupts MET transcription is associated with autism. *Proceedings of the National Academy of Sciences*, 103, 45 (November 2006), 16834–839.

Campbell et al. "Supporting Information." http://www.pnas.org/cgi/content/full/0605296103/DC1#T3 (accessed November 13, 2006).

Cantor, R. M. et al. 2005. Replication of autism linkage: Fine-mapping peak at 17q21. *American Journal of Human Genetics* 76, 1050–56.

Castel, Robert. 1991. Risk and danger. In *The Foucault effect: Studies in governmentality*, ed. G. Burchell, C. Gordon, and P. Miller. Chicago: University of Chicago Press.

Castles, Katherine. 2004. "Nice, average Americans": Postwar parents' groups and the defense of the normal family. In *Mental retardation in America: A historical reader*, ed. S. Noll and J. W. Trent. New York: New York University Press.

Chamak, Brigitte. 2008. Autism and social movements: French parents' associations and international autistic individuals' organizations. *Sociology of Health and Illness* 30: 76–96.

Chen, G. K., N. Kono, D. H. Geschwind, and R. M. Cantor. 2006. Quantitative trait locus analysis of nonverbal communication in autism spectrum disorder. *Molecular Psychiatry* 11, 214–20.

Clausen, Johs. 1966. Mental deficiency: Development of a concept. *American Journal of Mental Deficiency* 71(1): 727–45.

Collins, H. M., and Robert Evans. 2002. The third wave of science studies: Studies of expertise and experience. *Social Studies of Science* 32(2): 235–96.

– – – . 2007. *Rethinking expertise*. Chicago: University of Chicago Press.

Cone, Maria. 2009. Autism epidemic not caused by shifts in diagnoses; environmental factors likely. *Environmental Health News,* January 9. http://www.environmentalhealthnews.org/ehs/news/autism-and-environment. (Accessed August 25, 2009)

Coo, H., H. Ouellette-Kuntz, J. E. V. Lloyd, L. Kasmara, J. J. A. Holden, and M. E. Suzanne Lewis. 2007. Trends in autism prevalence: Diagnostic substitution revisited. *Journal of Autism and Developmental Disorders, Online First.*

Croen, Lisa A., Judith K. Grether, Jenny Hoogstrate, and Steve Selvin. 2002. The changing prevalence of autism in California. *Journal of Autism and Developmental Disorders* 32(3): 207–15.

REFERENCES

Cuccaro, Michael L., Harry H. Wright, Christina V. Rownd, and Ruth K. Abramson. 1996. Brief report: Professional perceptions of children with developmental difficulties: the influence of race and socioeconomic status. *Journal of Autism and Developmental Disorders* 26(4): 461–69.

D'Amato, Barbara. 2004. *Death of a thousand cuts.* Forge Press.

DeMyer, Marian K., Gerald D. Alpern, Sandra Barton, William E. DeMyer, W. Don Churchill, Joseph N. Hingtgen, Carolyn Q. Bryson, and William Pontius. 1972. Imitation in autistic, early schizophrenic, and non-psychotic subnormal children. *Journal of Autism and Developmental Disorders* 2(3).

Dewey Margaret A. 1991. Living with Asperger's syndrome. In *Autism and Asperger's Syndrome*, ed. Uta Frith. Cambridge: Cambridge University Press, 184–206.

Dewey, Margaret A., and Margaret P. Everard. 1974. The near-normal autistic adolescent. *Journal of Autism and Childhood Schizophrenia* 4(4): 348–56.

Dolnick, Edward. 1993. Deafness as culture. *The Atlantic Monthly.* September, 37–53.

Don, Y., and Y. Amir. 1968. Institutions in Israel. *Mental Retardation* 6(5): 29–31.

Douglas, Mary. 1966. *Purity and danger: An analysis of concepts of pollution and taboo.* New York: Praeger.

– – – . 1994. *Risk and Blame.* New York: Routledge.

Draaisma, Douwe. 2009. Stereotypes of autism. *Philosophical Transactions of the British Royal Society, B,* 364:1475–80.

Dreyfus, Hubert L., and Paul Rabinow. 1983. *Michel Foucault: Beyond structuralism and hermeneutics.* Chicago: University of Chicago Press.

Dworet, D., and S. Bennett. 2002. A view from the north: Special education in Canada. *Teaching Exceptional Children* 34: 22–27.

Edelson, Stephen M., and Bernard Rimland. 2003. *Treating autism: Parent stories of hope and success.* San Diego: Autism Research Institute.

Edelson, Stephen, and Bernard Rimland. 2006. *Recovering autistic children.* San Diego: Autism Research Institute.

Egg, Maria. 1964. *When a child is different: A basic guide for the parents and friends of mentally retarded children.* New York: The John Day Company.

Eisenberg, Leon. 1973. Psychiatric intervention. *Scientific American* 229: 116–27.

Eisenberg, Leon, and Leo Kanner. 1956. Early infantile autism 1943–1955. *American Journal of Orthopsychiatry* 26: 556–66.

Epstein, Steven. 1995. The construction of lay expertise: AIDS activism and the forging of credibility in the reform of clinical trials. *Science, Technology, and Human Values* 20(4): 408–37.

– – – . 1996. *Impure science: AIDS, activism, and the politics of knowledge.* Berkeley: University of California Press.

Ericsson, Kent. 2000. Deinstitutionalization and community living for persons with an intellectual disability in Sweden: Policy, organizational change and personal consequences. In *Disability Conference.* Tokyo: http://www.skinfaxe.se/ebok/tokyo.pdf.

Esping-Andersen, Gøsta. 1990. *The three worlds of welfare capitalism.* Princeton, N.J.: Princeton University Press.

Estroff, Sue E. 1981. *Making it crazy: An ethnography of psychiatric clients in an American community.* Berkeley: University of California Press.

291

Eurostat. 2008. *Basic statistics of the European Union.* Luxembourg: http://epp. eurostat.ec.europa.eu/portal/.

Exhorn, Karen Siff. 2005. *The autism sourcebook.* New York: Reganbooks.

Eyal, Gil. 2006. *The disenchantment of the Orient: Expertise in Arab affairs and the Israeli state.* Stanford: Stanford University Press.

Fairbanks, Amanda. 2009. Tug of war over costs to educate the autistic. *New York Times*, April 18, 2009.

Farmelo, Graham. 2009. *The strangest man: The hidden life of Paul Dirac, quantum genius.* London: Faber.

Feeley, Malcolm M., and Jonathan Simon. 1992. The new penology: Notes on the emerging strategy of corrections and its implications. *Criminology* 30(4): 449–74.

Fernald, Walter E. 1909. The imbecile with criminal instincts. *American Journal of Insanity* 65(4).

Fleischmann, Amos. 2005. The hero's story and autism: Grounded theory study of websites for parents of children with autism. *Autism* 9: 299–306.

Folstein, S. and M. Rutter. 1977. Infantile autism: A genetic study of 21 twin pairs. *Journal of Child Psychology and Psychiatry* 18: 297–321.

Fombonne, Eric. 1999. The epidemiology of autism: A review. *Psychological Medicine* 29: 769–86.

– – –. 2003. Epidemiological surveys of autism and other pervasive developmental disorders: An update. *Journal of Autism and Developmental Disorders* 33(4): 365–82.

Fombonne, Eric, Rita Zakarian, Andrew Bennett, Linyan Meng, and Diane McLean-Heywood. 2006. Pervasive developmental disorders in Montreal, Quebec, Canada: Prevalence and links with immunizations. *Pediatrics* 118(1): 139–50.

Foucault, Michel. 1972. *The archaeology of knowledge.* 1st American ed., *World of man.* New York: Pantheon Books.

– – –. 1984. Omnes et Singulatim: Toward a critique of political reason. In *Power (vol. 3, The essential works of Foucault 1954–1984).*

– – –. 2003. *Abnormal: Lectures at the College de France, 1974–1975.* Ed. A. I. Davidson. New York: Picador.

– – –. [1954] 1987. *Mental illness and psychology.* Berkeley: University of California Press.

– – –. [1961] 2006 *History of madness.* London: Routledge.

Freidson, Eliot. 1986. *Professional powers: A study of the institutionalization of formal knowledge.* Chicago: University of Chicago Press.

Frith, Uta. 1989. *Autism: Explaining the enigma.* Oxford: Basil Blackwell.

– – –. 1991. Asperger and his syndrome. In *Asperger and Asperger syndrome*, ed. U. Frith. Cambridge: Cambridge University Press, 1–36.

Gadamer, Hans-Georg. 1996. *The enigma of health: The art of healing in a scientific age.* Stanford: Stanford University Press.

Goddard, Henry H. 1915. *The criminal imbecile: An analysis of three remarkable murder cases.* New York: The Macmillan Company.

Goffman, Erving. 1961. *Asylums: Essays on the social situation of mental patients and other inmates.* 1st ed. Garden City, N.Y.

Goldstein, Herbert. 1959. Population trends in U.S. public institutions for the mentally deficient. *American Journal of Mental Deficiency* 63(4): 599–604.

Grandin, Temple. 1986. *Emergence: Labeled autistic.* New York: Warner Books.

REFERENCES

Grandin, Temple. 1995. *Thinking in pictures: My life with autism.* New York: Vintage.

Green, Vanessa A., Keenan A. Pituch, Jonathan Itchon, Aram Choi, Mark O'Reilly, and Jeff Sigafoos. 2006. Internet survey of treatments used by parents of children with autism. *Research in Developmental Disabilities* 27: 70–84.

Greenspan, Stanley I., and Nancy Thorndike Greenspan. 1985. *First feelings: Milestones in the emotional development of your baby and child.* New York: Viking.

– – –. 1990. *The essential partnership: How parents and children can meet the emotional challenges of infancy and childhood.* New York: Penguin Books.

Greenspan, Stanley I., and Jacqueline Salmon. 1993. *Playground politics: Understanding the emotional life of your school-age child.* Reading, Mass.: Addison-Wesley.

– – –. 1995. *The challenging child: Understanding, raising, and enjoying the five "difficult" types of children.* Reading, Mass.: Addison-Wesley.

Greenspan, Stanley I., and Serena Wieder. 2006. *Engaging autism: Using the Floortime approach to help children relate, communicate and think.* Cambridge: Da Capo Lifelong Books.

Griffith, Clarence S. 1971. How to work with your state legislation. In *Research and education: Top priorities for mentally ill children. Proceedings of the Conference and Annual Meeting of the National Society for Autistic Children, San Francisco June 24–27, 1970,* ed. C. C. Park. Rockville, Md.: U.S. Department of Health, Education, and Welfare.

– – –. 1973. Report of the President. In *Proceedings of the Conference and Annual Meeting of the National Society for Autistic Children, Flint MI, June 22–24,* ed. C. C. Park. Rockville, Md.: National Institute of Mental Health.

Grinker, Roy Richard. 2007. *Unstrange minds: Remapping the world of autism.* New York: Basic Books.

Groopman, Jerome. 2007. Medical dispatch: What's normal. *The New Yorker.* April 9.

Guthmann, Edward. 1988. Hoffman delves into autism in "Rain Man." *San Francisco Chronicle.* December 11, p. 19.

Habermas, Jürgen. 2003. *The future of human nature.* Cambridge: Polity Press.

Hacking, Ian. 1986. Making up people. In *Reconstructing individualism,* ed. T. Heller, M. Sosna and D. Wellberry. Palo Alto, Calif.: Stanford University Press, 222–36.

– – –. 1995. *Rewriting the soul: Multiple personality and the sciences of memory.* Princeton, N.J.: Princeton University Press.

– – –. 1998. *Mad travelers: reflections on the reality of transient mental illnesses.* Charlottesville: University Press of Virginia.

– – –. 1999. *The social construction of what?* Cambridge, Mass: Harvard University Press.

– – –. 2007. Kinds of people: Moving targets. *Proceedings of the British Academy* 151: 285–318.

– – –. 2007. On what has happened to autism, audiorecording of lecture presented at the Franke Institute, University of Chicago. April 18, 2007 [cited March 26, 2008]. Available from http://humanities.uchicago.edu/orgs/institute/wednesday-recordings/hacking/hacking-EW-0418.mp3.

293

– – –. 2009. Private thoughts in public language: The burgeoning autism narrative may reflect the pathology of our era. *Literary Review of Canada.* April 1.

– – –. 2009b. Autistic Autobiographies. *Philosophical Transactions of the British Royal Society, B,* 364: 1467–73.

Hatton, Chris, Eric Emerson, and Chris Kieman. 1995. People in institutions in Europe. *Mental Retardation* 33(2):132.

Hersch, Charles. 1968. The discontent explosion in mental health. *American Psychologist* 23: 497–508.

Hertz-Picciottoa, Irva, and Lora Delwiche. 2009. The rise in autism and the role of age at diagnosis. *Epidemiology* 20 (January): 84–90.

Hobbs, Nicholas. 1979. Helping disturbed children: Psychological and ecological strategies, II; Project Re-Ed, twenty years later. Center for the Study of Families and Children, Vanderbilt Institute for Public Policy Studies, Vanderbilt University.

Holmes, David L. 1990. Community-based services for children and adults with autism: The Eden family of programs. *Journal of Autism and Developmental Disorders* 20(3): 339–51.

Honda, H., Y. Shimizu, and M. Rutter. 2005. No effect of MMR withdrawal on the incidence of autism: A total population study. *Journal of Child Psychology and Psychiatry* 46(6): 572–79.

Howlin, P. 1997. Prognosis in autism: Do specialist treatments affect long-term outcomes? *European Child and Adolescent Psychiatry* 6: 55–72.

Houston, Rab, and Uta Frith. 2000. *Autism in history: The case of Hugh Blair of Borgue.* London: Wiley-Blackwell.

Hyman, Steven E. 2003. Diagnosing disorders. *Scientific American* (September): 97–103.

Isaev, D. N. and V. E. Kagan. 1974. Autistic syndromes in children and adolescents. *Acta Paedopsychiatrica,* 40: 182–90.

Jablensky, Assen. 1999. The concept of schizophrenia: Pro et contra. *Epidemiologia E Psichiatria Sociale* 8(4): 242–47.

– – –. 2007. Living in a Kraepelinian world: Kraepelin's impact on modern psychiatry. *History of Psychiatry* 18(3): 381–88.

Jasanoff, Sheila. 1991. Acceptable evidence in a pluralistic society. In *Acceptable evidence,* ed. D. G. Mayo and R. D. Hollander. New York: Oxford University Press.

Jolly, Donald H. 1952. When should the seriously retarded infant be institutionalized? *American Journal of Mental Deficiency* 57: 632–636.

Jones, Kathleen. 2004. Education for children with mental retardation: Parent activism, public policy, and family ideology in the 1950s. In *Mental retardation in America: A historical reader,* ed. S. Noll and J. W. Trent. New York: New York University Press.

Jones, Kathleen W. 1999. *Taming the troublesome child: American families, child guidance and the limits of psychiatric authority.* Cambridge, Mass.: Harvard University Press.

Kanner, L. 1943. Autistic disturbances of affective contact. *Nervous Child* 2: 217–50.

Kanner, Leo. 1941. *In defense of mothers: How to bring up children in spite of the more zealous psychologists.* New York: Dodd, Mead.

– – –. 1949. Feeblemindedness: Absolute, relative and apparent. In *Child care monographs.* New York.

– – – . 1958. The specificity of early infantile autism. *Acta Paedopsychiatrica* 25: 108–13.

– – – . 1964. *History of the care and study of the mentally retarded*. Springfield, Ill.: Charles C. Thomas.

– – – . 1965. Infantile autism and the schizophrenias. *Behavioral Science* 10(4): 412–20.

– – – . 1971. Follow-up study of eleven autistic children. *Journal of Autism and Childhood Schizophrenia* 1(2): 119–45.

– – – . 1973. The birth of infantile autism. *Journal of Autism and Childhood Schizophrenia* 3(2): 93–95.

Katz, A. 2006. The autism clause. *New York Magazine*. October 30: 51–53, 132.

Kephart, Beth. 1998. *A slant of sun: One child's courage*. New York: Norton.

King, Marissa D. 2008. Diagnosis, substitution, and diffusion in the autism epidemic. Ph.D. diss., Department of Sociology, Columbia University, New York.

Kirby, David. 2006. *Evidence of harm: Mercury in vaccines and the autism epidemic, a medical controversy*. New York: St. Martin's Press.

Kırcaali İftar, Gönül. 2007. Türkiye'de Gelişimsel Yetersizlik Alanı ve Özel Eğitim (The field of developmental disorder and special education in Turkey). Istanbul: Tohum Otizm Vakfı.

Kline, Wendy. 2001. *Building a better race: Gender, sexuality and eugenics from the turn of the century to the baby boom*. Berkeley: University of California Press.

Kogan, Michael D., Stephen J. Blumberg, Laura A. Schieve, Coleen A. Boyle, James M. Perrin, Reem M. Ghandour, Gopal K. Singh, Bonnie B. Strickland, Edwin Trevathan, and Peter C. van Dyck. 2009. Prevalence of parent-reported diagnosis of autism spectrum disorder among children in the U.S., 2007. *Pediatrics* 124: 1395–1403.

Koplewicz, Harold. 1996. *It's nobody's fault: New hope and help for difficult children and their parents*. New York: Random House.

Kraijer, Dirk. 1997. *Autism and autistic-like conditions in mental retardation*. Trans. E. v. Saane-Hijner. Lisse, The Netherlands: Swets and Zeitlinger B.V.

Krug, D. A., J. R. Arick, and P. Almond. 1980. Behavior checklist for identifying severely handicapped individuals with high levels of autistic behavior. *Journal of Child Psychology and Psychiatry* 21: 221–29.

Kugelmass, Judy. 1987. *Behavior, bias, and handicaps: Labeling the emotionally disturbed child*. New Brunswick: Transaction Books.

Kurita, Hiroshi. 2006. Disorders of the autism spectrum. *The Lancet* 368: 179–81.

Kurita, Hiroshi, Junji Shiiya, and Hiroto Ito. 1994. A nationwide survey of day-care for children with mental retardation in Japan. *The Japanese Journal of Psychiatry and Neurology* 48(1): 57–63.

Kustanovich, Vlad. Chair of Cure Autism Now advisory board discovers heritable risk factor for autism, http://www.cureautismnow.org/site/apps/nl/content2.as p?c=bhLOK2PILuFandb=1289189andct=3169231 (accessed November 13, 2006).

Kysar, John E. 1968. The two camps in child psychiatry: A report from a psychiatrist – father of an autistic and retarded child. *American Journal of Psychiatry* 125(1): 103–9.

295

Laidler, James R. 2005. U.S. Department of Education data on "Autism" are not reliable for tracking autism prevalence. *Pediatrics* 116(1): 120–24.

Lakin, Charlie K., Linda Anderson, and Robert Prouty. 1998. Decreases continue in out-of-home residential placements of children and youth with mental retardation. *Mental Retardation* 36(2): 165–67.

Lakin, K. C., G. C. Krantz, R. H. Bruininks, J. L. Clumpner, and B. K. Hill. 1982. 100 years of data on populations of public residential facilities for mentally-retarded people. *American Journal of Mental Deficiency* 87(1): 1–8.

Lakoff, Andrew. 2005. *Pharmaceutical reason*. Cambridge: Cambridge University Press.

– – – . 2000. Adaptive will: The evolution of attention deficit disorder. *Journal of the History of the Behavioral Sciences* 36(2): 149–69.

Landsman, Gail. 1999. Does God give special kids to special parents? Personhood and the child with disabilities as gift and giver. In *Transformative motherhood*, ed. Linda Layne. New York: NYU Press.

– – – . 2003. Emplotting children's lives: Developmental delay vs. disability. *Social Science and Medicine* 56(9): 1947–60.

Lane, Pam. 2008. A brief history of how we began. *Autism Matters* 1(2): 3–4.

Langone, John. 1974. *Goodbye to Bedlam: Understanding mental illness and retardation*. Boston: Little, Brown.

Lapin, Constance Lewis, and Anne Donnellan-Walsh. 1977. Advocacy and research: A parent's perspective. *The Journal of Pediatric Psychology* 2(4): 191–96.

Latour, Bruno. 1987. *Science in action: How to follow scientists and engineers through society*. Cambridge, Mass.: Harvard University Press.

Laumonnier, F., F. Bonnet-Brilhault, et al. 2004. X-Linked mental retardation and autism are associated with a mutation in the NLGN4 gene, a member of the neuroligin family. *The American Journal of Human Genetics* 74(3): 552–57.

Lerner, Barron. 2006. *When illness goes public*. Baltimore: Johns Hopkins University Press.

Lettick, Amy L. 1979. *Benhaven then and now*. New Haven, Conn.: Benhaven Press.

Liu, Kayuet, Noam Zerubavel and Peter Bearman. 2009. Social demographic change and autism. Unpublished manuscript.

Lockyer, L., and M. Rutter. 1969. A five to fifteen year follow up study of Infantile Psychosis. *British Journal of Psychiatry* 115: 865–82.

Lord, C., M. Rutter, S. Goode, J. Heemsbergen, H. Jordan, L. Mawhood, and E. Schopler. 1989. Autism diagnostic observation schedule: A standardized observation of communicative and social behavior. *Journal of Autism and Developmental Disorders* 19(2): 185–212.

Lotter, V. 1966. Epidemiology of autistic conditions in young children. *Social Psychiatry and Psychiatric Epidemiology* 1(3).

Lovaas, O. Ivar. 1971. Strengths and weaknesses of operant conditioning techniques for the treatment of autism. In *Research and education: Top priorities for mentally ill children. Proceedings of the Conference and Annual Meeting of the National Society for Autistic Children, San Francisco June 24–27, 1970*, ed. C. C. Park. Rockville, Md.: U.S. Department of Health, Education, and Welfare.

– – – . 1979. Contrasting illness and behavioral models for the treatment of autistic children: A historical perspective. *Journal of Autism and Childhood Schizophrenia* 9(4): 315–23.

– – – . 1981. *Teaching developmentally disabled children: The me book.* Baltimore: University Park Press.

– – – . 1987. Behavioral treatment and normal educational and intellectual functioning in young autistic children. *Journal of Consulting and Clinical Psychology* 55(1 February): 3–9.

– – – . 1993. The development of a treatment-research project for developmentally disabled and autistic children. *Journal of Applied Behavior Analysis* 26(4, Winter): 617–30.

Lovatt, Margaret. 1962. Autistic children in day nursery. *Children* 9(3): 103–8.

Luhrmann, Tania. 2000. *Of two minds: The growing disorder in American psychiatry.* New York: Alfred A. Knopf.

Lyons, Viktoria, and Michael Fitzgerald. 2007. Did Hans Asperger (1906–1980) have Asperger Syndrome? *Journal of Autism and Developmental Disorders* 37(10): 2020–21.

Macdonald, Van Bruce. 1998. How the diagnosis of Asperger's has changed my life. In *Asperger syndrome or high-functioning autism?*, ed. E. Schopler, G. Mesibov, and L. J. Kunce. New York: Plenum Press.

Mackie, Romaine P. 1969. *Special education in the United States: Statistics, 1948–1966.* New York: Teachers College Press.

MacMillan, D., and D. Speece. 1999. Utility of current diagnostic categories for research and practice. In *Developmental perspectives on children with high-incidence disabilities*, ed. R. Gallimore, C. Bernheimer, D. MacMillan, D. Speece, and S. Vaughn. Mahwah, N.J.: L. Erlbaum Associates.

MacMillan, Donald L., Gary N. Siperstein, and Frank M. Gresham. 1996. A challenge to the viability of mild mental retardation as a diagnostic category. *Exceptional Children* 62.

Madsen, K. M., M. B. Lauritsen, C. B. Pedersen, P. Thorsen, A. M. Plesner, P. H. Andersen, and P. B. Mortensen. 2003. Thimerosal and the occurence of autism: Negative ecological evidence from Danish population-based data. *Pediatrics* 112(3): 604–6.

Malzberg, Benjamin. 1952. Some statistical aspects of first admissions to the New York State schools for mental defectives. *American Journal of Mental Deficiency* 57: 27–37.

Mandell, David S., and Raymond Palmer. 2005. Differences among states in the identification of autistic spectrum disorders. *Archives of Pediatric and Adolescent Medicine* 159 (March): 266–69.

Mansell, J., M. Knapp, J. Beadle-Brown, and J. Beecham. 2007. *Deinstitutionalization and community living-outcomes and costs: Report of a European study.* Vol. 2. *Main report.* Canterbury: University of Kent.

C. Marshall, A. Noor, et al. 2008. Structural variation of chromosomes in autism spectrum disorder. *The American Journal of Human Genetics* 82(2): 477–88.

Martin, Emily. 2007. *Bipolar expeditions: Mania and depression in American culture.* Princeton: Princeton University Press.

Maryland Developmental Disabilities Council. 2008. Legislative history and evolution of the developmental disabilities act: Background and need for the legislation.

Matson, Johny L., and LoVulle Santino. 2008. A review of behavioral treatments for self-injurious behaviors of persons with autism spectrum disorders. *Behavior Modification* 32(1): 61–76.

Matson, Johny L., Sara Mahan, and LoVulle Santino. 2009. Parent training: A review of methods for children with developmental disabilities. *Research in Developmental Disabilities* 30: 961–68.

May, Jacques M. 1958. *A physician looks at psychiatry*. New York: John Day Company.

May, Jacques M., and Marie-Anne May. 1959. The treatment and education of the atypical, autistic child in a residential school situation. *American Journal of Mental Deficiency* 64: 435–43.

Mayes, Susan Dickerson, Susan L. Calhoun, and Dana L. Crites. 2001. Does DSM-IV Asperger's disorder exist? *Journal of Abnormal Child Psychology* 29(3): 263–71.

McCandless, Jacquelyn, Jack Zimmerman, and Teresa Binstock. 2003. *Children with starving brains: A medical treatment guide for autism disorder*. Putney, Vt.: Bramble Books.

McCarthy, Jenny. 2007. *Louder than words: A mother's journey in healing autism*. New York: Dutton.

Meyer, Jan. 2003. A non-institutional society for people with developmental disability in Norway. *Journal of Intellectual and Developmental Disability* 28(3): 305–8.

Mingroni, Michael. 2004. The secular rise in IQ: Giving heterosis a closer look. *Intelligence* 32: 65–83.

Molloy, C. A., M. Keddache, and L. J. Martin. 2005. Evidence for linkage on 21q and 7q in a subset of autism characterized by developmental regression. *Molecular Psychiatry* 10: 741–46.

Molteno, G., C. D. Molteno, G. Finchilescu, and A. R. L. Dawes. 2001. Behavioural and emotional problems in children with intellectual disability attending special schools in Cape Town, South Africa. *Journal of Intellectual Disability Research* 45(6): 515–20.

Moon, Elisabeth. 2003. *The speed of dark*. New York: Ballantine Books.

Moser, Dan, and Alan Grant. 1965. Screams, slaps and love: A surprising, shocking treatment helps far-gone mental cripples. *Life* (May 7): 90–96.

Mosse, Hilde L. 1958. The misuse of the diagnosis childhood schizophrenia. *American Journal of Psychiatry* 114 (March): 791–94.

Mnukhin, S. S. and D. N. Isaev. 1975. On the organic nature of some forms of schizoid or autistic psychopathy. *Journal of Autism and Childhood Schizophrenia* 5(2): 99–108.

Munir, Kerim, et al. 2006. Türkiye Cumhuriyeti Ruh Sağlığı Politikası (The mental health policy of the Turkish Republic). Ankara: T.C. Sağlık Bakanlığı.

Nadesan, Majia Holmer. 2005. *Constructing autism: Unravelling the "truth" and understanding the social*. London: Routledge.

Naon, Denise, Avital Sandler-Loeff, and Nurit Strosberg. 2000. Services for children with special needs: Coordination of treatment at child development centers. Jerusalem: Center for Research on Disabilities and Special Populations RR-352-00 -.

Nehring, Wendy. 2004. Formal health care at the community level: The child development clinics of the 1950s and 1960s. In *Mental retardation in America:*

A historical reader, ed. S. Noll and J. W. Trent. New York: New York University Press.

Neuer, H. 1947. The relationship between behavior disorders in children and the syndrome of mental deficiency. *American Journal on Mental Deficiency* 52: 143–57.

Neve, Michael, and Trevor Turner. 2002. History of child and adolescent psychiatry. In *Child and adolescent psychiatry*, ed. M. J. Rutter and E. A. Taylor. Oxford: Blackwell Publishing.

Nirje, B. 1969. The normalization principle and its human management implications. In *Changing patterns in residential services for the mentally retarded*, ed. R. B. Kugel and W. Wolfensberger. Washington, D.C.: President's Committee on Mental Retardation.

Nirje, B. 1972. The right to self-determination. In *Normalization: The principle of normalization*, ed. W. Wolfensberger. Toronto: National Institute of Mental Retardation.

Noll, Steven. 1995. *Feeble-minded in our midst: Institutions for the mentally retarded in the South, 1900–1940*. Chapel Hill: The University of North Carolina Press.

Norsworthy, Naomi. 1906. The psychology of mentally deficient children. *Archives of Psychology* 1(1): 1–111.

O'Donovan, Michael C., Nick J. Craddock, and Michael J. Owen. 2009. Genetics of psychosis: Insights from views across the genome. *Human Genetics* 126: 3–12.

Ong-Dean, Colin. 2005. Reconsidering the social location of the medical model: An examination of disability in parenting literature. *Journal of Medical Humanities* 26(2/3): 141–58.

– – – . 2006. High roads and low roads: Learning disabilities in California, 1976–1998. *Sociological Perspectives* 49(1): 91–113.

Ophir, Adi, Steven Shapin, and Simon Schaffer. 1991. The place of knowledge: The spatial setting and its relation to the production of knowledge. *Science in Context* 4: 3–218.

Ornitz, Edward M., and Edward R. Ritvo. 1968. Perceptual inconstancy in early infantile autism: The syndrome of early infant autism and its variants including certain cases of childhood schizophrenia. *Archives of General Psychiatry* 18(1): 76–98.

Ouellette-Kuntz, H., H. Coo, C. T. Yu, A. E. Chudley, A. Noonan, M. Breitenbach, N. Ramji, T. Prosick, A. Bedard, and J. J. A. Holden. 2006. Prevalence of pervasive developmental disorders in two Canadian provinces. *Journal of Policy and Practice in Intellectual Disabilities* 3: 164–72.

Parish, Susan L. 2005. Deinstitutionalization in two states: The impact of advocacy, policy, and other social forces on services for people with developmental disabilities. *Research and Practice for Persons with Severe Disabilities* 30(4): 219–31.

Park, Clara Claiborne. 1967. *The siege: A family's journey into the world of an autistic child*. Boston, Mass.: Little Brown.

– – – . 1970. Hands across the sea. *NSAC Newsletter* 2(2): 2.

– – – . September 1971a. Leo Kanner: Some answers around the corner. *NSAC Newsletter* 3(7): 7–8.

– – – . September 1971b. Schopler's developmental therapy to support unique public school program. *NSAC Newsletter* 3(7): 3–5.

299

Pedlar, A., P. Hutchinson, S. Arai, and P. Dunn. 2000. Community services landscape in Canada: Survey of developmental disability agencies. *Mental Retardation* 38(4): 330.

Perske, R. 1972. The dignity of risk. In *Normalization: The principle of normalization*, ed. W. Wolfensberger. Toronto: National Institute of Mental Retardation.

Pettus, Ashley. 2008. A Spectrum of Disorders: the urgent search to understand the biological basis of autism. *Harvard Magazine* 110(Jan./Feb., 3).

Powers, Michael D. 2000. *Children with autism: A parent's guide*. Bethesda, Md.: Woodbine House.

Prior, M. 2003. Annotation: Is there an increase in the prevalence of autism spectrum disorders? *Journal of Paediatrics and Child Health* 39: 81–82.

Prouty, R., G. Smith, and K. C. Lakin. 2007. Residential services for persons with developmental disabilities: Status and trends through 2006. Minneapolis: University of Minnesota, Research and Training Center on Community Living.

Prouty, Robert, K. Charlie Lakin, Kathryn Coucouvanis, and Linda Anderson. 2005. Progress toward a national objective of healthy people 2010: "Reduce to zero the number of children 17 years and younger living in congregate care." *Mental Retardation* 43(6): 456–60.

Prouty, Robert W., Gary Smith, and K. Charlie Lakin. 2001. Residential services for persons with developmental disabilities: Status and trends through 2000. Minneapolis: Research and Training Center on Community Living, University of Minnesota.

Rabeharisoa, Vololona, and Michel Callon. 2004. Patients and scientists in French muscular dystrophy research. In *States of knowledge: The co-production of science and social order*, ed. S. Jasanoff. London: Routledge.

Rapin, Isabelle. 1994. Introduction and overview. In *The neurobiology of autism*, ed. M. L. Bauman and T. L. Kemper. Baltimore: Johns Hopkins University Press.

Rapin, Isabelle, and Tuchman, Roberto F. 2008. *Current opinion in neurology* 21: 143–49.

Reichler, Robert J. and Schopler, E. 1976. Developmental Therapy: A Program Model for Providing Individual Services in the Community, In *Psychopathology and Child Development: Research and Treatment,* edited by E. Schopler and R.J. Reichler. New York: Plenum Press, 347–372.

Rellini, E., D. Tortolani, S. Trillo, S. Carbone, and F. Montecchi. 2004. Childhood Autism Rating Scale (CARS) and Autism Behavior Checklist (ABC) correspondence and conflicts with DSM-IV criteria in diagnosis of autism. *Journal of Autism and Developmental Disorders* 34(6): 703–8.

Ribot, T. H. 1910. *The diseases of personality*. Chicago: The Open Court Publishing Company.

Richards, B. W. 1963. Observations on accommodation for the mentally retarded in the province of Ontario. *Canadian Medical Association Journal* 89: 167–70.

Rimland, Bernard. 1964. *Infantile autism: The syndrome and its implications for a neural theory of Behavior*. New York: Appleton-Century-Crofts.

– – – . 1964b. Letter from Bernard Rimland to Joshua Lederberg. *Joshua Lederberg Papers* (July 31, 1964): 2. http://profiles.nlm.nih.gov/BB/A/L/Q/A/ (last accessed March 22, 2008).

– – –. 1971a. The Differentiation of childhood psychoses: An analysis of checklists for 2,218 psychotic children. *Journal of Autism and Childhood Schizophrenia* 1(2): 161–74.

– – –. 1971b. The ICBR study of high dosage vitamins as a method of treating severely mentally ill children. In *Research and education: Top priorities for mentally ill children. Proceedings of the Conference and Annual Meeting of the National Society for Autistic Children, San Francisco June 24–27, 1970*, ed. C. C. Park. Rockville, Md.: U.S. Department of Health, Education, and Welfare.

– – –. 1972. Operant conditioning: Breakthrough in the treatment of mentally ill children. In *Readings on the Exceptional Child*. 2nd ed., ed. E. P. Trapp and P. Himelstein. New York: Appleton-Century-Crofts.

– – –. 1987. Dr. Kitahara's school for autistic children. *Autism Research Review International* 1(2): 3.

– – –. 1988. Help needed! *Autism Research Review International* 2(2): 2.

– – –. 1992. Let's teach the kids to read. *Autism Research Review International* 6(3): 3.

– – –. 1993. Beware of the advozealots: Mindless good intentions injure the handicapped. *Autism Research Review International* 7(4): 3.

– – –. 1995. Lawsuit: Autism Research Institute vs. Autism Society of America. *Autism Research Review International* 9(2): 3.

– – –. 2003. Autism is treatable! *Autism Research Review International* 17(4): 3.

– – –. 2006. The history of the Autism Research Institute and the Defeat Autism Now! (DAN!) project. In *Recovering autistic children*, ed. S. Edelson and B. Rimland. San Diego: Autism Research Institute.

– – –. Letter from Bernard Rimland to Joshua Lederberg. http://profiles.nlm. nih.gov/BB/A/L/Q/A/ July 31, 1964 [accessed March 22, 2008].

Rimmerman, Arie. 2003. Out-of-home placement of children with intellectual disabilities: The need for a family support policy. In *The human rights of persons with intellectual disabilities: Different but equal*, ed. S. Herr, L. Gostin, and H. Koh. Oxford: Oxford University Press.

Ritvo, E. R., B. J. Freeman, and National Society for Autistic Children. 1978. National Society for Autistic Children definition of the syndrome of autism. *Journal of Autism and Childhood Schizophrenia* 8:162–67.

Roberts, Eric M., Paul B. English, Judith K. Grether, Gayle C. Windham, Lucia Somberg, and Craig Wolff. 2007. Maternal residence near agricultural pesticide applications and autism spectrum disorders among children in the California Central Valley. *Environmental Health Perspectives* 115(10): 1482–89.

Robinson, Franklin J., and Louis J. Vitale. 1958. Children with circumscribed interest patterns. *American Journal of Orthopsychiatry* 24(4): 755–66.

Roge, Bernadette. 1997. The development of services for people with autism and training for professionals (France). In *Education of children and young people with autism*, ed. R. Jordan: UNESCO.

Ronald, A., et al. 2006. Genetic heterogeneity between the three components of the autism spectrum: a twin study. *Journal of the American Academy of Child and Adolescent Psychiatry* 45, 691–99.

Rosch, Eleanor. 1978. Principles of categorization. In *Cognition and categorization*, ed. E. Rosch and B. B. Lloyd. Hillside, N.J.: Lawrence Erblaum Associates.

Rose, Nikolas. 1992. Engineering the human soul: Analyzing psychological expertise. *Science in Context* 5(2): 351–69.

Rosen, Bruce., Irit Elroy, and Nurit Nirel. 2007. Key findings from a national survey of mothers regarding preventive health services for children in the "Tipat Halav" framework. Jerusalem: Smokler Center for Health Policy Research RR-497–07.

Roszak, Theodore. 1968. *The making of a counterculture: Reflections on the technocratic society and its youthful opposition.* Garden City, N.Y.: Doubleday.

Rothman, David J., and Sheila M. Rothman. [1984] 2005. *The Willowbrook wars: Bringing the mentally disabled into the community.* New Brunswick: Aldine Transaction. Original edition, excerpted from *The Willowbrook wars* (1983).

Rutter, Michael. 1972. Childhood schizophrenia reconsidered. *Journal of Autism and Childhood Schizophrenia* 2(4):315–337.

– – –. 1978. Diagnosis and definition of childhood autism. *Journal of Autism and Childhood Schizophrenia* 8: 139–61.

– – –. 1983. The treatment of autistic children. *Journal of Child Psychology and Psychiatry* 26(2): 193–214.

Rutter, Michael, and Lawrence Bartak. 1971. Causes of infantile autism: Some considerations from recent research. *Journal of Autism and Childhood Schizophrenia* 1(1): 20–32.

Rutter, Michael, and Fraida Sussenwein. 1971. A developmental and behavioral approach to the treatment of preschool autistic children. *Journal of Autism and Childhood Schizophrenia* 1(4): 376–97.

Sarfatti Larson, Magali. 1977. *The rise of professionalism: A sociological analysis.* Berkeley: University of California Press.

Schellenberg, G. D. et al. 2006. Evidence for multiple loci from a genome scan of autism kindreds. *Moecular. Psychiatry* 11, 1049–60.

Schelly, David. 2008. Problems associated with choice and quality of life for an individual with intellectual disability: A personal assistant's reflexive ethnography. *Disability and Society* 23(7): 719–32.

Schopler, Eric. 1965. Early infantile autism and receptor processes. *Archives of General Psychiatry* 13(4): 327–35.

– – –. 1971a Parents of Psychotic Children as Scapegoats. *Journal of Contemporary Psychotherapy,* 4(1): 17–22.

– – –. 1971b. Introductory remarks. In *Research and education: Top priorities for mentally ill children. Proceedings of the Conference and Annual Meeting of the National Society for Autistic Children, San Francisco June 24–27, 1970,* ed. C. C. Park. Rockville, Md.: U.S. Department of Health, Education, and Welfare.

– – –. 1974. Questions, answers, and comments. *Journal of Autism and Childhood Schizophrenia* 4(2): 93–97.

– – –. 1978. On confusion in the diagnosis of autism. *Journal of Autism and Childhood Schizophrenia* 8(2): 137–38.

– – –. 1998. Conclusion: Premature popularization of Asperger syndrome. In *Asperger syndrome or high-functioning autism?,* ed. E. Schopler, G. Mesibov, and L. J. Kunce. New York: Plenum Press.

Schopler, Eric, Carol E. Andrews, and Karen Strupp. 1979. Do autistic children come from upper-middle-class parents? *Journal of Autism and Developmental Disorders* 9(2): 139–52.

Schopler, Eric, Gary Mesibov, R. Hal Shigley, and Anne Bashford. 1984. Helping autistic children through their parents: The TEACHH model. In *The effects of autism on the family*, ed. E. Schopler and G. Mesibov. New York: Plenum Press.

Schopler, Eric, and Robert J. Reichler. 1971. Parents as cotherapists in the treatment of psychotic children. *Journal of Autism and Childhood Schizophrenia* 1(1): 87–102.

Schopler, Eric, and Robert J. Reichler. 1972. How well do parents understand their own psychotic child? *Journal of Autism and Childhood Schizophrenia* 2(4): 387–400.

Schopler, Eric, Robert J. Reichler, and Barbara Rochen Renner. 1988. *The Childhood Autism Rating Scale (CARS)*. Los Angeles, Calif.: Western Psychological Services.

Schopler, Eric, Robert J. Reichler, DeVellis, and Daly. 1980. Toward objective classification of childhood autism: Childhood autism rating scale (CARS). *Journal of Autism and Developmental Disorders* 10(1):91–103.

Schopler, Eric, Michael Rutter, and Stella Chess. 1979. Editorial change of journal scope and title. *Journal of Autism and Developmental Disorders* 9(1): 1–10.

Schumacher, Henry C. 1946. A program for dealing with mental deficiency in children up to six years of age. *American Journal of Mental Deficiency* 51(1): 52–56.

Schwartzenberg, Susan. 2005. *Becoming citizens: Family life and the politics of disability*. Seattle: University of Washington Press.

Scull, Andrew T. [1977] 1983. *Decarceration: Community treatment and the deviant – a radical view*. 2nd ed. New Brunswick, N.J.: Rutgers University Press.

Sealy, Patricia, and Paul C. Whitehead. 2004. Forty years of deinstitutionalization of psychiatric services in Canada: An empirical assessment. *Canadian Journal of Psychiatry* 49: 249–57.

Seroussi, Karyn. 2000. *Unraveling the mystery of autism and pervasive developmental disorder: A mother's story of research and recovery*. New York: Simon and Schuster.

Sevin, Jay A., Johnny L. Matson, David A. Coe, Virginia E. Fee, B. M. Sevin. 1991. A comparison and evaluation of three commonly used autism scales. *Journal of Autism and Developmental Disorders* 21(4): 417–32.

Shafir, G., and Y. Peled. 2002. *Being Israeli: The dynamics of multiple citizenships*. Cambridge: Cambridge University Press.

Shao, Y. et al. 2002. Phenotypic homogeneity provides increased support for linkage on chromosome 2 in autistic disorder. *American Journal of Human Genetics* 70: 1058–61.

Shapiro, Joseph P. 1993. *No pity: People with disabilities forging a new civil rights movement*. New York: Times Books.

Shattuck, Paul T. 2006. The contribution of diagnostic substitution to the growing administrative prevalence of autism in U.S. special education. *Pediatrics* 117(4): 1028–37.

Shattuck, Paul T., and Maureen Durkin. 2007. A spectrum of disputes. *The New York Times* (June 11, 19)

Shnit, Dan. 2003. When legislation should take intellectual disabilities into account. In *The human rights of persons with intellectual disabilities: Different but equal*, ed. S. Herr, L. Gostin, and H. Hongju. New York: Oxford University Press.

Shore, Stephen M. 2003. *Beyond the wall: Personal experiences with autism and Asperger syndrome.* 2nd ed. Shawnee Mission, Kan.: Autism Asperger Publishing Co.

Siegel, Bryna. 1996. *The world of the autistic child: Understanding and treating autistic spectrum disorders.* Oxford: Oxford University Press.

Sigelman, Lee, Phillip W. Roeder, and Carol K. Sigelman. 1981. Social service innovation in the American states: Deinstitutionalization of the mentally retarded. *Social Science Quarterly* 62(3): 503–15.

Silberman, Steve. 2001. The geek syndrome. *Wired* 9:12 (December).

Silverman, Chloe. 2004. A disorder of affect: Love, tragedy, biomedicine, and citizenship in American autism research 1943–2003. University of Pennsylvania.

– – –. forthcoming. Desperate and rational: Of love, biomedicine, and experimental community. In *Lively capital: Biotechnology, ethics and governance in global markets*, ed. K. S. Rajan. Durham, N.C.: Duke University Press.

Silverman, C., and J. P. Brosco. 2007. Understanding autism: Parents and pediatricians in historical perspective. *Archives of Pediatric and Adolescent Medicine* 161(April): 392–98.

Sinclair, Jim. 2005. Autism Network International: The development of a community and its culture. http://web.syr.edu/~jisincla/History_of_ANI.html, quoted in Chloe Silverman, Brains, pedigrees, and promises: Lessons from the politics of autism genetics. In *Genetics and the Social Sciences: Making Biosociality*, ed. Sahra Gibbon and Carlos Novas, 2007. London: Routledge.

Spiegel, Alix. 2005. The dictionary of disorder: How one man revolutionized psychiatry. *The New Yorker* (Jan. 03): 56–63.

Spitz, Rene. 1971. The adaptive viewpoint: Its role in autism and child psychiatry. *Journal of Autism and Childhood Schizophrenia* 1(3): 239–45.

Stacey, Patricia. 2003. *The boy who loved windows.* Cambridge, Mass.: Da Capo Press.

Staub, Michael E. Forthcoming. *Madness is civilization: When the diagnosis was social, 1948–1980.* Chicago University of Chicago Press.

Stone, W. L. 1987. Cross-disciplinary perspectives on autism. *Journal of Pediatric Psychology* 12:615–630.

Stone, J. L. et al. 2004. Evidence for sex-specific risk alleles in autism spectrum disorder. *American Journal of Human Genetics* 75, 1117–23.

Strauss, Alfred A., and Newell C. Kephart. 1955. *Psychopathology and education of the brain-injured child*, vol. 2, *Progress in theory and clinic.* New York: Grune and Stratton.

Sullivan, Ruth Christ. 1971. Introduction. In *Research and education: Top priorities for mentally ill children: Proceedings of the Conference and Annual Meeting of the National Society for Autistic Children, San Francisco June 24–27, 1970*, ed. C. C. Park. Rockville, Md.: U.S. Department of Health, Education, and Welfare.

– – –. 1981. What does deinstitutionalization mean for our children. *Journal of Autism and Developmental Disorders* 11(3): 347–56.

– – –. 1984. Parents as trainers of legislators, other parents, and researchers. In *The effects of autism on the family*, ed. E. Schopler and G. Mesibov. New York: Plenum Press.

Szatmari, P., et al. 2007. Mapping autism risk loci using genetic linkage and chromosomal rearrangements. *Nature Genetics* 39: 319–28.

Tammet, Daniel. 2009. *Embracing the wide sky: A tour across the horizons of the mind.* New York: Free Press.

Takeshi, Yamamura. 2004. Study on function of institutions for people with physical and/or mental disabilities integrated with the idea of deinstitution-alization. Survey on institutions for mentally handicapped children. *Shogaisha (Ji) no Chiiki Iko ni Kanren saseta Shintai Shogai* 347: 349–83.

Tek, Saime. December 10, 2008. Telephone interview.

Tredgold, A. F. 1947 [1908]. *A textbook of mental deficiency.* Baltimore: Williams and Wilkins.

Trent, James W. 1994. *Inventing the feeble mind: A history of mental retardation in the United States.* Berkeley: University of California Press.

Tsuda, Eiji. 2006. Japanese culture and the philosophy of self-advocacy: The importance of interdependence in community living. *British Journal of Learning Disabilities* 34(3): 151–56.

Valverde, Mariana. 1998. *Diseases of the will: Alcohol and the dilemmas of freedom.* New York: Cambridge University Press.

Van Krevelen and D. Arn. 1963. On the relationship between early infantile autism and autistic psychopathology. *Acta Paedopsychiatrica* 30: 303–23.

– – – . 1971. Early infantile autism and autistic psychopathology. *Journal of Autism and Childhood Schizophrenia* 1(1): 82–86.

Van Krevelen, D. Arn, and Kuipers. 1962. The psychopathology of autistic pychopathy. *Acta Paedopsychiatrica* 29: 20–31.

Volkmar, Fred R., Domenic V. Cicchetti, Elisabeth Dykens, Sara S. Sparrow, Donald J. Cohen. 1988. An evaluation of the Autism Behavior Checklist. *Journal of Autism and Developmental Disorders* 18(1): 81–97.

Wadden, Norma P., Susan E. Bryson, and Robert S. Rodger. 1991. A closer look at the Autism Behavior Checklist: Discriminant validity and factor structure. *Journal of Autism and Developmental Disorders* 21(4): 529–41.

Wagner, Peter. 1994. *Liberty and discipline: A sociology of modernity.* London: Routledge.

Waldman, Michael, Sean Nicholson, and Nodir Adilov. 2006. Does television cause autism? In *National Bureau of Economic Research*: working paper #12632.

Wallin, J. E. Wallace. 1949. *Children with Mental and Physical Handicaps.* New York: Prentice-Hall.

Warren, Frank. 1984. The role of the national society in working with families. In *The effects of autism on the family*, ed. E. Schopler and G. Mesibov. New York: Plenum Press.

Waterhouse, L., D. Fein, L. Nath, and D. Synder. 1987. Pervasive developmental disorders and schizophrenia occurring in childhood: A critical commentary. In *Diagnosis and classification in psychiatry*, ed. G. Tischler. New York: Cambridge University Press.

Waterhouse, Lynn. 2008. Autism overflows: Increasing prevalence and prolifer-ating theories. *Neuropsychological Review* 18: 273–86.

Waterhouse, Lynn, Deborah Fein, and Emily G. W. Nichols. 2007. Autism, social neuroscience and endophenotypes. In *Autism and Pervasive Developmental Disorders*, 2nd ed., ed. F. Volkmar. Cambridge: Cambridge University Press.

Waterhouse, Lynne, Lorna Wing, Robert Spitzer, and Bryna Siegel. 1992.

305

Pervasive developmental disorders: From DSM-III to DSM-III-R. *Journal of Autism and Developmental Disorders* 22(4): 525–49.

Wing, L., and J. K. Wing. 1971. Multiple impairments in early childhood autism. *Journal of Autism and Childhood Schizophrenia* 1: 256–66.

Wing, Lorna. 1973. The handicaps of autistic children: A review of some aspects of work in the U.K. In *Research and education: Top priorities for mentally ill children. Proceedings of the Conference and Annual Meeting of the National Society for Autistic Children, San Francisco June 22–24, 1971*, ed. C. C. Park. Rockville, Md.: National Institute of Mental Health.

– – –. 1980. Childhood Autism and Social Class: A Question of Selection? *British Journal of Psychiatry* 137: 410–17.

– – –. 1981. Asperger's syndrome: A clinical account. *Psychological Medicine* 11: 115–29.

– – –. 1986. Clarification on Asperger's syndrome. *Journal of Autism and Developmental Disorders* 16(4): 513–15.

– – –. 1992. Brief note: Is autism a pervasive developmental disorder? *European Child and Adolescent Psychiatry* 1(2): 130–31.

– – –. 2005. Reflections on opening Pandora's box. *Journal of Autism and Developmental Disorders* 35(2): 197–203.

Wing, Lorna, and Judith Gould. 1979. Severe impairments of social interaction and associated abnormalities in children: Epidemiology and classification *Journal of Autism and Developmental Disorders* 9(1): 11–29.

– – –. 1979. Severe impairments of social interaction and associated abnormalities in children: Epidemiology and classification. *Journal of Autism and Developmental Disorders* 9: 11–29.

Winzer, Margret A. 1993. *The history of special education: From isolation to integration*. Washington, D.C.: Gallaudet University Press.

Wolf, Sula, and Jonathan Chick. 1980. Schizoid personality in childhood: A controlled follow-up study. *Psychological Medicine* 10: 85–100.

Wolfensberger, Wolf. 1972. *Normalization: The principle of normalization in human services*. Toronto: National Institute of Mental Retardation: Canadian Association for the Mentally Retarded.

Woodside, H. H. 1971. The development of occupational therapy 1910–1929. *American Journal of Occupational Therapy* 25(5): 226–30.

World Mental Health Atlas 2005. Geneva: World Health Organization.

Yazgan, Yankı. December 21, 2008. Telephone interview.

Yeargin-Allsopp, Marshalyn, Catherine Rice, Tanya Karapurkar, Nancy Doernberg, Coleen Boyle, and Catherine Murphy. 2003. Prevalence of autism in a U.S. metropolitan area. *JAMA* 289(1): 49–55.

INDEX

Page numbers in **bold** refer to tables and those in *italics* to figures.

307